THE COMPLETE
CLASSICAL MUSIC
GUIDE

THE COMPLETE
CLASSICAL MUSIC
GUIDE

GENERAL EDITOR
JOHN BURROWS
WITH CHARLES WIFFEN

and contributions from
Robert Ainsley, Duncan Barker, Karl Lutchmayer, Ivan Hewett, Lisa Colton,
Andrew Wilson, Nathanial Vallois, Ann Van Allen Russell, Jenny Nex,
Richard Langham-Smith, Sam Thompson, Simon Rees, Marcus Weeks

Previously published as *Eyewitness Companions: Classical Music*

LONDON ▪ NEW YORK
MUNICH ▪ MELBOURNE ▪ DELHI

Project Editor	Hannah Bowen
Designer	Joanne Clark
Production Editor	Rebekah Parsons-King
Jacket Designer	Mark Cavanagh
Managing Editor	Stephanie Farrow
Managing Art Editor	Lee Griffiths
US Editors	Jill Hamilton, Rebecca Warren

Dorling Kindersley (India)

Project Editor	Samira Sood
Editors	Rashmi Rajan, Pankaj Kumar Deo
Senior Art Editor	Rajnish Kashyap
Designers	Pooja Pipil, Aanchal Singal, Aanchal Awasthi
Managing Editor	Saloni Talwar
Managing Art Editor	Romi Chakraborty
DTP Manager	Balwant Singh
DTP Designer	Jaypal Singh Chauhan

First American Edition, 2012
Published in the United States
by DK Publishing
375 Hudson Street
New York, New York 10014
11 12 13 14 15 10 9 8 7 6 5 4 3 2 1
001 – 181271 – May/2012

Published in Great Britain by
Dorling Kindersley Limited.

A CIP catalog record for this book is available
from the Library of Congress.
ISBN 978-0-7566-9256-8

Based on content previously published in
Eyewitness Companions: Classical Music

DK books are available at special discounts when
purchased in bulk for sales promotions,
premiums, fund-raising, or educational use. For
details, contact: DK Publishing Special Markets,
375 Hudson Street, New York, New York 10014 or
SpecialSales@dk.com

Printed and bound in China
by Leo Paper Products Ltd

Discover more at **www.dk.com**

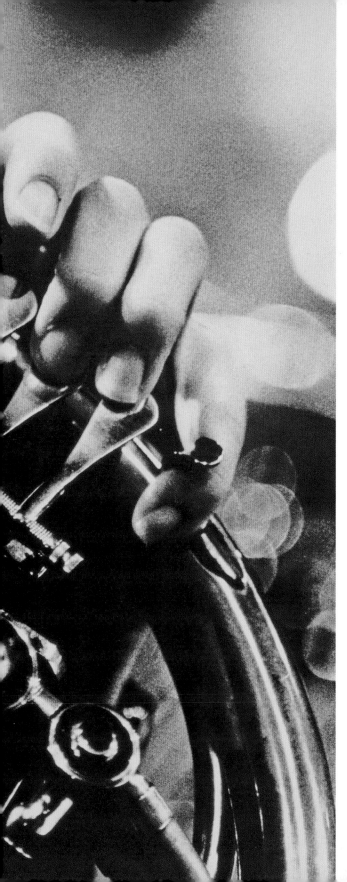

Contents

Key to symbols

- ● Birth and death dates
- ▣ Nationality
- ✍ Number of published works
- ✇ Approximate length of work
- ▦ Number of movements/acts/parts
- ◔ Scored for solo instrument
- ♔ Scored for ensemble
- ♫ Scored for orchestra
- ♙ Scored for choir/chorus
- ♦ Scored for solo voice

FOREWORD

I was first introduced by my Mother to the live performance of Classical music when I was ten years old, at the Albert Hall in Nottingham. Sir Malcolm Sargent was conducting the Halle Orchestra, with the soloist Moura Lympany playing the Rachmaninoff Piano Concerto No 2. The moment the orchestra began tuning up I was hooked and determined that music would play a vital role in my life. I played piano but it became obvious I was not cut out to be a professional musician, so I became a music promoter. My first Classical concert was in 1970 with the London Symphony Orchestra conducted by André Previn at the New Theatre, Oxford. Since then I have been privileged to work among many musicians of the highest international caliber.

For many years I had wanted to share my passion and commitment to Classical music in book form. I first approached DK when they were developing an illustrated handbook on Shakespeare. I instantly realised there was much scope for an imaginatively illustrated reference book that covered as much of the subject as would be usefully practical. The book should inform, excite, inspire and be very accessible to Classical music lovers of all ages and levels of knowledge. After several years of hard work I am delighted to present this book to the public and am thrilled that it is being read and used for music educational purposes in so many countries around the world. Many people have been involved with the creation of this book and I am indebted to them—it would not have happened without them. A big thanks to the creative team at Dorling Kindersley, to my dear friend Richard Havers, the Music Guru and a major author himself whose encouragement and help was vital to me; to my friend Lady Solti; and to Dr. Charles Wiffen and the many writers and academics who have collaborated on this book.

JOHN BURROWS
OBE HonRCM

INTRODUCING
CLASSICAL MUSIC

The Elements of Classical Music

The basic elements of music are pitch and rhythm. Conventions in Western music have arisen over the centuries by which composers and performers can organize and manipulate these elements. Some composers achieve memorable effects by breaking the "rules," others, by working imaginatively within them.

Musical notes are assigned different pitches, and are put together to form melodies. These may contain phrases, which can be thought of as musical sentences. Often, each phrase contains as many notes as can be sung comfortably in a single breath. The sound of a number of different notes played simultaneously creates harmony. The flavor of these melodies and harmonies often results from the types of scales (or collections of notes) that are used.

If the individual notes of a composition are bricks, then the rhythm is like mortar, holding them together. Rhythm, at its most basic, is the beat of a piece of music and the meter—or time signature—is the way in which the beat is grouped.

An entire piece of music can be constructed from these simple materials. It is like a building, designed by the composer according to a "form"—as with an architect's plan. A symphony is like a castle (with its own grand structure or form), whereas a short song will have a different and less complex form (more like a modest cottage). The

color or texture of a piece of music depends on how the voices or instruments are used, and how they are combined or orchestrated.

Pitch

For a sound to be produced, a vibration must be set up in the air. This may result from the motion of a taut string, the skin of a drum, or the column of air within a cylinder. If the vibration is regular, it is heard as an identifiable note of a certain pitch. If the vibration is fast, the pitch is heard as high; if it is slow, it will sound low or deep. As a general rule, the longer the string or column of air, the lower the pitch. The low threshold of human hearing is about 16–20 vibrations per second, while the upper threshold is around 20,000 vibrations per second.

The lowest notes of a pipe organ range from about 20 vibrations per second (or "cycles per second"), while a piccolo can reach about 4,176 cycles. An adult choir can produce anything from 64 to 1,500 cycles.

Standardized pitch

The letter-name "A" is given to the pitch of 440 cycles per second, which is produced by a key just to the right of the middle of the

The familiar piano keyboard, made up of the notes of the scale that form the basis for Classical melody and harmony, has come to symbolise the conventions of Western music.

piano keyboard (known as the note or "tone" a"). This is a standard universal measure of pitch. Without it, players would experience great difficulty adapting their instruments as they moved around the world.

Musical notation

In Western music, seven letters of the alphabet are assigned to different pitches, ranging from A to G. If you play all the white keys on the piano keyboard from one A up to the next A (eight notes) you will have covered an "octave." This particular series of notes corresponds to a scale known as the natural minor scale. Once you reach the next A you can repeat the cycle, and will hear higher

⊠ **The lengths** of the many pipes on a traditional organ determine the notes the instrument can produce.

⚠ **On the harp,** the shorter strings produce the higher notes, demonstrating clearly the relationship between the length of a vibrating string and its pitch.

versions of the same notes. If you start from C and repeat the procedure, you will hear the scale of C major.

If the length of a string is halved, a pitch is produced which is exactly double the frequency of the original pitch and sounds eight notes (or an octave) higher. In other words, if you halve the length of a string vibrating at 440 frequencies, you will hear the pitch of 880 frequencies, which corresponds to the next (or higher) A on the keyboard.

Although there are only seven letter names, other notes (the black keys on a piano, known as sharps or flats) exist in between some of these to produce a total of 12 notes.

Intervals

The gaps between the notes are known as "intervals," and moving from one note on the piano keyboard to its nearest neighbor covers the interval of a "semitone." Of course, with other instruments (such as the violin) it is possible to play in between these notes; indeed, it is common for string instruments and voices to slide between notes for expressive effect.

PITCH AND NOTATION

Western music uses horizontal lines and spaces against which to plot musical notes in graphic notation. Since the 17th century, five lines have been used, comprising a "staff" or "stave." A sign known as a "clef" is used at the beginning of each staff to indicate which line or space should be used to denote a particular note. The most common clefs are the treble (or G) and bass (or F) clefs, the former being used for higher pitches and the latter for lower pitches. Thus, a violinist would typically use the treble clef, while a double-bass player would usually use the bass clef. A pianist normally uses both, the treble clef being usually assigned to the upper half of the keyboard (played by the right hand) and the bass clef to the lower half. The diagram below shows the relationship of the piano keyboard to the treble and bass clefs.

Sharps and flats
These are used to raise (sharpen) and lower (flatten) a note by a semitone. The interval from, for example, G to A is known as a "tone," while the interval from a G to G♯ is a "semitone" (the smallest possible interval on the keyboard). Although the G♯ is a raised G, it is in fact the same note as an A♭ (in other words, a lowered A).

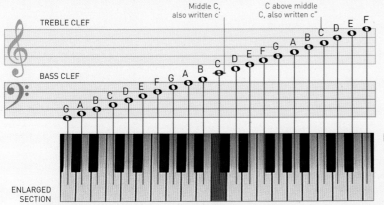

《 Middle C is colored brown on the full keyboard as well as on the enlarged section.

BASSOON
The range of the bassoon (the bass instrument of the woodwind family) is just over three octaves, similar to that of the male voice. Its lower notes correspond to the low notes of a bass singer, but its top notes are somewhat higher than a tenor. This range is similar to that of the cello and the trombone.

CLARINET
The range of the clarinet corresponds to the female voice. Its lowest notes are in the alto region while its high notes are close to those of a high soprano. It has a range of three and a half octaves and is most powerful in its upper register. The oboe, trumpet, and violin all have similar ranges to the clarinet.

PICCOLO
The piccolo (a small flute) is the smallest woodwind instrument and therefore produces the highest pitch of all the instruments of the family. Its range is nearly three octaves and it can reach higher pitches than the female voice. It often doubles lower instruments to provide brilliance and penetration in orchestral music.

⌃ **The simultaneous production** of musical tones in a complex interweaving of harmony and melody is one of the distinguishing features of Western music.

Harmony

Harmony is the result of combining musical notes, and when these are played simultaneously, they are said to form a "chord." Some chords sound dissonant, others harmonious or consonant. Harmony can be regarded as the resolution of tension. In conventional tonal music, certain phrases end in "cadences" (or closing progressions of chords). Common examples are the "perfect" cadence (which sounds conclusive), the "imperfect" (which sounds inconclusive and demands some kind of continuation), and the "plagal" (which sounds serious and final and is often used for the "Amen" of a hymn).

Rhythm and tempo

Many human activities, such as running, walking, or dancing, produce distinctive rhythms, which are often reproduced in music. Rhythm involves not only the positioning or spacing of notes in time, but also their duration, and both of these can be notated in Western music (see p.15). Composers can show duration in terms of sound or silence: for sound, note shapes are used;

PULSE AND TEMPO

ITALIAN	ENGLISH
Grave	Very slowly
Lento	Slowly
Largo	Broadly
Larghetto	Rather broadly
Adagio	Leisurely
Andante	At a walking pace
Moderato	Moderately
Allegretto	Fairly quickly
Allegro	Fast
Vivace	Lively
Presto	Very quickly
Prestissimo	As fast as possible

HARMONY AND INTERVALS

If two notes played together are separated by a consonant (harmonious) interval, the resulting sound will be pleasant or relaxing to our ears, whereas the notes of a dissonant interval clash with each other and demand to be resolved by a suitable consonance. The intervals considered dissonant have changed since the Middle Ages, but since the Classical and early Romantic eras the intervals illustrated below have been considered either consonant or dissonant.

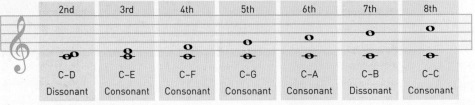

	2nd	3rd	4th	5th	6th	7th	8th
	C–D	C–E	C–F	C–G	C–A	C–B	C–C
	Dissonant	Consonant	Consonant	Consonant	Consonant	Dissonant	Consonant

EXAMPLES IN THE KEY OF C MAJOR

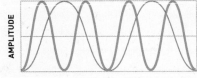

Interval of an octave
The waves shown are of two frequencies an octave apart, as in a consonant interval of the type C–C.

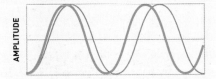

Interval of a second
These waves are of the two individual notes that are combined to produce a second, a dissonant interval of the type C–D.

NOTES, TIME, RHYTHM, AND METER

The chart below shows the time values of the notes used in Western music. For example, two half notes are equal in length to a whole and two quarter notes are equal to a half. All values are relative, however; a quarter is not an absolute length, such as a second, but varies according to the composer's instructions or a musician's instinct. In slow music, a quarter could be more than two seconds in length; in quick music, less than half a second. The UK uses different names for these values, such as "semibreve," and those are given below the American names.

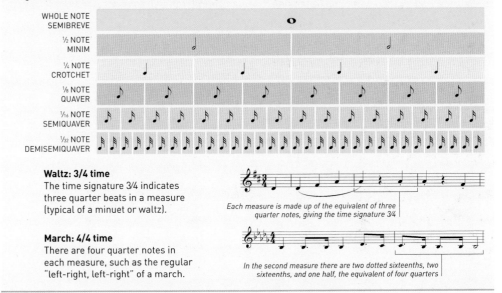

WHOLE NOTE SEMIBREVE		
½ NOTE MINIM		
¼ NOTE CROTCHET		
⅛ NOTE QUAVER		
¹⁄₁₆ NOTE SEMIQUAVER		
¹⁄₃₂ NOTE DEMISEMIQUAVER		

Waltz: 3/4 time
The time signature 3/4 indicates three quarter beats in a measure (typical of a minuet or waltz).

Each measure is made up of the equivalent of three quarter notes, giving the time signature 3/4

March: 4/4 time
There are four quarter notes in each measure, such as the regular "left-right, left-right" of a march.

In the second measure there are two dotted sixteenths, two sixteenths, and one half, the equivalent of four quarters

"rests," with corresponding values and names, are used to denote periods of silence.

The pulse (commonly known as the "beat") is a regular unit of time around which the rhythm of a piece is organized. In a march, this would be the position in time of each footstep. The composer decides whether the pulse should be a half or a quarter, or any other note value.

The speed of the pulse is the "tempo" of the work. Most composers have used Italian terms (see p.14) to indicate tempo.

« In nature, the sounds of horses cantering or of waves crashing on a beach create powerful, distinctive rhythms. Music owes much to such rhythmic sounds, not to mention more immediate rhythms, such as breathing and the beating of the human heart.

Since the early 19th century, musicians have also used metronome settings. (A metronome is a device that can be set to "tick" at varying speeds and is calibrated according to divisions of the minute—for example, 60 or 120 beats to the minute.

Meter

The meter corresponds to the grouping of the pulse. Much Classical music is grouped in twos or threes. Each group is known as a "measure" or "bar" and in notation is separated by a "barline." The meter is indicated by a "time signature," such as 3/4. The top number shows the number of beats in the measure, while the lower number shows the value assigned to each beat. The time signature 3/4 indicates that there are three quarter notes in a measure (typical of a dance such as a minuet or waltz). A march rhythm

could be given the time signature 2/4, in which there would be two quarter notes in every measure.

Scales and tonality

A scale (from the Latin *scala*, meaning steps) is a stepwise series of notes, usually between one note and the next note of that name an octave higher. In the West, scales may be traced back to medieval "modes," which were based on the musical ideas of the Ancient Greeks. These eventually came to be accepted as the principal scales for all music in the 16th century: the Ionian became the "major" scale, and the Aeolian the "natural minor" scale. Traditionally the associations of the major scale are positive— sometimes joyful, sometimes triumphant; Beethoven's "Eroica" Symphony, for example, is in the heroic key of E flat major. The minor

◘ **One of the most familiar time signatures** to dancers, the basic waltz meter (one-two-three, one-two-three) is three beats to each measure of music.

 **Across the world,** most cultures have their own scales, consisting not only of different notes from those used in the West, but of different numbers of notes.

scale is generally recognized as more somber in mood—sometimes plaintive and sometimes tragic. The Funeral March from Chopin's Piano Sonata No. 2 is in the key of B flat minor.

Musical form

All musical works—however short or long—are organized within a kind of frame, known as a "form." The two basic forms are "binary" (two sections, stated one after the other and sometimes repeated) and "ternary" (three sections, perhaps comprising section A, followed by section B, then section A again—musical sections or paragraphs are often identified by letters of the alphabet). Variants of these are to be found in more complex forms such as the "rondo," "variation," and "sonata" forms (see glossary).

Dynamics

Just as the pitch or rhythm of musical sound can be varied, so can the volume or intensity of that sound. In Western music, this variability has become known as "dynamics." As with tempo, it is common to use Italian terms to describe different dynamics, all of which are relative rather than absolute.

DYNAMICS

ITALIAN	ENGLISH
Pianissimo (pp)	Very quietly
Piano (p)	Quietly
Mezzo piano (mp)	Moderately quietly
Mezzo forte (mf)	Moderately loudly
Forte (f)	Loudly
Fortissimo (ff)	Very loudly

Classical Music Instruments

The design, construction, and acoustics of instruments change as musicians explore different ways of achieving what composers ask of them, and as instrument makers experiment with new materials and technologies. In the process, some instruments become obsolete, while those that fit in with new trends become popular.

Today's symphony orchestra has its roots in 16th-century instrumental consorts (see p.21) and 17th-century bands. The earliest orchestras, usually attached to a court, a church, or a theater, varied in structure from place to place. They were often directed from the keyboard or by the principal violinist.

During the 18th century, as popular works (such as those by Haydn and Mozart) began to be played all over Europe, some standardization of the orchestra became necessary. A string section comprising violins, violas, cellos, and double basses was usually joined by two oboes and two bassoons, with the occasional addition of two horns, two flutes, two trumpets, and timpani. The clarinet became a standard member of the orchestra only at the end of the 18th century.

The 19th century saw the rise of public concerts in large halls, which necessitated louder instruments and larger orchestras. As a result, instruments changed: woodwind key systems were redesigned; the brass acquired valves; string instruments were adapted to be able to project farther.

Larger and smaller versions of woodwind instruments, such as the piccolo, cor anglais, and bass clarinet, featured more frequently. Instruments were also added to the lower end of the brass section, with trombones and, later, tubas becoming standard members of the orchestra.

The orchestra today

The orchestra had more or less attained its present form, although in the 20th century a whole new range of percussion instruments became available. The Early Music revival has seen the recreation of historic styles of orchestra, but the dominant orchestral line-up remains the symphony orchestra under the direction of a conductor, with orchestras resident in most major cities throughout the world.

❮❮ **Instruments of the string family**—violins, violas, cellos, and double basses—form the backbone of the orchestra, but are also found in chamber ensembles such as the string quartet or as solo instruments.

" Music expresses that which **cannot be put into words** and that which **cannot remain silent. "**

Victor Hugo, French writer

Early Instruments

Many instruments from the past have disappeared from mainstream usage or have been replaced by modern equivalents. Over the last 50 years, however, makers and musicians have revived these instruments in an attempt to create historically informed performances. The ancestors of modern woodwinds usually have no keys, while those of the brass section include trumpets and horns without valves. Early stringed instruments, which have gut strings and lower tensions, tend to be softer in tone than their modern equivalents.

Strings

Viols have six or seven strings, with frets across the fingerboard. The outward-curving bow is held underhand. Some smaller viols, such as the **viola d'amore,** have additional sympathetic strings that run through the bridge and under the fingerboard. **Lutes** are plucked with the right hand and are often used as continuo instruments or to accompany singing. Some have additional bass strings known as diapasons. The **hurdy-gurdy** uses a wheel operated by a crank handle to "bow" the strings, and a small keyboard to stop the strings.

Second peg box for bass diapason strings

Tuning pegs

Fingerboard

Decorative carved head

Fretted fingerboard

Peg box

Tuning pegs

Cover over rosined wheel

Keyboard

Diapasons

Rose hole

Sympathetic strings

Bridge

Decorated keyboard

Handle

Tailpiece

HURDY-GURDY

VIOLA D'AMORE (1774)

18TH-CENTURY GERMAN BASS LUTE

ENGLISH-MADE BASS VIOL (1713)

18TH-CENTURY CLAVICHORD

Keyboards

The **harpsichord** is used in Early-Music ensembles as a continuo instrument, to add brilliance and rhythm to the texture. The strings, made of iron or brass, are plucked by small pieces of quill. The **virginal** and **spinet** are plucked in a similar way, while the **clavichord** uses small brass flags—tangents—to strike the strings. Clavichords are perfect domestic instruments as they are very quiet. In the **organ,** different sounds are produced by making pipes of different materials with a variety of cross sections, and by exciting the air in the pipes in various ways, such as blowing air across a fipple (as in the recorder) or by using reeds.

Brass

The **cornett** was a treble instrument with open finger holes, made from a single piece of ivory or two carved pieces of wood glued together. The **serpent** was used as a bass instrument in military and church bands in the 18th and 19th centuries. The earliest **trumpets** were "natural" instruments (without valves or keys) that played a single harmonic series. Various devices were added in the 18th and 19th centuries to enable them to play more notes. **Horns** were also originally natural instruments, sometimes equipped with crooks to enable them to be played in different keys.

Two carved pieces of walnut, bound with string and leather

"Acorn cup" mouthpiece

Keys used to change notes

Finger holes, placed for the convenience of the player's hands, were not acoustically correct

Crooks attached to extend length of horn

Open finger holes

LATE-18TH-CENTURY KEYED TRUMPET

18TH-CENTURY NATURAL HORN

19TH-CENTURY SERPENT

CORNETT

Woodwind

The earliest wind instruments were pipes made from wood or bone, with finger holes to change the sounding length and hence the pitch of the note produced. The **shawm** family are sounded by a double reed on a metal staple fitted into a "pirouette." Shawms were popular from the 13th to the 17th century and ranged from high soprano to a low bass called a pommer. Another double-reed instrument, the **crumhorn**, hides its reed within a cap. Its heyday was in the 16th and 17th centuries, when it was used to accompany religious ceremonies as well as secular dances. **Recorders** have a fipple or whistle-style mouthpiece and holes for one thumb and seven fingers. They were widely used as solo and consort instruments before the 19th century and have reemerged in the 20th century for teaching music in schools. Many early woodwinds were made of close-grained woods such as boxwood, but makers have also experimented with ivory, glass, and various metals.

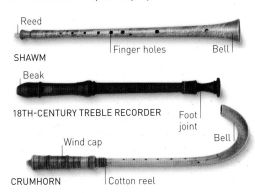

Reed

Finger holes

Bell

SHAWM

Beak

18TH-CENTURY TREBLE RECORDER

Foot joint

Bell

Wind cap

CRUMHORN

Cotton reel

A WIND CONSORT

Consorts were small groups of mixed instruments. The instruments played in a wind consort included the hautbois (ancestor of the oboe), cornett, and sackbut (ancestor of the trombone). In the 17th century, wind consorts would usually have been heard outside, often at gatherings of important people, with quieter string consorts used indoors.

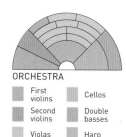

ORCHESTRA

First violins	Cellos
Second violins	Double basses
Violas	Harp

Strings

The string section is the largest group in the orchestra and forms its core, and the leading voice among the strings is the violin, an instrument of extraordinary range and versatility. Orchestral violins are divided into two sections: "firsts" and "seconds." Violins, violas, cellos, and double basses are primarily played with a bow but, like the harp, can also be plucked. The left hand is used to stop the strings in order to change their vibrating length and hence the pitch of the notes. A variety of tonal effects can be achieved by placing the bow closer to or farther away from the bridge, by damping the vibrations of the bridge using a mute, or by applying different bowing techniques. Since the early 19th century, many earlier stringed instruments have been altered to increase their volume and projection.

Scroll

Screw for adjusting tension of hair

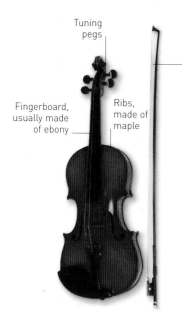

Tuning pegs

Rosined horsehair

Fingerboard, usually made of ebony

Ribs, made of maple

Table, made of pine

Carved wood, usually pernambuco

Bridge

Supporting spike

Violin

Characteristics: With four strings tuned in fifths, violins are agile and versatile, and can play two or three notes simultaneously.
History: Early violins were in use in Italy from the early 16th century. Cremona and Brescia became important centers of violin-making from 1550.

Viola

Characteristics: The alto of the family, the viola is tuned a fifth below the violin. It has a darker, richer sound than the violin.
History: Larger and smaller viola-type instruments were used for both tenor and alto lines from the early 16th century. Its modern role developed in the 18th century.

Cello

Characteristics: Tuned an octave below the viola, the cello is the tenor and bass of the violin family. It is also capable of playing virtuoso passages.
History: Appearing in the early 16th century, cellos were made by many of the famous Cremona violin makers.

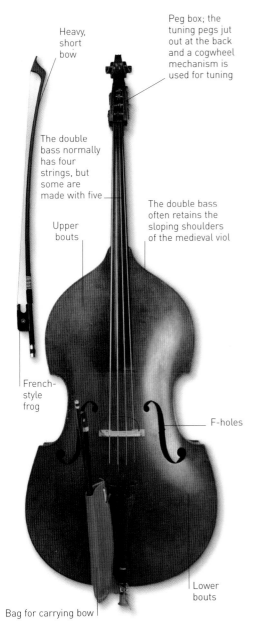

Heavy, short bow

Peg box; the tuning pegs jut out at the back and a cogwheel mechanism is used for tuning

The double bass normally has four strings, but some are made with five

Upper bouts

The double bass often retains the sloping shoulders of the medieval viol

French-style frog

F-holes

Lower bouts

Bag for carrying bow

Double bass

Characteristics: Although a member of the viols, the double bass has been adopted as the lowest-pitched voice of the violin family. There are two main styles of bow: French, held like a violin bow, and German, held with the hand upside-down like a viol bow.
History: Early double basses often had six strings, while many 18th-century examples had only three. Modern ones have four or five.

Harp

Characteristics: The modern orchestral harp has 47 strings stretched between the neck and soundboard, together with seven pedals for altering the pitches of the strings. As well as playing plucked chords, the harpist can use techniques such as glissandos and harmonics to create special effects. Harps are often associated with heavenly or ethereal music.
History: Small harps existed in ancient times and are still important in many folk traditions. The modern double-action pedal harp was developed in the 18th and 19th centuries by makers such as Cousineau and Erard in Paris and London.

The strings on a harp are attached at one end to the resonator; in the violin family they run above its surface

Pillar

Soundboard

Pedals for altering pitches of strings

ANTONIO STRADIVARI (c.1644–1737)

Stradivari emerged from a long tradition of violin makers in Cremona. Taught by Nicolo Amati, he educated his sons in the trade, and his family workshop produced violins, violas, cellos, pochettes, and guitars. Many consider his instruments the finest ever made. Debates continue concerning the woods and varnishes he used.

ORCHESTRA

Clarinets Bassoons

Flutes Oboes

Woodwind

Woodwind instruments are derived from basic blown pipes and can be made from a wide variety of materials. Many produce their sound by means of a vibrating "reed." They come in families, with larger and smaller versions of the main orchestral instrument, and are used to add a variety of colors to the orchestral sound. The standard woodwind section of the modern orchestra comprises two flutes, piccolo, two oboes, cor anglais, two clarinets, bass clarinet, two bassoons, and contrabassoon. In some works, composers may call for additional woodwind instruments, such as saxophones and smaller high-pitched clarinets.

Single reeds

Characteristics: Single reeds use a cane reed, held over a slot in the mouthpiece by a ligature and placed against the player's lower lip. The clarinet can produce a wide variety of tone colors. The saxophone appears occasionally in the orchestra but is more common in wind and jazz bands.
History: Johann Christopher Denner of Nuremberg is reputed to have invented the clarinet at the beginning of the 18th century. More keys were gradually added in the 19th century.

CLARINET REED

Feathered edge

THEOBALD BOEHM (1794–1881)

Born in Munich, Boehm was a professional flautist who also worked in the jewelry and steel industries. He spent over 30 years remodelling the keywork and bores of flutes, and his 1847 cylindrical flute is the pattern for most modern instruments. Boehm's successors have applied his principles to other woodwind instruments.

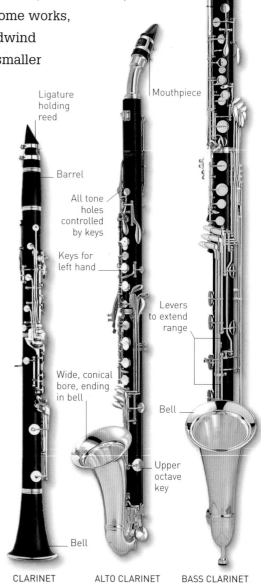

Crook

Ligature holding reed

Mouthpiece

Barrel

All tone holes controlled by keys

Keys for left hand

Levers to extend range

Wide, conical bore, ending in bell

Bell

Upper octave key

Bell

Bell

CLARINET   ALTO CLARINET   BASS CLARINET

Double reeds

Characteristics: The oboe and bassoon families have conical bores and a double reed, consisting of two pieces of shaped cane strapped together, which is held gently between the lips. The treble oboe is often given prominent melodies and requires a significant amount of air pressure to sound properly. The tenor voice of the cor anglais is popular as a solo instrument because it has a rich and sonorous quality. Forming the tenor and bass of the woodwind, the versatile bassoon has a bore which doubles back on itself. The large contrabassoon adds a deep bass to the woodwind section.

History: Both the oboe and the early bassoon first appeared in 17th-century France. While the oboe (from hautbois, meaning "high" or "loud wood") developed from the shawm, the bassoon's precursors were the dulcian ("sweet sounding") and fagot ("bundle of sticks").

Slender double reed

Reed attached to bent crook

Bell

The tubing of the contrabassoon is twice the length of the bassoon's

Crook (metal tube that holds reed)

Long levers to reach widely spaced finger holes

Staple (cork-covered tube)

Staple

Bore of oboe is conical

Distinctive bulbous bell

Hand support

Long wooden tube doubles back on itself

Butt

BASSOON REED

CLARINET

OBOE

COR ANGLAIS

CONTRABASSOON

BASSOON

Flutes

Characteristics: The air in a flute is set in motion by blowing across the edge of the embouchure hole. Usually providing the top woodwind voice, the flute also has a mellow low register. The smaller piccolo can cut through the entire orchestral texture to great effect.

History: Early flutes were usually made of boxwood or ivory and had open finger holes. The keywork of the modern flute (usually made of silver) is based on a 19th-century design.

PICCOLO

Embouchure

FLUTE

Brass

ORCHESTRA

■ Horns   ■ Trumpets

■ Trombones
and tubas

Brass instruments consist of a length of metal tubing ending in a flared bell. They use a slide mechanism or valves, which engage additional lengths of tubing to extend their range. The air column is set in motion by vibrating the lips against a cupped mouthpiece. Sound characteristics are partly a result of the width of the bore, as well as the shape and size of the mouthpiece and the bell. While they can be played subtly, brass instruments are often used for power and dramatic effect.

Mouthpiece

Rotary valves

Keys controlling rotary valves

Tuning slide

Bell

FRENCH HORN MOUTHPIECE

Small-cupped mouthpiece

French horn
Characteristics: The tubing of the modern horn is mostly conical. It usually has three or four rotary valves, operated by the left hand, while the right hand is inserted into the bell to shape the sound. Most horns are pitched in F (single) or a combination of F and B flat (double or "compensating"). Horn players sometimes specialize in playing either high or low parts.
History: The natural horn was used as a signaling instrument on the hunting field. Before the advent of valves, some players used hand stopping (partly closing the bell with the right hand) to play notes outside the harmonic series, a technique that also changes the timber of the note.

Valves

Mouthpiece

Cylindrical tubing

Bell

Cup

Shank

TRUMPET MOUTHPIECE

Trumpet
Characteristics: The bore of the orchestral trumpet is partly cylindrical and partly conical. It has three valves, which lower the pitch by a semitone, tone, or minor third. Different-sized trumpets (C, D, and B flat are most common) are used to make higher or lower parts easier to play. Inserting various mutes into the bell alters the timbre produced.
History: The early trumpet—a single length of tubing with a shallow flared bell—traditionally had a military or ceremonial function. From the late 18th century, various methods were developed to make more notes available, including the addition of crooks, slides, keys, or valves.

Water key

Slide to extend length of tubing

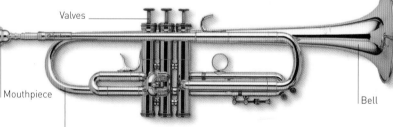

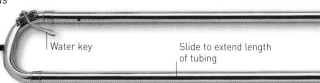

Tuba

Characteristics: Instruments of the tuba family (including euphoniums, sousaphones, and bombardons) have wide, conical bores and provide the bass of the brass section. Different shapes and sizes are used but the typical orchestral instrument has an upward-pointing bell, with three to six valves. The player uses a great deal of breath but less wind pressure than for smaller instruments.

History: First developed in Germany in the 1830s, the tuba was embraced enthusiastically by composers such as Berlioz. It had replaced its predecessor, the ophicleide (an early 19th-century invention) in most bands and orchestras by the 1870s.

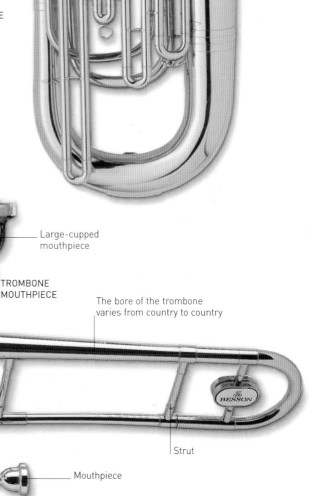

Bell

Mouthpiece

Valves

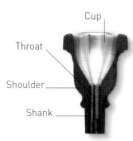

Cup

Throat

Shoulder

Shank

TUBA
MOUTHPIECE

Trombone

Characteristics: The cylindrical bored trombone has a telescoping slide rather than valves to change the tube length. Seven slide positions are used, each changing the pitch by a semitone. Sizes range from soprano to contrabass trombones, with the tenor and bass being the typical orchestral instruments.

History: When trombones, or sackbuts, first appeared in the late 15th century, they lacked the flaring bell of modern instruments. Valves were added in the 1820s, but it is the slide version that now predominates.

Large-cupped
mouthpiece

TROMBONE
MOUTHPIECE

Bell

The bore of the trombone
varies from country to country

Strut

Mouthpiece

ORCHESTRA

Drums | Other percussion instruments

Percussion and keyboards

Percussion instruments are divided into two main categories: membranophones (where a stretched membrane is struck, as with a drum) and idiophones (where an object made of resonant material is struck). Some idiophones, such as the xylophone and tubular bells, are tuned and capable of producing melody as well as rhythm. Other idiophones range from cymbals, triangles, and tambourines to the more exotic tam-tam (a large oriental gong), wood block, castanets, and maracas. Special sound-effect instruments, such as the whip (two wooden slats that are slapped together), sleigh bells, rattles, or sirens, can also be employed. To these, keyboard instruments, such as the piano and celesta, are often added.

Drums

Characteristics: Timpani (or kettledrums) can be tuned by altering the skin tension using turning screws or a pedal. The snare drum is smaller and has a set of gut or metal springs stretched across its lower drum head which vibrate when the upper head is struck.

History: Drums came into the orchestra in the late 17th century, initially in combination with trumpets.

Tensioned batter head

Tuning gauge

Tensioning screws

Copper or fiberglass shell

Tuning pedal

TIMPANUM AND DRUM STICK

Batter head

Metal frame

BASS DRUM

SNARE DRUM

Idiophones

Characteristics: Cymbals are made from metal and are sounded either with a stick or by clashing a pair together. Tambourines consist of "jingles" fitted in a ring of wood. They can be shaken, hit, or used to play a roll. The triangle—a steel bar bent to form an equilateral triangle—is hung from a string and may be hit with one or two metal beaters. Trills are played using quick strokes inside the top corner.

History: Many percussion instruments originated in China or Turkey and became regular members of the orchestra in the 19th and 20th centuries.

Jingles

TRIANGLE

TAMBOURINE

CYMBALS

Tuned idiophones

Characteristics: The glockenspiel consists of a series of metal bars tuned to a chromatic scale, laid out like a piano keyboard. Sticks with heads of wood, metal, rubber, or fabric can be used to create different tone qualities. A wooden equivalent, the xylophone, can have resonators fitted beneath its rosewood bars. Tubular bells, which are hit with a small mallet, are often used to evoke the sound of church bells.

History: Xylophones are found in many cultures, and, like tubular bells, were adopted by European composers in the 19th century. The first orchestral use of the glockenspiel is thought to be in Handel's *Saul* (1739).

Wooden bars

Resonators

XYLOPHONE

Tuned steel pipes

GLOCKENSPIEL | Metal plates

TUBULAR BELLS
AND MALLET

Keyboards

Characteristics: The piano, developed from the harpsichord in early-18th-century Florence by Bartolomeo Cristofori, is sometimes defined as a percussion instrument since its strings are struck by hammers. While early pianos are largely made of wood and have a delicate sound, modern grand pianos have metal frames, larger hammers, and heavier strings, and can be played much more loudly. The celesta, invented in 1886 by Auguste Mustel, is a keyboard instrument in which tuned metal plates are struck by hammers.

Metal frame supports tension of the strings

Keyboard

The left pedal ("una corda") moves the hammers so they strike only one of the two strings for each note in the treble and two of the three in the bass

Some pianos have a third central pedal which raises the dampers of those notes being played when depressed

The right pedal lifts all the dampers, allowing the strings to vibrate freely

GRAND PIANO

Classical Music
In Performance

A common perception of Classical music is that it is performed in the formal surroundings of a concert hall and usually involves a large symphony orchestra and world-famous soloists and conductors. However, Classical music can just as easily be brought to life in the home or outdoors.

The professional composer whose works are performed by professional musicians for a paying audience is a relatively recent phenomenon. The idea of attending an event specifically to listen to music—rather than to hear music in the course of a church service or an entertainment at court—would have been very unusual before the 17th century. In medieval times, most sacred music was performed by monks within the church and secular music was played and sung by wandering minstrels. Just as many early composers were anonymous, so too were most early performers.

During the Renaissance and Baroque periods, performers began to emerge from obscurity. Some of the first to achieve fame in northern Europe were organists; during his lifetime, J.S. Bach may have been better known as an organist than as a composer. Another group of "celebrity" performers to emerge during the Baroque period were opera singers. Some of Handel's sopranos were notorious for their capricious demands.

◀◀ **Live performance of Classical music,** whether a formal white-tie-and-tails concert or a more relaxed occasion, can be an unforgettable experience.

The concert

The word "concert" is probably derived from the Italian *concertare* ("to arrange" or "to get together"). In the 17th century, musicians would come together to perform both privately and publicly. An early example was in Lübeck, Germany, where it became fashionable in the 1620s for a performance of secular music to follow Evensong in a public building (such as the town hall). This came to be known as *Abendmusik*.

Concerts were enthusiastically taken up in England at the time of the Civil War, when hardly any music was performed in churches. Musicians responded to public demand by giving concerts for which listeners paid an admission fee. Many were held in taverns such as London's Mitre Inn.

A musical heritage

Until well into the 19th century, the composer and performer were often one and the same. The performance of "old" music (music composed by earlier generations) was rare until the 19th century. Until that time, almost all music heard was contemporary, often composed for specific events, whether sacred (as in the case of Bach's Cantatas) or secular (as in that of Handel's *Music for*

⏏ **A group of 14th-century musicians** performs on a range of instruments, including drum, pipe, shawm, vielle with a curved bow, and psaltery.

the Royal Fireworks). It was in England that performers began to take an interest in music of the past: the Academy of Ancient Music (established in 1726) performed music by such composers as Byrd and Purcell, whereas the rival Concerts of Ancient Music (founded in 1776) performed Baroque music, including that of Handel and Corelli.

Professional musicians

The music societies formed during the 18th century organized concerts in which amateur musicians could perform under the direction of professionals. The composer Telemann founded such a society in Hamburg in 1713, and another was to be found in Leipzig, directed by the Kantor of the Thomaskirche—the position held by J.S. Bach at the time of his death. The Leipzig society was named the Grosses Konzert in 1743, and by the middle of the 19th century, all its players were professionals. The organization—now the Leipzig Gewandhaus Orchestra—still exists today.

Many local music societies (as well as a few performers) began to sell admission to a series of concerts to the public, demanding payment prior to the first of the concerts. This became known as the "subscription concert." One of the first successful examples was that of J.C. Bach in London in 1765.

CONCERT HALLS

Initially, concert halls were limited in size, but London's Hanover Square Rooms (1775) held in excess of 600 people. The audience was free to move around during the performance and talk, or to sit on sofas around the hall. With the increased projection capabilities of new instruments, concert halls could become larger. In 1826, Berlin's Singakademie was built for an audience of 1,200. During the 19th century, cultural centers competed with each other to build larger, more elaborate halls, such as the Musikvereinsaal in Vienna (1870) and the Royal Albert Hall in London (1871).

⏏ **The Palau de la Música Catalana**, a richly decorated concert hall, was built in Barcelona in 1908 as a symbol of Catalan pride.

During the 18th and 19th centuries, concerts were long and diverse. The Gewandhaus subscription concerts would frequently contain an overture, an opera aria, an instrumental solo, and a choral finale in each half, and might last for three or four hours in total. Where vocal music had been at the centre of 18th-century programmes, during the 19th century it became more accepted

TIMELINE: CLASSICAL MUSIC IN PERFORMANCE

1715 Forerunner of Three Choirs Festival founded in Gloucester, Hereford, and Worcester, England

1764 Wolfgang and Nannerl Mozart tour Europe and perform for Louis XV

1791 Haydn's first visit to London for Salomon's concert series

1820 Spohr introduces baton at an orchestra rehearsal

1700	1740	1780	1820

1726 Academy of Ancient Music founded in London

1748 Holywell Room in Oxford opened for concert

1781 First Gewandhaus concert takes place in Leipzig

1810 Paganini undertakes first concert tour

1840 Liszt uses the term "recital" for a solo concert

to perform movements from concertos and symphonies, although concerts solely of instrumental music were still rare. The orchestra had emerged during the Renaissance as a group of players brought together for important occasions. During the 18th century, the modern string family replaced viols in this group and an important member was the keyboard player or "continuo"—a harpsichord, an organ, or, later, a piano that would play from the bass-line of the score.

By the 19th century, the continuo had disappeared and a standard layout had emerged. Violins were grouped into two sections and there were smaller groups of violas, cellos, and basses, while there was normally a pair each of flutes, oboes, clarinets, bassoons, trumpets, and horns ("double wind"), and timpani. During the 19th century, this group became extended so that piccolos, cor anglais, trombones, tubas, and further percussion were added.

The layout of orchestras has changed considerably over the years. Perhaps the most radical alteration in the course of the 20th century was the moving of the second violins next to the first violins and the cellos to the conductor's right.

As orchestras became established, a "canon" or core repertoire emerged—largely works by the Viennese composers (i.e. Mozart and Beethoven) as well as opera music by composers such as Gluck and Cherubini. By the end of the 19th century, concert activity had divided into solo recitals, chamber music performances, and orchestral performances.

The solo recital

Liszt was responsible for introducing the solo recital in the late 1830s. He toured Europe extensively, performing in towns and cities from Scotland to Russia. One of his innovations was that of playing from memory. In the 21st century this has become the norm for soloists, but in Liszt's time it was considered dangerously radical.

While Liszt was establishing his reputation across Europe, a market was developing for the celebrity performer in the United States.

MUSIC FESTIVALS

Festivals date back to about 1715 with the first meeting of the cathedral choirs of Gloucester, Hereford, and Worcester (the Three Choirs Festival). Many great composers have inspired festivals in their memory, notably Handel (1784) and Beethoven (1845). The 20th century saw the establishment of festivals such as the Maggio Musicale Fiorentino (from 1933) and the Lucerne Festival (1938). The composers Benjamin Britten and Sir Peter Maxwell Davies established their own festivals in Aldeburgh and Orkney respectively. American festivals include those at Aspen, Ravinia, and Tanglewood.

⌃ **The Boston Symphony Orchestra** has staged its summer festival at Tanglewood since 1940.

1880s Foundation of Berlin Philharmonic, Boston Symphony, and Amsterdam Concertgebouw Orchestras

1947 Amadeus Quartet founded

1983 The Canadian Opera Company is the first to use subtitles, for its production of *Elektra*

1995 The MP3 digital audio format is launched

1860　　　　**1900**　　　　**1940**　　　　**1980**

1877 Phonograph invented by Thomas Edison

1891 Carnegie Hall opens in New York; Paderewski tours USA for first time

1940 Tanglewood Music Center founded by Serge Koussevitsky

1976 Ensemble InterContemporain founded by Pierre Boulez

1983 The first commercial Compact Disk (CD) player is released by Sony in Japan

The singer Jenny Lind, for example, drew an audience of over 7,000 at Castle Garden in New York in 1850, while pianists such as Thalberg and Anton Rubinstein toured the United States from the mid-19th century onward, and Paderewski created a sensation with his tours there in the 1890s.

New orchestras

The Berlin Philharmonic Orchestra, founded in 1882, has set what many consider the finest standards in orchestral playing. Brahms's friend Joseph Joachim was appointed its first conductor and was succeeded by Liszt's pupil Hans von Bülow in 1887. Prestigious orchestras were established on the other side of the Atlantic by wealthy industrialists: the Philharmonic Symphony Society of New York (later the New York Philharmonic) in 1842 and the Boston Symphony Orchestra in 1881.

In recent years, new orchestras formed in response to social and political problems have revitalized the scene: Daniel Barenboim's West-Eastern Divan, founded in 1999, has brought together fine young performers from Israel and the Arab countries, and

the youthful Venezuelan Orquesta Sinfónica Simón Bolívar has stunned audiences with their exuberant virtuosity.

Wider audiences

In the 19th century, concert series were founded to make music available to people who could not afford to attend subscription concerts. London's Crystal Palace concerts were a typical venture of this kind. Two free concerts were given daily throughout the 1850s.

Military bands also brought music to wider audiences. Under J.P. Sousa in the 1880s, the Marine Corps Band would give free weekly concerts at the White House and the Capitol in Washington. At the same time there was a great increase in the number of choral societies, especially in industrial regions such as northern England, Wales, and Germany's Ruhr Valley.

Modern performers

Few 20th- or 21st-century composers have been known as performers, but Richard Strauss, Bernstein, Boulez, and others have combined the roles of conductor

 **The personnel and seating arrangement** of the modern symphony orchestra is now effectively standardized around the world. The picture below shows the Bournemouth Symphony Orchestra with its principal conductor, Marin Alsop.

THE CONDUCTOR

The conductor became a focal point of interest through the efforts of Hector Berlioz in the 1830s. The conductor's job is about far more than keeping time. In performance, he or she may give cues to the players to indicate their entries, and may need to control the balance between sections. However, much of the work—on issues such as phrasing, bowing, breathing, or the respective attack and decay of sound—is done before the performance. Some conductors (Leonard Bernstein, Valery Gergiev) have been known for their extrovert use of gestures on stage, while others (Pierre Boulez, Bernard Haitink) are far more restrained. The one thing that all great conductors have in common is a natural sense of authority.

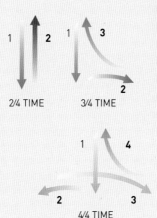

2/4 TIME   3/4 TIME

4/4 TIME

Whatever the time signature, the first beat of each bar is shown by a downward gesture (the downbeat) and the last by an upward gesture (the upbeat).

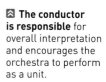

The conductor is responsible for overall interpretation and encourages the orchestra to perform as a unit.

and composer. Noncomposing performers, however, have influenced the repertoire of their instruments profoundly. The cellist Mstislav Rostropovich worked closely with Prokofiev, Shostakovich, Schnittke, and Britten; the singer Kathy Berberian inspired Berio to compose vocal music; and the pianist David Tudor worked with John Cage and other avant-garde composers.

Many performers have chosen to specialize in certain repertoires; Artur Schnabel, for example, was known for his renditions of the Beethoven piano sonatas. Some artists, such as the cellist Pablo Casals, are celebrated for the spirituality of their playing, while performers like violinist Jascha Heifetz and pianist Evgeny Kissin are noted for their technical prowess. Others, such as the pianist Alfred Brendel, seem to combine all these qualities with an intellectual integrity. Others still—violinists Maxim Vengerov and Nigel Kennedy, and the pianist Lang Lang, for example—are noted for their panache and conviction. Flamboyant artists who have raised the public profile of their instruments include

the flautist Sir James Galway, the percussionist Dame Evelyn Glennie, the trumpeter Håkan Hardenberger, the viola player Yuri Bashmet, and the trombonist Christian Lindberg. Some performers have looked to the east for inspiration; the violinist Yehudi Menuhin worked with sitar player Ravi Shankar, and the cellist Yo-Yo Ma has initiated an East-West collaboration through his Silk Road Ensemble.

RECORDING

Recording made music available to all. The first wax recordings, at the end of the 19th century, were dominated by opera arias by singers such as Caruso, as the voice could be reproduced much better than instrumental music.

Electric recording began in 1925, allowing longer excerpts of works to be recorded, and the arrival of LPs in 1948 allowed many works to be presented in their entirety. Stereo was introduced in 1958 and the CD in 1983.

In the 1990s computer technology advanced rapidly, and a new digital format for recorded music was developed. Recordings in the form of computer files were available as downloads from the internet, and could be played on a range of devices, from hi-fi systems to portable media players.

The availability of so many high-quality recordings means that new recordings of standard repertoire cannot be justified by the major record labels.

THE HISTORY OF
CLASSICAL MUSIC

Early Music
1000–1600

"Early Music" refers to the repertoire from historical periods less familiar to classically trained musicians and their audiences than those of the Classical and Romantic eras. This section covers the music of the Middle Ages and the Renaissance—a vast sweep of centuries of musical ideas, developments, and performance styles.

In terms of architecture, painting, and sculpture, the Renaissance can be said to have begun in 15th-century Florence. The transition between the music of the Middle Ages and the Renaissance is more difficult to identify, because musical styles developed gradually and in different ways across Europe. It is clear, however, that there were differences in the approach to musical composition as practiced by the French composer Machaut in the 14th century and the Italian Palestrina in the 16th century. Works by influential composers such as Dufay and Josquin changed musical style considerably in the late 15th and early 16th centuries, so 1450 is a convenient date to separate medieval from Renaissance music. What is usually referred to as Renaissance music may be seen to end at the point where Monteverdi and his contemporaries experimented with the new "Baroque" genres of opera, sonata, and concerto at the beginning of the 17th century, although countries such as England were still in a rich period of "Renaissance" music until perhaps two or three decades later.

◀◀ **This illustration of a minstrel** playing a vielle is from a 13th-century illuminated manuscript, *Cantigas de Santa Maria*, a collection of songs made for Alfonso X of Castile and León.

Church music

The music that has survived is heavily weighted in favor of the sacred. Plainsong was by far the most common kind of sacred music during this entire period, and was sung in every church, monastery, cathedral, and chapel. It was monophonic music—it had just a single line of melody—and could be sung by one voice or many. Most church musicians would have been expected to commit hundreds of chants to memory as part of their musical training, even after Guido d'Arezzo developed the music staff in the 11th century.

Secular monophonic music was created throughout this period, but only from the 12th century was it considered worthy of preservation in written collections. The most famous secular composers were the troubadours, trobairitz (female troubadours), and trouvères of medieval France, whose music and poetry usually expressed ideas of courtly love. Little is known about how their music was performed, but it is possible that their songs were accompanied by the vielle, a forerunner of the violin with five strings, one of which could produce a regular drone like that of a hurdy-gurdy or bagpipe. The vielle may thus have provided just a steady drone or more complex accompaniments to a solo singer.

Polyphony

The rise of polyphonic (literally "many-voiced") forms of composition from approximately the 12th century took place within the Church, as singers elaborated on the basic plainsong by the addition of other vocal parts on special occasions, such as Christmas or Easter. In the Cathedral of Notre-Dame de Paris, Léonin and Pérotin are credited with having written the first body of two-, three-, and four-part music to be circulated in manuscript form. By the 13th century, a large repertory of polyphony was found in major churches across Europe, and secular forms of music were also being written in more than one part. By the 15th century, polyphonic music was widespread and had become a necessary part of important religious and courtly celebrations.

The motet

The motet was one of the most popular sacred forms during the later Middle Ages, gradually making way for polyphonic settings of the Ordinary of the Mass (those parts of the Mass that remain the same every day). The motet was developed in the 13th century in northern France. The plainsong was placed into a strict rhythmic pattern, above which between one and three other lines were placed; these upper parts were each given a new text, resulting in a complex texture in which many different words sounded together.

Instrumental music

Along with new secular forms of song in the 16th century, such as the madrigal, instrumental music rose to such a status that it was more frequently copied down than it had been in the Middle Ages. The Renaissance saw a rise in the involvement of the merchant classes in the performance of music; the invention of music printing by Petrucci in 1501

PLAINSONG

Plainsong was the musical part of the liturgy in the Christian Church. Plainsong was monophonic, a single melodic line set in one of the eight church modes (scales based on a specific combination of intervals). These melodies might be short, regular, and simple, or more extensive, elaborate, and complex. The texts used for chants were religious, and written in Latin or Greek. Melodies were written down only from the 9th century, and there were regional variations in the chants used. Attempts were made to bring European churches into line so that all performed the same chants in the same way, but none were particularly successful.

≪ This Flemish manuscript score of 1522 is illuminated with a painting of clerics playing music in a garden.

TIMELINE: EARLY MUSIC

1054 Schism between Eastern Church and Church of Rome

c.1125 Rise of troubadours in southern France

c.1165–1200 Léonin and Pérotin compose significant body of church music for Notre-Dame de Paris

1000	1050	1100	1150

1030 Guido d'Arezzo describes the staff and uses the fingers and hand as aids to remembering music

1090 First Crusade: capture of Jerusalem

1150s Works of Hildegard of Bingen, earliest surviving set of compositions by a named author

⚠ **This scene,** showing nobles dancing in a garden, illustrates the great French medieval poem of courtly love, *Le Roman de la Rose.*

meant that music could be sold and distributed more easily, cheaply, and reliably than ever before, although much was still written down in manuscript (literally "handwritten") form.

Wealthy patrons of the 16th century demanded vocal and instrumental music for all sorts of musical combinations. In particular, "families" of instruments that comprised various sizes of one type of instrument (a consort of recorders, viols, or voices) flourished during the Renaissance period, although mixed or "broken" consorts of string, wind, and voice were also cultivated. Dances such as the stately pavan and the galliard, a lively dance involving leaps, became enormously popular.

Secular vocal music was written in vernacular languages, and very often had an amorous subject. The madrigal rose

» **French composers** produced the first complex polyphonic settings of the liturgy. This illumination, depicting monks singing, appears in a 13th-century French psalter.

c.1200 Completion of Notre-Dame de Paris

c.1250 Spanish *Cantigas de Santa Maria* written

c.1309 Papacy transfers to Avignon in southern France. The vast papal palace dominates the town

1338 Start of Hundred Years' War between England and France

c.1363 Machaut composes *Messe de Nostre Dame*

1200   **1250**   **1300**   **1350**

c.1200 Rise of German Minnesänger

c.1307 Dante starts work on *La divina commedia*

1320 Publication of *Ars Nova*, musical treatise attributed to Philippe de Vitry

1347 Black Death reaches Europe

⚠ **Monks in Gothic choir stalls** sing a funeral mass for the Holy Roman Emperor Maximilian I, who died in 1519.

to prominence in the 16th century and was notable for its use of subtle musical descriptions that matched the text, known as "word-painting." Composers delighted in devising ways to set the most expressive poetic phrases to music.

Composers and players

During the Middle Ages and the Renaissance, those who composed music were usually employed to do something else, such as work as a priest. To compose and write down

» **In this early 16th-century Flemish painting,** the young women are performing "Jouissance vous donnerai" (I Will Give You Happiness), a popular song of the time.

music, one had to be musically literate to some degree, especially for the composition of polyphony. People who received an education were usually employed by the Church, living within a religious foundation such as a monastery or nunnery, or were part of the nobility. During the Renaissance, the merchant classes valued an education for their sons and, to some extent, their daughters. There were relatively few female composers during this period, although many anonymous pieces may, in fact, have been written by women, and women certainly performed music written by men.

Religious division

The Protestant Reformation of the 16th century had inevitable musical consequences, largely because the Protestant reformers destroyed as much Catholic music as possible and replaced it with new, more direct styles, particularly in England. This made extraordinary demands of English composers of the period. Thomas Tallis, for example, wrote music for four different monarchs, each of whom required music with a different religious emphasis: from the elaborate, Latin-texted polyphony composed for Queen Mary to the direct, Protestant settings of English texts that were favored by her half-sister Elizabeth I.

TIMELINE: EARLY MUSIC

c.1436 Organ treatise by Henri Arnaut de Zwolle mentions use of reed stops

1453 Constantinople falls to Turks: end of Byzantine Empire

1500 Music printed by Ottaviano Petrucci in Venice

1517 Martin Luther's 95 Theses; start of Protestant Reformation

1425   **1450**   **1475**   **1500**

c.1430 Emergence of Flemish school of music, represented by Binchois and Dufay

1454 Gutenberg develops printing with movable type

1492 Columbus's first voyage to America; Spanish expel Moors from Granada

1524 Protestant hymnal by Luther and Johann Walter

Today, few musicians perform Early Music unless they use authentic reproductions of the instruments for which it was written. The quest for authenticity is supported by the exploration of early written and pictorial sources in search of clues as to how instruments were played, indications of pitch, tempo, phrasing, ornamentation, and accompaniment style, and what sort of improvisation might be appropriate. "Historically informed" performance gives a vibrant account of the possible sounds produced by early performers.

⏶ **The Dufay Collective,** a British ensemble, perform all kinds of medieval and Renaissance music, both instrumental and vocal. They are shown here playing on the harp and two vielles.

The simplest post-Reformation religious polyphony involved straightforward chanting in harmony, all voices moving together in the same rhythm as one another (homophony). Other polyphonic musical forms were contrapuntal. The idea of a musical texture where voices imitated one another in counterpoint became a distinguishing feature of sacred and secular music of the late Middle Ages and Renaissance, and is perhaps most recognizable in the choral music of Palestrina and the instrumental fantasies of English consort music at the end of the period.

Although musicians found new ways to compose, using an increasingly subtle palette of rhythmic, harmonic, and notational ideas, Early Music cannot be seen as a straightforward evolution from "primitive" plainsong to "sophisticated" polyphony. Fifteenth-century motets were often incredibly complex pieces of artistry, both notationally and in performance; instrumental dances in the 16th century were often delightfully simple.

The musical legacy

In appreciating Early Music, we are limited by our ignorance of how it sounded in its original context and just what the music meant to those who sang, played, or listened to it. On the other hand, the great variety of interpretations available is testament to how much there remains to discover in this seemingly distant repertoire and the myriad ways we may enjoy getting to know it better.

⏶ **One of the most popular instruments** of the Renaissance, the lute was probably introduced to Europe from Moorish Spain.

1534 Henry VIII declares himself head of the Church of England

1551 Palestrina appointed choirmaster by Pope Julius III

c.1555 Amati family of violin-makers established in Cremona, Italy

1525　　　**1550**　　　**1575**　　　**1600**

1540 Viol players from Venice, Cremona, and Milan employed by Henry VIII

1545 Council of Trent meets to determine Catholic response to the Reformation

1591 William Byrd's *My Ladye Nevell's Booke*, a compilation of music for the virginal

» **Hildegard experienced intense visions** (probably due to migraine), which she recorded in her books; she came to be known for her prophecies and miracles.

Hildegard of Bingen

◯ **1098–1179** ⚑ **GERMAN** ✎ **77**

Writer, poet, religious leader, diplomat, and composer, Hildegard's achievements were remarkable—and unique for a woman of her time. Promised to the Church by her noble family, she spent years living in religious contemplation. Through correspondence with popes and emperors, she became a significant political and diplomatic figure and wrote extensively on medicine, science, and theology. Her contemplative and ecstatic music comprises single-line settings of religious texts: not plainsong, but specially composed, using frequently repeated and varied short patterns.

MILESTONES

1136	Abbess of Disibodenberg Monastery
1150s	Lyrical poems and music, *Symphonia armonie celestium revelationum*, collected
1151	Writes *Ordo virtutum*, a morality play

Léonin (Leoninus)

◯ **DIED c.1201** ⚑ **FRENCH** ✎ **UNKNOWN**

The only written reference to a musician named Léonin was penned more than a century after his death by an anonymous English monk, who wrote that he was "the best composer of organum for the amplification of divine service." Léonin was a teacher, administrator, and poet who became a canon at the new cathedral of Notre-Dame de Paris. No music by him survives, but he is credited with the creation of the *Magnus liber*, the "Great Book" of chants used at Notre-Dame in the late 1100s. The book, later edited by Pérotin, laid the foundations for the idea of harmony and written-down composition.

MILESTONES

1150s	Cathedral administrator in Paris
1163	Construction of Notre-Dame begins
c.1192	Ordained as a priest
c.1200	Compilation of *Magnus liber*, a book of plainsong

Philippe de **Vitry**

◯ **1291–1361** ⚑ **FRENCH** ✎ **30**

From 1340, Vitry was one of France's leading intellectual figures—poet, philosopher, singer, composer, author, critic, bishop, and scholar. He traveled widely and was often involved in international relations. His motets—probably settings of his own Latin poems—enjoyed wide circulation and critical success, as did his poetry. The book of his teachings, *Ars nova*, established innovations such as the use of the half note and other short notes. Vitry may have invented the ballade, although no examples by him survive.

MILESTONES

1310s	Motets enjoy success
c.1320	Collection of his musical theories, *Ars nova*, published
1331	Accompanies the Duke of Bourbon to London
1342	Composes motet *Petre clemens*
1351	Created Bishop of Meaux

Pérotin (Pérotinus Magnus)

🌐 ACTIVE c.1200   📖 FRENCH   ✍ UNKNOWN

Pérotin, the first known composer of music in more than two independent parts, is a frustratingly shadowy figure. He is mentioned in late-13th-century documents as the man who edited and improved Léonin's *Magnus liber*, the book of music at Notre-Dame. He probably worked with the poet Philip the Chancellor, whose texts he set (in works such as *Beata viscera*), and he may have composed in the emerging genre of the motet, but very little is known about him for certain. However, Pérotin was certainly a pioneer: his two four-part settings of Latin texts have some startlingly modern-sounding touches.

MILESTONES

c.1198	Writes quadruple (four-voice) organum
c.1199	Setting of sacred text *Viderunt omnes*
c.1200	Working at Notre-Dame; setting of sacred text *Sederunt principes*
c.1207	Deputy Choirmaster at Notre-Dame
c.1210	Revises Léonin's *Magnus liber*

« **The composer known as Pérotin** may have actually been Petrus, a member of the hierarchy at the cathedral of Notre-Dame de Paris from about 1207 to 1238.

John **Dunstable**

🌐 1390–1453   📖 ENGLISH   ✍ c.52

So great was Dunstable's international reputation, both during his lifetime and for a long time afterward, that he was credited with many innovations for which other English composers had been responsible. A century after his death, some writers were even erroneously labeling him the "inventor of counterpoint." Nevertheless, Dunstable was a leading exponent of the mellifluous new English style, exploiting the smooth intervals of a third and a sixth, and his influence on continental composers was enormous. Many vocal works possibly written by him—including Mass movements, sacred Latin settings, dazzling motets, and English carols—survive, but their attribution and dating is very difficult because little is certain about Dunstable's career. However, it is known that he enjoyed great financial success, owning a series of properties around southern England and in London.

MILESTONES

c.1422	May have traveled to France with the Duke of Bedford
1436	Large income from property
1438	Working for the Duke of Gloucester
c.1440	Enjoys reputation as the leading English composer of his time
c.1449	Possibly purchased Broadfield Manor, Hertfordshire

« **Dunstable's epitaph** in St. Stephen Walbrook Church in London celebrates his skills as both musician and astronomer.

Guillaume de **Machaut**

◔ c.1300–1377   🏴 FRENCH   ✎ 143

Because he was a priest, it is perhaps surprising that Machaut's music contains so many songs on the theme of unrequited love. His ill-fated love for a young girl—the noble Péronne—was expressed in his secular music and poetry, including *Le voir dit,* and his distinctive musical style includes intricate melodies and bold dissonance. However, it is his four-part Mass that has defined his reputation as a significant composer.

Guillaume de Machaut's career was based in the Church, but he also worked for several secular patrons. Remarkably, his entire compositional output has been preserved. He was a great entrepreneur, passing on reliable copies of his music and poetry to noblemen and -women across Europe. Aside from his Mass, Machaut also produced an impressive collection of motets and songs, many of which take the theme of courtly love. The strict poetic structures used by authors of this period—rondeau, virelay, ballade, and lai— are all represented in his work.

MILESTONES

1323	Joins service of Jean de Luxembourg, King of Bohemia
1327	Travels to Lithuania
1340	Becomes canon of Reims Cathedral
1359	Reims besieged by the English
c.1363	Composes *Messe de Nostre Dame*
c.1363	Writes a collection of music, letters, and poetry in his autobiographical book, *Le voir dit*

KEY WORKS

⬆ **In recognition of his service** to the King of Bohemia, Machaut was appointed canon of Reims Cathedral.

DOUCE DAME JOLIE

SONG

This monophonic song describes an unnamed, unattainable woman to whom the poet pledges to dedicate his life. It is written in the poetic form of the virelay, one of the "formes fixes" that had become popular in the preceding century. The first two notes use the same pitch, creating a feeling of insistence, before the melody dips downward and back up again and the next two lines vary the first musical idea to new poetry. The second section of musical material raises the pitch higher than that at the opening, adding contrast.

MESSE DE NOSTRE DAME

MASS SETTING

Machaut wrote only one setting of the Mass Ordinary, from which he selected the Kyrie, Gloria, Credo, Sanctus, Agnus Dei, and "Ite missa est"

for polyphonic treatment. This music may have been performed regularly after its initial composition, as later copies contain some amendments to the music. Machaut's Mass is the earliest cyclic Mass to have survived with movements that are known to be by the same composer, and may have been the first of its kind.

The first and last three movements are set in a style usually associated with the isorhythmic motet, which involves the repetition of plainsong in long, slow notes in the tenor part, in a strict rhythmic pattern. The central movements use a more direct, chordal manner, all four voices moving more or less together. Several aspects of the *ars nova*, the musical style typical of Machaut's period, are detectable. These include the use of "hocket," where a pair of voices alternates notes of a single melody, causing a disjointed effect. The harmony sounds distinctive due to the frequent use of dissonance, when notes that clash are used to drive the music forward toward the end of a phrase.

Guillaume **Dufay**

🌐 1397–1474   📱 BELGIAN   ✍ c.200

Guillaume Dufay was a musician whose talents were greatly admired across Europe during his own lifetime. His compositions include examples of nearly every genre available at the time, including some of the finest early cyclic Masses, motets, and secular songs. Though he was a medieval composer, his works anticipate the more expressive style and greater harmonic range of the Renaissance. Little is known about his life, and writers continue to speculate about many details of his career. However, it is known that his parents were Marie Du Fayt and an unnamed priest, and his birth was thus illegitimate. He went on to become the most acclaimed composer of the 15th century.

Like many of his contemporaries, Dufay seems to have been aware not only of French compositional styles from the period (such as the works of Machaut) but also of English and Italian music. *Missa "L'homme armé"* is probably the earliest surviving Mass based on the famous secular song *"L'homme armé"* (*The Armed Man*), and it may have inspired later examples. The cantus firmus appears in the tenor part; singers who knew the original tune would certainly have spotted it although to modern ears it can seem carefully hidden.

The lyrics of the melancholy rondeau "Adieu ces bons vins de Lannoys," as well as dating evidence of its manuscript souce, help build a biographical picture of Dufay's early career. The title tells a story in itself: "Farewell to the Fine Wines of Laonnais." The song was written when Dufay left the town of Laon in France to take up an appointment in Bologna, Italy.

MILESTONES

1424	Perhaps moves to Laon, France
1428	Works in Rome
1435	Works at papal chapel in Florence
1436	Composes motet *Nuper rosarum flores*

🔼 **Dufay's early years** were spent as a chorister at Cambrai Cathedral, France, where he later went on to hold higher positions of authority.

Gilles **Binchois**

🌐 1400–1460   📱 BELGIAN   ✍ 120

Gilles de Bin—or simply "Binchois"—was one of the three great composers of the early 1400s, alongside Dufay and John Dunstable. From a middle-class Mons family, Binchois trained as a chorister and organist, served as a soldier, and possibly visited England before joining the court at Burgundy. Unlike Dufay and Dunstable, he is not known as an innovator, but he was a great melodist, and his sacred music, ballades, and rondeaus—which sometimes have an English influence—were clearly important in his lifetime. He held various church posts and retired in the early 1450s on a generous pension.

MILESTONES

1428	Music begins to be copied in Italy
1449	Travels to Mons with Dufay
c.1450	"Comme femme," rondeau, composed
1450s	Ockeghem's *Missa "De plus en plus,"* a Mass based on a Binchois melody

🔼 **Guillaume Dufay and Gilles Binchois** were the great masters of the early Flemish school. There is evidence that the two composers (and their works) were well known to each other.

Johannes **Ockeghem**

◯ c.1414–1497   🏳 **BELGIAN**   ✍ 50

Ockeghem appears in 1443 as a fully fledged composer of sublime, creative music. His year of birth is a mystery, although his close friendship with Binchois suggests Ockeghem wasn't much younger. Flemish by birth, most of his work was done at the French royal court, where he was a highly esteemed and well-rewarded employee of Charles VII. He held various ecclesiastical posts and even engaged in delicate diplomatic assignments abroad—something for which his likeable, wise, honest, and generous character suited him. Ockeghem was deeply mourned at his death (and long after) by his younger colleagues, such as Josquin Desprez.

MILESTONES

1446	Joins court of Charles I, Duke of Bourbon
1450s	Composes *Missa "L'homme armé,"* possibly his first Mass setting
1460	Composes the motet-chanson *Déploration on the Death of Binchois*

⌃ **According to a contemporary,** Ockeghem (shown here wearing glasses) was well known as an outstanding singer and master composer of "subtle songs, artful Masses, and harmonious motets."

Josquin Desprez

◯ 1440–1521   🏳 **FRENCH-FLEMISH**   ✍ c.240

⌃ **Probably born in northern Europe,** Josquin worked mostly in Italy. The recent invention of the printing press increased the influence of his music.

Josquin Desprez was celebrated both during and after his lifetime as one of the greatest musicians of the Renaissance period. He contributed to many genres, including motets, Mass settings, and French and Italian chansons. The widespread dissemination of his music was made possible by the invention of music printing at the beginning of the 16th century and he was a composer and singer whose skills were highly prized by the wealthiest patrons in Europe.

Josquin was the first composer to have printed volumes of music entirely devoted to his work. Many aspects of his early life and education are poorly documented: a major problem has been the frequent misattribution of pieces to Josquin that were not composed by him. His musical style displays great melodic invention and an enthusiasm for such techniques as canon, as well as a fondness for popular songs.

Josquin's Mass "Pange Lingua" is one of his most sophisticated and beautiful works. Its cantus firmus—a hymn in the plaintive Phrygian mode—indicates that it was written for performance on the feast of Corpus Christi, celebrated on the Thursday after Trinity Sunday.

Stabat Mater Dolorosa, Josquin's setting of the Crucifixion poem that describes Mary mourning at the foot of the Cross, is written in five parts, though only four carry the text. Perhaps in honor of the composer Gilles Binchois, this motet is based on the tenor line of *Comme femme desconfortée* (*A Woman in Distress*).

MILESTONES

1459	Becomes a singer at Milan cathedral
c.1475	Working for the King of Anjou
1484	Working in Milan
1495	Working at the Papal Chapel in Rome
1501	Petrucci publishes six chansons attributed to Josquin
1502	*First Book of Masses* published

Jacob **Obrecht**

1457–1505 **DUTCH** **c.100**

Obrecht spent most of his career working in churches in Bruges, Antwerp, and Bergen op Zoom, although he was eventually encouraged to move to Italy. His writing—full of long sequences and parallel motion—was more traditional than that of some of his contemporaries, but was nonetheless adventurous in other ways, particularly in his treatment of cantus firmus (fixed song). Obrecht's approach to setting texts to music remained contrapuntal, however. His work did not contribute to the new trend that was emerging in Italy during the 16th century—that music should meticulously express the actual meaning of the words. His secular works included inventive canonic pieces for instruments and he showed his national sentiment by arranging Dutch melodies.

Obrecht's scoring of *Missa "Sub Tuum Praesidium"* is unusual. After opening in only three parts, each new section of music adds another voice, until a seven-part texture is reached in the final portion of the Agnus Dei. His choral setting of the *Salve Regina* may have been performed both in church and at popular, secular festivities, perhaps with instruments. Despite its modest scoring, which allows references to the original antiphon to shine through, the texture is surprisingly rich and sonorous.

Missa "Super Maria Zart," Obrecht's four-part Marian Mass setting, is quite special. Lasting more than an hour, its massive scale shows his ingenuity when working on a large canvas. It is the longest Mass Ordinaries to survive.

MILESTONES	
1460s	Studies at University of Louvain
1484	Working at Cambrai Cathedral
1485	Leaves Cambrai to take up a position at Church of St. Donatien in Bruges
1487	Visits Ferrara
1488	Composes the motet *Mille quingentis* in honor of his father, Guillermus

Most of Obrecht's professional life was spent in religious employment; 27 of his surviving works are settings of the Mass.

Clément **Janequin**

c.1485–c.1558 **FRENCH** **250**

Although he never held an important regular music post at a cathedral or court, Janequin's music enjoyed popular success—his chanson "La bataille" was one of the most performed songs of the 16th century. Trained as a priest, he held a number of poorly paid church posts, but in 1530 his song to celebrate Francois I's entry into Bordeaux, "Chantons, sonnons, trompettes," established his reputation as a composer. Alhough his music was published widely and known across Europe, Janequin suffered recurring money problems and split with his family over an unpaid loan.

MILESTONES	
c.1515	Composes "La bataille," a chanson which imitates the noise of battle
1530	The chanson "Chantons, sonnons, trompettes" brings public fame
1530s	Most prolific period
1534	Choirmaster at Angers Cathedral

Janequin's songs often use short melodic fragments which imitate natural or man-made sounds. "Les cris de Paris" evokes the sound of Parisian street life.

Alexander **Agricola**

◔ c.1446–1506   ◪ **BELGIAN**   ✍ 120

Born Alexander Ackerman, the illegitimate son
of a wealthy Dutch businesswoman, Agricola was
an internationally popular composer in the 1490s.
He worked in courts and churches in Italy, France,
and the Low Countries, being in demand enough
to name his own salary. Technically, his sacred
Masses and motets, his secular songs, and his
instrumental pieces—which show the influence of
Ockeghem—are typical of the time, but the intense
and restless character of his music was described
by some contemporaries as "crazy and strange."

MILESTONES	
1470s	At court of Duke of Milan
1474	At court of Lorenzo de' Medici
1491	Leaves France for Florence
1490s	Songs gain international popularity
1500	Starts work for Burgundy court

Jacob **Arcadelt**

◔ c.1507–1568   ◪ **BELGIAN**   ✍ 250

French by upbringing, Arcadelt—after a tentative
start to his career in Italy—became a leading
composer of secular works. From the 1530s until
Lassus arrived in the 1550s, Arcadelt's simple,
clear French chansons were highly popular.
However, it was his 200-odd Italian madrigals,
especially the four-part ones, that established
his reputation in the 1530s: flexible, graceful,
singable music that sensitively illustrated the text.

MILESTONES	
1538	First book of madrigals
1540	Enters Papal Chapel in Rome
1544	Singing master at St. Peter's Basilica
1551	Returns to France
1554	Enters service of Charles, Duke of Guise, later Archbishop of Rheims
1560s	Six books of chansons published

John **Taverner**

◔ 1490–1545   ◪ **ENGLISH**   ✍ c.70

Taverner was a man of great influence in England
in the 16th century, both as a composer and
through his work as an associate of Thomas
Cromwell—Henry VIII's chief advisor who presided
over the dissolution of the monasteries. It is likely
that Taverner empathized with the spirit of the
Protestant reforms; one document records his
shame at writing "popish ditties"—music that
celebrated the Virgin Mary or Christian saints—
in his earlier career.

As well as being a composer, Taverner
worked as a singer, organist, and music
teacher, and may have been politically active,
too. In 1528, an investigation at Cardinal Wolsey's
college, where Taverner was choirmaster,
suspected him of circulating Lutheran literature
and briefly imprisoned him. If the caricatures
found in a copy of one of his works are accurate,
his appearance was not as becoming as the
beautiful choral works that form the major part
of his output, which included motets, Masses,
and secular items.

△ **Though he spent
most of his time in
Lincolnshire,** Taverner
was appointed to
instruct the choristers
at the newly founded
Cardinal College in
Oxford in 1528.

Taverner wrote eight Masses in all, and the
tune for the "In nomine Domini" section of his
Missa "Gloria tibi Trinitas" became one of the most
popular cantus firmus melodies for instrumental
music in England, in a genre known as the "In
nomine" in honor of Taverner's vocal original.

Magnificat à 4, for four adult male voices, may
be the latest of Taverner's three settings. The
text contains the words of the Virgin Mary at the
Annunciation, and it may have been performed for
the celebration of this feast in Boston, Lincolnshire.
The opera *Taverner* by Peter Maxwell Davies depicts
a popular account of the composer's life.

MILESTONES	
1515	*Missa "Gloria tibi Trinitas"* composed
1525	Working at Tattershall Collegiate Church, Lincolnshire
1528	Imprisoned for heresy
1530s	Works as agent of Thomas Cromwell
1537	Joins the Guild of Corpus Christi in Boston, Lincolnshire
c.1540	Composes *Magnificat à 4*

Thomas **Tallis**

● c.1505–1585   📖 ENGLISH   ✒ 100+

Thomas Tallis's musical career spanned the reigns of four English monarchs: Henry VIII, Edward VI, Mary (a Catholic), and Elizabeth I (a Protestant). The period saw enormous shifts in religious life and compositional style. Most of Tallis's output was for the Church, though he did write a handful of secular works. His flexibility as a composer undoubtedly ensured his survival as a leading figure in English music.

Tallis trained as a musician in the pre-Reformation Church. However, under a succession of rulers, he was required to write both Catholic and Anglican service music, all of which was of top quality. Tallis was a superb organist, but few of his keyboard pieces have survived. Dating his works is difficult, especially because he occasionally reworked old music for a new purpose. Well known for his florid Latin works, Tallis's simpler, Anglican music is equally well crafted and enjoyable to perform.

MILESTONES	
1538	Working at Waltham Abbey
1540	Waltham Abbey dissolved by Henry VIII; Tallis moves to Canterbury
1543	Employed by the Chapel Royal
1554	Composes Mass *Puer natus est nobis*
1575	Byrd and Tallis awarded license to print music; *Cantiones sacrae* published

KEY WORKS

SPEM IN ALIUM NUNQUAM HABUI

MOTET

Spem in alium is perhaps Tallis's best-known work. He uses spatial elements by arranging the voices into eight five-part choirs; the music can be heard to sweep around the full choir, or work with the sub-choirs singing across to one another. *Spem in alium* opens with a solo voice, but quickly builds as voices are layered on top of one another until the sound is rich and sonorous. The full choir sings only four times; a dramatic rest in all parts precedes the final full-choir section that ends the work.

LAUDATE DOMINUM

MOTET

This five-part psalm-motet was probably composed during the 1560s. Psalm-motets had been developed by Tallis's contemporaries, including Christopher Tye and Robert White. The feeling of celebration is created with the opening

idea, a rising phrase, in the contratenor for the word *laudate* (praise), imitated by the remaining voices as they enter one by one.

O NATA LUX DE LUMINE

CHORAL

Despite its Latin text, the carefully paced word setting of this work suggests it was composed during the reign of Elizabeth I. It appeared in *Cantiones sacrae*, a joint publication between Tallis and William Byrd, and the first collection of motets and hymns to be published in England.

IF YE LOVE ME

CHORAL

The style of this anthem immediately transports the listener to the heart of the Reformed liturgy of the 1540s. In two sections, the second of which is repeated, the message to keep God's commandments is communicated through carefully paced phrasing and delicate imitation.

⌃ **In 1575** Elizabeth I granted Tallis and Byrd a 21-year joint monopoly to print music.

Giovanni Pierluigi da **Palestrina**

● c.1525–1594   卿 ITALIAN   ✍ 650+

Palestrina's is perhaps the most familiar name of all late-Renaissance composers, and his sacred music is widely regarded as a pinnacle of contrapuntal style, rich and flowing in its sound. Hundreds of his works survive and many of these were published during his lifetime. Although the majority of them were produced for use in religious worship, he also wrote over 100 madrigals, both secular and sacred.

>> **Palestrina spent almost all his career** working and composing for the Catholic Church in Rome, much of it for the Vatican.

Life

Apart from the fact that he was born in the town of Palestrina in Italy, practically nothing is known about Giovanni Pierluigi's early history. His later career centered mainly on Rome, where he was trained and where he worked for most of his life. As far as is known, Palestrina began his musical life as organist and choirmaster in 1544 in his native city. His reputation grew and he gained his first Roman post in 1550 as a choirmaster at the Cappella Giulia, a subsidiary of the Sistine Choir. A brief spell at the Sistine Chapel itself in 1555 ended in his dismissal by the new pope, ostensibly for being married. His rejection made Palestrina fall ill, but after he recovered, he gained an appointment to the post of Maestro di cappella at the basilica of St. John Lateran. From 1561 to 1566 he worked at the more prestigious church of Santa Maria Maggiore, after which he enjoyed, until 1571, the patronage of the wealthy Cardinal Ippolito II d'Este. The remaining years of Palestrina's musical career were spent back at the Cappella Giulia. After the death of his first wife, he married a fur merchant, Virginia Dormoli. This marriage ensured him a steady income and he helped Virginia's business to flourish. Becoming a very wealthy man, Palestrina was financially able to publish 16 collections of his works.

Music

Given the sacred institutions that employed him, it is hardly surprising that most of Palestrina's output comprised music for the liturgy. His mastery of counterpoint led to subsequent generations using his works as a model for their own. His reputation was heightened by the composer Johann Joseph Fux's use of his music in his treatise *Gradus ad Parnassum* (1725) and by 19th-century biographies that praised his music without reservation.

Palestrina's music is characterized by elegant melodic lines in all the vocal parts, by the careful treatment of dissonance, and by a sensitivity to text-setting that foreshadows the *stile moderno* of the 17th century. While his music rarely contains overt word-painting, the meaning and accents of the Latin or Italian language are never lost. His most refined writing is to be found in his Masses, which are written in a variety of ways; some were settings of borrowed musical material, while others were entirely freely composed.

" The most **frivolous** and **gallant words** are set to exactly the **same music** as those of **the Bible**... "

Hector Berlioz on the music of Palestrina

MILESTONES

1547	Marries Lucrezia Gori on June 12	**1581**	Marries furrier Virginia Dormoli on February 28
1554	Publication of first book of Masses	**1588**	Lamentations published
1555	Publication of first book of madrigals	**1589**	Publication of hymns
1567	Publication of Masses, including *Missa "Papae Marcelli"*	**1591**	Settings for Magnificat published
1569	Publication of first book of motets for five voices	**1593**	Publication of litanies and offertories

KEY WORKS

MISSA BREVIS

MASS SETTING

The origin of the name *Missa brevis* (short Mass) for one of Palestrina's finest Mass settings is unclear. It was published in 1570. After a contrapuntal Kyrie, the Gloria opens with all four parts in homophony before the parts begin to weave an imitative texture, sometimes working in pairs or trios. The new section at "Qui tollis peccata mundi" brings the parts together in a chordal texture. In the Benedictus, the three voices that open the movement are rejoined by the bass at "Osanna in excelsis." The second part of the Agnus Dei divides the upper part, to give a five-part texture.

THE LAMENTATIONS OF JEREMIAH, LESSONS 1 TO 3

CHORAL

Palestrina's settings for three lessons from this piece were commissioned by Pope Sixtus V in 1587, and were published the following year. The opening of the first lesson of this serene setting for Maundy Thursday is chordal, but quickly moves to an imitative texture. The rhythm of the third lesson, from "Manum suam misit," is set in perfect complement to the stresses of the Latin text, briefly using a triple meter to achieve this.

MISSA "BENEDICTUS ES"

MASS SETTING

The probable model for this six-part Mass is a motet by Josquin Desprez (1520). The Kyrie opens with a rising scalic motive that passes from voice to voice. After the first words of the Gloria are intoned, the choir enters part by part, building a contrapuntal texture. At a new section, "Qui tollis peccata mundi," the movement becomes more reserved and penitential and closes with a relatively simple Amen. The lengthy Credo text ends with a much more elaborate and boldly dissonant "Amen." In the Sanctus-Benedictus, the highest voice opens with long held notes, while the lower parts move in steady but more active lines. The concluding Agnus Dei is a gentle, lyrical prayer for atonement.

MISSA "L'HOMME ARMÉ"

MASS SETTING

Palestrina wrote two Mass settings based on the melody "L'homme armé," a popular song that provided the foundation for at least 40 Masses in the 15th and 16th centuries. The five-part setting dates from 1570 and the four-part Mass from 1582.

MISSA "PAPAE MARCELLI"

MASS SETTING

This Mass, published in 1567, takes its name from Pope Marcellus II, who held the Papacy for just three weeks in 1555. It used to be said that this Mass safeguarded the future of Catholic music, a myth that has proved difficult to dispel. The music's sense of balance and poise is evident from the opening Kyrie. Traces of the "L'homme armé" melody can be heard in this work.

▲ **Palestrina presents** his work to Pope Julius III on the title page of his *Missarum Liber Primus* (first book of masses), published in 1554.

William **Byrd**

c.1540–1623   ENGLISH   c.500

A Catholic in a Protestant land, Byrd's reputation as a composer was such that he avoided the serious consequences of maintaining his faith under English law. His religious works show a polished contrapuntal technique, especially in their use of imitation. Byrd's verse anthems, motets, consort songs, and instrumental works are deeply expressive. His music rarely shows any influence of his teacher, Thomas Tallis.

Byrd is perhaps best known for his survival at the top of the establishment in Protestant England, despite his strong (and barely hidden) Catholic faith. His patrons, who included both wealthy Catholics and the "Virgin Queen," Elizabeth I, required a wide range of music from him for use in religious services and in the home. Apart from his Anglican music, Byrd composed and published many dangerously Catholic works that must have been performed only in a domestic context. He also produced much secular music, including some of the first notable repertoire for virginals.

MILESTONES	
1563	Appointed master of choristers and organist at Lincoln Cathedral
1572	Becomes Gentleman of Chapel Royal
1575	Elizabeth I grants Byrd and Tallis patent for publishing printed manuscript paper and music
1575	Byrd and Tallis jointly publish *Cantiones*, comprising 17 pieces by each composer
1588	Publication of *Psalmes, sonets and songs*
1605	Publishes *Gradualia*, Vol 1 (Vol 2 appears in 1607)

KEY WORKS

↗ **Byrd wrote many madrigals** and songs ideal for small social gatherings. Among them is "Ye Sacred Muses," a touching consort song in honor of his friend and colleague, Thomas Tallis.

GREAT SERVICE

LITURGICAL

Byrd was an innovator in form and technique in his liturgical works and contributed greatly to the developing genre of the English Anthem (including the newer "verse" style with organ accompaniment), composing his widely regarded *Great Service* in this format. The work takes its name from its massive scale; two choirs of five voices perform in different combinations across seven movements: Venite, Te Deum, Benedictus, Kyrie, Creed, Magnificat, and Nunc Dimittis. Unlike Byrd's three Mass settings in Latin, *Great Service* is in English, for use in the Anglican liturgy. Archbishop Thomas Cranmer's Lincoln Cathedral Injunctions (1548) had commanded that composers of Anglican music should seek clarity of textual expression, "a plain and distinct note for every syllable."

"QUI PASSE: FOR MY LADYE NEVELL"

KEYBOARD

The virginals were much favored by female musicians of the middle and upper classes throughout Europe. Most of Byrd's works for the instrument are collected in two books and the one dedicated to Lady Nevell contains the piece "Qui passe: for my Ladye Nevell," a wonderful transformation of a piece published 34 years earlier by the Venetian composer Filippo Azzaiolo, "Chi passa per questa strada" ("Who Walks Along This Street"). Byrd reworked the melody as a bass line, lacing the music with energetic rhythms and fast scales in both hands. The element of surprise is maintained throughout, through frequent changes between major and minor chords, and contrasting colors and textures. The effect is one of exuberant virtuosity.

Orlandus **Lassus**

● 1532–1594   🏴 BELGIAN   ✍ 1,600

In his youth, Orlandus Lassus traveled throughout Italy and Sicily in the service of various aristocrats. In the 1560s, when he was comfortably settled in Bavaria with a wife and children, he was the most celebrated musician in Europe. Various publishers spread his madrigals, chansons, and sacred music internationally, and he received several royal honors.

Lassus's prolific and versatile output includes some of the most beautiful examples of 16th-century church choral music (alongside those of Palestrina and Victoria), such as his Mass for double choir, *Missa Osculetur me*, plus hundreds of motets, madrigals, chansons, and Lieder—and even drinking ditties and comic songs—which reveal a likeable man of great humor and wit.

MILESTONES	
c.1544	In the service of the Viceroy of Sicily
1553	Becomes choirmaster in Rome
1556	Publication of first book of chansons
1556	Enters Bavarian court
1563	Promoted to chief Kapellmeister
1563	Begins work on *Seven Penitential Psalms*
1570	Rises to the nobility
1574	Receives order of the Golden Spur

« **Lassus composed many celebrated works** for the musicians of the Bavarian court. Here, he is captured in miniature, playing the spinet.

Giulio **Caccini**

● c.1550–1618   🏴 ITALIAN   ✍ c.80

Like the careers of many of his contemporaries, Giulio Caccini's career involved the composition, performance, and teaching of music. Though linked with the significant new genre of opera, his major musical achievement was arguably the collection of accompanied songs *Le nuove musiche*. He was among the first generation of virtuoso singers who became successful composers, and developed the new genre of opera alongside the Florentine composer Jacopo Peri. After moving from Rome to the important cultural city of Florence, Caccini's career was financed by the wealthy Medici family. There, he became a member of the music patron Giovanni Bardi's Camerata, a group of intellectuals interested in Ancient Greek ideals.

At a wedding between members of the Medici and d'Este families, Giulio Caccini was employed to sing, dressed as an angel, as part of an elaborate mechanized performance. In his songs, Caccini developed the monodic style that was to become a pillar of the Baroque era.

« **Caccini's opera *Eurydice*,** which tells the story of Orpheus's journey to the Underworld, was first performed in Florence in 1602.

MILESTONES	
1566	Living in Florence
1570s	Joins Florentine Camerata and develops the recitative
1586	Performs at wedding of Virginia de' Medici and Cesare d'Este
1600	First performance of Caccini's opera *Il rapimento di Cefalo*
1602	Publication of *Le nuove musiche*

Andrea **Gabrieli**

🌐 c.1510–1586   📖 ITALIAN   ✍ 400

Though generally thought of as an "uncle of the more accomplished Giovanni Gabrieli," one of his pupils, Andrea Gabrieli helped establish Venice's school of home-grown composers after domination by incomers from the Netherlands. An organist at St. Mark's Basilica, he composed everything from large sacred and theater works to songs and solo keyboard pieces, with popular success—many being republished decades after his death. Gabrieli's posthumous *Concerti* formed a collection of music for Venice's state functions.

MILESTONES

1536	Gains fame as singer at St. Mark's Basilica
1554	First published madrigal
1562	Friendship with Lassus begins
1578	Receives hardship payment to help maintain sister's family

Carlo **Gesualdo**

🌐 c.1561–1613   📖 ITALIAN   ✍ 150

Carlo Gesualdo's vocal music is notorious for its remarkable dissonance. A gentleman amateur at first, he gained a professional reputation with his later madrigals. Gesualdo's last years were spent in morbid isolation at his castle, music-making his only pleasure.

MILESTONES

1586	Marries Maria d'Avalos
1590	Wife and her lover murdered
1594	Marries noblewoman Leonora d'Este
1594	First book of madrigals published
1595	Retires to Gesualdo Castle, Avellino, outside Naples
1611	Three books of madrigals published

Tomás Luis de **Victoria**

🌐 1548–1611   📖 SPANISH   ✍ 200

Victoria started composing in Italy and became the greatest Spanish composer of the Renaissance. His work—all sacred music in Latin, including 20 Masses, 52 motets, and many other liturgical pieces—shows the subtlety and beauty of Palestrina, with whom he may have studied in Rome. After working in Italian churches, he returned to Spain in 1587 to serve Empress Maria, widow of the Holy Roman Emperor Maximilian II, as choirmaster and organist at a convent in Madrid. Supported by wealthy patrons throughout his life, he was able to publish his works in distinguished editions—and some were performed as far away as Mexico. Although many works are poignant and mystical, their prevailing mood—especially in his motets—is positive, as he was a cheerful man with strong family ties.

▶▶ **Victoria sang as a chorister** at the cathedral in his native Ávila, also the birthplace of Saint Teresa.

MILESTONES

1560s	Serves as a chorister in Ávila
1565	Leaves for Rome to study for priesthood
1572	Writes first collection of motets
1575	Ordained as a priest
1583	Writes first Requiem Mass
1594	Attends Palestrina's funeral
1603	Writes *Officium defunctorum* for funeral of Empress Maria

Giovanni **Gabrieli**

🌑 c.1554–1612 　　📖 ITALIAN 　　✍ c.250

Giovanni Gabrieli and his uncle, Andrea, were prolific and innovative composers during the late Renaissance period. Giovanni's polychoral works for voices and instruments, particularly those intended for performance in religious services, make use of a wide variety of acoustic textures and effects. Although much of his output is sacred and vocal, he also wrote many keyboard works and madrigals.

Gabrieli was possibly born in Venice, a thriving center of musical and religious activity. He may have been brought up by his uncle, before traveling to study with Orlandus Lassus in Munich. Aside from his compositional duties, Giovanni was employed as an organist and music teacher, and his published works reflect the diversity of the requirements of his patrons in Venice and northern Europe. His most famous publications are the *Sacrae symphoniae* and *Symphoniae sacrae*.

MILESTONES	
1564	Organist at St. Mark's Basilica, Venice
1585	Principal organist at St. Mark's Basilica, Venice
1593	Publication of organ intonations on the 12 church modes
1597	Publication of the *Sacrae symphoniae*
1615	Posthumous publication of the *Canzoni et sonate* and *Symphoniae sacrae*

KEY WORKS

SONATA PIAN' E FORTE, FROM SACRAE SYMPHONIAE

INSTRUMENTAL

Many of Gabrieli's works would have been performed by a rich combination of instruments, including strings, wind, organ, and plucked continuo. The antiphonal effects in the music were emphasized by the spatial arrangement of musicians in opposing organ lofts within the church—a divided-choir technique known as cori spezzati.

In the *Sonata pian' e forte*, one of three sonatas in the 1597 collection, the instrumental forces are divided into two choirs of four players each. As the title suggests, the dynamics are clearly marked by the composer, a relatively new practice at the time. The opening section consists of long, sustained homophony, but by the end of the piece the writing takes on a complex eight-part contrapuntal texture. Gabrieli's sonatas and canzonas were written for instruments only, perhaps for the accompaniment of church processions.

O MAGNUM MYSTERIUM

MOTET

A relatively early motet, *O magnum mysterium* is one of Gabrieli's finest pieces of music. The eight-part choir is divided into high and low voices. At the opening, the harmony is ambiguous, playing with major and minor chords, and the shifting between different tonal areas lends weight to the text, which focuses on the miracle of Christ's birth. The majority of the motet works steadily through the text, the phrases repeated by different combinations of voices.

INFLUENCES

Gabrieli's successor at St. Mark's Basilica in Venice was Claudio Monteverdi, whose reputation dwarfed that of his predecessor. However, Gabrieli's innovative instrumental and choral music proved extremely popular with German composers, and was championed by German musicians writing about music in the 19th century.

🔼 **Much of the sacred music** written for St. Mark's Basilica, Venice, in the polychoral style, was by Giovanni Gabrieli. As many as five choirs were placed in different galleries around the high altar.

Jacopo **Peri**

◔ 1561–1633   ᴘᴜ ITALIAN   ✍ 50

As the composer of the first surviving opera—
Euridice—Peri's place in music history is assured.
A musician at the Medici court, he gained a
reputation as an actor,
singer, and dazzling
chitarrone player. In
collaboration with
other Florentine

>> **Peri performed** in
many of his operas, and
his singing received
much praise.

musicians, poets, and philosophers throughout
the 1590s, Peri helped devise the idea of opera.
The result was *Dafne*, for which he set the text and
sang Apollo. It was a small-scale affair, performed
privately in a room. *Euridice* followed, first played
before an intimate royal audience to celebrate
the marriage of Maria de' Medici and Henri IV of
France. Continuing to work for the Medicis, Peri
became more in demand as a stage composer,
and his songs were published by popular request.
A slim, endearing man, he was nicknamed
"Zazzerino"—a reference to his attractive,
long blond hair.

MILESTONES

1579	Organist in Florence
1600	*Euridice*, opera, premiered October 6
1609	Song collection, *Le varie musiche*, first published
1620s	Writes three oratorios and two operas in collaboration with other composers

Jan Pieterszoon **Sweelinck**

◔ c.1562–1621   ᴘᴜ DUTCH   ✍ 320

Sweelinck's life was virtually
all spent in Amsterdam. A civil
servant, his personal life was
well regulated, comfortably
rewarded, and uneventful. He
was known across Europe as
a teacher, drawing pupils from
Germany in the 1600s, and his influence on north
German organ playing culminated in the music
of J. S. Bach. A perfecter of existing forms rather
than a pioneer, he wrote around 70 keyboard works,
such as fantasias—which led to the development

of the fugue—and toccatas. None were published
in his lifetime, but they were enthusiastically
copied by pupils. In contrast, his 250 vocal works,
which include chansons, madrigals, and motets,
were all published.

▲ **Sweelinck served** as an organist at Oude Kerk
in Amsterdam for over 40 years, and was renowned
for his brilliant improvisations.

MILESTONES

c.1577	Starts as organist at Oude Kerk
1594	First published work: book of chansons
1597	First psalm settings published
1606	Portrait painted by brother Gerrit
1619	*Cantiones sacrae*, Catholic motets for five-part choir, published

John **Dowland**

🌑 1563–1626　　📕 **ENGLISH**　　✍ 220

England's greatest composer of lute music and songs spent much of his career on the Continent, so he can have seen little of his family in London. Although he had patronage and enormous publishing success at home, and lasting influence abroad, he struggled for appointments in England. His involvement with scheming English Catholics in Italy didn't help his prospects, and he seems to have been a prickly, occasionally paranoid man. His *First Booke of Songs* was a bestseller and cemented his reputation. Its clever multidirectional layout, which enabled soloists or groups around a table to easily read parts singly or in combination, was a key to its success. Melancholy features strongly in his work: his bleak song "In darkness let me dwell" is remarkably dissonant and harmonically unstable.

» **Dowland's bittersweet melodies** were greatly admired in his lifetime, and the poet Richard Banfield wrote that his "heavenly touch upon the lute doth ravish human sense."

MILESTONES

1588	Listed among the major English composers
1594	Leaves England to work in Germany
1597	*Songs or Ayres* published
1598	Accepts position at Danish court
1604	*Lachrimae*, consort music, published
1612	Finally employed by the English court as one of the King's lutenists

Thomas **Weelkes**

🌑 1575–1623　　📕 **ENGLISH**　　✍ 75

After establishing himself as a fine madrigal composer while still a teenager, the future looked bright for Thomas Weelkes. In 1603 he held a lucrative post at Chichester Cathedral, composed fine Church music, had a wealthy wife, and his recent book of madrigals—expressive, rich, and brilliantly constructed—was one of the most important of the English tradition. However, he began to spend more time in the tavern than the church, and his personal life and quality of work went into a long decline. He was eventually dismissed from his post at the cathedral for unruly, drunken behavior.

MILESTONES

1597	First book of madrigals published
1598	Organist, Winchester College
1600	Composes madrigals for five and six voices
1617	Loses position at Chichester Cathedral

Thomas **Campion**

🌑 1567–1620　　📕 **ENGLISH**　　✍ 100

Campion was born into an affluent family in Essex and became a dilettante theorist, poet, and musician. After John Dowland, he was the most prolific of lute-song composers, with over 100 to his name, the lyrics of which are of outstanding literary merit. He attended Cambridge University, studied law at Gray's Inn and medicine at Caen, but preferred socializing and cultural activities to studying. He wrote masques, poems, and five books of songs—some self-published with friends—and was much in demand to supply both texts and music for entertainments at the royal court of James I.

MILESTONES

1586	Studies at Gray's Inn
1588	Works as an actor and singer
1601	First *Booke of Ayres* published
1605	Receives degree in medicine, Caen
1613	*Treatise on Counterpoint* published

The Baroque Era
1600–1750

The Baroque era saw the genesis of opera, the growth of the orchestra, and a flourishing of instrumental music, especially for the violin and keyboard. Most new fashions originated in Italy and Italian musicians dominated the field, but, by the end of the period, distinctive national styles had evolved.

The word "baroque" was originally a pejorative term for a style of architecture and art produced between the end of the 16th and the mid-18th centuries, but by the time music scholars adopted the term it had lost most of its negative connotations.

The period was one of great creativity—from Shakespeare and Cervantes in literature to Newton and Galileo in science. Music, too, blossomed. By the 1590s a new musical style had emerged in contrast to the lush polyphony of Palestrina and his contemporaries. Instead of complex intertwining parts, the new style (dubbed *stile moderno* to distinguish it from the *stile antico* ("old style") of earlier Renaissance compositions) placed a solo voice or instrument above a simple accompaniment consisting of a bass line with the chords lightly filled in above it (the basso continuo, a "continuous bass"). There were usually two instruments playing the continuo—a keyboard, lute, or guitar along with a low-ranged melodic instrument such as a cello, bass viol, or bassoon reinforcing the bass line.

◀ **This painting** by Dutch Baroque artist Hendrick Terbrugghen (1588–1629) shows a boy playing an early form of violin and singing.

The term "monody" (from the Greek meaning "one song") is used to describe this new combination of solo voice and basso continuo. Monody allowed the performer the freedom to embellish and ornament the melodic line at will, something unthinkable in the older polyphonic style.

The birth of opera

This new style of singing allowed composers to convey the text clearly through a solo voice, while singers could interpret the words more dramatically. It was monody that made musical drama—opera—possible. The invention of opera is credited to a group of Florentine musicians and poets known as the Camerata, particularly the composers Giulio Caccini and Jacopo Peri and the poet Ottavio Rinuccini, who were trying to recreate the singing style of Ancient Greek drama. This new style was first seen in *intermedi*—short musical dramas performed between the acts of spoken plays—but in 1598 the three collaborated on *Dafne*, the first true opera. Two years later, both Peri and Caccini wrote operas on the Orpheus myth, *Euridice*, but it was Monteverdi's *L'Orfeo* (1607) that is seen as the true benchmark for early opera. The new art form would combine a variety of musical styles—speechlike recitative, moving arias, choral and instrumental interludes—into one large narrative structure.

The Catholic Church frowned on the "immoral" plots of some operas and banned their performance during Advent and Lent. The void was filled by another kind of dramatic vocal music: the oratorio. Operas and oratorios both employed recitative, arias, duets, and instrumental pieces, but oratorios were unstaged, with no costumes or sets, and tended to be about biblical subjects. Comic

opera was a later development, gaining ground in the 1730s. It developed from short comic pieces (*intermezzi*), performed in the intervals between the acts of serious operas.

Instrumental music

Opera was not the only musical form to flourish. Major and minor courts across Europe maintained chamber ensembles as a mark of prestige. This created a demand for instrumental sonatas and concertos to entertain the noble patrons and their guests.

⊠ **This painting** (c.1690) by Anton Domenico Gabbiani shows a small chamber ensemble. A number of violinists and a cellist are gathered around the harpsichord player.

TIMELINE: THE BAROQUE ERA

1600 *Euridice*, early opera by Peri and Rinuccini

1618 Start of 30 Years' War, which devastates much of central Europe

1637 First public opera house opens in Venice

1661 Italian-born Lully appointed superintendent of music to Louis XIV

| 1600 | 1620 | 1640 | 1660 |

1607 Monteverdi's opera *L'Orfeo* performed in Mantua

1644 Birth of violin-maker Antonio Stradivari

1649 English Civil War (1642–49) ends with execution of Charles I

In the sonata, the violin (which could emulate certain qualities of the singing voice) gained a whole new repertoire and generated an increased interest in its potential. This was also the age of the great violin makers of Cremona: Amati, Stradivari, and Guarneri.

The 17th century also saw the birth of the orchestra, driven in large part by the growth in opera, the size of the ensemble growing along with the visual spectacle onstage. Keyboard music (mainly for harpsichord and organ) also flourished, and virtuosi such as Johann Pachelbel and the Couperins attracted much attention in court and church circles.

Although the innovations of the early Baroque came out of Italy, distinctive national styles began to emerge. The Italian style was one of melodic dominance, virtuosity, and a strong sense of metre, while the French style, developed by Lully at the court of Louis XIV,

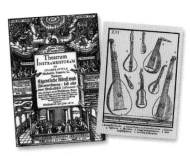

⌃ **Michael Praetorius, a prolific German composer,** published his *Syntagma Musicum* in 1619. It includes an encyclopedic guide to the instruments of the day.

was strongly influenced by dance rhythms. The German style, taken to its greatest heights by J.S. Bach, was a hybrid of the two, with the addition of a contrapuntal element.

THE STAGING OF OPERA

Opera began as a court entertainment, usually for specific private occasions such as a marriage between two noble households. Venice opened a public opera house as early as 1637 and other cities, such as Hamburg (1678), gradually followed. The high ticket prices, however, restricted attendance to the merchant classes and above. Public demand ensured that performances grew more and more spectacular. Large amounts of money were spent on lavish costumes, lighting, and staging, with special effects including airborne chariots, gods descending from the heavens by means of complex systems of ropes and pulleys, and ornate group dances.

⌃ **The opera *Giunio Bruto*—the first act of** which was by Cesarini, the second by Caldara, and the third by Alessandro Scarlatti—was first performed in 1707.

1703 Vivaldi made violin master at the Pietà orphanage, Venice

1722 Johann Sebastian Bach takes position as cantor in Leipzig

1731 First public concerts given in Boston

1742 First performance of Handel's *Messiah* in Dublin

1680 1700 1720 1740

1689 Purcell's *Dido and Aeneas*

c.1709 Bartolomeo Cristofori builds first pianoforte

1722 Rameau's *Traité de l'harmonie*

1732 Royal Opera House opens at Covent Garden

1750 Death of J.S. Bach

Claudio **Monteverdi**

◔ *1567–1643*   ⫿ **ITALIAN**   ✍ *254*

More than any composer, Claudio Monteverdi defined the transition from the Renaissance style to the Baroque. Although his early madrigals reflect the lush chromatic style of the late Renaissance, Monteverdi not only embraced the simplified new style but was also its greatest advocate. His opera *L'Orfeo* marked the beginning of a new era.

» **A prolific songwriter,** Monteverdi is best known for his secular madrigals on the theme of love.

Life

Monteverdi began his musical career young, publishing his first book of madrigals at age 15 and his second eight years later. At this time he was making a living performing, eventually securing a position as a lowly court musician for the Duke of Mantua. It was here that he met his wife Claudia Cattaneo, the daughter of a colleague in the string band. Although his time in Mantua was productive, Monteverdi felt undervalued as a composer, and eventually left for his home town of Cremona. A year later, he moved on to the more prestigious position of maestro di cappella at St. Mark's Basilica in Venice. In addition to his duties he also continued to take on outside commissions, including several from his old employer, the Duke of Mantua. He often wrote

music for the annual Venetian Carnival, most notably the stage work *Il combattimento de Tancredi e Clorinda* for a commedia troupe in 1624. Monteverdi cultivated his relationships with wealthy patrons and with other composers (Heinrich Schütz visited in 1628–29) and enjoyed a quiet middle age until 1630, when plague and a war in Mantua rocked Venice; subsequently he entered the priesthood. His final years were spent revising his earlier works, completing his treatise on *seconda prattica* (*stile moderno*), and composing new music. His final book of madrigals was published posthumously in 1651.

Music

Monteverdi's early madrigals may have been firmly in the traditional style, but by 1600 he had already begun to incorporate elements of the new, more austere style into his works, a practice that made him the target of criticism from conservative music critic Giovanni Artusi. Monteverdi responded by including a manifesto on *seconda prattica* as a preface to his fifth book of madrigals in 1605. His published madrigals were already known as far as Copenhagen when he wrote his first opera, *L'Orfeo*, in 1607. A second opera, *Arianna*, followed the next year, fueled by his grief over the loss of his wife. *Arianna* proved even more popular than *L'Orfeo*, particularly the Lament, which is the only surviving portion of the opera. Following his appointment to St. Mark's Basicila in 1613, the focus of Monteverdi's writing shifted to sacred choral music, although he continued to write madrigals and dramatic music throughout his life, including *Il Ritorno d'Ulisse in Patria* (1640) and *L'Incoronazione di Poppea* (1642) for the new opera in Venice.

> " The **end** of all **good music** is to **affect** the **soul.** "   **Claudio Monteverdi**

MILESTONES

1587	First of nine books of madrigals published	**1608**	Writes *Arianna*
1590	Becomes string player for Duke of Mantua	**1610**	Composes Mass and Vespers, dedicated to Pope Paul V
1599	Marries singer Claudia Cattaneo		
1600	Travels to Austria, Hungary, and Italy as part of Duke's entourage	**1613**	Appointed maestro di cappella at St. Mark's Basilica in Venice
1607	Writes *L'Orfeo*; wife Claudia dies	**1624**	Writes *Il combattimento de Tancredi e Clorinda*

KEY WORKS

L'ORFEO

OPERA   ⧖ 118:00   ▭ 6   🎻🥁🎵

Although not his first opera, Monteverdi's *L'Orfeo* was the first to gain broad acceptance and to popularize the elements of *seconda prattica*. Based on the ancient Orpheus myth, the opera presents a variety of styles: "dry" and fully accompanied recitative, florid arias, choruses, and instrumental interludes. Also, in keeping with the traditions of Classical Greek drama, he makes use of *deus ex machina* ("god from a machine") in the final act.

VESPRO DELLA BEATA VERGINE (VESPERS)

CHORAL   ⧖ 72:00   ▭ 14   🎤🥁🎵

Monteverdi's *Vespers for the Blessed Virgin* was written during his service for the Duke of Mantua, although his duties did not include composing sacred music. In fact, the work is dedicated to Pope Paul V and was published in a volume that also included his *Mass in illa tempore* as well as several Vespers psalm settings and motets. It is possible that he later used these as "audition pieces" to obtain the position at St. Mark's Basilica in Venice. The work contains a mixture of both *stile antico* and *moderno*, and a reworking of an instrumental toccata from *L'Orfeo*.

LUCI SERENE E CHIARE

CHORAL   ⧖ 3:30   ▭ 1   🥁

This is a transitional madrigal, with elements of both the old and new styles. The five-part text setting is clear and uncomplicated; this may be in part to allow instruments to either replace or double vocal parts, as a later arrangement with basso continuo suggests. The poem "Eyes serene and clear / You inflame me" by Ridolfo Arlotti is on the subject of suffering from the pangs of love.

SI, CH'IO VORREI MORIRE

CHORAL   ⧖ 3:00   ▭ 1   🥁

Another five-part madrigal, *Si, ch'io vorrei morire* hides a much more earthy message. The references to dying in the text are an allusion to a much more pleasant "ending," as supported by both other portions of the lyrics ("Ah mouth! Ah lips! Ah tongue!") and the rather unsubtle rising and falling of the music.

CRUDA AMARILLI

CHORAL   ⧖ 2:30   ▭ 1   🥁

From the fifth book of madrigals, this five-part madrigal is more harmonically stable than *Luci serene*, although elements of the older polyphonic style remain. This madrigal was specifically cited by Artusi as an example of the "Imperfections of Modern Music." The text ("Cruel Amaryllis") is taken from Giovanni Guarini's play *Il pastor fido*, a popular source for contemporary composers.

INFLUENCES

Monteverdi's writings on *seconda prattica* and his madrigals, sacred music, and operas in that style make him the most influential composer of his time. His music also shows a slow movement from modal harmonies to the key-based tonal system we use today.

🔼 **Cremona Cathedral,** where Monteverdi began his musical career as a choirboy.

Gregorio **Allegri**

🌑 **1582–1652**   🏳 **ITALIAN**   ✍ **c.30**

Although Allegri composed and published a steady stream of sacred works throughout his lifetime, he is remembered largely for his *Miserere*, an elaborate sacred motet sung by the papal choir during Holy Week every year until 1870. The details of the work were a closely guarded secret, although Mozart at the age of 14 reputedly reproduced the work from memory after one hearing.

Allegri's position as singer and maestro di cappella of the papal choir crowned a career that began as a boy chorister at age nine. He commenced his studies in composition with G.M. Nanino, the maestro di cappella at Rome's San Luigi dei Francesi. After appointments at cathedrals in Fermo and Tivoli, Allegri returned to Rome, eventually joining the papal choir. The music that he wrote for the Sistine Chapel, unlike his previous work, was old-fashioned for the time, following in the *stile antico* ("old style") of Palestrina, but, like that of Palestrina, demonstrating great subtlety and clarity of style. Allegri also published eight books of sacred motets in a more modern style between 1618 and 1639, which were intended for wider usage.

MILESTONES	
1607	Active as singer and composer at Fermo and Tivoli cathedrals
1618	Publishes first book of motets; *Concertini, libro I* published (now lost)
1619	*Concertini, libro II* published
1628	Appointed maestro di cappella of St. Spirito in Sassia, Rome
1629	Joins papal choir in Rome
c.1638	Composes *Miserere Mei Deus*
c.1640	Publication of *Lamentationes Jeremiae prophetae I*, sacred vocal work
1650	Elected maestro di cappella of papal choir; composes *Sinfonia a 4*
c.1651	Publication of *Lamentationes Jeremiae prophetae II*, sacred vocal work

KEY WORKS

MISERERE MEI DEUS

PSALM SETTING   ⏱ **12:10**   📖 **1**   🎵

Allegri's famous *Miserere* and the shroud of secrecy surrounding it contain a larger story. The work itself is relatively simple, alternating between five-part and four-part choir sections

▶▶ **Allegri joined the choir** of the Sistine Chapel as composer and singer in 1629, and remained a member until his death.

separated by plainsong, and would have been performed with one singer on each part. What the Vatican did not wish to have copied were the added embellishments above the basic chords; whereas with other similar compositions the singers would have added their own ornaments to the written music, often changing them with each performance, the embellishments for the *Miserere* (including the haunting high C) were also written down and had to be memorized by the choir, who would have been singing in the dark. The text is taken from Psalm 51 and begins "Have mercy upon me, O God." The psalm setting is traditionally sung as part of the Holy Week services leading up to Easter as a penitential song.

Johann Jacob **Froberger**

⬤ **1616–1667**   𝄞 **GERMAN**   ✍ **100**

A virtuoso on the harpsichord and organ as well as a composer, Froberger wrote almost exclusively for keyboard instruments. He was one of the most highly regarded musicians of his time, and traveled widely throughout Europe performing his work.

Born in Stuttgart, he moved to Vienna as a young man, where he worked as a court organist, and later went to Rome to study with Frescobaldi. His

cosmopolitan life influenced the development of his musical style, which combined elements of German, Italian, and French styles—a feature that was to be very influential on German composers of the following generation. As well as writing fantasias, toccatas, canzonas, and other conventional works for the harpsichord and organ, mainly in the Italian style, Froberger was an early pioneer of the keyboard suite, a group of pieces that incorporated dances and other movements in a French style. These suites for harpsichord contain some of his most expressive music, and are sometimes programmatic, describing a particular event or scene, or referring to something more personal such as the "Plainte, written in London to dispel melancholy," written after he had lost all his money to pirates.

Very little of his music was published during his lifetime, but manuscript copies survived and his music continued to be performed and studied after his death, having an enormous influence on the German late Baroque keyboard style associated with composers such as Handel and J.S. Bach.

MILESTONES	
1634	Moves to Vienna
1637	Appointed court organist to Emperor Ferdinand III
1649	Publishes set of ricercares; starts three-year tour of Europe
1653	Starts work for Imperial Chapel at Regensburg
1656	Ricercares use new types of tuning
1662	Arrives penniless in London

Orlando **Gibbons**

⬤ **1583–1625**   𝄞 **ENGLISH**   ✍ **c.100**

Born in Oxford and educated at Cambridge, where he sang with the King's College choir, Gibbons worked for the Chapel Royal from 1603 until his untimely death. He was recognized as one of the finest organists of his age; as a composer he mastered all the forms and styles of his time,

including consort and keyboard music, but is remembered mainly for his fine church pieces and hymn tunes. What survives of the second of his two services, and his many verse anthems such as *This is the Record of John*, contain outstanding music, full of vitality and deft counterpoint that typifies the Baroque style. Most of his secular songs were written before he was 30, and the beautiful "Silver Swan," from the *First Set of Madrigals and Motetts*, has become well known. So sudden was his death that he never made a will; his widow died before his estate was settled.

MILESTONES	
1598	Enters Cambridge University
1605	Becomes Gentleman of the Chapel Royal
1612	*First Set of Madrigals and Motetts*
1619	Chamber musician to James I
1622	*O Clap Your Hands*, 8-part anthem
1623	Organist and chorus master at Westminster Abbey
1625	Dies suddenly from brain haemorrhage

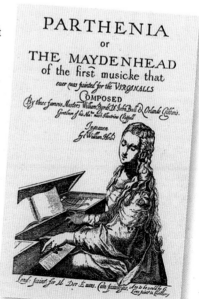

》 Along with his contemporary William Byrd, Orlando Gibbons contributed to the first book to be published containing music for the virginal.

Girolamo **Frescobaldi**

● 1583–1643   ⚑ ITALIAN   ✍ 35

As the child prodigy of a rich family, the young Frescobaldi had his musical skills displayed throughout Italy. A virtuoso keyboard player, he went on to enjoy prestigious court and church posts in Ferrara, Rome, and Mantua. After turning out some early madrigals, Frescobaldi focused on keyboard music, becoming the first major composer to face the challenges of developing a musical narrative. An outstanding improviser on harpsichord and organ, he produced an imaginative body of work covering every keyboard genre of the time, while also pioneering new techniques, especially in his capriccios and toccatas. Frescobaldi's influence was wide and long-lasting.

MILESTONES

1607	Makes only trip abroad, to Flanders
1608	Becomes organist at St. Peter's, Rome
1613	Marries the mother of his illegitimate child
1627	Publishes his second *Libro di toccate*, (*Book of Toccatas*) for keyboard
1635	Publishes *Fiori musicali* (*Flowers of Music*), organ music for Mass

⬢ **A virtuoso organist** and imaginative improviser, Frescobaldi spent much of his musical career delighting court and Church with his keyboard skills.

Francesco **Cavalli**

● 1602–1676   ⚑ ITALIAN   ✍ c.70

⬓ **The daily round** of religious ritual at St. Mark's Basilica inspired much of the drama and vivacity in Cavalli's music.

Cavalli was a close associate (and possibly pupil) of Monteverdi, on whose death he took over as the leading composer and performer in Venice. Born Francesco Caletto, he was an outstanding singer, and entered St. Mark's Basilica choir under Monteverdi, eventually becoming the organist. Early on he composed Church music (much of it lost), but after marrying into money, he turned to stage projects. Public opera was booming, and he wrote 40 or so with great success, with *Equisto*, *Giasone*, *Xerxes*, and *Erismena* being staged throughout Italy. In contrast to early academic operas, Cavalli's were fast-paced and comic, and he developed the contrast between recitative and aria. His box-office appeal declined toward his death, but his reputation remained high.

MILESTONES

1616	Joins the choir of St. Mark's Basilica, Venice
1639	Stages his first opera, *Le nozze di Teti e di Peleo* (*The Marriage of Teti and Peleo*)
1662	Stages *Ercole amante* (*Hercules in Love*), opera, for Louis XIV in Paris
1665	Made principal organist at St. Mark's Basilica

Giacomo **Carissimi**

● 1605-1674   ♙ ITALIAN   ✍ c.280

From the age of 23 until his death 46 years later, Carissimi was maestro di capella (chapel master) at Sant' Apollinare, the church of the Jesuit Collegio Germanico in Rome, renowned for its musical tradition. With his simple but effective style, he established the features of the Latin oratorio, using music as a kind of musical sermon, to vividly illustrate a religious point. He is famous, also, for having practically invented the cantata, whose text usually dealt with the pain of unrequited love. Carissimi was a prolific composer of motets and cantatas, although how prolific is hard to pinpoint because many of his pieces were destroyed or lost. Although melancholy, Carissimi was a kind, well-respected man, and he supplemented his income by loaning money on generous repayment terms.

MILESTONES	
1628	Becomes maestro di capella at Assisi
1630	Appointed maestro di capella at Sant' Apollinare, Rome
c.1650	Composes *Jephtha*, oratorio
1654	Teaches Marc-Antoine Charpentier
1659	Funds two college sopranos from his own pocket

◄ **The Church of Santa Maria de Apollinare** in Rome provided the inspirational setting for the first of Carissimi's oratorios, stimulating worship through the beauty of music.

Heinrich **Schütz**

● 1585-1672   ♙ GERMAN   ✍ 500

Spotted by a musician staying at the family inn, the young Schütz was encouraged to take up music, and went on to become the leading German composer of his time. After studying music in Venice, Schütz was appointed musical director at the Dresden court, where he composed for religious and political occasions. Although his huge output—mostly sacred—is strongly influenced by Italian styles, his dramatic choral works, inspired by the ideals of Martin Luther, put German music on the map. Schütz enjoyed a long and fruitful life, despite the early death of his wife and child.

MILESTONES	
1609	Studies under Giovanni Gabrieli
1615	Starts work at the Dresden court
1627	Stages the first German opera, *Dafne*
1629	Publishes his first book of *Symphoniae sacrae* (*Sacred Symphonies*)
1633	Starts work at the Copenhagen court
1636	Publishes his first *Geistliche concerte* (concertos for voices and instruments)

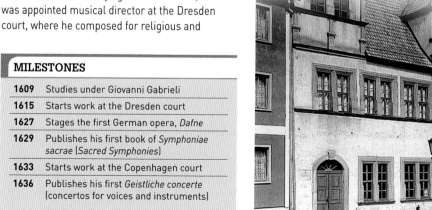

◄ **At the family house** in Weissenfels, Germany, the gifted young Schütz impressed a visiting musician with his precocious vocal and keyboard skills.

Jean-Baptiste **Lully**

◔ **1632–1687**   ⚏ **FRENCH**   ✍ **119**

Jean-Baptiste Lully began life as the son of an Italian miller, but, after moving to France, his rapid ascension to a prestigious position in the court of Louis XIV (the Sun King) made him the most influential composer in the history of French music. For about a quarter of a century, he had almost total control over French musical life, including opera, ballet, and theatrical music, as well as music publishing.

Lully entered the French court at the age of 13 as a page and tutor, but soon joined the music establishment there. He became first a composer, and then Superintendent of the King's Chamber Music, with responsibilities that included direction of the King's prestigious string ensemble, the "24 violons du Roi." Much of his later career was devoted to composing ballets and grand operas for the court. Lully's death is famous: while conducting by pounding out the beat with a cane, he stabbed his toe; gangrene set in and he died soon after.

MILESTONES	
1646	Taken to Paris by Chevalier de Guise as tutor to his niece, Louis XIV's cousin
1652	Becomes ballet dancer at Louis' court
1662	Marries Madeleine Lambert, daughter of composer Michel Lambert
1670	Writes *Le bourgeois gentilhomme*
1672	Establishes Académie Royale de Musique for the performance of opera
1674	Composes *Alceste*, opera

KEY WORKS

ARMIDE

OPERA   ⏱ **160:00**   ▭ **5**   ♫ ♪ ♩

Armide was the last of a series of lyric tragedies by Lully and his long-time librettist, Philippe Quinault. They had worked together since Lully's first opera, *Les fêtes de l'Amour et de Bacchus* in 1672. Quinault retired after *Armide*, which premiered in 1686, although Lully wrote two more operas before his death the following year.

Based on an epic poem by Italian poet Torquato Tasso and set during the First Crusade, the story is that of the sorceress Armide who falls in love with her sworn enemy Renaud. Unusually for the era, the opera centers almost entirely on the title character and her conflicting emotions. The work was an immediate success and became a staple of the French repertoire.

The opera opens with a Prologue in which the goddesses Glory and Wisdom summarize the plot and (obliquely) praise the king.

LE BOURGEOIS GENTILHOMME

COMEDY-BALLET   ⏱ **103:00**   ▭ **5**   ♫ ♪ ♩

This work came out of a renewed interest in Turkish culture in France following a rare visit to the French court by the Turkish envoy. Lully and the playwright Molière had collaborated on other comedy-ballets—theatrical works that combined music and dance into the spoken drama—but it was with this work that they reached the pinnacle of the genre. The work features musical interludes between acts which, in effect, form part of the play.

INFLUENCES
As the sole composer of French opera for 15 years, Lully created a national style. His operas and opera-ballets were performed all over Europe, and inspired later composers such as Rameau and Gluck. Publication of his instrumental overtures and dance suites led to the development of the French suite genre used by Bach and Handel.

⌃ **Most of Lully's operas** included prologues that glorified the Sun King or the concept of kingship. Supernatural plots gave scope for lavish and ingenious stage effects.

Barbara **Strozzi**

● **1619–1677**   ⚐ **ITALIAN**   ✍ **8**

The adopted, possibly illegitimate, daughter of Giulio Strozzi, the respected Venetian poet, Barbara Strozzi (alias Valle) was a singer much in demand at Venice's cultural events and meetings who became a composing professional. A student of Francesco Cavalli, she sang in many of his operas. She must also have performed her own compositions, many of which were for solo female voice on themes of love and emotional conflict. Strozzi published eight works, most after her father's death in 1652, suggesting she had to compose for her livelihood. She never married but had four children.

MILESTONES	
1637	Performing at Accademia degli Unisoni, Venice
1644	Begins composing
1651	Cantatas, Ariettas, and Duets, Op. 2
1654	Cantatas, Ariettas, and Duets, Op. 3

Giovanni Battista **Vitali**

● **1632–1692**   ⚐ **ITALIAN**   ✍ **35**

A composer, cellist, and singer, Vitali spent his life working in Italy's vibrant court, church, and institutional music scene. His relatively modest output includes some innovative instrumental music, and his ideas—such as linking themes and keys across movements, and the use of dance rhythms in all movements—laid the foundations of the Baroque trio sonata for successors such as Arcangelo Corelli and Henry Purcell. A pioneer in music publishing, Vitali also wrote important textbooks on musical composition, such as *Artifici musicali*, first published in 1689.

MILESTONES	
1674	Joint maestro di capella at Modena
1684	Sonata da chiesa, Op. 9
1684	Promoted to maestro di capella

Dietrich **Buxtehude**

● **c.1637–1707**   ⚐ **DANISH**   ✍ **275**

Buxtehude was effectively director of music for the city of Lübeck, Germany, and such was his reputation that J. S. Bach walked 185 miles to hear him play. Only two major collections of his work (sets of ensemble sonatas) were published in his lifetime; his music was circulated mainly in manuscript copies. Although he wrote a wide range of vocal music, including the secular cantata "Alles, was ihr tut" (All That You Do), he is now remembered for his organ works—Lutheran chorales, wide-ranging improvisatory preludes, and the ostinato pieces that inspired Bach. He had four daughters, and a condition of employment for his successor was to marry one; Johann Mattheson, a candidate in 1703, lost interest in the job when he realized this.

» Buxtehude was organist at Lübeck's Marienkirche but also ran concert series in the church, at which sacred dramatic works were performed.

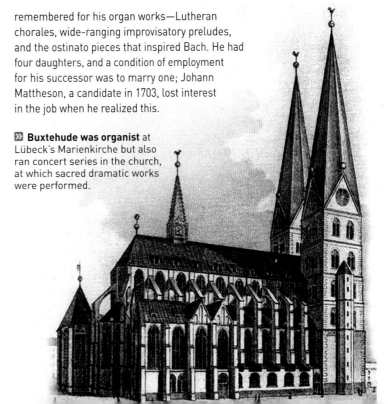

MILESTONES	
1668	Becomes organist at Lübeck; marries daughter of predecessor
1678	Introduces sacred dramatic works in *Abendmusiken* (evening concerts)
1680	Writes set of cantatas *Membra Jesu nostri*
1703	Handel and Mattheson visit
1705	J. S. Bach visits

Marc-Antoine **Charpentier**

◔ 1643–1704   ⌘ FRENCH   ✍ 548

Unusually for a French composer of his time and talent, Charpentier never achieved a position at Louis XIV's court. Instead, he produced a wide variety of music for theater and Church, collaborating with the dramatist Molière and producing several Masses, motets, and sacred dramas, including his "Christmas Oratorio." Seen as too "Italian" in his lifetime, his unique style is now coming to be fully appreciated.

Unlike his contemporary Lully, an Italian who came to epitomize French music, Charpentier was a Parisian who went to Italy to study composition, bringing back with him not only the works of Italian composers but also a unique hybrid writing style. He also enjoyed the patronage of Mademoiselle de Guise, a well-connected French noblewoman with a large private musical entourage, while his reputation as a composer of sacred music not only helped him procure a position at the Jesuit church of Saint-Louis in Paris, followed by Sainte-Chapelle, but also won him commissions for the chapel of the Dauphin.

MILESTONES

1662	Travels to Rome, possibly to study with Giacomo Carissimi
1673	Collaborates with Molière on his final play, *Le malade imaginaire*
1679	Begins composing for the Dauphin
1680s	Director of Music at Saint-Louis
1693	Premiere of *Médée* at the Académie Royale de Musique, Paris
1698	Appointed choirmaster of Sainte-Chapelle, Paris

KEY WORKS

THE CHRISTMAS ORATORIO
FRIGIDAE NOCTIS UMBRA, H414

ORATORIO   ⏱ 29:20   📖 7   ♫ ♬ ♪

Charpentier wrote four short Christmas oratorios in his lifetime; this one may have been composed for his patron, Mademoiselle de Guise, in the mid-1680s. Written for six voices, two violins, and basso continuo, the work comprises seven movements beginning with an introductory prelude for instruments alone. Throughout the oratorio one can hear elements of the older polyphonic style, particularly in the central chorus, reflecting Charpentier's Italian training.

MESSE DE MINUIT POUR NOËL, H9

MASS SETTING   ⏱ 29:20   📖 6   ♫ ♬

Charpentier's *Midnight Mass for Christmas* is quintessentially a work of light to be performed at the darkest hour. Each of the six movements, set to the text of the traditional Latin liturgy, is based on popular French carol tunes of the period (some of which may still be known to audiences today). The Mass as a whole alternates between upbeat tunes and gentle lilting melodies, reflecting the contemplation of the Christ child.

》 Charpentier's work with Molière led directly to his long-term involvement with the newly-formed Comédie-Française, which is currently the oldest national theatre company in the world.

Arcangelo **Corelli**

● 1653–1713   ᴾᵁ ITALIAN   ✍ c.82

Among his contemporaries, Corelli was the most famous violinist-composer of the Baroque period, and one of the most influential after Monteverdi. Although not a prolific composer—his entire output consisted of six collections—his instrumental writing was admired for its harmonic refinement and brilliance of style, and was highly influential to many composers, including Bach and Handel.

There is still very little known about Corelli's background, although he did spend most of his working life in Rome. There he gained the patronage of several prominent aristocratic and royal supporters of the arts, including the exiled Queen of Sweden. He was regularly employed to direct performances of operas, oratorios, and other large works, including those by Handel. Today, Corelli is primarily known for his 12 *Concerti grossi*, which represented a new form of composition. As a violin virtuoso, he contributed to establishing modern bowing techniques and was one of the earliest performers to use double-stopping and chordal

effects on the instrument. As a teacher of the violin his achievements were also outstanding, and his pupils included Francesco Geminiani and Vivaldi.

MILESTONES	
1679	Becomes chamber musician to the exiled Queen Christina of Sweden
1681	First set of 12 trio church sonatas, *Sonate da chiesa*, Op. 1, published
1687	Appointed music master to Cardinal Pamphili
1694	Composes *Sonate da camera*, Op. 4

KEY WORKS

SONATE A VIOLINO E VIOLONE O CIMBALO, OP. 5, NO. 12, "LA FOLIA"

CHAMBER   🕭 12:00   ▥ 4   ⚏ ✇

Corelli's sonata known as "La Folia" concludes with a set of 24 variations on a simple melodic and harmonic sequence thought to have originated in Spain in the late 15th or early 16th century. The basic melody and harmony are elementary, comprising two short, virtually identical phrases. It is this simplicity, along with the compelling harmonic sequence, that is the likely source of its popularity, lending itself well to variation and improvisation. Corelli, virtuoso violinist that he was, incorporates numerous coloratura violin techniques throughout, ranging from florid passagework and arpeggiation to the messa di voce, a sustained note that swells from soft to loud and then fades slowly away again. In addition to the notated ornaments, the

composer leaves ample room for improvisation on the part of the individual performer; in fact, several editions of the work, published by others after the 1700 edition, claim to incorporate ornaments used by Corelli himself in performance. Many editions of Corelli's "Folia" Sonata were published in his lifetime, including an arrangement for recorder and bass.

CONCERTO GROSSO, OP. 6, NO. 8

ORCHESTRAL   🕭 15:00   ▥ 6   ♫

Corelli's Op. 6 collection, published posthumously as a set of 12, are considered by many to be the epitome of the concerto grosso form. The first eight are set in "sonata da chiesa" or church sonata-style, the last of which has been dubbed the "Christmas Concerto," largely due to Corelli's label of "Pastorale" for the final movement, and would have been performed on Christmas Eve.

⌂ **In 1675** Corelli settled in Rome, where he became one of the city's leading violinists. As a performer, he was admired for the exquisite tone of his playing.

Johann **Pachelbel**

1653–1706   **GERMAN**   c.346

Pachelbel was one of the dominant figures of late 17th-century European keyboard and chamber music. Although chiefly known today for his Canon in D, he was well known during his lifetime as both an organist and a prolific composer.

Pachelbel's career is marked by a series of posts as organist at increasingly prestigious places, and by his growing influence as a teacher and composer. When work dried up at one position he moved on to the next, joining the courts at Eisenach and Stuttgart and then moving to Gotha as town organist. He was then invited by his home town, Nuremberg, to return to take up the prestigious post at St. Sebaldus, where he remained until his death.

The Magnificat plays an important role in the Protestant liturgy of the vespers services, and Pachelbel wrote several different settings of the text during his lifetime. Traditionally the organ was used in this context either to play alternate verses of the chant in some form, or to play a short prelude as a means of determining the opening pitch for the singers. Pachelbel's 95 Magnificat Fugues had the latter, more utilitarian role in the daily services: to bring the singers in. This large body of short fugues in different keys, styles, themes, and moods represents possibly the most impressive collection of organ music until J. S. Bach's a generation later.

In the now famous Canon in D, three violins play the canon, while a basso continuo plays a ground, a short, simple passage of eight notes repeated over and over again: 54 times in this instance. The Canon in D remained relatively obscure until recently.

⬆ **Pachelbel's *Hexachordum Apollinis*,** six sets of variations for harpsichord, had a title page engraved by the composer and organist Nicolaus Schurtz.

MILESTONES	
1673	Becomes deputy organist of St. Stephen's Cathedral in Vienna
1681	Marries Barbara Gabler
1683	Wife and infant son die of plague
1685	Marries Judith Drommer
1692	Flees French invasion; goes to Gotha
1695	Invited to take up position at St. Sebaldus in Nuremberg; writes *Magnificat Fugues*
1699	Writes *Hexachordum Apollinis*, harpsichord

Alessandro **Scarlatti**

1660–1725   **ITALIAN**   950

A maestro di cappella at 18, and with six successful operas performed in Rome's aristocratic circles by 23, Scarlatti's career had a remarkable start. He moved to Naples and by the 1690s was at the peak of his fame. By 1700 the city rivalled Venice as the leading operatic center, but Scarlatti was by then running into money problems—partly due to his large family—and, in looking for freelance work, he often ignored his contractual duties. After problematic spells in Rome and Venice, he returned to Naples, but, despite his fine reputation, his later, more complex operas achieved only a lukewarm success. Routinely called the founder of Neapolitan opera, it seems his style was mostly pan-Italian; only one of his 110-plus operas, *Trionfo dell'onore*, is Neapolitan in music and text. He died in poverty, and is remembered as the father of the composer Domenico Scarlatti.

⬆ **It was at the Teatro Capranica** in Rome that Scarlatti produced some of his finest and most expressive operas, including *Telemaco* (1718), *Marco Attilio Regoló* (1719), and *Griselda* (1721).

MILESTONES	
1679	Writes *Gli equivoci nel sembiante*, opera
1680	*L'honestà negli amori* performed for the Queen of Sweden
1706	Admitted to Arcadian Academy, Rome
1721	Composes the *St. Cecilia Mass*

Domenico **Scarlatti**

🌑 **1685–1757**   🏳 **ITALIAN**   ✒ **c.717**

Son of Alessandro Scarlatti, harpsichordist and composer Domenico Scarlatti's greatest contribution were his single-movement keyboard sonatas, yet only a small number were published in his lifetime. Although born in the same year as Bach and Handel, Scarlatti's light, homophonic compositional style is more characteristic of the early Classical period, and reveals his innovative approach to harmony.

Very little is known about Domenico Scarlatti's life, despite the vast amount that has been written about him. Much of his early life was spent traveling with his father, who managed his career closely. However, Scarlatti soon established his own name as a keyboard virtuoso and composer (one story—possibly apocryphal—tells of a performing competition between Domenico and Handel). His appointment to the household of the exiled Queen of Poland led to more prestigious positions: first at the Vatican, then at the Portuguese court, and finally at the Spanish court in Madrid, where the majority of his keyboard works were written.

MILESTONES	
1700	Becomes organist and composer of Capella Reale in Naples
1708	Appointed maestro di cappella to Maria Casimir, exiled Queen of Poland, in Rome
1714	Employed as maestro di cappella at Cappella Giulia at the Vatican
1719	Becomes mestre of the Royal Chapel to King João of Portugal
1728	Composes *Festeggio armonico*
1738	*30 Essercizi per gravicembalo* published, bringing Scarlatti international recognition
1754	Composes *Missa quattuor vocum*

KEY WORKS

STABAT MATER

CHORAL	⏳ 26:45	📖 7	👥 🎻

Scarlatti may be best known for his 500 or more essercizi, or keyboard sonatas, but in the years before his appointment to the Spanish court he composed a variety of music, including 13 operas (now largely forgotten) and several sacred works for the maestro di cappella positions he held. Of the latter, his Stabat Mater for ten voices and basso continuo stands out as a work of great grandeur, depth of expression, and harmonic color.

Composed in Rome for the Cappella Giulia sometime between 1713 and 1719, it is thought that this work may have been intended for private devotions. The subject matter is full of pathos, describing the anguish of the Virgin Mary at the foot of the Cross; the name refers to the first line of the text "Stabat Mater dolorosa" ("There stood the Mother grieving"). The second half of the text becomes a prayer to the Virgin herself, followed by a brief prayer to Christ in the final stanzas.

The composition is divided into seven sections in contrasting styles, each section comprising one to five stanzas of the text.

SONATAS IN A MAJOR, K181, K182

SOLO PIANO	📖 2	🎵

Scarlatti's keyboard sonatas have a distinctive style that is immediately recognizable, despite their extremely simple binary form. Despite the similarity of key and tempo (Allegro) and the use of repeated motives throughout, these two pieces are entirely different in character: K181 is marked by the repetition of strikingly dissonant chords, while K182 is more nimble and dancelike, with great leaping arpeggios.

⌃ *Festeggio armonico* celebrates the betrothal of Scarlatti's pupil Maria Barbara to the Spanish crown prince.

François **Couperin**

◓ 1668–1733   ⟨ℙ⟩ FRENCH   ✍ 126

François Couperin eclipsed the reputation of his famous composer uncle, Louis, from an early age, first as an organist and then as a composer of works for keyboard. His *Pièces de clavecin*, miniature character works for harpsichord, were described as "national treasures." They continue to be staples of the keyboard repertoire today as well as the epitome of French Baroque instrumental music.

Couperin was the most famous of a very distinguished family of musicians, and became known as "Couperin le Grand." He was only 11 when he inherited the prestigious organist's post at St. Gervais in Paris on the death of his father, Charles. Church composer Michel-Richard Delalande took the post until Couperin could assume his duties at 18. From then on Couperin's star continued to rise. He won an appointment to the royal court at 25 and became one of the leading teachers of harpsichord and organ of his generation.

Couperin wrote a vast amount of sublime keyboard music, including his 27 famous suites (*ordres*) of harpsichord music, giving many of them evocative titles. He also produced several chamber and vocal works, and some

key theoretical writings. His *L'art de toucher le clavecin* (*The Art of Playing the Harpsichord*), published in 1716, was much admired by Bach, with whom he corresponded.

MILESTONES

1690	Obtains a *privilège du Roi* (printing license) to publish his organ Masses
1693	Louis XIV appoints him as one of the four court organist-composers
1694	Becomes tutor to the king's children
1702	Ennobled as *chevalier*
1703	Publishes psalm settings for the Chappelle du Roi (Royal Chapel)
1713	Publishes first book of *Pièces de clavecin*, harpsichord pieces

KEY WORKS

VINGT-CINQUIÈME ORDRE

SOLO HARPSICHORD   ⧖ 17:00   ▭ 5

This multipart suite for harpsichord first appeared in print in 1730 in Couperin's fourth book of *Pièces de Clavecin*, his last published work. As with most of Couperin's harpsichord works, these are character pieces with descriptive (and sometimes enigmatic) titles evoking images and reminiscences.

The opening work, *La visionaire* (*The Visionary*), describes a religious fanatic, and features the dotted rhythms and ornate elaborations

common to French music of the period. (His embellishments are always written exactly into the music, excluding performer improvisation.) *La misterieuse* (*The Mysterious One*) is a contrasting piece, more elegant and lilting, while *La Monflambert*—named after the wife of a local councillor, whom it might describe— is more melancholy in mood.

Another shift comes in the fourth piece, *La muse victorieuse* (*The Victorious Muse*), with its triumphal flourishes in C major. Couperin finished the *Ordre* in a darker vein, perhaps because of his own declining health: both the title and the music of *Les ombres errantes* (*Wandering Shades*) have a pensive, almost funereal aspect.

◖ **Couperin's treatise** on harpsichord-playing technique was extremely influential.

Henry **Purcell**

● 1659–1695　　　🏴 ENGLISH　　　✍ 515

Despite his relatively short life, Henry Purcell remains one of the most important English composers. His facility in writing for all genres and audiences, his popularity at court through the reigns of three different monarchs, and his vast output of court odes, theatrical music, sacred anthems, secular songs and catches, chamber music, and organ voluntaries are clear testament to his prodigious talent.

Henry Purcell moved in exalted Church and Court circles from an early age, becoming a chorister in the Chapel Royal at age ten, an (unpaid) member of Charles II's musical retinue at 14, a court composer at 18, and an organist at Westminster Abbey at 20. Considering this meteoric career, perhaps it is unsurprising that Purcell produced so much music for Church and Court services, including numerous sacred choral works and odes for courtly occasions (including several "welcome songs" for Charles II and James II). Purcell also composed secular songs throughout his lifetime, and wrote dramatic musical works for the stage from 1688 onward.

MILESTONES

1677	Composes elegy *What Hope For Us Remains Now He Is Gone?* on the death of English composer, Matthew Locke
1680	Composes first music for the stage
1683	Keeper of the King's Instruments; composes first *Ode for St. Cecilia's Day*
1691	Composes music for Dryden's play *King Arthur*
1692	Composes music for *The Fairy Queen*, an adaptation of Shakespeare's play, *A Midsummer Night's Dream*

KEY WORKS

DIDO AND AENEAS

OPERA	⏱ 60:00	📖 3	🎭🎻🎵

Full opera was uncommon in 17th-century England, so it is not surprising that Purcell composed only one, *Dido and Aeneas*, deciding to concentrate instead on incidental music for existing theatrical works. With a libretto by Nahum Tate, *Dido* owes much to the tradition of courtly masques, and in particular John Blow's *Venus and Adonis* of 1682.

The opera consists of three short acts, each comprising several brief arias, recitatives, and dances. The action begins with the arrival in Carthage of Prince Aeneas, who is fleeing the fall of Troy. Dido, Queen of Carthage, knows that Aeneas is fated to found Rome, but nevertheless falls for the prince. Dido's nemesis, the Sorceress, along with her minions, plot to trick Aeneas into leaving Carthage by sending a witch disguised as

Mercury to order him to leave the city. Aeneas bids a difficult farewell to Dido. After a final broken-hearted lament, Dido kills herself.

I GAVE HER CAKES

CATCH	⏱ 1:00	📖 1	🎵

Purcell produced several secular catches (where the same music is sung by each singer in turn), some of which are quite ribald. This example, on a theme of drinking and flirting, dates from 1701.

INFLUENCES

Purcell studied composition under John Blow (who he succeeded as organist at Westminster Abbey), Christopher Gibbons, and Matthew Locke (who he succeeded as court composer). He also copied Continental styles; French dance rhythms are common in his works, and his trio sonatas are a conscious imitation of the Italian style.

⬆ **As court composer,** Purcell was called upon to write music for royal celebrations, including the coronation of Queen Mary and William of Orange in 1685.

Tomaso Giovanni **Albinoni**

◐ 1671–c.1751   ▥ ITALIAN   ✍ c.300

Due to his privileged background, Albinoni composed freelance, and knew more noble patrons than he did musicians. His prolific output includes 55 operas and 59 concertos, in which he was probably the first to use the three-movement form consistently.

Albinoni mass-produced his music but, thanks to his melodic gifts and individual style, he was as popular in his lifetime as Corelli and Vivaldi, and J. S. Bach used his Trio Sonatas as teaching material. But his popular fame rests on a piece he didn't write: "Albinoni's Adagio" was composed by Remo Giazotto around 1945; only the bass line was Albinoni's.

⏏ **As the eldest son** of a prosperous merchant in Venice, Albinoni didn't need to compose for a living and cultivated music more for pleasure than for profit.

MILESTONES	
1694	Composes 12 Trio Sonatas, Op. 1
1705	Marries operatic soprano Margherita Raimondi
1715	Oboe Concerto, Op. 7, published
1722	Supervises *I veri amici*, opera, Munich
1741	Writes last work, *Artamene*, opera

Jeremiah **Clarke**

◐ c.1674–1707   ▥ ENGLISH   ✍ 60

The "Trumpet Voluntary" familiar from wedding ceremonies, once thought to be by Henry Purcell, in fact came from a harpsichord piece by Clarke, a prominent composer in the generation just after Purcell. Clarke served as organist at the cathedrals of Winchester and St. Paul, and at the Chapel Royal, and his output includes church music, odes, songs, and theater music. He committed suicide in 1707, apparently after an unhappy love affair.

MILESTONES	
1685	Becomes chorister at Chapel Royal
1692	Organist at Winchester College
c.1697	Writes *Prince of Denmark's March* ("Trumpet Voluntary")
1699	"Vicar-choral" at St. Paul's Cathedral
1700	Becomes "Gentleman-extraordinary" at the Chapel Royal
1702	Writes "Praise the Lord," anthem, for Queen Anne's coronation

Francesco **Geminiani**

◐ 1687–1762   ▥ ITALIAN   ✍ 80

In the 1710s, the English were highly enamored of Italian culture and inspired by the virtuosity of Italian violinists such as Geminiani, who spent his working life in England. He promoted himself as "Corelli's pupil" and enjoyed early success with his brilliant and expressive Corelli-like Op. 1 sonatas, and even more with his Op. 3 concerti grossi. Admired mainly as a player, Geminiani performed to nobility rather than to the public, and was a prominent figure in London musical circles.

MILESTONES	
1716	Composes Sonatas for Violin, Op. 1
c.1732	Writes concerti grossi, Opp. 2 and 3
1751	*The Art of Playing the Violin* published
1756	*The Enchanted Forest* performed, Paris

Jean-Philippe **Rameau**

● **1683–1764**   🏳 **FRENCH**   ✍ **76**

Jean-Philippe Rameau was not only the most important French composer of the 18th century but was also an influential music theorist. His style of operatic writing ended the posthumous reign of Lully, whose model had been followed for half a century. Also a harpsichordist and organist, Rameau wrote many works for the keyboard. His highly ornamented compositions stand out as the epitome of Rococo style.

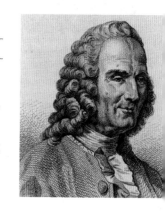

Rameau composed only a few small keyboard and sacred works prior to 1722, but the publication of his treatise on harmony that year marked the beginning of a productive period. His *Pièces de clavecin* were published in 1724, followed by a new theory book in 1726 and sets of keyboard works and cantatas in 1729. He wrote his first opera, *Hippolyte et Aricie*, at the age of 50. It drew the interest of Louis XV and Rameau later received several royal commissions as a result. His music is characterized by a musical dynamism that contrasts with the more staid style of Lully—Voltaire once dubbed Rameau "our hero of the semiquavers" (sixteenth notes).

MILESTONES	
1702	Appointed organist of Clermont-Ferrand Cathedral
1722	Publishes the highly influential *Traité de l'harmonie*; settles in Paris
1726	Marries Marie-Louise Mangot; publishes *Nouveau système de musique théorique*
1736	Completes *Les indes galantes*, opera
1739	Premiere of *Dardanus*, opera
1754	*Observations sur notre instinct pour musique* is published
1764	Is ennobled; dies a few months later

KEY WORKS

HIPPOLYTE ET ARICIE

OPERA	⏱ 165:00	📖 5	🎭 🎻 🎵

Despite Rameau's characteristically frenetic compositional style, this, his first opera (or properly, *tragédie en musique*) is very much in the French tradition: five acts in length, with a divertissement (a dance or other spectacle) in each act, and a plot based on figures from Classical mythology or history. Nonetheless, the style of music received both enthusiastic praise and critical dismissal. Many felt its vigorous passage work was too "Italian" and ornate. This opera may have been the first work to which the term "Baroque" was applied, though this would have been meant as an insult. Ironically, 20 years later, Parisian supporters of Italian opera would accuse Rameau of not being Italian enough. The libretto by Abbé Simon-Joseph Pellegrin is

based on Racine's play *Phèdre* of 1677, with elements of the tragedies of Euripides and Seneca. It concerns the incestuous love of Phèdre (Phaedra) for her stepson Hippolyte (Hippolytus). Despite the title, much of the action centers on Hippolyte's father, Thésée (Theseus), King of Athens.

PIÈCES DE CLAVECIN (1724)

KEYBOARD	⏱ 24:00	📖 9	🎵

In this, his second set of harpsichord works, Rameau first demonstrated his characteristic florid style, with dramatic runs of scales, and rapid and complex passages that fully exploit the harpsichord keyboard. The influence of Couperin is sometimes evident, but Rameau's athletic style takes these character pieces to a new level.

✉ **Rameau's satirical comedy-ballet *Platée*,** featuring a grotesque swamp nymph, was written for the wedding of the dauphin to a reputedly plain Spanish princess.

Antonio **Vivaldi**

● 1678–1741   ⁐ ITALIAN   ✎ 811+

Vivaldi was the most celebrated of all the Italian Baroque composers, and probably one of the most prolific. In addition to more than 500 concertos, he produced several operas, sacred vocal works (including his famous *Gloria*), and numerous other instrumental works, while his virtuoso violin playing earned him international fame. Like his father, he had fiery red hair, earning him the nickname "the Red Priest."

» **One of the most prolific composers** of his day, Vivaldi is best known for his poetic work *The Four Seasons*.

Life

In many respects Antonio Vivaldi's life was as flamboyant as his music. The son of a violinist, he worked as a violinist himself while training to be a priest. In 1703 he obtained a post at the Pio Ospedale della Pietà, an institution for abandoned (although highly talented) girls, where he taught and earned his students international fame. He rapidly made a name for himself as a composer as well, and publications of his music were widely praised and emulated. In 1713, the governors of the Ospedale commissioned several sacred works from him, and he began to write operas for the Venetian stage. He traveled a great deal, writing operas for Carnival in Mantua and Rome from 1723 onward, while in Venice the governors requested two concertos a month from him. Vivaldi soon became associated with singer Anna Giraud, who appeared in many of his operas. In 1737, during a public contracts dispute, the rumors about their relationship, and his refusal to say Mass (due to asthma) caught up with him, and he was barred from Ferrara. After some opera performances fared badly he began to lose public favor, and as a final ignominy he fell ill and died on a trip to Vienna, only to be buried in a pauper's grave.

Music

Arcangelo Corelli may have created the model for the Italian concerto but it was Antonio Vivaldi who showed what could be done with it. Vivaldi's skill as a violinist and orchestrator can be seen in the challenging roles he gives both to the solo instruments and ensembles, and having the talented performers of the Ospedale available allowed him to tailor his works to specific virtuosi and combinations of instruments. His vocal works also demonstrate a deft (and prolific) touch: his sacred solo and choral works range from the energetic to the sublime and show many of the same extravagances of his instrumental writing, and his operas were briefly the toast of Rome. Apart from the works published during Vivaldi's lifetime, the vast majority of his works are undated. Indeed, many have yet to be catalogued, although the current catalog lists more than 800 works.

" **I have heard him boast of composing a concerto faster than a copyist could write it down!** "

Charles de Brosses, 1739

MILESTONES

1693	Begins studies for the priesthood	**1716**	Appointed maestro de' concerti at the Pietà
1703	Following ordination, takes post teaching violin at the Ospedale della Pietà, an orphanage for girls	**1718**	Appointed music director to the court of Mantua
1705	Writes 12 Sonatas for Violin, Op. 1	**1725**	*Le quattro staggioni* (*The Four Seasons*), Op. 8, Nos. 1–4, published
1711	Publishes *L'estro armonico*, Op. 3, a collection of concerti grossi	**1740**	Becomes music director to the court of Charles VI in Vienna

KEY WORKS

THE FOUR SEASONS, OP. 8, NOS. 1–4, RV 271

ORCHESTRAL ⏱ **36:00** 📖 **16**

These four concertos for violin and orchestra—"Spring", "Summer", "Autumn", and "Winter"—are part of a set of 12 published in Amsterdam in 1725 titled *Il cimento dell'armonia e dell'inventione*, or *The Trial of Strength Between Harmony and Invention*. Unlike most of Vivaldi's concertos, these four have a clear programme: each concerto was accompanied by an illustrative sonnet printed in the principal violin's partbook, each on the theme of the respective season. The author of these poems is unknown, although there is some speculation that Vivaldi himself may have written them. The concertos remained popular long after Vivaldi's death, particularly in France (where "Spring" was a favourite of the French court), and today they are some of the most frequently recorded and performed works ever.

GLORIA, RV 589

CHORAL ⏱ **60:00** 📖 **12**

Written for the Ospedale, Vivaldi's *Gloria* contains a wealth of Baroque styles and contrasts. The opening choral annunciation is followed by a more contemplative "Et in terra pax" in B minor, which in turn is followed by a lively duet for women's voices. The work alternates choral sections and solos throughout; after a brief reprise of the opening music, an energetic choral fugue

based on an earlier *Gloria* by Giovanni Maria Ruggieri brings the piece to a rousing conclusion.

NULLA IN MUNDO PAX SINCERA

CHORAL ⏱ **13:30** 📖 **4**

The opening Larghetto may sound familiar to many listeners, having appeared in many soundtracks. The motet was written for less dramatic purposes, however; the text is a devotional prayer to Jesus and his peace. In the final Alleluia, the soprano demonstrates the type of florid virtuosity usually reserved for the strings, finishing with a flourish.

CONCERTO FOR FLUTE, OP. 10, NO. 3, RV 428, "THE GOLDFINCH"

ORCHESTRAL ⏱ **10:00** 📖 **3**

The "Goldfinch" Concerto is well-known for its more overt representations of birdsong, the composer making use of an instrument for which he rarely wrote. The simple slow movement, set only for flute and continuo, is particularly fine.

⌂ **Vivaldi was associated** for much of his life with the Ospedale della Pietà in Venice.

INFLUENCES

The qualities of Vivaldi's music—concise themes, clarity of form, rhythmic vitality, homophonic texture, balanced phrases, dramatic dialogue between soloist and ensemble—directly influenced many composers including J. S. Bach, who transcribed several of Vivaldi's concertos for keyboard.

Georg Philipp **Telemann**

● **1681–1767**   ▣ **GERMAN**   ✍ **c.3,700**

Telemann was one of the most prolific composers of the Baroque period. He gained an international reputation through both the quality of his music—which always reflected the current musical fashion—and the wide dissemination of his works: his innovative German periodical *Der getreue Music-Meister* provided amateur musicians with instrumental and vocal pieces for domestic music-making.

After holding several Church and Court positions in Poland and Germany, Telemann was appointed music director and cantor at Hamburg in 1721, a prestigious post that he held until his death. Today he is chiefly known for his solo and trio sonatas, but his instrumental works include many orchestral suites, concertos, quartets, trios, and compositions for keyboard, and his cantatas and larger Church works number over 1,000. There are also some 50 operas, including his delightful comedy *Der geduldige Socrates* (*The Patient Socrates*).

A contemporary of J.S. Bach and Handel, and a good friend of both of them, Telemann was in many ways the most modern of the three, developing a style that bridged the gap between the late Baroque and the early Classical periods. As well as composing cantatas, Passions, and instrumental music in the conventional German style, he was attracted to the forms and styles of French and Italian music that had recently become fashionable, and without losing his own distinctive voice he composed suites and overtures in the French style, concertos and sonatas in the Italian style, and even incorporated elements of Polish folk song into his work. This ability to write in the popular idioms of the time ensured frequent performances, and during his lifetime he was the best-known composer in Germany, supplying demand for his work with a seemingly never-ending stream of compositions.

MILESTONES

1701	Enrols as law student at the university in Leipzig; meets Handel
1702	Becomes director of the Leipzig Opera
1704	Appointed director of the New Church in Leipzig
1708	Appointed Konzertmeister in Eisenach; forms friendship with J.S. Bach
1721	Composes *Der geduldige Socrates*, opera
1728	*Der getreue Music-Meister* first published
1733	*Musique de table* published

KEY WORKS

NOUVEAUX QUATUORS EN SIX SUITES

CHAMBER   🎵 **78:00**   📖 **28**   ✿

A collection of six multi-movement chamber works, this set contains two concertos, two sonatas, and two ballets. While the works reflect the French style, the structure is more Italian. Unlike the trio sonatas, which were scored for four instruments, these are true quartets for three melody instruments (flute, violin, viola da gamba, or cello) and accompaniment (harpsichord).

MUSIQUE DE TABLE

CHAMBER   🎵 **270:00**   📖 **68**   ♫ ✿ ⦿

This set of works, considered by scholars to be Telemann's magnum opus, was published in three separate anthologies, each containing an orchestral suite, trio, quartet, concerto for solo instruments, a solo sonata, and a single-movement piece the composer titled "Conclusion."

In 1722, Leipzig city council failed to secure Telemann as Cantor of the Thomaskirche; the post was offered to their third choice, J.S. Bach.

BOURLESQUE DE QUIXOTTE

ORCHESTRAL	20:10	7	

Telemann popularized the French orchestral suite in Germany, gaining much inspiration from the works of Lully, whom he much admired. There is no standard organization for these multi-movement works, except that they open with the typical overture in the French style: a Grave slow section dominated by dotted rhythms, followed by an Allegro fugal section which leads to a return to the slower opening section. This opening movement is followed by a selection of dance movements, with the only criteria being that they are arranged to contrast with one another. Telemann also modeled the French fashion of giving programmatic titles to the suites. With this suite he provides six programmatic movements (following the French overture) based on Cervantes's "Knight of the Doleful Countenance" and his servant Sancho Panza.

Overture (*grave-allegro-grave*, 5:33) The first movement follows the familiar French overture style, as described in more detail above.

Le reveil de Quixotte (*adagio*, 2:50) *The Knight's Awakening* characterizes our hero Don Quixote's slow wakening through the use of long notes, pauses, and simple lyrical minuet rhythm.

Son attaque des moulins à vent (*vivace*, 1:46) In high relief is *Attack on the Windmills* with its quick eighteenths and repeated notes representing Don Quixote attacking his imagined enemies.

Ses soupirs amoureux après la Princesse Dulcinée (*andante*, 3:11) *Sighs of Love for the Princess Dulcinea* reflects Don Quixote's love, with the inclusion of sighing motifs and musical suspensions representing his yearning for Dulcinea.

Sanche Panche berné (*allegro*, 1:50) This movement is an imaginative musical description of Quixote's servant Sancho Panza through the inclusion of octave jumps, with ornamented turns, within a strict rhythm.

La galope de Rosinante/Celui d'ane de Sanche (*allegro*, 2:14) The penultimate movement is a description of Don Quixote's horse Rosinante galloping along in 3/8 time contrasting with Panza's donkey whose stubbornness is reflected by pauses and dotted rhythms.

Le couché de Quixotte (*andante*, 2:46) Telemann puts our hero to sleep in this final movement, *The Sleep of Quixote*, with a simple, lyrical melody—just the opposite of the previous movement, and returning full circle to the beginning of the story.

Telemann's chamber music was often written for amateur music-makers to play at home, rather than for the concert hall.

George Frideric **Handel**

🌐 **1685–1759**   📖 **GERMAN/ENGLISH**   ✍ **487**

Handel was the consummate 18th-century artist, traveler, and entrepreneur. In his lifetime he came to represent not only a unique synthesis of German instrumental and Italian operatic writing, but also an entire era of music in England. Although largely known today for his *Water Music*, *Music for the Royal Fireworks*, and *Messiah*, it was his dramatic works that were the focus of much of his career, and that made his name.

» Handel became a British citizen in 1727. He wrote four anthems for the coronation of King George II that year, including *Zadok the Priest*, which has been sung at every British coronation since.

Life

Handel began studying law before devoting his full attention to a career in music. After a brief period at the university of Halle, he moved to Hamburg and an orchestral position at the opera house, where he composed his first opera (*Almira*). From Hamburg he traveled to Italy in 1706, and then to Hanover, where he took the position of Kapellmeister at the Electoral court. The post allowed for extensive travel so he went to London, where Italian opera was gaining in popularity. His opera *Rinaldo* was a great success; although he returned briefly to Hanover he received permission to travel again to London on the condition he return within a reasonable time. He never did; instead, in 1714, his employer the Elector of Hanover succeeded to the English throne as George I, and Handel entered the service of the Royal Court. The next decade saw his fortunes rise and fall as he competed with the Italian opera and as opera itself gained and lost the interest of the public. His oratorios and other choral works, however, enjoyed more success. During the last decade of his life he suffered from declining health. He had had two strokes earlier, but in his 60s his sight began to fail irreparably. Nevertheless, he continued to compose, arrange earlier works, and supervise productions until his death.

Music

Handel's operas owe much to the popular Italian style, with lyrical, virtuosic arias, dynamic string writing, and a simple, sturdy approach to harmonic progression that belies his Germanic roots. Even the most contrapuntal passages in his choral works contain a clarity not found in the works, of his contemporary J. S. Bach.

Handel's versatility enabled him to write for all kinds of occasions. Despite his Lutheran upbringing, he produced a number of sacred works for the Catholic Church during his time in Italy, and likewise during a brief period spent in the service of James Brydges, Duke of Chandos, he composed the "Chandos Anthems" in the English style.

Handel's large-scale choral works are perhaps his most significant legacy. They were his most consistently successful works and enjoyed multiple revivals even in his lifetime.

> **"Handel** understands **effect** better than any of us; when he **chooses,** he **strikes** like a **thunderbolt."**
>
> **Wolfgang Amadeus Mozart**

MILESTONES

1697	Appointed assistant organist at Halle Cathedral
1703	Moves to Hamburg
1706	Travels to Italy; composes operas and first oratorios
1708	In Italy performs with an orchestra led by Arcangelo Corelli
1710	Appointed Kapellmeister to the Elector of Hanover (later George I)
1711	First trip to London
1712	Settles in England
1717	*Water Music*, HWV348–50
1720	Appointed musical director of Royal Academy of Music
1723	Appointed composer of the Chapel Royal; composes *Giulio Cesare*, HWV17
1735	*Esther*, HWV50, first English oratorio
1742	*Messiah*, HWV56, premiered in Dublin
1749	*Music for the Royal Fireworks*, HWV351, performed in Green Park, London
1751	Suffers from failing sight, which leads to total blindness by 1753

KEY WORKS

WATER MUSIC, HWV348–50

INSTRUMENTAL　　🎵 45:00　　📖 3　　🎼

On July 17, 1717, a royal event of unusual splendor took place on the Thames River in London. King George I and a large number of nobles traveled up the Thames from the royal palace at Whitehall to Chelsea on open river barges, serenaded by 50 musicians playing three instrumental suites composed by Handel for the occasion. The guests feasted at Chelsea until the early morning, then returned to the barges and to Whitehall to the same music with which they had arrived. These works were mere light entertainment, yet Handel employs his usual deft touch as a composer, presenting a happy juxtaposition of traditional minuets and English country dances. *Water Music* also marks the first appearance in an English orchestra of the French horn, an instrument well suited to outdoor performance.

MESSIAH, HWV56

ORATORIO　　🎵 142:00　　📖 16　　👥♦♫

In 1741 Handel received an invitation from the Lord Lieutenant of Ireland to help raise money for three major Dublin charities through performances of his music. Although Handel was in poor health at the time, he was determined to compose a new sacred oratorio for the occasion, and turned to Charles Jennens, his librettist for *Saul* and *Israel in Egypt*, for an appropriate subject. Jennens responded with a collection of Old and New Testament verses arranged into a three-part "argument" (as the librettist himself described it). The result was the best known and best loved of all Handel's oratorios.

The text was not without controversy, with newspapers weighing in with debates as to its "blasphemous" nature. The finished product, however, enjoyed a very different reception, earning critical praise first in Dublin and then in London. Handel made several subsequent revisions to the work, including a version created for Thomas Coram's Foundling Hospital in 1754. Although the work remains a perennial favorite, nowadays most Christmas performances include only the first part plus the Hallelujah Chorus from Part two.

GIULIO CESARE IN EGITTO, HWV17

OPERA　　🎵 240:00　　📖 3　　👥♦♫

Giulio Cesare in Egitto (*Julius Caesar in Egypt*) premiered in 1724 in London at a time at which Handel's operatic career was at a peak. It starred many leading Italian singers of the day, including the soprano Francesca Cuzzoni as Cleopatra and the castrati Senesino and Gaetano Berenstadt as Caesar and Ptolemy respectively. The libretto by Nicolo Haym portrays the various characters as strong, complex individuals, giving Handel a wide emotional range to play with.

ORGAN CONCERTOS, OP. 4, NO. 4 IN F, HWV292

ORCHESTRAL   ⏲ 14:45   📖 4   🔊 ▣

Handel was a talented organist, and his organ concertos, originally intended to be performed between the sections of his oratorios, gave him a chance to demonstrate his virtuosity. The Op. 4, No. 4 concerto (1735) was intended for a performance of *Athalia*. Previous concertos had accompanied *Esther*, *Deborah*, and *Alexander's Feast*.

ZADOK THE PRIEST

CHORUS AND ORCHESTRA   ⏲ 5:30   🔊 ▣

One of the four Coronation Anthems Handel was commissioned to write for the coronation of George II in 1727 (the others being *My Heart Is Inditing*, *The King Shall Rejoice*, and *Let Thy Hand Be Strengthened*), this is, other than the *Hallelujah Chorus*, probably the best known of Handel's choral numbers, and certainly one of the most dramatic. It begins quietly with a repetitive introduction on the strings, building slowly to a climactic entry of the chorus and wind instruments. A quieter middle section in a 3/4 dance time is followed by another tutti section to the words "God save the King! Long live the King!" and the piece ends with a rousing "Allelujah." *Zadok the Priest* has been performed at the coronation of every British monarch since its first performance.

✉ **In this 19th-century engraving** Handel and King George I of England listen to the *Water Music* from the royal barge on the Thames.

ACIS AND GALATEA

MASQUE   📖 2   ⚜

One of Handel's first works in the English language, *Acis and Galatea* was written for the Duke of Chandos in about 1718, with a libretto by the dramatist John Gay. It was originally written as a one-act "little opera," but it was so popular that Handel revised and expanded it into a three-act version (incorporating numbers from an earlier version, in Italian, of the same story), and later into the two-act masque most often performed today.

The plot is a conventional mix of pastoral and mythology: the nymph Galatea's love for the shepherd Acis is threatened by the jealous interference of the giant Polyphemus who kills Acis, but all ends well with Acis immortalized as a spring. One of Handel's most successful dramatic works during his lifetime, and still popular with audiences today, it contains the well-known duet "Happy we" and the aria "O ruddier than the cherry."

MUSIC FOR THE ROYAL FIREWORKS

INSTRUMENTAL   ⏲ 17:30   📖 5   🔊

Originally scored for a large wind band (24 oboes, 12 bassoons including a contrabassoon, nine trumpets, nine French horns, three pairs of kettledrums, and snare drums) to suit its first performance accompanying fireworks to celebrate the end of the War of Austrian Succession in 1749, this suite was later arranged by Handel for full orchestra, and it is this version that is most usually heard today.

Like the *Water Music*, it begins with a French-style *Overture*, which is followed by a *Bourrée* (a quick dance), and then two movements relevant to the celebration of the Treaty of Aix-la-Chapelle: *La Paix* (the Peace), and *La Réjouissance* (the Rejoicing). The suite ends with a movement of two minuets. It was first performed as a public rehearsal in Vauxhall Gardens to appreciative crowds a week before the firework display, which was less successful because the building housing the fireworks caught fire.

Guiseppe **Tartini**

🌐 1692–1770   📖 ITALIAN   ✍ c.350

Unusual for his time, Tartini composed almost solely for violin, writing concertos and sonatas—including his famous "Devil's Trill" Sonata—and resisting invitations to write operas. His early music is influenced by Corelli. Something of a mystic, he theorized about the relations between music and emotions. After gaining international fame as a violin virtuoso (his technique sharpened by three years' practice while hiding in a monastery), he set up a highly regarded violin school.

MILESTONES

1710	Marriage disapproved of; flees Padua
1723	Performs in Prague for coronation
1734	Violin Sonatas, Op. 1, published
1754	First music treatise published

Domenico **Paradies**

🌐 1707–1791   📖 ITALIAN   ✍ UNKNOWN

Critical and popular reaction to the operas of Paradies, from *Alessandro in Persia* staged in Lucca in Italy to *Fetonte* in London, was lukewarm: Charles Burney, the music historian, described his music as ill-phrased and graceless. Nevertheless, Paradies always found work, such as supplying individual arias to various productions, although he enjoyed more success as a teacher of harpsichord and composition. His fame rests on one progressive, sophisticated set of sonatas conceived for harpsichord, the *Sonate de gravicembalo*. Mozart's father admired these pieces, and they achieved rapid fame throughout Europe.

MILESTONES

1738	Writes *Alessandro in Persia*, opera
1746	Emigrates to London
1754	Writes 12 *Sonate de gravicembalo*
1770	Returns to Venice

Thomas Augustine **Arne**

🌐 1710–1778   📖 ENGLISH   ✍ UNKNOWN

Although now best remembered as the composer of "Rule, Britannia!", Arne was a prolific composer of theater music (operas, masques, and incidental music) and books of songs. Arne enjoyed huge popularity in London's theatre land during the 1740s, but his music was of variable quality, and much of it is now lost. He was a stage man through and through: his sister was the finest tragic actress in the country and his wife a renowned singer. Arne's innovations included all-sung comic opera and the first use in England of the clarinet (in *Thomas and Sally*).

MILESTONES

1740	*Alfred*, masque, with "Rule, Britannia!"
1760	Writes *Thomas and Sally*, comic opera
1762	*Artaxerxes*, the first English opera seria

William **Boyce**

🌐 1711–1779   📖 ENGLISH   ✍ c.180

A rival of Arne in London's 18th-century music theaters, Boyce also enjoyed national popularity with his instrumental music, songs, and secular choral works, often written in an Italianate, late-Baroque style. A mild, diligent man, his music varies in quality, but his best works, such as *Solomon* or his 12 Sonatas, show technical accomplishment and a gift for melody.

MILESTONES

1736	Appointed composer to Chapel Royal
1747	Writes 12 Sonatas for Two Violins and Bass
1749	Boyce Festival held in Cambridge
1761	Composes for George III's coronation
1770s	Deafness forces him to give up work

Johann Sebastian **Bach**

● 1685–1750   ♫ GERMAN   ✍ 972

During his lifetime, Johann Sebastian Bach was known mostly as an organist, and was outshone as a composer by his sons. By the end of the 18th century, however, his musical oeuvre of vocal, choral, keyboard, and instrumental works—both sacred and secular—had been rediscovered by a new and more appreciative audience who admired their unique quality and spirit. Since then his star has not stopped rising.

» **A master of counterpoint,** J.S. Bach composed numerous orchestral pieces, plus seminal works for cello and harpsichord.

Life

Orphaned at age 10, Bach moved in with his brother, Johann Christoph, who taught him the organ. After studying briefly in Lüneburg, he was appointed organist at the Bonifaciuskirche at Arnstadt, although he proved quarrelsome; first he almost dueled with a student, then he angered the town consistory by overstaying his leave. Bach stayed until 1707, when he moved to Mühlhausen; in short order he married his cousin Maria, fought with his new students, and left for the ducal court in Weimar. The new post paid well and Bach thrived until internal court politics made his position untenable. He left to become Kapellmeister at the Cöthen court in 1717, although the duke had him imprisoned for a month for disloyalty. Bach's wife died in 1720 and he married singer Anna Wilcke the next year. In 1723 he became Kantor at the Thomasschule in Leipzig, and in 1729 he became Director of the Collegium Musicum at the university. In 1737, critic Johann Scheibe criticized Bach's music, accusing him of bombast and artificiality, but he continued to compose and perform until failing eyesight made writing difficult. Following two unsuccessful eye operations, his health deteriorated and he died three months later.

Music

Bach was ultimately a pragmatic man, and much of his output relates directly to the demands of his life at the time. His early tutelage on the organ sparked his interest in the works of other north German organ composers, such as Buxtehude and Reincken (both of whom he later met). He continued to develop his organ compositions at Arnstadt and Weimar, also producing cantatas on a regular basis for chapel. In Cöthen, his courtly duties demanded more secular fare, and many of his instrumental works date from this period, including the six "Brandenburg" Concertos, the *Clavierbüchlein* for his new wife, Anna, and the *Orgel-Büchlein*.

It was as Kantor at Leipzig that Bach held the widest remit for composition. His duties included producing and directing music for civic events and

> " The **aim and final end** of all **music** should be none other than the **glory of God** and the refreshment of the **soul.** "
>
> **Johann Sebastian Bach**

⌃ **The town of Eisenach,** where Bach was born. The hilltop castle (Wartburg) is where Martin Luther translated the New Testament into German in 1521.

for organizing music for the four main town churches, plus whatever was required for his teaching duties at the Thomasschule. His Leipzig period saw a tremendous outpouring of sacred and secular cantatas and motets for all occasions and church feasts, including five complete cycles of cantatas for the entire church year.

In contrast, his instrumental writing waned until he took on the directorship of the Collegium Musicum; Bach revised several of his earlier instrumental works for their weekly concerts and produced new music as well, most notably the comic *"Coffee Cantata"* (until 1741 the Collegium met in Gottfried Zimmermann's coffeehouse). Works from his final decade include the *Goldberg Variations*, *The Art of Fugue*, and *The Musical Offering* (the latter dedicated to Frederick the Great). His sacred writing continued as well; this period saw the composition of the Mass in B minor, the *"Christmas" Oratorio*, and the *St. Mark Passion*.

Bach's compositional style demonstrates a profound understanding of both harmonic progression and the intricacies of Baroque counterpoint; indeed, he was regarded during his life as the greatest contrapuntalist ever. His early studies in organ and composition gave him a thorough understanding of the fugue and the dense, cerebral north German style. His interest in the Italian concerto and the French overture and dance suites came later, and were synthesized into a cohesive style.

Bach was a craftsman in both good and bad senses; his formal and harmonic structures were intricate in detail (Friedrich Nietzsche said that

Bach's music gave him a sense of "the higher order of things"), but he was often accused of being overly formalistic as well, creating complex works at the expense of emotional expression. When the lighter, more "natural" courtly style began to gain wider popularity in the 1730s, Bach's music fell out of fashion. Ironically it was his composer sons Carl Philipp Emanuel and Johann Christian Bach who came to prominence as the leading representatives of the new style.

After Bach's death, his music remained synonymous with the old style. However, it had its proponents, most notably Baron Gottfried von Swieten, who organized concerts of Bach's music in Vienna. Beethoven is known to have played the "48"; one cannot hear the choral fugue in his Symphony No. 9 without speculating on Bach's influence.

⌃ **Prince Leopold of Anhalt-Cöthen** was 23 years old when he hired Bach as his Kapellmeister in 1717.

≪ **The Thomasschule in Leipzig,** where Bach was Kantor from 1723 until 1729. For Bach this was a time of great productivity.

MILESTONES

1692	Enters Eisenach's Lateinschule
1695	Father dies; lives with brother Johann Christoph, who teaches him the organ
1700	Becomes chorister at Lüneburg
1703	Appointed violinist in court orchestra of Duke of Weimar; leaves to become organist at Arnstadt
1705	Walks some 215 miles to Lubeck to meet Dietrich Buxtehude
1707	Appointed organist at Mühlhausen; marries his cousin Maria Barbara Bach
1708	Becomes court organist and chamber musician (later concertmaster) to the Duke of Weimar
1714	Son Carl Philipp Emanuel born
1717	Becomes Kapellmeister (director of music) at court of Cöthen; many of his instrumental works are written in this period, including the "Brandenburg" Concertos
1721	Wife dies; marries Anna Wilcke
1723	Prince Leopold of Anhalt-Cöthen dies. Bach's position as Kapellmeister is terminated; appointed Kantor of Thomasschule, Leipzig, after Telemann (the most famous composer of the day) turns down the post; the majority of his cantatas are composed in this period; produces *Magnificat*
1724	First performance of *St. John Passion*
1729	Becomes Director of Collegium Musicum; first performance of *St. Matthew Passion*
1733	Writes a portion of the Mass in B minor
1735	Birth of his youngest son Johann Christian Bach (the "London Bach")
1747	Visits son C.P.E. Bach in Potsdam and plays for the king, Frederick the Great; one of the works improvised during this visit becomes *A Musical Offering*
1749	Finishes Mass in B minor; completes *The Art of Fugue*
1750	Ill health leads to fatal eye operations

KEY WORKS

Bach wrote a series of sonatas which explored the full range and character of the harpsichord.

A MUSICAL OFFERING, BWV 1079

CHAMBER	⏱ 49:00	📖 16	♟

On Sunday, May 7, 1747 (so the story goes), Bach arrived at the royal court in Potsdam and was immediately summoned to the King's presence. Frederick the Great was an avid musician himself and often played the flute alongside his court musicians (including Bach's son Carl Philipp Emanuel). Frederick sat at the keyboard and played Bach the "royal theme"; Bach listened and then freely improvised a three-part fugue on the same theme. The next night Bach was invited back, but was challenged to provide a six-part fugue on the same theme—a daunting task. Bach demurred, instead improvising a six-part fugue on another theme, but subsequently wrote out a similar fugue on the King's theme. He then elaborated a series of other pieces on the same theme, including a full trio sonata for flute, violin, and continuo, had the music bound and inscribed with an extended dedication, and presented it to the delighted monarch.

THE WELL-TEMPERED CLAVIER, BWV 846–893

KEYBOARD	⏱ 255:00	📖 96	🎧

Also known as the *48 Preludes and Fugues*, *The Well-Tempered Clavier* represents a lifetime of work by Bach. The first collection of 24 preludes and fugues dates from 1722, while the second set of 24 was finished some twenty years later. Each prelude is a freely composed work, exploring a particular musical idea without specified form. Conversely, the fugues follow a stricter set of rules. The juxtaposition of the two adds both effective color to the performance and a broader challenge to the performer. These may have been intended as technical exercises, but if so they remain complex, elegant pieces, exploring all areas of the keyboard.

GOLDBERG VARIATIONS, BWV 988

KEYBOARD ⏱ 78:00 📖 32

As the story goes, during a trip to Dresden in 1741, Bach presented to Count von Keyserlinck his *Aria mit verschiedenen Veränderungen* (*Aria with Sundry Variations*) for use by the resident harpsichordist in the Count's household, one Johann Gottlieb Goldberg. Goldberg had studied with Bach as well as with Bach's eldest son, Wilhelm Friedemann (then resident in Dresden). Because Goldberg was only 14 in 1741, the story may well be apocryphal; if not, that Bach would present such a difficult work to such a young performer implies either great talent on Goldberg's part or great optimism on Bach's. The variations were published as Part IV of Bach's *Clavier-Übung* (*Keyboard Works*) collection the next year. The 30 so-called *Goldberg Variations* (plus the aria and final reprise)

are one of the most complex sets of theme and variations ever written. The "aria," or main theme, is a sarabande in two sections; the theme, unusually, lies in the bass line. Each of the variations follows the same bass line and harmonic progression in some form, albeit often with additional notes interjected. Bach presents a surprising array of forms: gigue (No. 7), fugue (No. 10), French overture (No. 16), and of course a few flashy showpieces. As an added level of complexity, every third variation is a canon, written at increasingly broad intervals: in No. 3 the second part enters one bar later at the unison, in No. 6 the second part enters a major second up from the first entry, and so forth to the interval of a ninth in No. 27. The final variation is a quodlibet—a contrapuntal combination of two popular tunes set above the main theme in the bass.

☑ **A string ensemble,** featuring violinists Itzhak Perlman and Pinchas Zukerman, perform the sixth of Bach's "Brandenburg" Concertos.

A page from the second fugue of Bach's *The Well-Tempered Clavier*.

THE BRANDENBURG CONCERTOS, BWV 1046–1051

CHAMBER   90:00   6

This set of six varied concertos was dedicated to Margrave Christoph Ludwig of Brandenburg in 1721. The works were shelved in the Margrave's library and lay there unplayed.

Concerto No. 1 (20:00) In the first concerto, Bach borrowed from his earlier "Hunt" Cantata, hence the prominent horn part. The last movement comprises a series of dances.

Concerto No. 2 (11:15) The opening movement offers in quick succession the same solo phrase played by violin, oboe, recorder, and trumpet.

Concerto No. 3 (11:00) The first and last movements are pure Italian-style string ensemble writing, while the second was notated by the composer as just a few unornamented chords.

Concerto No. 4 (13:45) Here, Bach combines a solo violin concerto with a concerto grosso, with the violin vying for attention with two recorders.

Concerto No. 5 (19:35) The fifth concerto marks Bach's first use of the transverse flute. The harpsichord plays a prominent role throughout.

Concerto No. 6 (15:00) The final work of the collection features a string ensemble throughout.

Canadian pianist Glenn Gould made a critically acclaimed recording of the *Goldberg Variations* in 1955. A second, equally brilliant recording came in 1981.

ST. MATTHEW PASSION, BWV 244

ORATORIO   160:00   68

The Lutheran Passion oratorio, a sacred drama popular in Germany, already existed in the 17th century as a mixture of Lutheran chorales, strophic arias, and choruses. By the next century, composers (including Bach) had added the flair of operatic recitative and aria to the genre. Bach wrote three Passions during his career: the *St. Matthew*, the *St. John*, and the *St. Mark*, although the *St. Mark* has largely been lost. The first two, however, remain favorites of the choral repertoire and are frequently performed in concert during the Easter season. The *St. Matthew Passion*, for double chorus, double orchestra, two organs, and soloists, is a grand work first performed on Good Friday 1727. The text is taken from the Gospel According to Matthew, chapters 26 and 27, with added recitative and aria texts by local poet Christian Friedrich Henrici. The narrative structure is thus: the Evangelist narrates the unfolding events as they occur in recitatives, with occasional lines of dialogue sung by soloists. Solos are also used for prayers and commentary on the story, as in the alto solo "Buss und Reu" ("Grief and Sin"). The chorus sometimes take a direct participatory role, presenting dialogue by the crowds in the drama, for example, and sometimes offer detached commentary or prayer, including the interjected chorales. While Bach never wrote an opera, the Passions are very much in the same theatrical vein.

Part one (68:00) The work opens with a prologue in which the chorus lament the events to come. The narrative proper begins in Bethany with Christ prophesying his own imminent crucifixion. The story then follows the biblical story of Judas's collusion with the Pharisees, Jesus's appeals to God, and finally the betrayal and arrest. After each section of narrative, a commentary is inserted in the form of a recitative and aria or a chorale.

Part two (92:00) After another prologue, which bemoans the arrest of Jesus, the second part begins with the interrogation before Caiaphas, Peter's denial, and the judgment by Pilate. Bach concludes the work with Jesus's crucifixion, death, and entombment, and a final choral lament.

SIX SUITES FOR SOLO CELLO, BWV 1007–1012

SOLO CELLO   140:00   36

Each of these cello suites has a prelude and five dance movements comprising a wide variety of styles. They are remarkably sophisticated and self-contained works, and form the foundation of the solo cello repertoire.

CHRISTMAS ORATORIO, BWV 248

ORATORIO   150:00   6

The *"Christmas" Oratorio* is properly a six-part cycle: six sacred cantatas to be performed on the three days of Christmas, New Year's Day, the Sunday after the New Year and the Feast of the Epiphany. Much of the music is reworked from earlier secular cantatas which were written for the Collegium Musicum in Leipzig.

MASS IN B MINOR, BWV 232

MASS SETTING   106:00   27

The Mass in B minor was an ongoing work; the Sanctus was written in 1724, while the Credo dates from near the end of Bach's life. The Kyrie and Gloria are taken from a 1733 Mass dedicated to the Dresden court, and the last four movements are parody works, based on other music and added later.

> ### INFLUENCES
>
> Bach passed on a technical mastery of keyboard playing and musical form to his sons, but his music was seen as unfashionable by the end of his life. Later revivals of his music, most notably by Mendelssohn, brought new interest in his compositional style and in Baroque counterpoint in general.

The Monteverdi Choir and the English Baroque Soloists sing Bach's Mass in B minor at London's Royal Albert Hall, 2004.

The Classical Era
1750–1820

Between 1750 and 1820, composers such as Haydn, Mozart, and Beethoven developed a new, simpler musical style, whose maxims—clarity, restraint, and balance—mirrored contemporary intellectual and artistic values. Almost every subsequent development in Western art music can be traced back to this period.

Among the forerunners of the Classical era were composers such as C.P.E. Bach, Johann Quantz, and Baldassare Galuppi. Their works were a reaction against the complexity of Baroque music—its intricate polyphony, counterpoint, and ornamented melody. Instead, composers aimed for a style in which a simple melody was accompanied by harmonic progressions.

The Enlightenment, with its focus on rational, human ideals, played a major part in this shift in esthetic values. So, too, did interest in the simple elegance of Greek and Roman art and architecture, inspired in part by the discovery of the ruins of Pompeii in 1748. Socially and politically, this was a time of great change, with the effects of the Industrial Revolution and colonization creating a larger middle class keen to become consumers of the arts. At the same time, the aristocracies of Europe, suffering from the ravages of the Napoleonic Wars, were less able to support musicians, and the old patronage system started to crumble.

◀ **In the Classical era,** composers developed new forms such as the symphony and string quartet. In this engraving, Josef Haydn directs a rehearsal of one of his quartets.

Professional musicians

Traditionally, musicians employed by aristocratic courts were numbered among the servants—below the valets. However, as public concerts became more common, they were able to earn money from their performances, and publishing their compositions ensured a further income. Haydn, who was employed by the Esterházy family, was given frequent leave to travel, and toward the end of his life he had transcended his lowly position to become part of the court. Mozart, employed by the Archbishop of Salzburg, was not given the same freedoms and, resenting his servile position, moved to Vienna to become one of the very first freelance musicians. However, the music world could not yet support such an ambition, and he suffered considerable financial hardship. When Beethoven moved to Vienna in 1794, he succeeded in gaining the support of wealthy patrons and never had to hold an official appointment.

Evolving genres

As instrumental music became more popular than vocal music for the first time, composers had to develop ways of creating larger musical canvasses that could support more intense listening. The result was the "Sonata Principle" (sometimes known as Sonata Form), a musical structure consisting of three sections. Its use became almost synonymous with the first movements not only of sonatas, but also of symphonies and indeed most instrumental music of the era. It has remained in use until the present day.

The symphony evolved from the small-scale Baroque sinfonia into an iconic art form. Usually in four movements, the symphony would start with a gripping "sonata allegro"

THE SONATA PRINCIPLE

Music structured according to the "Sonata Principle" begins with an Exposition, which introduces the musical material and tends to be repeated. Two themes are usually presented, the second in a key a fifth higher than the original (tonic) key. The next section—the Development—alters the themes, frequently fragmenting them and playing them in different keys before leading the music to the third section, the Recapitulation. Here the opening themes are played again, but this time all in the tonic key. This structure allows a large span of music to be built from relatively little material with a minimum of repetition.

◀◀ **Beethoven's Waldstein Sonata,** Op. 53, is a brilliant example of the Classical sonata form.

⌃ **Between 1762 and 1767** the prodigious Mozart and his sister Nannerl toured all the main musical centres of Germany as well as Switzerland, Paris, and London.

movement, followed by a slow movement. The third movement was usually an elegant minuet, but this evolved into the scherzo, which could be humorous, or express a more ironic, elemental passion. The finale was frequently a rondo, in which repetitions of a catchy, upbeat melody were interspersed with contrasting themes.

Other genres were also redefined. The three-movement concerto became a vehicle for just one soloist in which the ideals of balance and elegance were matched by instrumental virtuosity, while the sonata

TIMELINE: THE CLASSICAL ERA

1753 C.P.E. Bach starts work on *The True Art of Keyboard Playing*

1762 First performance of Gluck's *Orfeo ed Euridice*; Mozart begins touring Europe aged 6

1774 Start of reign of Louis XVI. Court life was one of elegant formality, expressed in dances such as the minuet

1786 First performance of Mozart's *The Marriage of Figaro* in Vienna

1750　　　　　　　　**1760**　　　　　　　　**1770**　　　　　　　　**1780**

1759 Voltaire's *Candide* published

1763 Ruins of Pompeii identified

1775 Start of the American Revolution

1781 Haydn composes 6 String Quartets, Op. 33

1789 French Revolution

developed into a more formal composition for one or two instruments. The rise in domestic music-making created a market for new forms of chamber music, such as the string quartet – invented by Haydn—and the piano trio.

The symphony orchestra became a broadly standardized entity, smaller but not very different from the orchestra of today. With the orchestra's fuller sound, the role of the continuo gradually died out; instead, the first violin directed the orchestra until eventually displaced by a specialist conductor. Orchestras now had a far greater dynamic range. In the 1740s, the crescendos and diminuendos of the Mannheim Court orchestra, under Johann Stamitz, caused a sensation and were soon a staple of all symphonic writing.

The opera

In opera, notably in the works of Gluck and Mozart, plots were now chosen for greater dramatic realism and music was written to serve the drama rather than decorate it. Gradually, Italian began to lose its dominance as important works were written in German and French.

◀ **This painting shows** the performance of Haydn's great oratorio, *Creation*, given in honor of the composer in the festival hall of Vienna's Old University.

1791 First performance of *The Magic Flute* in Vienna; death of Mozart

1803 Beethoven completes the "Eroica" Symphony

1808 First performance of Beethoven's Symphonies No. 5 and No. 6; Goethe publishes *Faust* part 1

1824 Premiere of Beethoven's Symphony No. 9 in Vienna

1790   1800   1810   1820

1795 First performance of Haydn's "London" Symphony, No. 104; Beethoven publishes Op. 1 trios

1798 Haydn's *Creation* first performed in Vienna

1804 Napoleon made Emperor

1827 Death of Beethoven

Christoph Willibald **Gluck**

● 1714–1787   ⬚ GERMAN   ✍ 93

Although lacking the musical finesse of his rivals, Gluck earned himself a place in music history with the reforms he brought to opera. Espousing a more continuous texture in which music served the poetry and drama of the libretto rather than the singer's virtuosity, he employed vivid characterization, simple plots, and large-scale planning of music to bring universal human themes and emotions to life.

Largely self-taught, Gluck became an organist and cellist in Prague before moving to Vienna, and then Milan, where he joined an orchestra and studied composition with Sammartini, a leading symphonist. The success of his first opera ensured commissions that took him all over Europe. Gluck and the poet Ranieri Calzabigi drew up a manifesto of operatic reform, eschewing stylized convention in favor of a symbiosis of music and drama. Starting with *Orfeo*, his work changed operatic norms, while causing some controversy, particularly in conservative Paris.

MILESTONES	
1741	Debut opera *Artasere* is an instant success
1745	Presents two operas in London befriends Handel
1750	Marries the heiress Marianna Bergin
1754	Employed at Vienna Opera
1774	Stages opera *Iphigénie en Aulide* in Paris; made Kapellmeister of Vienna Opera
1779	Suffers a stroke and retires

KEY WORKS

ORFEO ED EURIDICE

OPERA	⏱ 120:00	▭ 3	♫ ♯ ♪

In this, the first of Calzabigi and Gluck's "reform operas," their aim was to conjure a "beautiful serenity." Choosing a simple Greek tragedy in preference to the labyrinthine plots employed in opera seria, and using three rather than six soloists, they created a work of unprecedented directness. The role of Orpheus was originally written for a castrato, but recast as a high tenor when the opera was extended and rewritten in French as *Orphée* for Paris in 1774. Later rearranged by Berlioz, it is now usually performed by a mezzo soprano.

ALCESTE

OPERA	⏱ 135:00	▭ 3	♫ ♯ ♪

The second of the "reform operas," *Alceste* was published with a preface that declared Gluck's new principles of opera. It tells of Alceste's sacrifice of her own life to save her dying husband King Admetus.

LA RENCONTRE IMPRÉVUE

OPERA	⏱ 110:00	▭ 3	♫ ♯ ♪

Also known as *Les pèlerins de la Mecque*, this was Gluck's last work in the opéra comique style, incorporating spoken dialogue. Set in Cairo, it features a "harem escape," a plot much in vogue in an 18th-century Vienna fascinated by Islam and by Turkish music.

IPHIGÉNIE EN TAURIDE

OPERA	⏱ 102:00	▭ 4	♫ ♯ ♪

Probably Gluck's finest work, *Iphigénie en Tauride* was written at the same time as Piccinni's opera on the same theme, splitting Paris into Gluckists and Piccinnists. Its first performance in 1779 was Gluck's greatest triumph, and much later it inspired Berlioz to become a musician. The music is dramatic, expressive, and almost symphonic in its orchestration.

⬆ **This fine score** is of the Italian version of *Orfeo ed Euridice*. The 1774 French version includes the famous "Dance of the Blessed Spirits".

Carl Philippe Emanuel **Bach**

● 1714–1788   ⁍ GERMAN   ✍ 875

Possibly the most important composer of his generation, C. P. E. Bach bridged the gap between the Baroque style of his father, J. S. Bach, and the Classical style of Haydn and Mozart. The main exponent of the *empfindsamer Stil*, an expressive musical style, he also developed the sonata, and was renowned as a keyboard player whose *True Art of Keyboard Playing* is the major treatise on 18th-century music.

The second son of J. S. Bach, C. P. E. Bach studied with his father until appointed court harpsichordist to Frederick II of Prussia. Although poorly paid, Bach composed, taught, and performed at the courts of Berlin and Potsdam for some 30 years before leaving to succeed his godfather, Georg Philipp Telemann, as Kantor and music director in Hamburg. Bach became responsible for 200 performances a year at five churches and started to write non-secular vocal music. The bulk of his works are, however, instrumental.

MILESTONES

1731	Studies law at Leipzig university
1744	Marries Johanna Danneman
1749	Writes Trio Sonata in C minor, "Sanguineus and Melancholicus," WQ161/1
1755	Composes Flute Concerto in G major, WQ169
1757	Writes Symphony in E flat major, WQ179

KEY WORKS

MAGNIFICAT IN D MAJOR, WQ215

MASS SETTING   ⏱ 45:00   📖 9

Bach modeled his first major choral piece on his father's Magnificat (BWV 243). Although adapting the same key and text, he achieved rather more homophonic and melodious effects. Scored for trumpets, drums, flutes, oboes, horns, and strings, with four vocal soloists, it is one of the few major choral pieces to be written after J. S. Bach and before Haydn.

FLUTE CONCERTO IN G MAJOR, WQ169

ORCHESTRAL   ⏱ 24:00   📖 3

One of five flute concertos adapted from Bach's keyboard compositions, this piece is perhaps the most virtuosic. After a vigorous opening with some "sighing" motifs, the flute enters with music of a much gentler nature. The strings set the scene for a pleading slow movement, while the flute responds with long, rhetorical

phrases culminating in a tender cadenza. In the elegant finale, the flautist has frequent opportunities to relish the highly virtuosic writing.

SYMPHONY IN E FLAT MAJOR, WQ179

ORCHESTRAL   ⏱ 11:15   📖 3

This piece clearly reflects the new Classical style, with its light homophonic (rather than complex polyphonic) effects. The symphony opens with an arresting movement, followed by a particularly sensitive Larghetto, and closes with a jaunty finale, showcasing the horns.

INFLUENCES

When Carl Czerny went to study with Beethoven, he was immediately required to purchase C. P. E. Bach's *True Art of Keyboard Playing*. Perhaps now better known than any of his music, it codified contemporaneous musical style and established technical norms—including fingering—which underpinned most later keyboard playing.

 An autographed score from C. P. E. Bach's notebook. Original scores can offer invaluable insights into his intentions and views on performance.

Johann Adolf **Hasse**

● 1699–1783   🏳 **GERMAN**   ✍ 1,600

In the mid-1700s, Hasse's operas—staged in high-quality productions and tailored to individual singers—made him famous throughout Europe. His emphasis on beauty rather than complexity paved the way for the Classical style. Fêted by the nobility and royalty of Vienna, Naples, Paris, London, and Berlin, he was also admired by both J.S. Bach and Mozart. One of Alessandro Scarlatti's last pupils in Naples, he went on to serve for 30 years as musical director at the Dresden court, where music flourished. Hasse's vast output, very often composed at speed, includes 63 operas, 90 cantatas, and 80 flute concertos written for Frederick II of Prussia.

⏩ **Hasse staged lavish productions** at the Dresden Semperoper, often with the help of the librettist Pietro Metastasio.

MILESTONES	
1730	*Artaserse*, opera, performed in Venice; marries famous Italian mezzo-soprano, Faustino Bordoni
1731	*Cleofide*, opera, performed in Dresden; it impresses J.S. Bach
1742	*Lucio Papiro*, opera, staged in Dresden

Johann Joachim **Quantz**

● 1697–1773   🏳 **GERMAN**   ✍ c.600

The son of a blacksmith, Quantz started learning music at the age of only 11. After training in Italy, France, and England, he switched from the oboe to become one of the first professional flute players in Europe. A star member of the Dresden orchestra, he was spotted by the future Frederick II of Prussia, whom he went on to serve for over 30 years as a hard-worked but richly rewarded flute teacher, maker, composer, and performer. Quantz's massive output, mostly for Frederick, includes 300 flute concertos and 235 flute sonatas, of variable quality, but all craftsmanlike. His book on the flute made him famous throughout Europe.

MILESTONES	
1718	Appointed court oboist in Dresden
1719	Specializes in the flute
1727	Adds a second key to the flute
1739	Begins making flutes
1741	Starts work for Frederick II of Prussia
1752	Publishes *On Playing the Tranverse Flute*

☑ **A skilled flautist,** Frederick II of Prussia performed for his courtiers under the expert guidance of his tutor, Johann Quantz.

Johann Wenzel Anton **Stamitz**

◯ **1717–1757**   ▥ **CZECH**   ✍ **150**

The Classical symphony developed at intensely musical centers, such as the Electoral Court at Mannheim in Germany, where Stamitz served as violinist, composer, and musical director. A star contributor, he brought international fame to the orchestra with its impeccable and dynamic renderings of his symphonies. Although he wrote countless concertos, he is known for his 58 surviving symphonies, which established the four-movement pattern and the Classical style. Four other members of the Stamitz family, including his sons, Carl and Johann (Anton), became prominent musicians.

MILESTONES	
1741	Works at the court of Mannheim
1750	Serves as musical director at Mannheim
1754	Enjoys a season in Paris
1755	Publishes Orchestral Trios, Op. 1

Leopold **Mozart**

◯ **1719–1787**   ▥ **GERMAN**   ✍ **c.550**

The father of Wolfgang Amadeus, Leopold was a noted court composer and violin teacher. Despite supporting his gifted son—as teacher, agent, and editor—he found time to pursue his own career. Haughty and hard to please, he was nevertheless a man of wit and wisdom who wrote copious concertos, symphonies, serenades, and church music, but probably not the "Toy" Symphony often credited to him.

MILESTONES	
1743	Becomes court violinist at Salzburg
1747	Marries Anna Maria Pertl
1756	Publishes popular violin tutor
1757	Becomes court composer at Salzburg
1769	Writes Symphony in G major, G16, "Neue Lambacher" ("New Lambach")

François-Joseph **Gossec**

◯ **1734–1829**   ▥ **BELGIAN**   ✍ **160**

Gossec started his career as a court employee and ended up as the foremost musical representative of the French Revolution. He had come to Paris as a protégé of Jean-Philippe Rameau, and worked for both private and court orchestras while composing comic operas, with mixed success. However, he became a key musician in Paris after founding the Concert des Amateurs, an independent orchestra, before directing the renowned Concerts Spirituels and organizing the École Royale. During the Revolution, he resigned his post at the Opéra and wrote pro-Revolutionary works. Though overshadowed by other composers, he stimulated a revival of instrumental music in dance-dominated France.

☑ **French rebels** stormed the Bastille in Paris in 1789, inspiring Gossec to create dramatic instrumental works celebrating the Revolutionary ideals.

MILESTONES	
1751	Becomes a chorister at Antwerp
1754	Composes Symphony No. 1
1766	Les pêcheurs (The Fishermen), opera, first performed
1770	Founds the Concert des Amateurs
1773	Directs the Concerts Spirituels
1795	Appointed Professor of Composition at the Paris Conservatoire

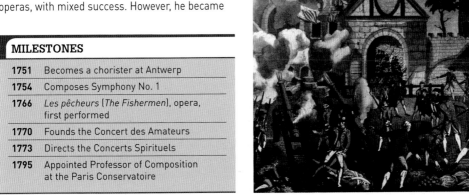

Franz Joseph **Haydn**

● 1732–1809   ▥ AUSTRIAN   ✍ 1,195

Born in the Baroque era and still alive when Beethoven composed his "Pastoral" Symphony, Haydn was a key figure in the evolution of the Classical style. Writing a vast oeuvre within the protective confines of the Esterházy court, and establishing the standard forms of the symphony, sonata, and string quartet, he emerged as an international musical figure who both influenced Mozart and taught Beethoven.

>> **The music of Haydn** is full of bold effects, but also has an intimate lyricism, as can be seen in his greatest work, *The Creation*.

Life

Possessing a fine singing voice, Haydn received elementary music training as a choirboy, but when his voice broke he had to earn a meagre living from performing in ensembles and teaching children. He continued his studies by reading treatises, until the singer Nicola Porpora helped him hone his compositional skills. He was introduced to a number of influential people, and became Count Morzin's music director in 1759. On the strength of his Symphony No. 1, Haydn was appointed Vizekapellmeister at the court of one of the richest and most influential Hungarian families, the

Esterházys, and by 1766 had taken full responsibility for their music. Composing new instrumental works for the twice-weekly concerts, as well as for festivities, church, and theater, he developed his skills unmolested by market forces. When Prince Nicolaus died in 1790, Haydn's music had already been published all over Europe. An invitation from the impresario J. P. Salomon to present new works in England swiftly followed, and during two extended stays Haydn amassed a fortune and was awarded a doctorate from Oxford University. He was recalled to the Royal Court in 1795, following the accession of Prince Nicolaus's grandson, and remained active as a composer in Vienna until 1803.

Music

Mostly self-taught and largely cut off at court from mainstream music, Haydn later suggested that this very isolation had forced his originality upon him. While his oeuvre includes practically every genre of music, from folk-song arrangements to opera, it is through his innovations in instrumental music that Haydn had the greatest influence. Although frequently referred to as the "father of the symphony," he did not invent the form, but his 108 works in the genre pioneered its evolution, from a three-movement Baroque overture for fewer than 20 players to the dramatic four-movement form for as many as 60, which became the Classical period's finest legacy. Haydn's finest achievement, however, was in the creation of a new medium: the string quartet. Whereas orchestral works had sometimes been performed by four players, and some pieces had been composed for the same combination with the accompaniment of a continuo part, Haydn established a genre in which each instrument was equal and independent.

❝❝ My **Prince** was always **satisfied...** and I was in a position to **improve, alter,** and be as **bold** as I pleased. **❞❞**

Franz Joseph Haydn, on his employer, Prince Nicolaus

MILESTONES

1740	Becomes a choirboy at St. Stephen's Cathedral, Vienna	**1791**	First visit to England, where he remains for 18 months; composes six symphonies including "Surprise" Symphony, No. 94
1753	Starts work as an accompanist to singer Nicola Porpora	**1792**	Meets and starts teaching Beethoven
1759	Composes Symphony No. 1	**1794**	Returns to England for a further 18 months; composes "English" Sonata, and is commissioned to write oratorio *The Creation*
1760	Marries Maria Keller, but they later separate after an unhappy marriage		
1762	Assumed date for String Quartet No. 1	**1796**	Composes Trumpet Concerto for Anton Weidinger's new keyed trumpet
1765	Composes Cello Concerto No. 1		
1772	First performance of "Farewell" Symphony, No. 45	**1798**	First performance of *The Creation* is given in Vienna and is an immediate success; composes "Nelson" Mass

KEY WORKS

STRING QUARTET NO. 63, "SUNRISE," OP. 76, NO. 4

CHAMBER   ⏱ 22:00   📖 4   ♟

Haydn returned to Esterháza in 1795, where his duties were now far lighter, and his international fame made him more of a trophy than a servant. No longer composing sonatas and symphonies, he turned once again to the more private medium of the string quartet, distilling the experiments of a long career into eight final works that demonstrate his total mastery over the genre which he had himself invented. The spacious improvisatory violin ascending over a single chord that opens this piece led to comparisons with a sunrise, giving the work its nickname. The later passages have an expansiveness that is almost Romantic.

THE CREATION

ORATORIO   ⏱ 99:00   📖 3   ♟ ♙ ♙

After hearing performances of Handel's oratorios in London, Haydn was inspired to write a similarly large-scale biblical work. The piece was an instant success in both England and Germany, and it became his most performed work. The opening representation of chaos is possibly the most extraordinary music of the period. Conjuring timelessness, Haydn juxtaposed seemingly incongruous ideas, allowing harmonies to meander until, with a blaze of glory, the chorus sings, "Let there be light."

SYMPHONY NO. 104 IN D MAJOR "LONDON"

ORCHESTRAL   ⏱ 26:30   📖 4   ♟

Twelve of Haydn's later symphonies are known collectively as the "London" Symphonies. This was his final work in the series—and in the genre. Taking advantage of a far larger orchestra than he was used to in Vienna, this work features some of his most majestic music.

After a solemn introduction in the minor key, the main theme of the allegro is surprisingly lyrical. This is swiftly usurped by faster, more exuberant music that makes frequent use of trumpets and drums. After the charmingly poised opening melody, the sudden entry of the full orchestra in the second movement is a real

⬆ **The string quartet,** in which each instrument plays an equal part, was Haydn's greatest achievement.

surprise. After this disquieting display of drama and passion, the return to gentility is never quite assured. Far faster than earlier minuets, the third movement with its frequent syncopations, surprises, and the orchestral timbre of the Trio, point firmly in the direction of Beethoven. Claimed both as a traditional Croatian folk tune and as a London street seller's cry, the earthy melody used in the final movement brings Haydn's career as a symphonist to a joyful end.

TRUMPET CONCERTO

ORCHESTRAL	⌛ 13:00	📖 3	

In this, the first work written for the newly invented keyed trumpet, Haydn took full advantage of the instrument's ability to play all the notes within its compass by boldly presenting running passages and cantabile melodies in its lower range. Premiered in Vienna in 1800 by the instrument's inventor, Anton Weidinger, the concerto remains a cornerstone of every trumpet player's repertoire.

 Renowned mezzo-soprano Cecilia Bartoli appeared in Haydn's opera *L'anima del filosofo* at the Royal Opera House, London.

"ENGLISH" SONATA, HOB.XVI/52

SOLO PIANO	⌛ 13:00	📖 3	

Numbering over 50, Haydn's piano sonatas have a staggering variety and originality. Featuring a rather whimsical first movement, the "English" Sonata (1794) is notable for its use of some of the first notated pedal effects, while the breadth of its adagio was made possible by the mellow tone and resonating capacity of a new piano by John Broadwood. The amusing finale takes great pleasure in sending the pianist down numerous wrong turns.

INFLUENCES

Although he was a musician's musician, after his death in 1809 Haydn's music was frequently dismissed as inferior to that of Mozart and a mere precursor to Beethoven's compositions. However, it has rightly been said that few music innovations in the century following Haydn's death could not be traced back to his works.

Johann Christian **Bach**

🌐 1735–1782   ♫ GERMAN   ✍ c.360

The most versatile and cosmopolitan of J. S. Bach's composing sons, "the London Bach" composed operas in Milan before moving to England and becoming music master to the royal family. He helped establish the Classical era, partly with music in the new lighter style—especially his symphonies and piano concertos—and also with the acclaimed public concerts he organized with the celebrated harpsichord player Carl Friedrich Abel, taking musical emphasis away from the church and into the concert hall. After enjoying financial success, fame, and respect, his reputation faded: his concerts lost money, he was defrauded, and he suffered a long and debilitating chest illness.

MILESTONES

1760	Becomes cathedral organist in Milan
1763	Writes variations on *God Save the King*
1764	First Bach–Abel concerts performed
1768	Plays first piano solo in public
c.1781	Composes Symphonies for Double Orchestra, Op. 18

◀ **Concerts performed** at the Hanover Square Rooms in London, featuring many fashionable musicians, were popular in the 18th century.

Johann **Albrechtsberger**

🌐 1736–1809   ♫ AUSTRIAN   ✍ 750

Many, including his friend Mozart, viewed Albrechtsberger as one of the world's greatest organists. He was also a prolific composer, writing keyboard pieces, church compositions with fine oratorios, and a range of other works, including a curious Concerto for Jew's Harp. As a composition teacher, known for his skill in counterpoint, he was in great demand. One of his pupils was Beethoven, whose later fugues reflect Albrechtsberger's enthusiasm for the form.

MILESTONES

1772	Becomes court organist, Vienna
1790	Publishes popular textbook: *Fundamentals of Composition*
1793	Kapellmeister at St. Stephen's, Vienna
1794	Tutors Beethoven

Karl Ditters von **Dittersdorf**

🌐 1739–1799   ♫ AUSTRIAN   ✍ c.200

A prolific composer of more than 100 symphonies, 40 concertos, as well as several comic operas, Karl Ditters (ennobled in 1773 with the title "von Dittersdorf") mainly wrote accessible, craftsmanlike music in the popular genres of the time, spanning the development of the Viennese Classical style. He held various court appointments and was a virtuoso violinist, gaining considerable celebrity through performing his own concertos.

MILESTONES

1764	Writes Mass for Frankfurt coronation of Archduke Joseph
1786	*Doktor und apotheker*, opera, performed; composes twelve symphonies based on Ovid's *Metamorphoses*
1795	Sacked by Schaffgotsch, Prince of Breslau

Giovanni **Paisiello**

◉ **1740–1816**   🏛 **ITALIAN**   ✍ **180**

The most popular opera composer of the late 1700s was not Mozart but Paisiello, a Neapolitan whose reputation brought him lucrative posts with Catherine the Great, Napoleon, and the King of Naples. More than 30 of his operas were successes. His light, rhythmic style and melodic turns of phrase, as in his *The Barber of Seville* (the first opera setting of the story), influenced Mozart's *The Marriage of Figaro* and *Don Giovanni*, as well as Rossini, Bellini, and Donizetti.

MILESTONES	
1776	Works for Catherine II in St. Petersburg
1782	Writes *The Barber of Seville*, opera
1789	Composes *Nina*, opera
1802	Works for Napoleon in Paris

Jean Paul **Martini**

◉ **1741–1816**   🏛 **FRENCH**   ✍ **150**

Born in Germany, Martini established a successful career as a court musician in France. There he adapted shrewdly to the changing regimes throughout the Revolution, first directing concerts for the Queen, later writing music for Napoleon's marriage, and finally writing for the restored Royal Chapel. At best a minor innovator, Martini's melodic operas had mixed success, but *L'amoureux de quinze ans*, written in 1771, enjoyed considerable popularity, while his highly regarded church music combined old forms with modern theatricality, and his chansons, such as "Plaisir d'amour," were influential. In 1800 he became professor of composition at the Paris Conservatoire.

MILESTONES	
1783	Writes *Le droit du seigneur*, opera
1793	"Prière pour le Roi," political song
1814	Composes *Scene héroïque pour Napoléon*

Luigi **Boccherini**

◉ **1743–1805**   🏛 **ITALIAN**   ✍ **c.600**

After studying in Rome and gaining acclaim as an outstanding cello virtuoso in Italy, Boccherini toured Europe to seek his fortune. Following success in Paris, he was invited to Madrid to be court chamber composer to the Infante Don Luis. There he wrote quintets—for his cello with Don Luis's existing quartet. Though still popular in Paris, Boccherini—who saw both wives and several of his children die—was dogged by illness and bad luck in his last years, and died in obscurity and poverty in a tiny apartment.

MILESTONES	
1767	Success in Paris; publishes his first chamber music
1771	Writes String Quintet in E major
1786	Appointed court composer for Friedrich Wilhelm II of Prussia

» **"There is perhaps no instrumental music** more ingenious, elegant, and pleasing than his quintets," Charles Burney wrote of Boccherini in 1770.

Carl **Stamitz**

◉ 1745–1801   ▥ **GERMAN**   ✍ 250

Son of Johann, head of the renowned Mannheim orchestra, Carl Stamitz was a violinist who became a prolific composer of lyrical, flowing orchestral music. He wrote 50 symphonies, around 25 symphonies concertante, and over 60 concertos. He went to Paris to work as a court composer, performing at Le Concert Spirituel and publishing his music. He then worked around Europe, spending three years in London, where he worked with J. C. Bach. After a period at the court of William V, Prince of Orange, and more travelling, he ended up as music director and teacher at Jena University.

MILESTONES	
1762	Gains position as second violin in Elector of Mannheim's court orchestra
1770	Moves to Paris; begins concert career as virtuoso of violin and viola d'amore
1780	Goes to work in The Hague
1790	Goes on working visit to Russia

Domenico **Cimarosa**

◉ 1749–1801   ▥ **ITALIAN**   ✍ 110

Shortly after leaving composition classes, Cimarosa burst onto the scene with his comic opera *Le stravaganze del conte* in Naples. After that, his 60 light, elegant operas, mostly comic, with witty and lively ensembles, were staged all over Europe. He also wrote chamber music in a Mozart-like style. When Napoleon occupied Naples in 1799, Cimarosa, then organist at the royal chapel, wrote a song of praise that was sung at the burning of the royal flag—only to see the king retake the city and throw him in jail. His reputation saved his head, but he was exiled and died soon after in Venice.

MILESTONES	
1772	*Le stravaganze del conte*, opera, premiered
1780	*L'Italiana in Londra* staged at La Scala
1787	Visits court at St. Petersburg
1792	*Il matrimonio segreto*, opera, staged while Kapellmeister in Vienna for two years
1793	Returns to Naples; accepts royal post

⌃ **Cimarosa was probably** the most successful Italian opera composer until Rossini. His biggest triumph was *Il matrimonio segreto* (*The Secret Marriage*).

Muzio **Clementi**

◉ 1752–1832   ▥ **ENGLISH**   ✍ 178

Largely forgotten today, Clementi was one of the first piano virtuosos. A child prodigy, Clementi was "bought" from his Italian father at the age of 13 and taken to a wealthy household in the southwest of England, where he occupied himself entirely with studying the harpsichord for seven years. Moving to London in 1774, he became England's preeminent keyboard player, but after two European tours and a piano "duel" with Mozart, he retired from the concert stage and concentrated on teaching. He codified his intimate knowledge of the new instrument in *Gradus ad Parnassum*, a seminal work of 19th-century piano teaching consisting of 100 piano studies.

Among the finest of Clementi's 64 piano sonatas, Piano Sonata in F sharp minor, Op. 25, No. 5 was certainly written for the concert stage rather than the drawing room. Although pianistically varied, its mood is unusually dark, and with all three movements in the minor mode, this is an intense and brooding work of considerable pathos.

Also a successful publisher and piano manufacturer, Clementi was much celebrated in his lifetime and was buried in Westminster Cathedral, where his epitaph reads, "The father of the pianoforte."

MILESTONES	
1779	Publishes Piano Sonatas, Op. 2
1787	Completes Two Symphonies Op. 18
1790	Retires from the concert stage; completes Six Piano Sonatas, Op. 25
1798	Establishes Longman, Clementi & Co.
1802	Begins eight-year tour of Europe on behalf of his firm
1807	Publishing contract with Beethoven
1813	Becomes director of newly founded Philharmonic Society in London
1816	Symphonies performed in Paris

⌃ **Abandoning traditional** two-movement sonatas, Clementi initiated three-movement forms.

Antonio **Salieri**

● 1750–1825   ℙ **ITALIAN**   ✍ c.350

When the Viennese court composer F.L. Gassmann saw Salieri's talent in Venice, he took him to Vienna to complete his training. Once there Salieri blossomed, proved adept at making the right friends (such as Emperor Joseph II), and was a major contributor to Viennese musical life from 1770 to 1820. Many of his operas—rich, theatrical, and combining German power and Italian sweetness—enjoyed great success in Italy (the comedies), Paris (the tragedies), and across Europe. His later operas had a lukewarm reception and he devoted himself to teaching. Salieri's relationship with Mozart—contrary to myths created by Pushkin's play *Mozart and Salieri* (1831) and Peter Schaffer's film *Amadeus* (1984)—was no more than respectful rivalry.

MILESTONES

1779	Writes *La scuola de'gelosi*, comic opera
1781	*Der Rauchfangkehrer*, singspiel, published
1784	Composes *Les Danaïdes*, opera
1788	Writes *Axur re d'Ormus*, opera, with Lorenzo da Ponte; Hofkapellmeister to Joseph II
c.1804	Concentrates on writing sacred music

⏶ **Salieri wrote his opera** *Europa riconosciuta* (*Europa Revealed*) for the grand opening of Theatre Alla Scala, Milan, in 1778. It includes several arias of great brilliance.

Luigi **Cherubini**

● 1760–1842   ℙ **ITALIAN**   ✍ 300

After a modest early career in Italy and London, Cherubini moved to Paris, becoming a dominant figure in the music world as a conductor, publisher, composer, and teacher. His music—especially in his successful Revolution-era operas—could be self-expressive, dramatic, and dark. He adroitly rode changing circumstances, both stylistic (mixing comic and serious styles) and political (he wrote a piece celebrating Louis XVI's execution, then one praising his memory). After 1816 he wrote almost exclusively religious music. Beethoven called Cherubini the greatest living composer, but his reputation faded after his death, possibly due to the lack of a clear Italian national identity until Unification in 1861.

≫ **Jean Auguste Dominique Ingres** admired the music of Cherubini and, in recognition of his many talents, painted *Luigi Cherubini and the Lyric Muse* in 1842.

MILESTONES

1780	Produces his first opera, *Quinto Fabio*
1786	Arrives in Paris
1791	Composes *Lodoïska*, opera, and achieves first international success
1797	*Medée*, opera, published
1815	Superintendent of French royal chapel
1822	Director of Paris Conservatoire
1836	Writes Requiem in D minor

Jan Ladislav **Dussek**

◉ 1760–1812   ♫ CZECH   ✎ c.280

Something of an early Romantic, Dussek was fêted from London to St. Petersburg as a touring piano virtuoso and composer. His accomplished concertos and sonatas sold very well, and in many ways are more harmonically adventurous than Mozart's, or even Beethoven's. However, they have been surprisingly neglected since his death. A piano innovator, he first placed the instrument sideways to improve the audience's view, and worked with a manufacturer to extend the keyboard. Dussek played for Marie Antoinette in Paris, and during the French Revolution fled to London. Forced to leave England after a publishing failure, he went on to lead a wild and reckless life, following his patron the Prince of Prussia into battle. In his final years he returned to Paris.

MILESTONES	
1786	Moves to Paris; meets Marie Antoinette and Napoleon
1790	First known performance in London
1797	Piano works increase in complexity
1800	Flees London for Hamburg
1806	Writes *Elégie harmonique sur la mort du Prince Louis Ferdinand de Prusse*, sonata

⬇ **The most well-known of Dussek's sonatas,** *Elégie harmonique sur la mort du Prince Louis Ferdinand de Prusse*, was inspired by his patron's death at the battle of Saalfeld in 1806.

Samuel **Wesley**

◉ 1766–1837   ♫ ENGLISH   ✎ c.430

Wesley was a child prodigy who became something of a maverick celebrity in London music circles: he never held court appointments or official posts, but made a haphazard living as a teacher and writer, and as an organist known for his extraordinary improvisations. Most of his output is Latin church music, combining old and new styles.

MILESTONES	
1774	Composes *Ruth*, oratorio, aged eight
1799	Writes *The Death of Abel*, oratorio
1802	Symphony in B published
1813	Becomes regular organ soloist at Covent Garden, London
1817	Institutionalized after jumping out of a window

Franz Xaver **Süssmayr**

◉ 1766–1803   ♫ AUSTRIAN   ✎ 160

Known as the composer who completed Mozart's Requiem, Franz Süssmayr—whose limitations are highlighted clearly next to Mozart's work—was nevertheless a craftsmanlike composer who enjoyed stage success in Vienna. Songs from his *Magic Flute*-like *Der Spiegel von Arkadien* were sung in cafés and taverns, and circulated in pirate copies. He held various institutional posts and wrote in many national styles—French and Italian comic idioms, Italian opera seria, and popular German forms—and his melodic gifts were at their best in his solos, duets, and trios. He was Kapellmeister of Vienna's National Theater from 1794 until his death.

MILESTONES	
1791	Copyist and pupil of Mozart
1799	*Solimann II*, singspiel, published
1802	Writes *Il noce di Benevento*, ballet

Wolfgang Amadeus **Mozart**

● 1756–1791   🏳 AUSTRIAN   ✍ 655

⌃ **Although his greatest love** was opera, Mozart was the most brilliant pianist of his age. He took the piano concerto to new heights of richness and virtuosity.

Probably the most prodigious musician ever born, Mozart's early tours around Europe made him famous and also familiarized him with many musical styles, which he then synthesized in his own cosmopolitan works. Unique in musical history for his accomplishment in all forms and genres and possessed of an astonishing compositional fluency, he was the first important composer to attempt to establish a "freelance" musical career.

⏩ **Leopold Mozart** took his children on tour at early ages; in 1762, they played for the Bavarian elector in Munich and the imperial family in Vienna.

he had to settle for the realities of a court appointment, where his social status was between the valets and the cooks. Never happy at the small court of Salzburg and convinced of his own musical superiority, Mozart attempted to obtain other positions, but, failing so to do, left to become one of music's first "freelance" professionals. Arriving in Vienna in 1781, he married Constanze Weber and started to give concerts, publish music, and receive commissions, particularly for operas. Over the next ten years Mozart wrote over 200 works and consolidated his reputation, but he had to give piano lessons, take in boarders, and borrow money to maintain the lifestyle he desired. His death was probably from rheumatic fever. He was buried in a mass grave according to Viennese custom, without mourners, but obituary notices unanimously hailed his greatness.

Life

The son of a gifted musician, Mozart's first musical experiences were hearing his child-prodigy sister, Nannerl, at her lessons. His own gifts soon surpassed hers and, proud of their accomplishments, their father gave up his career to promote their talents before the astounded royalty and cognoscenti of Europe. Despite extensive tours, Mozart composed and studied continually, but, by 1772, no longer a child prodigy,

Music

The range of Mozart's musical output is extraordinary, and it has been said that no other composer has been equally accomplished in so many different media, but it is his operas that hold the key to his essential style. Building on the operatic reforms of Gluck, Mozart combined vivid vocal characterization and supreme melodic gifts with an emphasis on orchestral expressivity and color to achieve a far more dramatic conception than had previously been encountered. The resulting depictions of character, psychology, and human interaction evince a subtle complexity that blurred the lines between opera seria and opera buffa, particularly in the three operas written with Italian poet, Lorenzo Da Ponte, as librettist: *The Marriage of Figaro, Don Giovanni,*

❝ We **cannot despair about mankind** knowing that **Mozart** was a man. ❞   **Albert Einstein**

and Così fan tutte. Mozart also wrote several operas in German, of which *The Magic Flute* has been the most enduringly popular. It combines joyous tunes with noble choruses and includes the *tour de force* coloratura aria of the Queen of the Night.

Mozart wrote a substantial amount of solo vocal and choral music, ranging from the short motet *Ave Verum Corpus*, a piece of utterly serene beauty, to the dazzlingly spirited *Exsultate, jubilate* for soprano and orchestra. Of his large-scale choral works, the *Missa solemnis* and the Requiem (both unfinished) show him in a serious, darker mood, interspersed with sections of exultation or grandeur. Mozart's symphonies, concertos, and chamber works show a particular attention to instrumental color. His peers were frequently amazed by the way he matched experimental combinations of instruments, such as those in the Quintet for Piano and Winds (oboe, clarinet, bassoon, and horn) and the *Kegelstatt Trio* (clarinet, viola, piano) with subtleties of orchestration, particularly in the use of wind instruments, the latter helping to establish the clarinet as a regular in the orchestra.

His refinement of the concerto, especially the piano concerto, brought the genre to a new level of sophistication, establishing it as no less important than the symphony, which had far-reaching effects in the 19th century. In 1782, he began a period of concentrated piano concerto writing. The 15 (Nos. 11–25) he produced by the end of 1786 became ever more symphonically rich and pianistically virtuosic. Mozart had written most of his symphonies in his youth, but his last, "Jupiter," was the summation of his symphonic development, ending with undiluted orchestral brilliance.

Composed in already well-established forms, Mozart's music is seldom regarded as revolutionary, but contemporaneous audiences certainly found some of his work difficult to appreciate, particularly in its startling contrasts, complexity, and sometimes dissonant harmony. Having assimilated the major European musical styles as a boy, his mature work allied a fusion of Italian lyricism, French brilliance, and Middle-European compositional processes with a very natural sense of symmetry, which has come to be regarded as the epitome of Classical refinement.

⌃ **Mozart fell in love** with Constanze Weber in 1781 and married her in 1782. Of their six children, only two survived.

MILESTONES

1761	Composes Andante, K1a, Allegro, K1b		**1785**	Composes Piano Concerto No. 21
1764	Composes Symphony No. 1, K16		**1786**	Opera *The Marriage of Figaro*, produced; composes Piano Concertos Nos. 23–25, *Kegelstatt Trio*, "Prague" Symphony
1767	Travels to Vienna and catches smallpox			
1768	Singspiel *Bastien and Bastienne* is staged			
1772	Appointed Konzertmeister at Salzburg		**1787**	Visits Prague twice: *Figaro* is success; "Prague" Symphony and *Don Giovanni* premiered, composes *Eine kleine Nachtmusik*
1773	Fails to gain post in Vienna; composes many string quartets, symphonies, and motet *Exsultate, jubilate*			
1778	"Paris" Symphony performed in Paris; his mother dies there; writes Concerto for Flute and Harp, Piano Sonata, K 310		**1788**	Severe financial problems: starts borrowing; composes his three greatest symphonies (Nos. 39, 40, 41), three piano trios, and "Coronation" Piano Concerto
1779	Becomes court organist; composes *Coronation Mass*, *Sinfonia Concertante*		**1789**	Travels to Dresden, Leipzig, Potsdam, and Berlin trying to obtain post or commissions; composes Clarinet Quintet
1780	Receives commission from Munich for opera *Idomeneo*; rehearses it there			
1781	*Idomeneo* is a success; leaves his post to become freelance musician in Vienna		**1790**	Opera *Così fan tutte* premiered in Vienna; gives concerts in Germany
1782	Marries Constanze Weber; opera *Die Entführung aus dem Serail* is acclaimed		**1791**	Premiere of *La Clemenza di Tito* in Prague; opera *The Magic Flute* is a success in Vienna; Clarinet Concerto; begins Requiem, which is left incomplete at his death
1784	Gives series of public concerts for which composes Piano Concertos Nos. 14–19			

⌃ **Mozart became a Freemason** in Vienna in 1784. The influence of their ideology is strongly felt in his sensationally successful comic opera *The Magic Flute*.

KEY WORKS

DON GIOVANNI, K527

OPERA	⏱ 174:00	📖 5	

Asked to write an opera for Prague after the success of *The Marriage of Figaro*, Mozart decided on the story of Don Juan. Notable for the vivid musical depiction of characters and emotions, and just as serious in emotion as it is comic in plot, *Don Giovanni* is still considered to be among the greatest operas ever composed.

PIANO CONCERTO NO. 21, K467

ORCHESTRAL	⏱ 28:30	📖 3	

> **When he died,** Mozart had the score of the Requiem on his bed and had been explaining to Süssmayr his ideas on how to finish it.

This is one of Mozart's six 1785–86 concertos, probably performed at his subscription concerts in Vienna. With some of the most complex piano writing of the time, even Mozart's father commented that "the new concerto is astonishingly difficult."

EINE KLEINE NACHTMUSIK, K525

ORCHESTRAL	⏱ 16:30	📖 4	

Mozart's most famous work, and one of several divertimenti and serenades written for social occasions, *A Little Night Music* is scored for only strings and may even have been intended as a quintet. Originally in five movements, a second minuet was later removed from the manuscript.

SYMPHONY NO. 41, "JUPITER," K551

ORCHESTRAL	⏱ 36:50	📖 4	

Mozart wrote his last three symphonies without a commission, or any prospect of performance, in the summer of 1788. The "Jupiter" is now recognized as one of Mozart's greatest symphonies, but it was never played during his lifetime. As a tribute to Mozart after his death, Haydn quoted the theme from the slow movement in his Symphony No. 98.

REQUIEM, K626

MASS SETTING	⏱ 54:30	📖 8	

The "gray messenger" who commissioned Mozart's final work was actually an emissary for Count Walsegg-Stuppach, who wished to perform the Requiem in memory of his wife and required anonymity because he wished to pass the work off as his own. Mozart started it in good spirits, but his health began to fail and he became obsessed with the idea that he was writing it for his own death. Death did indeed strike when the work was far from complete. His widow, needing the outstanding half of the fee to support their family, asked Mozart's assistant, Franz Xaver Süssmayr, to complete it.

PIANO SONATA NO. 8, K310

PIANO SOLO	⏱ 16:30	📖 3	

Mozart wrote this sonata in Paris at the time of his mother's death. It is among the finest piano works of the early Classical period. One of only three minor-key sonatas in his output, its drama is immediate in the orchestral textures of its opening. A restrained slow movement lulls the listener before the dark pathos of the finale.

SYMPHONY NO. 38, "PRAGUE," K504

ORCHESTRAL   ⏱ 30:00   📖 3   ⚜

Following the success of *The Marriage of Figaro* in Prague, Mozart introduced this symphony there in 1787. Unusual in that it had only three movements, it opens in a dark, majestic mood, which is immediately dispelled by the arrival of the faster main body of the music. An expressive slow movement balances the lively finale, in which, to the delight of the symphony's first audience, Mozart used a theme borrowed from *The Marriage of Figaro*.

STRING QUARTET NO. 19, "DISSONANT," K465

CHAMBER   ⏱ 30:30   📖 4   ⚜

This is one of six quartets that Mozart dedicated in 1785 to Haydn, whose recent Op. 33 quartets had brought the form to a new level of sophistication. Mozart's equally finely wrought response seems effortless in its mastery of Haydn's innovations, but according to the composer was "the fruit of long and laborious endeavor." This, the last of the set, is named after its surprisingly dissonant introduction, which gives way to work of a graceful charm.

CLARINET CONCERTO, K622

ORCHESTRAL   ⏱ 28:00   📖 3   ⚜

Mozart first met Anton Stadler in 1783 and, immediately taken by his virtuosity on the newly invented clarinet, they formed a friendship that

inspired the *Kegelstatt Trio*, the Clarinet Quintet, and this lyrical concerto. Mozart capitalized on the clarinet's mellifluous tone quality, especially in the operatically inspired slow movement. Mozart made his final public appearance conducting the Viennese premiere of this concerto.

INFLUENCES

While always noted for its formal beauty and elegance, Mozart's music was usually dismissed in the century after his death as a historically interesting precursor to Beethoven's. Only more recently, as an antidote to Romanticism and Modernity, has his name become a byword for musical perfection.

◁ *The Magic Flute* tells the beguiling story of the victory of love over adversity and light over darkness, set against the machinations of the Queen of the Night.

◁ Written in Italian, *The Marriage of Figaro* contains music of great beauty. The Countess's poignant aria, *Porgi amor* (*Grant me love*), is one of Mozart's greatest.

Ludwig van **Beethoven**

● 1770–1827 　　▨ GERMAN 　　✍ 398

The supreme iconic figure of Western music, Beethoven established the popular concept of the artist, who, separate from society, transcends personal tragedy to achieve his goal and becomes a hero. Calling himself a "Tondichter," or "poet in sound," his music mirrored his beliefs in the prevailing spirit of individualism by emphasizing personal expression over traditional form, and thus paved the way for musical Romanticism.

》 **Beethoven's invariably intense music** visits all points on the emotional scale, from the bleakest melancholy to the most joyful celebration.

growing deafness would become total and, while staying in the village of Heiligenstadt, wrote a letter detailing his desperate unhappiness. Overcoming the crisis, he returned, determined to "seize Fate by the throat," and launched himself into an unprecedented period of creativity that bore many of his most famous works. By 1812, his deafness had engendered further depression and isolation and a lapse in creativity, but his final years, in a spirit of resignation, brought forth his most spiritual and exalted music. Suggestions that he died with a fist raised, though appropriate, are possibly apocryphal, but his death was mourned by all of Vienna.

Life

Showing early musical talent, Beethoven was given a thorough music grounding by the Bonn court organist, Christian Gottlob Neefe, and was soon acting as his deputy. Aged 17, he left for Vienna to further his studies, but returned within weeks when he discovered his mother was dying. Impressed by his music, Haydn invited him to study in Vienna. There, Beethoven was soon invited into aristocratic circles, where the beauty and virtuosity of his playing and his compositional prowess won him many patrons who subsequently became devotees of his works. However, by 1802 he realized that his

Music

Beethoven's compositional battles were hard fought, with certain works spending many years in labored gestation. Once fully formed, however, the majority of them were instantly successful. The growing middle class enjoyed their immediacy, power, and dramatic virtuosity, while the cultural elite was equally impressed by the thorough absorption and subsequent transcending of 18th-century musical styles.

Although Beethoven's output is usually divided into three periods, a fourth, before his arrival in Vienna, should also be considered, because by then he had already composed a number of vocal and chamber works, and a very accomplished set of variations for piano. These early works are all catalogued with "WoO" numbers (*Werke ohne Opus*—works without opus). His early reputation and fame rested on his phenomenal gifts of improvisation at the keyboard, which some said were even greater than Mozart's.

❝ Keep your **eye on him;** one day he will make the **world talk of him.** ❞ **Mozart,** on hearing the 17-year-old Beethoven

Beethoven's usually designated "early" period began after his arrival in Vienna in 1792 at the age of 22. There he assimilated—and then began to transform—the sonata principle from a balanced, archlike structure to a more dynamic, urgent form, where the recapitulation (the third section after the exposition and the development sections) was a culmination rather than a repetition. At first tending toward exploration and elaboration of the initial musical ideas—and preferring four movements to the customary three—Beethoven's solo piano works were highly successful. But, as his accomplishment grew, his compositions—including the Op. 18 string quartets, three piano concertos, two symphonies, and the *Pathétique* and "Moonlight" piano sonatas—became more expressive and concentrated. The *Pathétique* sonata, with its French name meaning "passionate" or "emotional" (given to it by Beethoven himself), is regarded as his first masterpiece.

Beethoven's "middle" period dates from 1803—the year after he realized the seriousness of his growing deafness and rejected suicide in favor of giving the world, he said, "all the music I felt was within me." From this time, his music took on a new, heroic style whose dimensions, range, and power were a watershed in music history. Its first manifestation was the epic "Eroica" Symphony, a work of colossal energy and, at 50 minutes, the longest that had thus far been written, revealing new developments of the symphonic form.

Beethoven's new "symphonic ideal" was applied to all genres and resulted in a torrent of productivity. From this period come four more symphonies, the Violin Concerto, Piano Concertos Nos. 4 and 5, and an opera, *Fidelio*. However, his increasing isolation through deafness marked the change into his "late" period. By 1813 Beethoven was exploring more intimate modes of expression, often emphasizing the lyrical and veiled. With an increasing fondness for variation and fugue (such as in the *Diabelli Variations*), and further experimentation with sonata forms—which resulted in three final piano sonatas of great intellectual and expressive depth—his music left the Classical world of Haydn and Mozart behind and entered the Romantic era. His *Missa Solemnis* and Symphony No. 9 were also innovative, combining symphonic choral writing "from the heart" as never before.

⊠ **In 1808,** Beethoven was granted an annuity for life by his pupil and friend, the Habsburg Archduke Rudolf of Austria.

MILESTONES

1778	First public performance in Cologne
1781	Takes lessons in organ and violin
1783	Composes Three Sonatas, WoO 47
1787	Studies briefly in Vienna with Mozart
1792	Returns to Vienna to study with Haydn
1795	First public concert in Vienna: performs Piano Concerto No. 1 in B Flat, Op. 19
1800	Symphony No. 1 and Septet performed in Vienna; composes Piano Concerto No. 3; ballet *Prometheus* successfully staged; publishes "Moonlight" Piano Sonata
1802	Depressed by failing hearing, writes *Heiligenstadt Testament*; composes Symphony No. 2 and *Kreutzer* Violin Sonata
1804	Completes "Eroica" Symphony; composes "Waldstein" Piano Sonata
1805	Opera *Fidelio* premiered, but withdrawn after three performances owing to Austrian occupation of Vienna; composes "Appassionata" Piano Sonata
1806	Completes Violin Concerto, Symphony No. 4, *Razoumovsky Quartets*
1808	Symphonies Nos. 5 and 6, Piano Concerto No. 4, and *Choral Fantasy* premiered together in four-hour concert
1809	Writes "Emperor" Piano Concerto
1811	"Archduke" Trio written
1812	Completes Symphonies Nos. 7 and 8
1814	Revised *Fidelio* produced successfully; his final appearance as pianist in "Archduke" Trio is disastrous owing to his deafness
1816	Granted custody of his nephew, Karl—leads to legal battle with sister-in-law; writes song cycle *An die ferne Geliebte*
1818	Is sent Broadwood piano from London; "Hammerklavier" Piano Sonata completed
1822	Finishes Piano Sonata No. 32
1823	Completes Mass in D (*Missa solemnis*) and *Diabelli Variations*
1824	Finishes "Choral" Symphony
1826	Writes String Quartet Op. 130
1827	Falls ill with dropsy and pneumonia; dies in March and some 10,000 people attend his funeral

KEY WORKS

VIOLIN CONCERTO, OP. 61

ORCHESTRAL ⧖ 45:15 ▢ 3 ♫ ⊚

The score for this concerto was finished only two days before the first performance, and was virtually read at sight. Not an immediate success, Beethoven arranged it for piano, but the original became popular after the 13-year-old Joseph Joachim performed it in London with Mendelssohn in 1844.
First movement (*allegro ma non troppo*, 25:45) Beethoven developed Mozart's concerto style on an unprecedented scale in this movement, unusually giving prominent roles to the timpani and woodwind.
Second movement (*larghetto*, 10:00) Beginning with an ethereal set of variations accompanied by muted strings, the movement ends with a brief cadenza which leads directly into the finale.
Third movement (*rondo, allegro*, 9:30) This is a cheerful and traditional ending, with only a brief moment of Beethovian pathos in the minor key.

SYMPHONY NO. 9, "CHORAL," OP. 125

ORCHESTRAL ⧖ 69:00 ▢ 4 ♫

Possibly the most iconic work of Western music, the "Choral" still stands as a colossus against which all subsequent symphonies have been judged. Opening

mysteriously, the first movement settles into a dark and forceful sonata style. Among many surprises is a fortissimo repeat of the opening bars in the major key at the recapitulation. After experimenting with timpani as a feature in the Violin and "Emperor" concertos, here he gives them a major role in the second movement. In the third movement, the sublime adagio is actually two sets of variations on two alternating themes. Two startling interruptions for the new valved horn come near the end. In the fourth movement, fragments of earlier movements are heard before instruments, then voices, settle on Schiller's *Ode to Joy* in a hitherto unprecedented choral addition to a symphony.

PIANO SONATA IN F MINOR, "APPASSIONATA," OP. 57

PIANO SOLO ⧖ 23:00 ▢ 3 ⊚

In this sonata, composed in 1804–05, Beethoven brought piano virtuosity to a new level of complexity, powerfully fusing it with his new, heroic style. Although the subtitle was not his own (it was added by the publisher), Beethoven seems to have approved of it. This violent, impassioned piece was one of his favorite works in that particular medium.
First movement (*allegro assai*, 9:00) Almost using the keyboard as an orchestra, Beethoven elicited a new kind of musical drama in this movement with its sudden changes in volume, register, and pace.
Second movement (*andante con moto*, 6:20) Starting with a chordal theme, this calm movement develops into a series of three variations, each higher and more decorative than the last. Its serenity provides a brief respite from the mood of tragic despair that dominates the rest of the work. It ends with a version of the opening interrupted by a mysterious arpeggio.
Third movement (*allegro ma non troppo*, 7:40) Unusually, the third movement of the sonata flows directly from the second. The arpeggio gives way to a forceful outburst leading into a relentless finale, which the performer should keep reined in, until the explosive coda and the abrupt and violent ending.

» **Beethoven dedicated his "Eroica" Symphony** to Napoleon in admiration of his ideals, but removed the name in disgust when Napoleon made himself emperor.

FIDELIO, OP. 72

OPERA ⏳ 124:00 📖 2 🎵🎭♿

For his only opera, Beethoven set the story of an old French libretto, *Léonore, ou L'amour conjugal*, which reflected his belief in the triumph of free will, liberty, and human goodness. He revised *Fidelio*, as he renamed it, twice over ten years and wrote another three overtures.

The opera tells the story of Marcelina, the jailer's daughter, who is in love with Fidelio, her father's employee. However, Fidelio is really Leonora— a woman in disguise looking for her husband, Florestan, whom the prison governor is holding illegally. Leonora overhears the governor's decision to murder Florestan and decides to rescue him. When the governor enters Florestan's cell to kill him, Leonora holds him off with a pistol. The government minister's arrival ensures Florestan's freedom and the townspeople rejoice as the corrupt governor is arrested.

SONATA NO. 9 FOR VIOLIN AND PIANO, "KREUTZER," OP. 47

DUO ⏳ 35:00 📖 3 🎻

Beethoven dedicated this piece to Rudolphe Kreutzer, a famous violinist living in Paris. Avoiding the piano-centered style of his previous works in the genre, here there is a real equality in the virtuosity of the two instruments; indeed, the score bore the subtitle "written in a molto concertante style, as though a concerto."

PIANO CONCERTO NO. 5, "EMPEROR," OP. 73

ORCHESTRAL ⏳ 40:00 📖 3 🎵🎹

Beethoven's final work in this genre was nicknamed the "Emperor" by the composer J. B. Cramer in response to its grandeur. Unusually starting with flourishes for piano, it also broke with tradition by dispensing with an improvised cadenza in favour of an already written one. Too deaf to perform it himself, Beethoven had it premiered by his pupil, Carl Czerny. It was instantly hailed as a masterpiece.

SYMPHONY NO. 6, "PASTORAL," OP. 68

ORCHESTRAL ⏳ 40:00 📖 5 🎵

Although the five country scenes, including a vivid storm, were inspired by Beethoven's love of nature, he emphasized that this was "more the expression of feeling than tone-painting." The symphony was first given in December 1808 at an epic concert that included the premieres of the Symphony No. 5, Piano Concerto No. 4, and *Choral Fantasy*.

INFLUENCES

The first composer to establish a freelance career from the outset, Beethoven's refusal to be subservient to aristocratic patrons marked the change in the role of the musician from servant to autonomous cultural arbiter, and thus created a model of aspiration that was followed by almost every subsequent Classical musician.

The British pianist John Ogdon (1937–89) gave many highly original and moving interpretations of Beethoven's piano music.

Johann Nepomuk **Hummel**

● **1778–1837**   ▥ **AUSTRIAN**   ✍ **c.450**

A prodigy who, like Mozart, toured Europe as a boy, Hummel was idolized as a composer and fêted as Europe's greatest pianist. A warm person whose business acumen helped secure better copyright laws for composers and more financial security for his family, he wrote all types of music (except symphonies, deferring to Beethoven) in a polished late-Classical style. His bestselling folk songs for Scottish publisher George Thomson show how well he wrote for the market.

MILESTONES

1804	Becomes Konzertmeister at the court of Prince Nikolaus Esterházy
1810	*Mathilde von Guise*, opera, staged
1819	Kapellmeister at Weimar court
1828	Piano tutor sells out in days

Antonín **Reicha**

● **1770–1836**   ▥ **CZECH**   ✍ **c.260**

Though his operas never found success, Reicha's instrumental works, often exploring aspects of technique, were eventually published and widely performed. His good reputation as an author on music theory led to a professorship at the Paris Conservatoire, and it was as a teacher, rather than as a prolific composer, that he became best known. He befriended Haydn and Beethoven, and both Berlioz and Liszt admired his forward-looking ideas. Reicha's wind music was popular, and his colourful quintets proved models of the genre.

MILESTONES

1794	Teaches music in Hamburg
1803	Composes 36 Fugues
1818	Professor at the Paris Conservatoire

John **Field**

● **1782–1837**   ▥ **IRISH**   ✍ **70**

By the age of 18, Field was an established piano virtuoso on the London concert scene. When he visited St. Petersburg with his teacher, Muzio Clementi, he was so at home in the artistic and aristocratic milieu that he remained in Russia. There, he developed a distinctive style of piano playing (Chopinesque, but pre-Chopin), while also pioneering the nocturne, of which he wrote 16. Field's name spread across Europe, and as a teacher he was influential. By the 1830s, however, his music had fallen out of fashion. After an outrageous, Byronesque lifestyle of excess—quite unlike his serene music and delicate performing style—his health rapidly declined.

MILESTONES

1792	First public performance in Dublin
1793	Field's family sets up home in London
1803	Visits St. Petersburg, Russia
1811	Composes Piano Concertos Nos. 1–3
1812	Writes Nocturnes Nos. 1–3
1822	Settles in Moscow
1832	Visits London

⌃ **The moonlit Thames,** as depicted by the painter Henry Pether, conveys the serene mood of Field's atmospheric nocturnes.

Louis **Spohr**

● 1784–1859   🏳 GERMAN   ✎ 208

One of the most celebrated musicians of his time, Spohr's instrumental compositions were favorably compared with those of Beethoven—and admired both by his peers—such as Mendelssohn, Schumann, and Chopin, and by the later Romantics Brahms and Tchaikovsky. A virtuoso violinist considered second only to Paganini, he also achieved great success as a teacher, his *Violin Tutor* being widely read.

From a musical family, Spohr started his career as a court chamber musician at Brunswick before touring throughout Germany as a virtuoso violinist. Appointed Konzertmeister at Gotha, he began to compose, and also became one of the first conductors to use a baton. After further touring with his harpist wife, Dorette Scheidler, and public success with two operas, he finally settled in Kassel where, as Kapellmeister, he wrote more operas and symphonies for orchestra, presented works by Bach and Wagner, and taught violinists from all over Europe. Heavily influenced by Mozart, his music combines Classical forms with early Romantic modes of expression.

MILESTONES	
1799	Embarks on first concert tour to Hamburg; joins the Brunswick court
1813	Directs Theater an der Wien
1816	Writes Violin Concerto No. 8
1826	Composes Six Songs, Op. 72
1836	Marries pianist Marianne Pfeiffer
1840	Composes Symphony No. 6

◀ **A consummate performer** and natural showman, Spohr delighted his friends and family at his lively musical gatherings with his virtuoso technique and Romantic panache.

KEY WORKS

SYMPHONY NO. 6 IN G MAJOR, "HISTORIC," OP. 116

ORCHESTRAL   ⏱ 26:00   📖 4   🎻

Wishing to satirize grand opera, Spohr wrote each of the first three movements of this symphony as a pastiche of earlier musical styles and periods (1720, 1780, and 1810) while parodying the music of his contemporaries in the finale.

SIX SONGS, OP. 72

SONG CYCLE   ⏱ 14:00   📖 6   🎵

As a teacher, Spohr advocated a vocal approach to playing the violin, and he clearly loved writing songs, turning out more than 90.

In the six songs here, Spohr sets a variety of Romantic poetry and an "exotic" Persian love sonnet, with great passion and broad lyricism.

VIOLIN CONCERTO IN A MINOR, OP. 47

ORCHESTRAL   ⏱ 17:50   📖 1   🎻

Of his 15 concertos and numerous solo works for the instrument, this is one of Spohr's few violin works still heard today.

Written for performance in Italy, in the form of a vocal scene, its use of several operatic formulae in one instrumental movement made it an instant success.

The Romantic Era
1810–1920

The Romantic movement emerged at the end of the 18th century in art and literature, and somewhat later in music. The Romantics rejected the confines of Classical convention; for them, originality was of paramount importance. They celebrated the emotional and the instinctive, and looked toward nature for inspiration.

Beethoven cast a long shadow over the 19th century. The emotional power of his music made him the chief precursor of what we now label Romanticism. His lifetime coincided with a watershed in history: the French Revolution of 1789 had been the most visible expression of the rights of the individual in the 18th century. Despite the oppressive regimes of the post-Napoleonic period, the Romantic cult of the individual flourished, along with an increasing awareness of the rights of nations to govern themselves and take pride in their own culture. In this climate of self-expression, women came nowhere near to winning equal rights, but a few were able to become composers and publish their works—Clara Schumann and Fanny Mendelssohn being the most celebrated examples.

Some music of the Romantic period was characterized by the virtuoso performer—for example, Liszt. A parallel trend was for intimate music intended for the salon—such as the shorter works, or "miniatures," of Chopin and Schumann. There lies a conflict here between the public character of many

of the great Romantic solo and orchestral works and the solitude of such works as Schubert's song cycle *Winterreise*.

Past and future

The Romantic era was one of extremes, with composers not only looking back to the past but also abandoning classical conventions and experimenting with new and daring harmonic language and form. This progressive style is especially evident in Berlioz's *Symphonie fantastique*, with its extraordinary narrative of desire and destruction, or in Liszt's Sonata in B minor of 1852, with its snakelike one-movement form, or in the strange harmonies of the same composer's quasi-impressionistic late piano pieces, such as *Nuages gris*.

The Romantic period can claim to have "rediscovered" music from the past. When in 1829 Mendelssohn organized a performance of J.S. Bach's *St. Matthew Passion*, he unlocked a great treasure trove of music that was revived in the next few decades. Not only did this alert musicians and audiences to the significance of Bach's own music, but it also encouraged musicians to perform music of the past and composers such as Brahms to use its materials and forms.

◀◀ **The suffering** so poignantly expressed in Schubert's greatest songs contrasts with the image of the cheerful evenings he apparently spent playing for his friends.

Connections

Whereas musicians of earlier periods had tended to concentrate on their craft alone, the Romantics blurred the lines between disciplines: Berlioz and Schumann both published criticism as well as music; Weber wrote a novel; Liszt wrote essays on a wide range of interests; and Wagner wrote his own libretti as well as the music for his operas. Romantic composers therefore frequently referred to ideas beyond music itself—for example, landscape and nature became important themes, from the songs of Schubert to 20th-century works such as Richard Strauss's "Alpine" Symphony and Vaughan Williams's "Sea" Symphony.

With constant theorizing about the direction music should take, it is not surprising that the Romantic era was one of bitter disputes. One of the most celebrated feuds was that between the followers of Brahms and those of Wagner. Brahms was seen by his partisans as a traditionalist, while Liszt and Wagner were believed by their supporters to represent the musical future. In fact, Brahms's musical language was at times highly adventurous, just as Wagner often looked to the past (most clearly in the music of *Die Meistersinger von Nürnberg*).

Music in the home

If there is one instrument that symbolizes the Romantic period, it is the piano. Most Romantic composers composed not only concert music for the instrument but also music intended for amateur use. A measure of the political and social changes of the time was that far more homes now owned a piano. There was a

◨ **The Romantics** were often mocked for their style and excesses, in the case of Berlioz (pictured here in an 1846 cartoon) the vast orchestras required to perform his works.

TIMELINE: THE ROMANTIC ERA

1827 Schubert composes great song cycle *Winterreise* in year before his death

1834 Schumann founds the review *Neue Zeitschrift für Musik*

1840 Marriage of Schumann to Clara Wieck

1848 Revolutions across Europe

1820 — **1830** — **1840** — **1850**

1824 Death of Byron at Missolonghi during Greek War of Independence

1832 Chopin gives first Paris concert

1839 Berlioz's dramatic symphony *Romeo and Juliet*

1840s Liszt tours the length and breadth of Europe to wild adulation

1853 Schumann champions music of the young Brahms

consequent demand for music that could be played in the home, and many orchestral and operatic works were arranged for the piano.

A living legacy

Music from the Romantic era has remained perennially popular with listeners. It continues to be enjoyed for its richness of melodic and harmonic invention, its poignancy and grandeur, as well as its extra-musical associations. Many late-20th-century composers have adopted certain characteristics of Romantic style—for example, in his score for the film *Star Wars*, the composer John Williams used music in a Romantic symphonic style to represent the future. The American composer John Adams could likewise be called a neo-Romantic with regard to his great orchestral works, such as *Harmonielehre*. Romanticism survives in our time.

LITERATURE AND ROMANTIC MUSIC

Literature substantially influenced music during the Romantic period, from Berlioz's use of Byron in *Harold in Italy* to Schubert's settings of the poets Heine and Goethe to Schumann's references to novels by Jean Paul and E.T.A. Hoffman in his piano works. Hoffmann's strange stories also inspired Offenbach's *The Tales of Hoffmann* and Tchaikovsky's *Nutcracker Suite*, and he voiced the feelings of many Romantics when he asserted that "Music is the most Romantic of all the arts—in fact, it might be said to be the sole purely Romantic one."

» The English poet Byron inspired the Romantic movement across Europe.

⌃ This painting of a solitary wanderer by Caspar David Friedrich (c.1818) embodies the mood evoked by many early Romantic composers.

« The lighter side of Romanticism was to be found in salons across Europe. Here Johann Strauss Jr. provides the musical entertainment at an evening party in Vienna.

1867 Johann Strauss Jr first performs "Blue Danube" Waltz

1877 Phonograph invented by Edison

1889 First performance of Mahler's Symphony No. 1 in Budapest

1893 Tchaikovsky completes Symphony No. 6, the "Pathétique"; dies soon after in St. Petersburg

1860   1870   1880   1890

1868 Brahms's *German Requiem*

1874 First French Impressionist exhibition in Paris

1890 Richard Strauss's symphonic poem *Death and Transfiguration*

Niccolò **Paganini**

◔ 1782–1840   ▥ ITALIAN   ✍ c.250

Paganini's total mastery of the violin, demonic charisma, and personal mystique created the benchmark for the Romantic virtuoso. Most of his well-crafted, imaginative music, including a large body of chamber works, is now seldom heard. However, he influenced a generation of composers, including Liszt, Chopin, and Schumann, to use instrumental virtuosity as an essential expressive element in their music.

Paganini's talent was rigorously nurtured by his father, who forced him to practice obsessively, depriving him of food and water when he faltered. Thus acquiring an extraordinary facility, it was surprisingly not until 1809, after a long period as a court musician, that he became a traveling virtuoso. Even after a triumphant debut in Milan in 1813, he continued to tour Italy sporadically, only launching his career as an international artist at the age of 46—mesmerizing audiences across Europe and amassing great wealth.

MILESTONES	
1794	Gives first public performance
1795	Goes to Parma to study violin and composition
1796	Returns to Genoa to practice
1801	Leads an orchestra in Lucca
1809	Leaves Lucca to become a "free artist"
1820	Six Sonatas for Violin and Guitar, Op. 3
1834	Settles in Parma; health deteriorates

KEY WORKS

24 CAPRICES

SOLO VIOLIN   ▥ 24   ◉

Although Paganini had probably composed his caprices by 1805, he published them only in 1820, when he provocatively dedicated them "to the artists," knowing that few, if any, of his contemporaries would be able to play them. Each is a mini-masterpiece, exploring a different aspect of violin technique, and together they provide an almost complete compendium of the instrument's possibilities. The theme of the final caprice has been used for famous works by composers as diverse as Brahms, Rachmaninoff, Lutoslawski, and Andrew Lloyd Webber.

LE STREGHE

ORCHESTRAL   ⏱ 9:30   ▥ 1   ⚛ ◉

After four years as a traveling virtuoso, Paganini finally felt ready to make his debut at La Scala in Milan. At the ballet, he heard the melody of

Süssmayr's *Le streghe* (*The Witches*) and decided to capitalize on its popularity by writing a set of variations. After a majestic orchestral introduction, the violin enters, teasing the audience with a simple, gracious melody which is not the expected theme. Only after a repeat of this section does the actual witches' tune begin, but again performed quite unassumingly, raising expectation even higher before the first variation, where the fireworks finally begin. Listeners are subjected to a rollercoaster ride demonstrating Paganini's astounding techniques.

VIOLIN CONCERTO NO. 1

ORCHESTRAL   ⏱ 36:00   ▥ 3   ⚛ ◉

Opening with a theatrically expectant orchestral introduction rather reminiscent of the Italian operas of Rossini, the violin entry is virtuosic, but ultimately vocally inspired, and frequently lyrical. The tragic and operatic slow movement reminds us that Paganini was equally renowned for his ability to move as to dazzle.

▣ **Paganini amazed audiences** in London with his extraordinary violin techniques and his showman's ability to astonish.

Franz **Schubert**

⬤ **1797–1828**   🏳 **AUSTRIAN**   ✎ **1,009**

One of music's greatest melodists, Schubert had a tragically short life, constantly belied by his optimistic music. Achieving compositional maturity by the age of 17, his vast output evinces astounding fluency allied to an extraordinarily rich and varied musical imagination. The epitaph on his tombstone reads, "The art of music here entombed a rich possession, but even fairer hopes. Franz Schubert lies here."

Life

Born into a musical family, Schubert showed a precocious talent for the violin and piano. By the age of ten he was studying harmony and the following year became a chorister at the Court Chapel in Vienna, where he studied composition with Salieri, who had also taught Beethoven. Leaving in 1813, he was already an accomplished composer, having written numerous works, including a symphony, and even started an opera, but following his father's wishes he became a schoolteacher. Schubert continued to compose, however, and eventually he felt confident enough to give up school teaching, although he did become music teacher to the Esterházy family, who had formerly employed Haydn. Still not well known in Vienna, Schubert was in considerable financial difficulty, and when he caught syphilis in 1822 his unhappy situation threw him into despair. However, his creativity continued undiminished and by 1825 he was published and becoming known in Vienna— even the dying Beethoven requested a meeting. He gave his only public concert in 1828, but by the end of the year his health had deteriorated markedly, and he died on November 19. His estate was valued at 63 gulden, while his unpaid bills amounted to nearly 1,000 gulden.

Music

Whether to place Schubert's music within the context of the Classical or Romantic period has always been a topic of contention. Certainly subjective in its emotions, his work is far more dependent on the hedonism of melody for its own sake than that of Haydn, Mozart, or Beethoven, and is more adventurous. Sacrificing the Classical tenets of balance in favor of spontaneous imagination, his

◀ **Many of Schubert's songs** and solo works were first performed by the composer at evening parties hosted by his cultured and influential friends.

music, however, invariably displays Classical forms and, with the exception of the songs, is almost entirely missing any external allusion or descriptive title. While formerly considered Romantic, perhaps influenced by the changing fortunes in his personal life, more recent commentators have placed his work alongside Beethoven's in historical context. His huge output includes sacred and choral works, orchestral music comprising overtures and nine symphonies, over 70 chamber music works, and works for piano including 21 sonatas and some 60 works for piano duet. However, he was first known for his songs. Schubert was the central figure in the creation of the German art-song, or Lied. Frequently combining the very greatest poetry with accompaniments made possible by advances in piano design, his imagination was able to capture in music both the essential mood and the detail of the narrative. Furthermore, by setting narrative poetry cycles, he developed the genre to create the song cycle. It is therefore rather surprising that his many works for the stage are still almost unknown.

MILESTONES

1802	Studies violin with his schoolmaster father and piano with his brother	**1818**	Gives up school teaching and becomes music teacher to the Esterházy family
1808	Accepted as chorister at the Court Chapel, where he becomes a pupil of Antonio Salieri	**1819**	Spends summer in Steyr; commissioned to write the "Trout" Quintet, D667
1813	Completes Symphony No. 1, D82; starts work on an opera; commences teacher-training	**1822**	Writes the "Unfinished" Symphony, No. 8, D759, and the "Wanderer" Fantasy, D760
1814	"Gretchen am Spinnrade", D118	**1823**	Admitted to Vienna hospital; composes song cycle *Die Schöne Mullerin*, D795
1815	Becomes a schoolmaster; composes Symphonies No. 2 and No. 3, and the song "Erlkönig", D328, which in his lifetime becomes his best-known work	**1827**	Torchbearer at Beethoven's funeral; composes first part of *Winterreise*, D911
1816	Completes Symphony No. 5, D485, and more than 100 songs, including "Der Wanderer", D493	**1828**	Public concert receives no press due to the arrival in Vienna of Paganini; completes "Great" Symphony No. 9, D944 and *Winterreise*, D911

KEY WORKS

PIANO QUINTET, "DIE FORELLE" ("THE TROUT"), D667

CHAMBER   🎵 **42:20**   📖 **5**   ⚓

This masterpiece adds a double bass, rather than the more usual second violin, to the piano-quartet ensemble. With its unquestioned joy and natural simplicity, this piece has an irresistible appeal.

With the double bass providing a sonorous foundation, the piano doesn't need to provide a bass line in the first movement, and so is frequently used as a purely melodic instrument.

In the second movement, a gentle dialogue between instruments which threatens to come to an end in mid-movement is immediately repeated in its entirety in a different key.

Brisk and vigorous, with a number of humorous silences as well as sudden changes of dynamic and register, the Scherzo third movement is tempered by a wistful Trio section.

The fourth, "extra" movement which gives the work its name is a set of variations on Schubert's 1817 song "Die Forelle". In increasingly inventive variations, each instrument gets the melody in turn, and the movement ends with a fully collaborative reprise of the opening.

The fifth movement contains surprising juxtapositions of elegance and rustic vitality, and the odd false ending, giving the work a mercurial if slightly unsatisfying conclusion.

WINTERREISE, D911

SONG CYCLE   🎵 **73:00**   📖 **24**   🎧♪

This song cycle is set to *Posthumous Papers of a Travelling Horn Player* by Wilhelm Müller, in which a traveller journeys out of town, dwelling on memories of an unfaithful lover. Poetically, the songs explore the psychological journey as much as the actual one, charting the loneliness of the protagonist through desolate winter scenery. Musically, the hypnotic rhythms of the sparse accompaniments form a desolate background to the subdued melancholy of the vocals. Schubert's genius lay in providing infinite variety within this unity of mood— 24 vivid shades of grey.

☑ **The Vienna Philharmonic Orchestra** has recorded many of Schubert's works. Recommended recordings include Symphonies No. 3 and No. 8. Here Joseph Krips conducts the "Unfinished" in 1969.

The German baritone Dietrich Fischer-Dieskau is a pre-eminent Lieder singer, and has performed and recorded both of Schubert's major song cycles.

SYMPHONY NO. 8 IN B MINOR, "UNFINISHED", D759

ORCHESTRAL   ⏱ 24:30   📖 2   ♫

The "Unfinished" Symphony, written in 1822, was not heard until the manuscript was rediscovered and performed in 1865. Sketches exist for a third movement, quashing theories that Schubert thought the work complete. It is actually the most complete of a number of unfinished symphonies by the composer.

It has been suggested that the dark turmoil of the first movement mirrors Schubert's state of mind when he found out that he had contracted syphilis. Unlike the "Wanderer" Fantasy of the same period, this is introverted music, with each of the principal themes being introduced as quietly as possible. The movement is marked by passages of gentle lyricism interrupted by fierce outbursts. The music of the second movement repeatedly tends towards agitation. Until the last few moments of the ethereal coda, it never quite recaptures the serenity of the opening. Even the beautiful clarinet melody is usurped by its syncopated string accompaniment.

SYMPHONY NO. 9, THE "GREAT", D944

ORCHESTRAL   ⏱ 62:00   📖 4   ♫

Visiting Schubert's brother in 1828, Schumann discovered this symphony, and sent it to Mendelssohn, who premiered it the following year. Nicknamed the "Great" for its size, its Classical form and proportions encompass a Romantic lyricism and richness of harmonic and orchestral colour that bridge the gap between Beethoven and Bruckner.

INFLUENCES

At his death, little of Schubert's music had been published, except for a number of songs and some mature works. Its slow dissemination in the 19th century limited its influence, as harmonic turns—surprisingly advanced for the 1820s—appeared commonplace at their first hearing 40 years later.

> **❝** Schubert's **life** was one of **inner, spiritual thought,** and was seldom **expressed** in words but **almost entirely in music. ❞**
>
> **Franz Eckel,** Schubert's friend from childhood

Hector **Berlioz**

🌑 **1803–1869**   🏳 **FRENCH**   ✍ **124**

Little appreciated in France during his lifetime, Berlioz's music and life embodied Romantic ideals perhaps more than any other composer barring Liszt. His imagination, grandiose conceptions, and extraordinary skill in orchestration brought a new pictorialism to music. The first major composer who was not an instrumental performer, he became one of the first modern conductors, as well as a perceptive critic.

⚠ **Berlioz's final years** saw the publication of his fascinating memoirs. On his deathbed he whispered, "At last, they will now play my music."

Life

Expected to become a doctor like his father, Berlioz received only a rudimentary early music training and, lacking a piano, had to study harmony in secret from treatises. In Paris, his medical studies succumbed to frequent visits to the Opéra and private musical study and, against his parents' wishes, he enrolled at the Conservatoire. There he heard Beethoven's symphonies and read Goethe's *Faust*, but his most formative experience was attending performances of Shakespeare, where his passion for the Bard was eclipsed only by his obsession for the leading lady, Harriet Smithson. Her initial rejection inspired the *Symphonie fantastique*, but they were later married for nine disastrous years. Winning the Conservatoire's highest award, the Prix de Rome, did little to increase acceptance of his music, and in spite of a generous gift from Paganini, Berlioz turned to music journalism to support himself, where his erudite but acerbic wit did little to endear him to his peers. A third career beckoned when, unhappy with performances of his works, he started to conduct them himself, and then found himself in demand as an international conductor. For the following 20 years he toured extensively, and wrote some of his most important operatic and choral works.

» **Berlioz first saw Harriet Smithson** in 1827 when she played Ophelia in *Hamlet* by Shakespeare. He finally met her in 1832 and they married in 1833.

Music

Unaccomplished as an instrumentalist, Berlioz instead made the orchestra his instrument. Eschewing the popularity of chamber and solo works, he expressed his intense personality in dramatic and often epic orchestral, operatic, and choral forms. His works blurred formal boundaries by frequently incorporating programmatic elements, as in the operatic choral symphony *Romeo and Juliet* and the symphonic concerto *Harold in Italy*. More revolutionary still was his use of orchestration. Not afraid to employ huge forces and newly invented instruments, and to redistribute players around the hall, even offstage, he was able to paint both subtler and more blazing colors than had previously been imagined. His melodies fall naturally, avoiding the regular beat and stylized ornamentation of Italianate music, while his harmony encompasses surprising dissonances for dramatic ends. As he wrote in his memoirs, "The ruling characteristics of my music are passionate expression, intense ardor, rhythmical animation, and unexpected turns."

❝ Every **composer knows** the **anguish** and **despair** occasioned by **forgetting ideas** which one has no time to write down. ❞   **Hector Berlioz**

MILESTONES

1821	Enters medical school in Paris; makes first visits to the Opéra	**1834**	Composes *Harold in Italy*, viola concerto
		1837	Writes *Grande messe des morts*
1824	Gives up medicine; composes *Messe solonnelle* (lost in 1835, found in 1991)	**1841**	*Les Nuits d'été*, vocal work, composed
		1842	Begins first of many international tours
1828	Hears Beethoven's symphonies and reads Goethe's *Faust*	**1849**	Composes Te Deum
1830	*Symphonie fantastique* wins Prix de Rome	**1858**	Writes *The Trojans*, opera

KEY WORKS

SYMPHONIE FANTASTIQUE, OP. 14

ORCHESTRAL   ⏲ 56:00   📖 5   ♫

Inspired by Beethoven, Berlioz decided to become a symphonist himself. This work became a Romantic autobiography about his obsession with Harriet Smithson, who is musically portrayed by an *idée fixe*. His concert notes described a young musician of great sensibility and imagination, in despair because of hopeless love. Opium plunges him into a heavy sleep accompanied by weird visions. Ranging from calm and melancholy to passion and despair, the artist recalls the time before love, then its delirious effect, and religious consolation. A brilliant and sumptuous waltz halts dramatically as the beloved's theme is heard once again. Offstage players depict far-off shepherds piping. The melancholy artist almost achieves tranquillity, but the beloved is recalled and distant thunder sounds. To rasping brass and winds, the artist is condemned to death for his beloved's murder. We hear her plaintive theme, the blade drops and crowds cheer. Grotesquely parodied, the beloved joins the devilish orgy while the ancient plainsong "Dies Irae" is intoned, surrounded by tolling bells.

TE DEUM, OP. 22

CHORAL   ⏲ 47:00   📖 6   ♫

Written to be heard in church, Berlioz described this piece as being not only the ceremonial hymn of thanksgiving usual in a Te Deum, but also an offering of prayers whose humility and melancholy contrast with the majesty of the hymns. His placing of the orchestra and chorus (including a large children's choir) at the opposite end of the church

to the organ was essential to the musical effect. Berlioz also reordered the traditional text to control the overall tension of the work. In addition to the six choral movements, there are two instrumental movements—originally designed for ceremonial purposes—that are not always included in modern performances.

THE TROJANS

OPERA   ⏲ 240:00   📖 5   ♫

Berlioz based his magnum opus, *Les Troyens*, on Virgil's *Aeneid*, completing both libretto and music in two years. The first two acts depict the story of the Trojan Horse, and the remainder, Dido and Aeneas in Carthage. It was first performed in 1863 as two separate operas as is often the case today.

GRANDE MESSE DES MORTS (REQUIEM), OP. 5

MASS SETTING   ⏲ 76:00   📖 10   ♫

Berlioz's forceful and vivid setting of the Requiem, with its massive orchestra including 12 horns, 16 timpani, and four brass ensembles, immerses the listener in the drama of the text.

INFLUENCES

Apart from the *Symphonie fantastique*, Berlioz's works were seldom heard until the 1880s, when they were revived in France as an antidote to Wagner. Only after the 1950s did his music become widely disseminated, although logistical difficulties still prevent regular performances of some of his works.

Felix **Mendelssohn**

● 1809–1847   ♩ GERMAN   ✍ 321

One of the most naturally gifted and accomplished musicians in the history of music, Mendelssohn preserved Classical ideals of harmony and form. As such, he was admired by conservative music lovers for his charm, craftsmanship, and picturesque imagination, particularly in staid Victorian drawing rooms, but his music was eclipsed as soon as the public fully embraced the ideals of Romanticism.

>> **Until his sister Fanny's death,** Mendelssohn's life was relatively free of torment, struggle, or frustration, a fact that is mirrored in his sunny, cheerful music.

Life

Born into a wealthy, cultured family, Mendelssohn had the finest private education available. His musical training was so thorough that it included the hiring of orchestras to try out his compositions. Felix showed talents not only as a violinist, pianist, organist, composer, and conductor, but also in fine art and poetry, and in his teens he became a protégé of Goethe. One of the first musicians to be fully aware of musical history, at the age of 20

> " A **Romantic** who felt at ease within the **mold of Classicism.** "
>
> **Pablo Casals,** cellist and conductor

he conducted the second-ever performance of Bach's *St. Matthew Passion*, leading to the 19th-century Bach revival. As he later recalled, "It was a Jew who restored this great Christian work to the people" (the Mendelssohns had actually converted to Christianity in 1816). There followed three years of travel and concert-giving. His love of all things British drew him back for ten lengthy visits to England and Scotland. He returned to conducting posts in Düsseldorf and then Leipzig, where he conducted the Gewandhaus orchestra. Here he established the now universal concept of programming both historical and modern works. Following the death of his sister Fanny, also a gifted pianist and composer, Mendelssohn suffered a series of strokes, and died at the age of 38.

Music

Mendelssohn's style does not fit easily with other Romantic music, and it has been suggested that he could be called neo-Classical. He drew on the fugal technique of Bach, the textures and clarity of Mozart, and the orchestration of Beethoven. By his mid-teens, his style, as evinced by the overture to *A Midsummer Night's Dream*, had crystallized. Unlike his radical contemporaries, Mendelssohn used well-established forms, adapting them to his needs, but retaining their underlying principles. Neither sensuous nor flamboyant, his natural melodic gifts were always coupled with the very highest levels of craftsmanship. Where his music is specifically Romantic is in its use of extra-musical stimuli. Literary, artistic, and geographical inspiration drew forth the best from his picturesque imagination, and descriptive, rather than psychological, imagery informs much of his finest work.

MILESTONES

1818	First public performance	1835	Director of Leipzig Gewandhaus
1821	First visit to Goethe	1837	Marries Cécile Jeanrenaud
1823	Grandmother gives him a score of J. S. Bach's *St. Matthew Passion*	1839	Conducts first performance of Schubert's "Great" Symphony No. 9
1825	*Octet*, Op. 20, is published	1841	Conducts first performance of Schumann's Symphony No. 1
1826	Overture to *A Midsummer Night's Dream*, Op. 21; attends Hegel's course on esthetics	1842	*Variations Sérieuses*, Op. 54; premiere of the "Scottish" Symphony
1829	Conducts *St. Matthew Passion*; first visit to England and Scotland	1844	Violin Concerto, Op. 64, is published
1832	First volume of *Lieder Ohne Worte* (*Songs Without Words*), Op. 19	1846	First performance of *Elijah*, Op. 70

KEY WORKS

VIOLIN CONCERTO, OP. 64

ORCHESTRAL	⧖ 25.00	📖 3	🔹 🔊

This famous and popular concerto in E minor was the last of Mendelssohn's orchestral works, and the last of his three violin concertos. The composer was too ill to conduct his friend Ferdinand David at the premiere, and was replaced by the Danish composer Niels Gade. The work was innovative in a number of ways, and the piece's three movements are played without interruption.
First movement (*allegro molto appassionato*, 11:00) Flying in the face of convention, Mendelssohn allowed the violin to present the memorable opening theme before the orchestra. This move influenced the majority of composers who followed him. He also moved the cadenza forward from the end of the movement, presumably to allow the tension to subside before the seamless entry of the second movement accompanied by the bassoon.
Second movement (*andante*, 8:00) A simple "song without words" with a more agitated central section, this slow movement gives the soloist nothing to hide behind but his own tone, intonation, and musical imagination.
Third movement (*allegro non troppo*, 6:00) Opening with its own fanfare, in this movement all our Mendelssohnian expectations of gossamer-light fantasy are fulfilled with effervescent virtuosity.

A MIDSUMMER NIGHT'S DREAM, OP. 21, 61

INCIDENTAL MUSIC	⧖ 35:00	📖 9	🔹

The overture and incidental music in this suite come from opposite ends of Mendelssohn's life, but use much of the same musical material.
Overture (*allegro di moto*, 12:00) Mendelssohn orchestrated this precocious answer to the magic of Shakespeare's play at the age of 18. Opening with chords to depict the procession of Oberon and Titania, we are swiftly immersed in the scurrying fairy world. A touching melody describes the lovers, while a rustic dance for the "mechanicals" is interrupted by frequent donkey brays.
Incidental music (23:00) Four of the eight pieces were conceived as entr'actes (music between acts), most famously the fleeting fairy Scherzo. Also set are two songs, "You Spotted Snakes" and "Through This House Give Glimmering Light..." for soprano, mezzo, and chorus. Finally, the ubiquitous *Wedding March* first saw the light of day here.

INFLUENCES

Numerous musicians over the past two centuries have been admirers of the work of Mendelssohn, but few, if any, can be said to have been influenced by it. However, Mendelssohn's part in the great 19th-century Bach revival turned a cult into a popular movement whose effect on subsequent generations is impossible to overestimate.

🖼 Mendelssohn's *Wedding March* was first officially used at the wedding of the Princess Royal of Great Britain in 1858.

Frédéric **Chopin**

◉ 1810–1849   ▨ POLISH   ✍ 219

Exiled by revolution, abandoned by his mistress, dying of consumption, but always elegantly dressed, the frail image of Chopin fulfills all the stereotypes of the Romantic artist. The first poet of the piano, his music was immediately popular and has always transcended the vagaries of fashion. A national hero, his music announced the liberation of his native Poland and still accompanies international statesmen to their graves.

⏩ **Chopin's exquisitely crafted piano music is** highly regarded for its lyricism, purity, and delicate charm.

Life

Exiled from Poland by the Russian capture of Warsaw in 1831, Chopin made his home and his name in the piano capital of the world—Paris. Preferring private performances in the salons of Parisian nobility to the strain and artistic compromises of courting the general public, he also developed a very lucrative career teaching ladies of aristocratic birth. In 1836 Liszt introduced him to George Sand, the novelist who had outraged Paris with her cigar-smoking and trouser-wearing. A nine-year relationship followed, during which Chopin wrote the majority of his most important works, starting with the Preludes, completed during the couple's stay in Majorca. However, his health began to wane, and following the couple's separation in 1847, it deteriorated rapidly and he wrote almost no more music. Following an extended visit to England and Scotland in 1848, he died the following year in Paris; 3,000 people attended his funeral.

Music

All of Chopin's music includes a piano, and most of it is for that instrument alone. His works seem to have sprung fully formed onto the page. Notation was simply the last stage of a process of improvisation at the keyboard, and it was not unusual for a work to evolve further after publication.

His early music was written for his own concerts, and is fairly typical of the virtuoso material of the day, but after giving up the concert platform he found his unique voice, and every single work is a masterpiece. A simple, melodic style was refined and extended in numerous miniatures written primarily for his pupils, while virtuosity was sublimated into lofty drama in the more complex, large-scale concert works. Chopin was particularly drawn to dance forms—the waltz is evident in many works. Chopin was particularly drawn to dance forms—the waltz is evident in many works—but it was with the mazurka and the polonaise that he was able to assert his true, Polish identity.

❝ After **playing Chopin,** I feel as if I had been **weeping over sins** that I had **never committed,** and mourning over **tragedies** that were **not my own.** ❞

Oscar Wilde, 1891

MILESTONES

1818	Gives first concert	**1836**	Becomes engaged to Maria Wodzinska; meets George Sand
1826	Becomes a student at Warsaw Conservatory		
1829	Two concerts in Vienna; Variations, Op. 2, favorably reviewed by Robert Schumann	**1837**	Engagement broken; visits London; Etudes, Op. 25, published
1830	Debut of Piano Concerto No. 2, Op. 21	**1838**	Goes to Majorca with George Sand
1831	Arrives in Paris, meets Liszt	**1839**	Preludes, Op. 28, completed
1832	Meets Mendelssohn and Berlioz	**1846**	Composes *Barcarolle*, Op. 60
1835	Meets Robert Schumann, composes *Andante Spianato*	**1847**	Separates from Sand
		1848	Last concert in Paris, tours Britain

KEY WORKS

PIANO CONCERTO NO. 2 IN F MINOR, OP. 21

ORCHESTRAL   ⏱ 26:15   📖 3   🎵

Chopin wrote his piano concertos to launch the virtuoso career that he later found so distasteful. **First movement** (*maestoso*, 11:00) After the first performance in 1830, Chopin wrote: "The first Allegro of my concerto, which relatively few could grasp, called forth applause, but it seems to me that people felt they had to show interest and pretend to be connoisseurs."
Second movement (*larghetto*, 8:00) Inspired by his feelings for Constantia Gladkowska, Chopin wrote that the slow movement "belonged" to her. With its distinctive harmony, poetic lyricism, and ornate decoration it stands in sharp relief to other concertos of the period.
Third movement (*allegro vivace*, 7:15) Virtuosic yet always elegant, the finale pays tribute to the mazurka of Polish folk music. The horn call that ushers in the exciting coda was a great surprise to early audiences.

PRELUDES, OP. 28

SOLO PIANO   ⏱ 35:00   📖 24   🎵

There is a breathtaking variety in these 24 pieces, perhaps the most forward-looking of all Chopin's music. Exploring every key, they are full of harmonic surprises and enigmatic melodies. Among the many later composers inspired by the Preludes were Debussy and Rachmaninoff.

BARCAROLLE, OP. 60

SOLO PIANO   ⏱ 8:40   📖 1   🎵

Originally named after the *barcarole* sung by Venetian gondoliers, the barcarolle was probably first popularized as a musical form outside its native city by travelers returning from the Grand Tour. Beloved by Romantic audiences for its gentle evocations of love, it was soon appropriated by composers for solo and operatic vocal works, perhaps most famously in Offenbach's *The Tales of Hoffmann*.

The form also became associated with the piano, as Mendelssohn, Liszt, and Fauré penned a number of fine examples, but none is more celebrated than Chopin's. His last major work, it was premiered by the composer at his last recital in Paris in 1848. Although it was written not long before his final estrangement from George Sand, it shows no signs of melancholy. Featuring an almost continuous lilting rhythm, the bass conjures the ebb and flow of the water, while the rich harmony supplies the scene's shimmering, shifting colors. Two long alternating melodies evoke the vocal origins of the genre, evolving from beautiful simplicity to sublime radiance. Foreshadowing the music of Alexander Scriabin over 40 years later, the complex harmonies of the coda create one of the most extraordinary moments in the piano repertoire.

≫ **Frédéric Chopin completed the Preludes** in this cell in an abandoned monastery in Majorca in January, 1839.

Robert **Schumann**

● **1810–1856**   ♙ **GERMAN**   ✍ **268**

Schumann's deep and sensitive musicianship makes little attempt to play to the gallery, instead drawing the listener into the composer's remote and enigmatic inner world. Perhaps the most elusive composer of the Romantic period, his music is at turns fanciful, introspective, and bombastic. Daringly original, and frequently impractical, he captured, as no other did, the innocent spirit of early German Romantic literature.

》 By turns whimsical, fantastic, and grotesque, Schumann's music is the apotheosis of Romanticism, rich in literary allusions.

attempt to strengthen his fingers, but probably as a result of a cure he was taking for syphilis, he gave up hope of a concert career and devoted himself to composition. In 1834, as editor of a new music journal, the *Neue Zeitschrift für Musik*, he brought the music of the young Chopin and Brahms to popular attention.

In spite of their age gap, Clara and Robert fell in love, exchanging their first kiss in 1835. Her father banned the liaison, but they took him to court, and were eventually married in 1840. They started a large family (seven children survived), but Schumann, in whose family mental illness ran, started to suffer badly from depression. In 1854, he attempted suicide by throwing himself into the River Rhine. Rescued, he entered an asylum where he died.

Life

Obsessed equally by music and literature as a boy, though receiving no thorough education in either, Schumann was persuaded by his mother to become a lawyer. While studying in Leipzig he heard Paganini play, and decided instead to become a musician. Enrolling with a local piano teacher, Friedrich Wieck, whose 11-year-old daughter, Clara, was already a piano prodigy, he gave up his law studies and moved into Wieck's home. When he injured his hand, allegedly in an

Music

Between 1830 and 1840 Schumann published several piano masterpieces. Happiest when capturing moods and ideas in the white heat of inspiration, he showed a love of miniatures, and grouping several together around a common musical or conceptual theme, he created the Romantic piano suite. He was less accomplished in the structuring of large-scale movements. Of his more expansive piano works, only the Fantasy in C makes a lasting impression. Following in the footsteps of Schubert, he then focused on the art song, completing 19 song cycles in one year alone. Chamber music, largely ignored by his contemporaries, was his next target. It drew forth some of his finest mature work, including three string quartets and works for piano and strings. He also penned four symphonies, which are among the most impassioned symphonic music of their time.

" I am **affected by everything** that goes on **in the world...** and then **I long to express** my **feelings** in **music. "**

Robert Schumann

MILESTONES

1828	Enters Leipzig University	**1838**	Composes *Kinderszenen*, Op. 15, and *Kreisleriana*, Op. 16
1830	Hears Paganini; gives up law for music		
1831	*Abegg Variations*, Op. 1, and *Papillons*, Op. 2, published	**1839**	Discovers Schubert's "Great" Symphony No. 9
		1840	Marries Clara; composes songs
1832	Injures hand	**1842**	Completes three string quartets, the Piano Quintet, Op. 44, and the Piano Quintet, Op. 47
1834	First edition of the music journal *Neue Zeitschrift für Musik*		
1835	Completes *Carnaval*, Op. 9	**1844**	Suffers from depression and a nervous breakdown; moves to Dresden
1836	Is forced to break off all relations with Clara	**1853**	Meets Brahms

KEY WORKS

FANTASY IN C, OP. 17

SOLO PIANO   ⏱ 30:00   📖 3   👁

Dedicated to Liszt, the superlative 1838 Fantasy in C was originally Schumann's tribute to Beethoven. At a time when he was forbidden to see his beloved Clara, the lines by the poet Friedrich von Schiller that preface the work were certainly intended for her eyes: "Through all the sounds of Earth's mingled dream, lies one quiet note for the secret listener."

Ruins (*Durchaus phantastisch und leidenschaftlich vorzutragen*, 12:00) This impassioned and kaleidoscopic outpouring finds little peace even in the earthbound central interlude. Only at the end do we achieve tranquillity, when Schumann quotes a song from Beethoven's *An die ferne Geliebte*. It is no coincidence that its opening words are "Take then these songs, my love."

Triumphal arch (*Mässig*, 7:00) An overwhelmingly extrovert march whose infectious drive is produced by an almost constant stream of asymmetric rhythms even in the graceful middle section. In the maniacally exuberant leaps of the final pages, joy is unconfined. "It makes me hot and cold all over," Clara wrote.

Wreath of stars (*Langsam getragen*, 11:00) Unusually, a calm, slow movement ends the piece. Schumann's mercurial nature manifests itself in a vast musical landscape suggesting both serene peace and utter despair.

DICHTERLIEBE, OP. 48

SONG CYCLE   ⏱ 28:00   📖 16   👁 🎵

For Schumann it was a small step from writing cycles of piano music such as *Carnaval*, where moods are swiftly captured, to distilling the essence of a poem in a song. Until 1840 he claimed that song was an inferior medium to instrumental music and ignored it, but once he had started, before the year was out he had written more than 150 individual songs.

The song cycle *Dichterliebe* (*A Poet's Love*) explores the journey from the joy of new love, through failure, to renunciation. The setting of Heinrich Heine's frequently bitter words is quietly compelling yet heart-rending in its lyrical pathos. Equally striking is his use of the piano; no longer an "accompanist," it is an equal partner, which sets the scene and then adds to and comments upon the narrative. In the majority of the songs, Schumann adds a piano postlude, in which he sums up the mood, most poignantly at the end of the cycle, where he reflects on all that has passed. It is astounding that Schumann completed this entire masterpiece in only nine days.

INFLUENCES

Schumann's most important music was too subtle and quirky to gain much popularity in his own lifetime, and he met with very little success as a conductor and teacher. It was mainly through performances by his widow, and by friends such as Joseph Joachim and Brahms, that his music eventually entered the musical canon.

⌂ **Schumann's workroom in Zwickau,** where he lived until leaving for Leipzig to study law. While at school he read Schiller, Goethe, Byron, and Jean Paul.

Clara Josephine **Schumann**

● 1819–1896   ⚑ GERMAN   ✑ c.45

Under her father's tuition, Clara Wieck became a great pianist, championing the music of Chopin, Schumann, and Brahms. She received widespread praise for her technique and bold repertoire, and for her thoughtful interpretations and pianistic singing tone, but marriage to Schumann, against her father's wishes, and numerous pregnancies curtailed her career. After Schumann's death she resumed touring and teaching, and also edited his music.

Originally composing showpieces for her own concerts, her attitude to composition became increasingly ambivalent, and she wrote nothing after 1854. Clara's best work shows imagination and craftsmanship, but lacks melodic individuality. Her intimate friendship with Brahms is generally believed to have been platonic.

MILESTONES	
1828	First public performance in Leipzig; meets Robert Schumann
1835	Composes *Piano Concerto*, Op. 7
1838	Appointed Kammervirtuosin to the Austrian court
1844	Tours Russia
1846	*Piano Trio*, Op. 17 published

⌃ **When Robert Schumann first heard** Clara's charming *Romances* he wrote, "I can hear that we are destined to be man and wife. You complete me as a composer."

Charles Valentin **Alkan**

● 1813–1888   ⚑ FRENCH   ✑ c.100

Born Charles Henri Valentin Morhange, one of six Jewish children who all went on to become musicians, Alkan was a child prodigy, having his first compositions for piano published at age 14. During his youth he was a close friend of Chopin

and Liszt, but over time he became reclusive and often disappeared for long spells. His concert appearances before 1873 were few, and although they established him as a virtuoso pianist, he preferred not to play his own compositions.

Alkan's music is original, brilliant, and often hugely demanding—his Op. 39 includes a full "symphony" and "concerto," but scored for unaccompanied piano.

MILESTONES	
1819	Enrolled in Paris Conservatoire
1838	*Le Chemin de Fer*, Op. 2, for piano
1847	25 Preludes, Op. 31, published
1857	Compiles 12 Études in all the Minor Keys, Op. 39
1860s	Disappears from public life
1873	Reappears to give concerts

« **Enrolled in the Paris Conservatoire** at age six, Alkan won many prizes for his piano playing there, one of the most prestigious being the Conservatoire first prize for piano, which he won at age 11.

Charles-François **Gounod**

🔘 **1818–1893** 📖 **FRENCH** ✏️ **c.500**

Remembered today mainly for his operas *Faust* and *Roméo et Juliette*, Gounod was enormously popular in France and Britain during his lifetime, and his elegant, graceful style influenced many French composers at the turn of the century, including Massenet, Bizet, and Saint-Saëns.

A devout Catholic, Gounod considered becoming a priest, and his early works were nearly all choral church music, inspired by his study of Palestrina's music in Italy. The best known of his settings of the mass, the *Messe Solennelle de Ste. Cécile*, brought him to public attention in 1855 and marked the turning point in his career. At this time he also began to write orchestral music, including two Symphonies, and operas. Gounod's first success came with *Le médecin malgré lui*, performed at the Théatre-Lyrique in 1858, and was followed by *Faust* the year after, and culminated with *Roméo et Juliette* in 1867.

Gounod sat out the Franco-Prussian War in England, where he wrote a great deal of music for the choral societies popular there. He also became involved (probably platonically) with a married woman, Georgina Weldon, and the public scandal began to eclipse his reputation as a composer. He returned to Paris in 1874, and went back to writing mainly religious choral music. In all, he wrote more than 20 settings of the mass, 12 operas, and over 100 songs.

MILESTONES

1852	Conducts Orphéon Choral Society
1858	Composes *Faust*, opera
1867	*Roméo et Juliette*, opera, performed
1886	*Mors et vita*, oratorio, performed for Queen Victoria in London

Franz Adolf **Berwald**

🔘 **1796–1868** 📖 **SWEDISH** ✏️ **80**

The startling originality and modern-sounding harmonies of Berwald's music met with little enthusiasm in his lifetime; he had more success running his orthopedic institute. Marriage, and small triumphs in Vienna, inspired him again. His music—bold, cheerful, and generous, like the man—has since established him as Sweden's first major composer.

Born into a family of musicians in Stockholm, Franz Adolf Berwald became a violinist in the court orchestra and opera when he was a teenager, with an ambition to become a full-time composer. He got a scholarship to study in Berlin, but found it difficult to get his music performed and after some years of frustration and financial difficulty he gave up composition to set up an orthopedic clinic.

By 1841, Berwald had made enough money to move to Vienna, where he married and resumed composing. Encouraged by the reception of his music in Austria, he wrote a number of orchestral works, including four symphonies, hoping for a similarly positive reception in Sweden. Unfortunately, only his first Symphony was given a performance, and it was not well received.

In order to make a living, he took a job at a friend's glassworks, and only in the last few years of his life was his talent recognized by his appointment as professor at the Stockholm Conservatory and performance of his work.

MILESTONES

1812	Violinist in court orchestra
1835	Abandons composing for orthopedics
1845	Symphony No. 3 (unperformed)
1855	Piano Concerto (unperformed)
1862	*Estrella de Soria*, opera, finally performed

Johannes **Brahms**

◉ 1833–1897　　🕮 GERMAN　　✍ 135

Brahms is a towering figure in 19th-century music, perhaps the last great composer in the Classical tradition. Once regarded as the unfashionable antithesis of Wagner and Liszt, his music has proven itself to be not only powerfully affecting, but also an important influence on the development of 20th-century music. A sometimes difficult man, he composed masterpieces in all genres except opera.

» **Though the music of Brahms** was rooted in the Classicism of past masters, its expressive and gigantic nature was Romantic at its core.

Life

Born to a poor family in Hamburg, Brahms showed early promise as a musician. From around the age of 13, however, he made extra income for the family by playing in bars and houses of ill repute. Attempting to make a career as a pianist, in 1853 Brahms toured with the violinist Eduard Reményi and during the trip he made three of the most important acquaintances of his life: the violinist Joseph Joachim, the composer Robert Schumann, and the latter's wife, Clara, herself a renowned pianist. Schumann was so impressed with Brahms's compositions that he wrote a glowing article proclaiming him to be Beethoven's heir. This gave Brahms's career an immediate boost, but heaped expectation upon him. When Schumann suffered a breakdown the following year, Brahms went to Düsseldorf to help Clara and her family. He fell deeply in love with her, and their relationship after Schumann died has been a source of great speculation. They were undoubtedly intimate friends, and Brahms entrusted Clara with the first reading of many of his greatest works. Brahms was famously abrasive and often made tactless remarks; this hid a sensitive and thoughtful character who could be very generous with his time (and money), and inspired great loyalty from his friends.

Music

Brahms is often considered to be the last great composer in the Germanic Classical tradition, which stretches back through Beethoven, Mozart, and Haydn to Bach. When the trend in composition was toward programmatic music, he refused to see himself as a "modern" composer. Instead, he stuck to the Classical forms used by the masters and often spoke of the pressure he felt composing in their shadow. This dichotomy between Brahms's Classicism and the "progressive" music of Wagner, Liszt, and Bruckner has become a key theme in 19th-century music history. But, as Schoenberg first showed in a now infamous essay titled "Brahms the progressive," Brahms's music was nonetheless extremely innovative. The key to his innovation is the "developing variation," the constant reworking of small fragments of musical material as a composition progresses, epitomized in late works such as the Clarinet Quintet. This style of writing paved the way for music in which every aspect of a composition arises from the same thematic cell. Rarely rhetorical, Brahms's music is frequently described as "autumnal"—passionate and romantic, yet controlled, refined, and infused with melancholy.

> ❝ **Without craftsmanship, inspiration** is a **mere reed shaken** in the wind. ❞ **Johannes Brahms**

MILESTONES

1845	Studies piano with Otto Cossel and theory with Edward Marxsen
1854	Schumann institutionalized; Brahms moves to Düsseldorf to help Clara
1857	Composes Piano Concerto No.1, Op. 15
1863	Director of the Vienna Singakademie
1867	Composes *Ein Deutches Requiem*, Op. 45
1872	Conductor of Vienna Gesellschaftskonzerte
1876	Premiere of Symphony No. 1, Op. 68
1877	Symphony No. 2, Op. 78
1878	Violin Concerto, Op. 77

1881	Piano Concerto No. 2, Op. 83
1883	Symphony No. 3, Op. 90
1885	Symphony No. 4, Op. 98
1887	Writes Double Concerto for Violin and Cello, Op. 102
1890	String Quintet, Op. 111
1891	Hears clarinetist Richard Mühlfeld and writes Clarinet Quintet Op. 115 and Clarinet Trio Op. 114
1896	Clara Schumann dies; composes *Vier Ernste Gesänge*, Op. 121

⏏ **Brahms spent his adolescence** in and around the docks of Hamburg, where he made money in taverns and brothels performing piano tricks for the locals.

KEY WORKS

CLARINET QUINTET, OP. 115

CHAMBER   ⏱ **36:00**   📖 **4**   ♟

On completing the String Quintet No. 2 in 1890, Brahms resolved to retire from composition. However, inspired by the playing of clarinetist Richard Mühlfeld, he wrote both the Clarinet Trio and the Clarinet Quintet. The Quintet has come to be seen as his very finest chamber work.

First movement (*allegro*, 12:00) All the melodic material in this sonata-form movement stems from the opening theme, presented by the two violins.

Second movement (*adagio*, 12:00) The adagio begins with a peaceful clarinet melody. The central section is a remarkable imitation of Hungarian folk music, with wild arpeggios.

Third movement (*andantino—presto non assai, ma con sentimento*, 4:00) The movement begins as an intermezzo, but quickly reveals itself to be a lively sonata-form movement based on a scurrying figure introduced by the violins.

Fourth movement (*con moto*, 8:00) After the dark and unsettled theme is explored in five variations, the opening phrase from the first movement makes an unexpected return, giving a sense of finality.

SYMPHONY NO. 3, OP. 90

ORCHESTRAL   ⏱ **33:00**   📖 **4**   ♫

The most compact of his symphonies, and perhaps the most immediately accessible, in Brahms's lifetime the popularity of his Symphony

 Although Brahms was seen as old-fashioned by admirers of Wagner and Liszt, he was highly regarded by many of his peers.

No. 3 was such that the composer took to describing it as "unfortunately over-famous." As is so common with Brahms, the key to the whole first movement is in the first few bars. The majestic first theme has been seen by some critics as a direct reference to Schumann's Symphony No. 3. The simple folklike theme of the second movement spoke to Clara Schumann of "worshippers kneeling about their little forest shrine." In the third movement, one of Brahms's most beautiful creations, the heart-wrenching theme appears first on cello before returning after the somber Trio section, now on the French horn. The Finale begins in brooding fashion before more animated development leads eventually to a quiet, satisfying close, replete with ghostly hints of the first movement's opening theme.

EIN DEUTCHES REQUIEM, OP. 45

BIBLICAL SETTING ⏳ 70:00   📖 7   🎵 ♙ ♟

A German Requiem, first performed in its complete form in 1868, made Brahms's reputation in Vienna, and remains one of his most consistently popular works. Rather than use the standard Requiem texts, Brahms chose his own passages from the Lutheran Bible, avoiding reference to Christianity and—notably—omitting the Last Judgment entirely. Although a believer, he was not overtly religious, and later said that he would have liked to replace the word "German" with "Human" in the title. This has led some writers to suggest that the real motivation for the work was an expression of his pain at the deaths of his mother and of Robert Schumann.

A German Requiem contains some of the composer's most haunting and poignant music. The fourth part, "Wie schön sind deine Wohnungen" ("How Lovely are thy Dwellings Fair") is the emotional core of the work, with the remaining six parts forming a huge arch structure around it. The final part, "Selig sind die Toten" ("Blessed are the Dead"), recalls material from the first to give a sense of closure. By making use of choral fugues (in the second and sixth parts), Brahms deliberately evokes the spirit of Bach's sacred choral works.

SYMPHONY NO. 1, OP. 68

ORCHESTRAL   ⏳ 50:00   📖 4   🎵

Brahms had often spoken of hearing the "footsteps" of Beethoven behind him, and this self-imposed expectation is perhaps the reason it took him so long to write his first symphony (he began the work in 1862, but did not complete it until 1876). Immediately dubbed "Beethoven's Tenth," its lineage is plain to hear, but it is an epic and individual work.

>> **The influence of violinist Joseph Joachim** led Brahms to include Hungarian folk rhythms in some of his work. Joachim also introduced Brahms to the Schumanns.

Many of the piano works of Brahms, from the solo pieces to the concertos, have been performed or recorded by Russian pianist Evgeny Kissin.

VARIATIONS ON A THEME BY HANDEL, OP. 24

SOLO PIANO   ⏱ 27:00   📖 27   👁

Like Beethoven, Brahms was attracted to the variation form and wrote several sets of variations on themes from other composers. The "Handel Variations," based on an air from one of Handel's keyboard suites, are perhaps his most appealing.

PIANO QUARTET NO. 1, OP. 25

CHAMBER   ⏱ 40:00   📖 4   ♟

Brahms appeared as pianist in the premiere of his first piano quartet, the first time he had presented himself as such to a Viennese audience. A stormy, passionate, and youthful work, it displays typical Brahmsian hallmarks, particularly in the way that material is derived from the opening 4-note figure.

VIOLIN CONCERTO, OP. 77

ORCHESTRAL   ⏱ 38:00   📖 3   ♫ 👁

Brahms wrote this concerto for his great friend Joseph Joachim. It is a large-scale work, ferociously difficult for the violin soloist.

SYMPHONY NO. 4, OP. 98

ORCHESTRAL   ⏱ 42:00   📖 4   ♫

Perhaps lacking the melodic appeal of his earlier symphonies, this work has a rugged charm that epitomizes Brahms's own character. A critic once described hearing the first movement as akin to "being beaten by two very clever men."

VIER ERNSTE GESÄNGE, OP. 121

SONG   ⏱ 20:00   📖 4   👁 ♪

Brahms's contribution to the Lieder tradition is often overlooked, if only because his legacy is so significant elsewhere. In fact Brahms wrote a great many songs, of which the *Four Serious Songs*, composed as a response to the death of Clara Schumann, are perhaps his most affecting.

INFLUENCES

In one sense, Brahms was the last "Classical" composer, even in his own time viewed by some as an anachronism. Composers such as Dvořák and Reger were directly influenced by his music, although his indirect influence on the development of 20th-century music, through the advocacy of Schoenberg, is perhaps more significant.

Franz **Liszt**

◔ 1811–1886　　⚑ HUNGARIAN　　✎ 749

Liszt can truly be said to have been the central figure of the Romantic movement. As a young man he set Europe on fire with his astonishing pianistic gifts. He slowly gained recognition as a composer, developing the potential of the piano and the role of the pianist. As famous for his life as for his music, he worked tirelessly to promote his colleagues' work, and to teach subsequent generations of pianists and composers.

⌃ **Liszt was one of the first** in a long line of composer/musicians to gain celebrity as much for their stagecraft as for their music.

Life

By the age of 12, Liszt had already performed throughout Europe, but ill health and religious contemplation during his late teens saw him withdraw from public life. Only after hearing Paganini did he return to the piano, dazzling listeners with the unprecedented complexity of his music. Fame and fortune followed, but in 1835 he shocked Paris by eloping with the already married Countess Marie d'Agoult. Living in Switzerland and Italy they had three children, while Liszt focused on composition. Returning to the concert platform in 1838, he established the prototype of the modern concert pianist by performing from memory and giving the first solo recitals (indeed inventing the term). For eight years he toured extensively, but by 1847 he longed to settle and marry his new lover, Princess Carolyne Sayn-Wittgenstein. He became Kapellmeister at the court of Weimar, where until 1861 he wrote or revised most of his important works and taught the next generation of great pianists. However, when the Vatican stopped the annulment of the Princess's previous marriage, and following the deaths of two of his children, Liszt again sought solace in the Church. He became an abbé, but continued to compose, teach, and perform without income until his death.

Music

As a young virtuoso writing piano music to astound the public, Liszt's early works were showpieces that took piano technique to new heights of difficulty. Liszt incorporated virtuosity as an essential dramatic element of his music. However, his knowledge of the piano's evolving capabilities bore fruit in his transcriptions of operatic and symphonic music. Particularly in the symphonies of Beethoven and Berlioz, he found ways to transform the piano into a substitute orchestra.

Following his retirement from concert life, Liszt studied composition intensively. He became a true composer, whose harmonic language influenced Ravel and Wagner. During this period he produced his most important works—not only piano pieces, but also two symphonies and 12 symphonic poems, a genre he invented. In his final years, Liszt's experiments foreshadowed the music of the 20th century in its unstable harmonies and sparse textures.

MILESTONES	
1821	Studies with Beethoven's pupil, Carl Czerny
1822	First public concert in Vienna
1831	Hears Paganini play
1833	Transcribes Berlioz's *Symphonie fantastique*
1853	Composes Sonata in B Minor, S178
1857	Premiere of *Faust-Symphonie*, S108
1861	Moves to Rome, composes *Mephisto Waltz No. 1*, S110/514
1865	Takes minor orders of the Catholic Church, becoming an abbé

❝ My **mind** and **fingers** have worked like **two damned ones.** Unless I go mad, you will find an **artist in me.** ❞

The 21-year-old Liszt in a letter to a friend, 1832

KEY WORKS

PIANO CONCERTO NO. 1, S124

ORCHESTRAL   ⏱ 18:20   📖 4

Once one of the most popular works in the piano repertoire, Liszt's Piano Concerto No. 1 belongs to the unabashed virtuoso pianist. Now heard infrequently, suffering in part from its brevity, it was premiered in 1855 with Berlioz conducting and Liszt himself at the piano.

First movement (*allegro maestoso*, 5:15) Pianist and orchestra vie for attention with abrupt musical interjections in this kaleidoscopic movement.

Second movement (*quasi adagio*, 4:30) Simply the greatest nocturne Chopin never wrote. After presenting the exquisite melody, the piano destroys the mood, only to melt away as an accompaniment for the woodwinds.

Third movement (*allegretto vivace*, 4:20) Liszt's novel use of the triangle in this Scherzo drew much derision. The soloist's role gradually changes from one of restrained virtuosity to that of unchallenged protagonist.

Fourth movement (*allegro marziale animato*, 4:15) In a controlled series of gear changes, themes are brought back as pulses are inexorably raised.

FAUST-SYMPHONIE, S108

ORCHESTRAL   ⏱ 71:00   📖 3

Liszt wrote this work in 1854, having been introduced to Goethe's play *Faust* by Berlioz in 1830. The three movements depict the main characters: Faust, Gretchen, and Mephistopheles. The work ends with the addition of a tenor soloist and male chorus, for a setting of Goethe's "Chorus Mysticus."

MEPHISTO WALTZ NO. 1, S110/514

ORCHESTRAL/SOLO PIANO   ⏱ 10:00   📖 1

Written first for orchestra and then arranged for piano, the program for this work comes from Austrian poet Nikolaus Lenau's *Faust*, which differs from Goethe's play. In Lenau's version, Faust and Mephistopheles arrive at a tavern where, seeing a black-eyed beauty, Faust is overcome with reticence. Bored with the rustic music, Mephistopheles plays a diabolical waltz on the violin that inspires Faust and his inamorata to dance, then disappear into the woods. A spectacular and daring concert piece, the devilish outer sections are tempered by a seductive core, where the score explains that "they sink into the ocean of their own lust."

TRANSCENDENTAL ÉTUDES, S139

PIANO SOLO   📖 12

Exploring the possibility of orchestral sounds at the piano, this monumental cycle opened new doors, requiring pianists to use not just their fingers, but also their arms, shoulders, and backs to master the necessary combination of speed and power.

⬆ **Long after retiring from public performance,** Liszt would treat listeners to private recitals at his house in Weimar—now a museum devoted to the composer.

INFLUENCES

While Liszt's codification of the possibilities of the piano influenced nearly every piano composer who followed, only a few of his less important works were heard with any regularity after his death. Only in the 1960s was his music reassessed and given its rightful place in the musical pantheon.

Johann **Strauss Sr.**

◔ 1804–1849   ▥ AUSTRIAN   ✍ 251

Founder of the "Strauss Waltz Dynasty," Johann Strauss Sr. helped take the waltz—then a traditional Austrian folk dance—out of the village tavern and into Europe's finest ballrooms. He was famous for the rhythmic verve of his music and the finesse of his conducting, but his music has been eclipsed by the more memorable melodic gifts of his sons. He is now principally known for the stirring *Radetzky March*.

Of humble origins, Strauss learned to play the violin in his teens while apprenticed to a bookbinder, spending the evenings performing traditional dances in local taverns. Following the lead of Carl Maria von Weber's 1819 piano piece *Invitation to the Dance*, he expanded the Viennese waltz into a chain of dances framed by an introduction and coda, and was soon presenting these works with his own orchestra. A six-year contract to play at the prestigious Sperl dance hall consolidated his fame, and he was soon in demand at ballrooms across Europe.

MILESTONES	
1819	Joins Joseph Lanner's small band
1825	Marries Maria Anna Streim; forms own orchestra; Johann Strauss Jr born
1842	Writes *Beliebte Annen Polka*, Op. 137
1843	Composes *Loreley Rheinklänge*, Op. 154, and *Kunstlerball Tanze*, Op. 150
1846	Appointed first ever Royal and Imperial Hofballmusikdirektor

KEY WORKS

RADETZKY MARCH, OP. 228

DANCE   ⌛ 3:00   ▥ 1

On August 31, 1848, to celebrate the Austrian army's victory over an Italian revolutionary uprising at Custozza, an open-air victory festival was held in Vienna. The concert was dedicated to the 82-year-old Commander-in-Chief of the Imperial Austrian army, Count Radetzky von Radetz, and a special march had been commissioned from Strauss to celebrate the occasion. The march quickly became a Habsburg anthem, ensuring frequent performances and eventually bestowing immortality on a composer whose other works posterity has judged ephemeral.

The march actually incorporates two popular Viennese melodies which would have been very familiar to its first audiences. The outer, martial sections include a common street song, while the more gentle trio section features one of the previous season's most popular dance melodies.

CACHUCHA GALOP, OP. 97

DANCE   ⌛ 2:00   ▥ 1

In 1837, the Austrian ballerina Fanny Elssler performed "the cachucha"—a Spanish dance then very popular in Paris—for the audience of the Viennese Court Opera. After three performances of this "lascivious" dance, Vienna caught "cachucha fever." Strauss realized the financial potential of the situation and promptly wrote this hair-raising galop. The main section of the galop and the coda feature a castanet accompaniment to original melodies from the cachucha dance, while the central trio section is original Strauss.

LORELEY RHEINKLÄNGE, OP. 154

DANCE   ⌛ 5:40   ▥ 1

Echoes of the Rhine Lorelei was one of Strauss's most popular waltzes, and was performed to great acclaim in 1844 by his son Johann Strauss Jr., who went on to steal his father's crown.

⏏ **The partnership** between Strauss (violinist on left) and Joseph Lanner (violinist on right) began with a small band of Viennese musicians in 1819.

César Auguste **Franck**

🌑 **1822–1890**　　📛 **BELGIAN**　　✍ **97**

Franck's rejection of the frivolous and spectacular music of his contemporaries, in favor of symphonic and instrumental forms of high seriousness, strongly influenced successive generations of French composers. A late developer compositionally, his finest works—notable for their rich Wagner-inspired harmonies, innovative structures, and noble lyricism—were all written in his final years.

Franck toured Belgium as a pianist at the age of 11, but in maturity concentrated on composition. He later attracted considerable fame as an organist, and was subsequently appointed professor of the organ at the Paris Conservatoire, where his lofty music ideals inspired a group of young composers, including d'Indy and Dukas. A deeply religious man, Franck composed numerous sacred works, but his true legacy lies in the orchestral, keyboard, and chamber works written in the last years of his life. Harmonically rich, but based on traditional forms, these include some of the greatest French music of the Romantic period.

MILESTONES	
1837	Enrols at the Paris Conservatoire
1846	First performance of a large-scale work, biblical oratorio *Ruth*
1848	Marries actress Félicité Desmousseaux
1861	Appointed organist at Sainte-Clotilde Basilica, Paris
1862	First important work, *6 Pièces*, organ
1880	First performance of Piano Quintet, and *Les Béatitudes*, oratorio
1884	*Prelude, Chorale, and Fugue* published
1885	Writes *Variations symphoniques*
1886	Composes Violin Sonata in A major

KEY WORKS

PRELUDE, CHORALE, AND FUGUE

SOLO PIANO　　⏲ 18:40　　📖 3　　🎧

Franck's organ-loft is never far away from this noble work. The improvisatory Prelude leads directly into a chaste Chorale, where the octave bass line imitates the organ's pedals. From this emerges the implacable Fugue, which climaxes with the return of the theme from the Chorale, before ending joyfully in the major key.

VIOLIN SONATA

DUO　　⏲ 27:00　　📖 4　　⚜

Written as a wedding gift for Franck's countryman, the violinist Eugene Ysaÿe, this is one of the most popular Romantic violin sonatas. Arranged over four very different movements, Franck uses his own innovation, known as cyclic form, to unify the whole by bringing back the transformed opening theme in subsequent movements.

VARIATIONS SYMPHONIQUES

ORCHESTRAL　　⏲ 15:40　　📖 1　　🎼 🎧

Often regarded as Franck's masterpiece, this set of six variations and a finale form one of the most beautiful and compact piano concertos in the repertoire. Ranging from melancholy lyricism to glittering elegance, the solo part is sufficiently restrained to allow the piano and orchestra to be fully equal partners.

🔺 **When Eugene Ysaÿe first performed** Franck's Violin Sonata in Brussels, the room was so dark he had to play from memory.

Anton **Bruckner**

● 1824–1896   🏴 AUSTRIAN   ✍ 36

Anton Bruckner was an important figure in the development of the symphony. Although a Romantic composer, he made use of, and expanded, Classical structures such as sonata form in his symphonies, and he was particularly influenced by the work of Wagner. Bruckner was also an organist, and in addition to the composition of nine symphonies, he produced a number of instrumental and sacred choral works.

» A devout Catholic born in rural Austria, Bruckner produced works that were at once solemn and transcendent.

Life

Born in Ansfelden, Austria, in 1824, Bruckner was largely self-taught as a composer. He was very dedicated and also worked as an organist, often practicing for 12 hours a day. His first job as an organist was at the Abbey of St. Florian near Ansfelden in 1851, and he later went on to Linz Cathedral, where he worked from 1856 to 1868. He was a very religious man and his first surviving work is the *Requiem Mass*, written in 1849. Bruckner was from a peasant background and he had a strong provincial accent that was looked down upon in cosmopolitan Vienna. He was also a rather solitary figure and was reluctant to explain or discuss his music with others. However, his musical outlook was very modern for its time, and he took on many of the harmonic innovations of Wagner, a move that was held against him by many critics loyal to the more conservative figure of Brahms. His three Mass settings and Symphony No. 1 were all written during his tenure at Linz, and in 1868 he became court organist and a teacher at the Vienna Conservatory. He went on to write eight more symphonies, in addition to a number of other sacred works and substantial pieces for organ, piano, and choir. His Symphony No. 9 was left incomplete on his death in 1896.

Music

Bruckner's music in many ways bridges the stylistic gap between early and late Romantic music, paving the way for major later figures such as Mahler and Sibelius. In his symphonies he relied on many Classical structures (including sonata form) and Baroque techniques, but he expanded the length and harmonic range of themes and the extent of their development. Bruckner's music is particularly unusual for the long durations of its sections and movements, although this allowed him to achieve a great subtlety in form, with many sections containing a number of related subsections. This, together with an often gradual rate of change, lends the music its famous transcendent or "otherworldly" quality. Bruckner's international reputation has grown enormously in recent decades and his works are particular favorites of many conductors and orchestras.

❝ Bruckner! He is my man! ❞   **Richard Wagner**

MILESTONES

1837	Sent to Abbey of St. Florian near Ansfelden; becomes choir boy	**1866**	Mass No. 2 in E minor; writes Symphony No. 1
1849	*Requiem Mass*	**1867**	Mass No. 3 in F minor
1851	Organist at Abbey of St. Florian	**1868**	Becomes court organist and teacher at the Vienna Conservatory
1856	Organist at Linz Cathedral, Austria	**1873**	Symphony No. 3 first performed in Vienna
1861	Makes first concert appearance as composer at Linz	**1887**	Composes Symphony No. 8
1864	Composes Mass No. 1 in D minor	**1891**	Receives honorary doctorate from the University of Vienna
1865	Hears *Tristan und Isolde* in Munich; becomes a devoted Wagnerian	**1896**	Dies while working on Symphony No. 9

KEY WORKS

SYMPHONY NO. 9

ORCHESTRAL   ⏱ 60:30   📖 3   🎵

This piece, Bruckner's last, has a quality of isolation and intense spirituality that is not present in his other works. The chromaticism and dissonance are further heightened by the lack of an affirmative ending (the work is unfinished), which contributes to its dark and foreboding quality.

TE DEUM

CHORAL   ⏱ 23:15   📖 5   🎵 🎶 🥁 🎤

This work of 1884 shares many qualities with Bruckner's Masses of the 1860s and was one of his favorite pieces. The Latin title is taken from the first line of the text "Te Deum laudamus" ("We praise thee, O God"). The work is scored for the forces of solo soprano, contralto, tenor, and bass, a four-part choir, orchestra, and optional organ.

MASS NO. 1 IN D MINOR

MASS SETTING   ⏱ 43:50   📖 6   🎵 🥁

This Mass has quite symphonic proportions and the accompanying orchestra has a prominence reminiscent of Mozart and Haydn. Another principle that Bruckner took from the Classical era is that of cyclic form, and here themes from earlier movements are used in the Agnus Dei, the final movement. Inspired by Wagner's *Tannhäuser*, this work represents Bruckner's first piece as a fully mature composer.

SYMPHONY NO. 3

ORCHESTRAL   ⏱ 1:00:00   📖 4   🎵

Often called Bruckner's "Wagner" Symphony, this work's earliest version (of 1873) contained quotations of Wagner's music and many remained in the published score of 1890. Two extra-musical ideas also appear in the piece. The first is the slow, dancelike theme in the adagio, written as an elegy for Bruckner's mother. The other concerns his view of the opposing factors of life.

⬆ **Bruckner studied** at the Augustinian Abbey of St. Florian, Austria, as a boy and he went on to become organist there in 1851.

INFLUENCES

Bruckner's historical position is of great importance. Incorporating Liszt's thematic developments and Wagner's harmonic boldness with the Classical principles of Haydn and Mozart, he laid the groundwork for many later figures. Schoenberg's early style owes a lot to Bruckner.

Pyotr Ilyich **Tchaikovsky**

● 1840–1893   Ⓝ RUSSIAN   ✍ 159

Tchaikovsky's intensely emotional music combines many influences in an individual style: Russian folk song with Western European technique; nationalism with a personal agenda; the bombastic with the haunting and beautiful. The effects of the composer's homosexuality on his music and the mystery surrounding his death still cause speculation and controversy, but his music remains perennially popular.

》 Though a master of many forms of musical composition, Tchaikovsky is perhaps best known for his romantic ballets.

Life

A sensitive and highly strung boy, Tchaikovsky was born into a large middle-class family in provincial Russia. After law school in St. Petersburg, he became a civil servant, studying music privately but showing only average ability. However, he left his job to concentrate on music at St. Petersburg Conservatory, and during five years under Anton Rubinstein his technique progressed rapidly. He moved to Moscow to teach and enjoyed celebrity in artistic and homosexual circles.

At the age of 37 he entered into a platonic marriage of convenience with an infatuated student, Antonina Milyukova, but the effects that this had on his emotional state and his ability to compose were so destructive that they separated after two months. For the next 14 years Tchaikovsky corresponded with Nadezhda von Meck, a wealthy widow and lover of his music, who became his financial supporter (although by mutual agreement they intentionally never met). Nevertheless, by his early 50s Tchaikovsky was ill, depressed, and facing his own mortality. In 1893 he died of cholera.

Music

Critics were divided by Tchaikovsky's early work (his Violin Concerto and Piano Concerto No. 1 received very unfavorable reviews), but it was clear from the beginning that he could write "masterpieces" (such as his Symphony No. 6 and *The Queen of Spades*). Some of his music seems to reflect his life: in *Eugene Onegin*, the fifth of his ten operas, the "Letter scene" has Tatyana declaring her love to Onegin by letter, just as Antonina did to Tchaikovsky (although Onegin declines). Following on, the despair at Fate in his Symphony No. 4 is a commentary on his state of mind during the disastrous marriage that resulted, whereas his freewheeling orchestral suites evoke his sense of freedom during the traveling years after his separation. However, this idea is all too easy to overplay.

The influence of Schumann and Beethoven, as well as Glinka, can be heard in Tchaikovsky's orchestral music, and there is often a strong sense of a psychological program in which motto themes undergo transformation (as in the last three symphonies); he also made extensive use of folk tunes (especially in his Symphony No. 2, the "Little Russian"). His Violin Concerto and the first of his three concertos for piano are familiar showpieces that stretch the performer to the limit.

❝ I am Russian in the **completest** possible **sense** of that **word. ❞**

Tchaikovsky in a letter to Mme. von Meck, 1878

MILESTONES

1865	Appointed professor of harmony at new Moscow Conservatory	**1877**	*Swan Lake* produced; begins Symphony No. 4 and *Eugene Onegin*; starts eight years of international travel
1866	Symphony No. 1, Op. 13, composed	**1878**	Violin Concerto, Op. 35, composed; Symphony No. 4 and *Eugene Onegin*, Op. 24, completed
1869	*Voyevoda*, Op. 3, opera, produced; *Fatum*, Op. 77, for orchestra, performed; begins *Romeo and Juliet* overture	**1880**	*1812 Overture*, Op. 49, written
1873	Symphony No. 2, Op. 17, performed in Moscow to great success	**1881**	Violin Concerto, Op. 35, premiered in Vienna, to terrible reviews
1874	*The Oprichnik*, opera, produced; String Quartet No. 2, Op. 22, and Piano Concerto No. 1, Op. 35, composed	**1890**	*The Sleeping Beauty* produced in St. Petersburg; *The Queen of Spades*, Op. 68, composed, premiered triumphantly; *Souvenir de Florence*, Op. 70, composed
1875	Piano Concerto No. 1, Op. 23, premiered in Boston, US; Symphony No. 3, Op. 29, premiered in Moscow	**1892**	The ballet *Nutcracker*, Op. 71, produced
1876	Starts corresponding with Nadezhda von Meck		

⬆ **Still displaying his piano** and various personal effects, this is the house in Klin, near Moscow, where Tchaikovsky spent the final year of his life.

KEY WORKS

EUGENE ONEGIN, OP. 24

OPERA   ⏱ **140:00**   📖 3   🎭👥♦

Completed in 1878, and based on a verse novel by Pushkin, this story of a bored, Byronic young aristocrat's desultory and damaging love affairs constantly reminds us that "real life is not like a novel"; yet its "Letter Scene" eerily reflects the composer's own personal struggles at the time.

Themes (including pre-Revolutionary Russia, town versus country, social convention, and death of inspiration) abound in this enduring opera, which in many ways is "about" Tatiana, the only character who grows, rather than the superficial, irredeemable Onegin.

Act one (65:00) Russia, c.1820. Eugene Onegin, having inherited his uncle's country estate outside St. Petersburg, is introduced by his poet friend Lensky to the Larin sisters: the flighty Olga, and the brooding, novel-reading Tatiana. Tatiana declares her love for Onegin by letter, but he brushes her off.

Act two (40:00) Onegin, provoking his hot-headed friend, takes Lensky's beloved Olga to a ball. A duel results in which Onegin kills Lensky.

Act three (35:00) Onegin falls in love with Tatiana, now married to his cousin Prince Gremin. She still loves him but stays with her husband, suspecting that her attraction is now only as a challenge.

SWAN LAKE, OP. 20

BALLET   ⏱ **140:00**   📖 4   🎭

After its unsuccessful Moscow premiere in 1877, *Swan Lake* was revised in 1895, two years after Tchaikovsky's death. That version, with choreography by Petipa and Ivanov, to a tighter libretto by Tchaikovsky's brother Modest (complete with happier ending), is the basis of the ballet we know today.

Act one (50:00) At the royal palace, Prince Siegfried celebrates his coming-of-age. Various dances entertain the party to now-familiar themes, and a flight of swans appears, marked by the main oboe melody of the ballet.

Act two (30:00) Siegfried and friends are hunting swans, denoted by the oboe melody. However, one swan—Odette—tells him she is a woman, turned into a swan by the evil magician Rotbart.

Act three (45:00) At the royal castle, Siegfried has to choose a wife at a ball, entertained by various dances. He thinks he sees Odette there, but she is actually Odile, Rotbart's daughter. Siegfried dances with her and nominates her as his bride, spelling doom for Odette.

Act four (15:00) Back at the lake, Odette is about to die—but Siegfried battles with Rotbart, breaks the spell, and is reunited with her, as the swan theme triumphantly reappears.

⬆ **Tchaikovsky's three ballets**—*Swan Lake*, *The Sleeping Beauty*, and *Nutcracker*—show off his trademark lusciously scored melodies.

SYMPHONY NO. 4 IN F MINOR, OP. 36

ORCHESTRAL ⏱ 46:00 📖 4 ♫

Begun in 1877 before his marriage and finished the following year after his separation, the symphony is an emotional diary in music.
First movement (*andante*, 18:00) An ominous brass fanfare, denoting fate, is followed by a string theme reminiscent of decisive moments in Bizet's *Carmen*. The composer's comment on the recurrence of the fanfare was: "All life is an unbroken alternation of hard reality and swiftly passing dreams of happiness."
Second movement (*andantino*, 12:00) A lament for oboe becomes a warmly nostalgic string theme, which passes through noble desperation to a quietly resigned conclusion.
Third movement (*scherzo*, 6:00) After the lament of the second movement recedes, the sprightly scherzo features pizzicato strings alternating with blocks of jaunty woodwind and brass in a good-natured jumble.

Fourth movement (*allegro con fuoco*, 10:00) A hectic, clattering theme is contrasted with variations on a Russian children's song about hopeful brides, evidently a reference to Antonina. The work ends in boisterous determination.

PIANO CONCERTO NO. 1, OP. 23

ORCHESTRAL ⏱ 35:00 📖 3 ♫ 🎻

Ukrainian folk themes, French song, a grand opening tune that promptly disappears, occasionally inexpert piano writing—it seemed an unsuccessful mix to potential performers, but proved another winner after its triumphant premiere.

NUTCRACKER, OP. 71

BALLET ⏱ 102:00 📖 2 ♫

Tchaikovsky acknowledged that *Nutcracker* was twee compared to *The Sleeping Beauty*, but his setting of Hoffman's fairy tale has proved better box office, thanks to effects such as the Sugar Plum Fairy's celesta.

» **This cartoon by Franklin McMahon** shows Sir Georg Solti conducting Tchaikovsky's Symphony No. 4 with the Chicago Symphony Orchestra.

1812 OVERTURE, OP. 49

| ORCHESTRAL | ⏳ 16:00 | 📖 1 | 🔱 |

The "Solemn Overture" was composed in 1880 for the consecration of Moscow's Cathedral of Christ the Savior, built in thanks for the Russian victory over Napoleon in 1812.

SOUVENIR DE FLORENCE, OP. 70

| CHAMBER | ⏳ 35:00 | 📖 4 | ♟ |

The unusual scoring—two violins, two violas, two cellos—gave Tchaikovsky problems, but he ended up producing a lyrical and warm masterpiece. Despite the title (recalling his Italian holidays), the work is richly Russian in character.

VIOLIN CONCERTO, OP. 35

| ORCHESTRAL | ⏳ 35:00 | 📖 3 | 🔱 🎻 |

Denounced as "unviolinistic" by early players and "stinking music" by critics, this noble, virtuosic showpiece injects Russian passion into the "Euro-style" concerto with hugely successful results.

THE QUEEN OF SPADES, OP. 68

| OPERA | ⏳ 170:00 | 📖 3 | 🔱🎵👥 |

Tragedy is literally on the cards in this rich, dense masterpiece, which hints at Mozart, Bizet, Orthodox music, Russian folk song, French song, and more, yet remains a cohesive, powerful whole.

SYMPHONY NO. 6, OP. 74

| ORCHESTRAL | ⏳ 45:00 | 📖 4 | 🔱 |

Tchaikovsky's dark, despairing farewell—possibly an attempt to confront his demons—was prophetically named "Pathétique" by his brother Modest. The second movement's love "waltz" has an undanceable five beats.

INFLUENCES

Tchaikovsky greatly encouraged the young Rachmaninoff, but his heartfelt style soon became old-fashioned outside Russia as composers looked for a more radical language. However, many of his works are cornerstones of the Romantic repertoire, and are constantly performed and recorded.

▲ **The Bolshoy Zal (Great Hall)** in the Moscow Conservatory, where Tchaikovsky was made Professor of Harmony in 1865.

◀ **Rudolf Nureyev made his debut** in the West performing *The Sleeping Beauty*. Written in 1889, it was Tchaikovsky's first successful ballet.

Gustav **Mahler**

⬤ **1860–1911**   🏳 **AUSTRIAN**   ✍ **18**

Known chiefly as a conductor in his short lifetime (he directed the Vienna Opera for ten years), Mahler composed in his spare time. His large-scale songs with orchestra and nine epic, intense, emotionally exhausting symphonies (plus beginnings of a tenth) are among the most recorded and performed of his repertoire. He is now seen as a link between the 19th-century Austro-German tradition and 20th-century Modernism.

» **Successful in his career** because of his driving ambition, Mahler exacted the highest standards of music-making in both himself and others.

Life

Mahler was born to a large German-speaking Jewish family in Bohemia, factors that made him feel like an outsider throughout his life. His father was a rough but successful man in the liquor trade. Mahler's musical talent showed early: he gave local recitals at ten and, at 15, he entered the Vienna Conservatory, soon winning prizes for piano and composition. Gradually he developed an international reputation as a conductor as he progressed—despite quarrels with authority en route—through Kassel, Prague, Leipzig, Budapest, and Hamburg, before spending ten years at the Vienna Opera and finally four in New York. An innovator in opera presentation, especially in Wagner's music, he was a demanding conductor, disliked by some musicians and respected by others. He suffered institutional anti-Semitism, despite converting nominally to Catholicism in Vienna. At 41, he met 22-year-old Alma Schindler and married her four months later, ordering her to give up her own composing ambitions to raise the two daughters she soon produced. However, one died aged six. That year, Mahler was diagnosed as having a serious heart condition, drastically curtailing his beloved walking, swimming, and cycling. Alma's affair in 1910 with the architect Walter Gropius (whom she eventually married) destroyed Mahler, who was now enjoying recognition as a composer. Six months later he contracted a serious blood infection of which he died.

Music

Apart from lost student chamber works, Mahler's output is virtually all symphony and vocal; although an outstanding opera conductor, he completed none of the three he started. His style is late-Romantic, but he expanded the orchestra in both sound and size (his Symphony No. 8 requires 1,000 participants). However, what really distinguishes a Mahler symphony is more theatrical: the feeling of many voices at work and a sequence of events. There is often an atmosphere of tension and *fin-de-siècle* angst contrasted with love and joy; Mahler consulted with Freud, and a strong psychoanalytical—some say self-pitying—aspect runs through much of his music. Sarcasm, parody, and irony abound in Mahler's mix of the sublime and the ridiculous, which may explain the popularity of his symphonies in the "knowing" era of the late 20th century.

> ❝ The symphony must be like **the world.** It must **embrace everything.** ❞
>
> **Gustav Mahler,** 1907

MILESTONES

1875	Enters Vienna Conservatory
1880	First conducting experience; completes cantata *Das klagende Lied*
1884	Starts Symphony No. 1
1888	Music director, Budapest opera; starts Symphony No. 2
1891	Starts conducting at Hamburg
1897	Begins at Vienna Hofoper
1901	Starts Symphony No. 5; meets Alma Schindler
1902	Marries Alma; finishes Symphony No. 5
1905	Song cycle *Kindertotenlieder* first performed
1906	Begins Symphony No. 8
1907	Daughter Maria dies; he joins Metropolitan Opera, New York
1909	Completes song-symphony *Das Lied von der Erde*
1910	Finishes Symphony No. 9; learns of Alma's affair

KEY WORKS

SYMPHONY NO. 5

ORCHESTRAL   80:00   5

Mahler met Alma while composing this symphony. Its five movements progress from tragedy to triumph. The fourth movement, the Adagietto, is Mahler's most popular work.

DAS LIED VON DER ERDE

SONG-SYMPHONY   65:00   6

The Song of the Earth is a symphony-like work based on translations of ancient Chinese poems and set for two solo singers and orchestra. Filled with sadness and longing yet ultimately uplifting, simple yet profound, and achingly beautiful, it is possibly Mahler's greatest piece.

SYMPHONY NO. 8

ORCHESTRAL   75:00   21

The "Symphony of a Thousand" (1,030 performers were needed to play in the 1910 premiere) is a tribute to enlightenment and divine love, orchestrated for eight solo singers, massive choir, and large orchestra.

SYMPHONY NO. 9

ORCHESTRAL   70:00   3

Like Beethoven and Bruckner, Mahler died jinxed on nine numbered symphonies; his last—in many ways an extension of *Das Lied von der Erde*—was finished in 1910 and only performed after he died.

KINDERTOTENLIEDER

SONG CYCLE   25:00   5

Grimly prophetic of the death of Mahler's own daughter, *Songs for Dead Children* is a setting for baritone voice of poems by Friedrich Rückert, who lost two children, and is contemplative rather than dramatic.

Mahler was a conductor at the Vienna Opera from 1897 to 1907, a significant achievement considering this appointment's reputation as a stressful and demanding position.

INFLUENCES

Mahler's works fell into obscurity after his death, partly because of opposition in Hitler's Germany to Jewish musicians, but became very popular in the last third of the 20th century. The dramatic and multi-layered nature of his symphonies can also be found in those of Dmitri Shostakovich.

Richard **Strauss**

◔ 1864–1949   🏳 GERMAN   ✍ 189

Richard Strauss began his career composing songs and symphonic poems, and ended it as the greatest opera composer of his day. His career, which rarely escaped controversy, spanned the last days of the Austrian Empire and all of Hitler's Nazi Germany, in which the composer allowed himself to become embroiled. His masterpieces are his orchestral tone poems, his songs, and his great operas.

⭡ **The early tone poems of Strauss,** such as *Also Sprach Zarathustra*, are works on a grand scale, full of flamboyant, dramatic gestures.

Life

Richard Strauss was born in Munich, the son of a horn-player in the court orchestra. He began composing at six and studied music privately, but did not attend a conservatory. He became assistant to Hans von Bülow in Meiningen, then traveled to Italy, and later worked in Munich at the Opera. He married the soprano Pauline de Ahna, a general's daughter, who inspired many of his songs, which they performed together. His early operas, *Guntram* and *Feuersnot* (*Fire Emergency*) were not as successful as his tone poems, and *Salome* and *Elektra* caused an international scandal. The latter brought him together with the poet Hugo von Hofmannsthal: the two were to collaborate on five further operas. In 1908, the successful Strauss built himself a large villa at Garmisch in Germany. He conducted widely and was the conductor of the Berlin Royal Opera, resigning from this post in 1918 to become Joint Director of the Vienna Opera the next year. When the Nazi party came to power in 1933, Strauss was appointed President of the Reichsmusikkammer,

⏩ **The villa in Garmisch-Partenkirchen,** Germany, where Strauss spent the final years of his life. He moved here after several years of exile in Switzerland.

though he lost the post two years later because of his collaboration with the Jewish librettist Stefan Zweig. Strauss spent much of World War II in Vienna, then returned to Garmisch, where he died in 1949.

Music

Strauss's early career as an orchestral conductor gave him enormous knowledge of the potential of the post-Wagnerian symphony orchestra, and he expanded this still further, using unusual timbres and combinations of instruments for the vivid and original characterizations of his great tone poems. The success of *Don Juan* established his reputation, and he built on it with *Till Eulenspiegel*, *Also Sprach Zarathustra*, *Don Quixote*, and *Ein Heldenleben*. His earliest attempts at opera were not successful, but *Salome* (and the scandal it caused with its New Testament subject and its libretto based on Oscar Wilde's play) gave him a new reputation as an opera composer. *Elektra* pushed the boundaries of operatic music, and many reacted against its dissonances and the huge, blatant waltz tune of its finale. Waltzes also run all through his next work, *Der Rosenkavalier*, in homage to his namesake and to the city of Vienna where it is set. His later collaborations with Hugo von Hofmannsthal brought about philosophical works such as *Die Frau ohne Schatten*. After Hofmannsthal's death, Strauss turned to Stefan Zweig and other librettists for his final operas, written first in the shadow of World War II, and then during the war itself. Strauss mourned the bombed-out theaters of Europe in *Metamorphosen*, but a chance meeting with an American soldier inspired one of his greatest instrumental works, the Oboe Concerto. *Four Last Songs* was his last musical testament.

MILESTONES

1875	Studies theory with Meyer	1905	Writes *Salome*, Op. 54
1881	Symphony No. 1 and String Quartet No. 1 performed in Munich	1909	*Elektra*, Op. 58, produced
1884	Symphony No. 2 performed in New York	1910	Writes *Der Rosenkavalier*, Op. 59, with von Hofmannsthal
1885	Becomes assistant conductor to Hans von Bülow in Meiningen	1912	*Ariadne auf Naxos*, Op. 60, performed
1887	*Aus Italien* performed in Munich	1919	*Die Frau ohne Schatten*, Op. 65, produced in Vienna
1889	Becomes third conductor at Weimar Opera	1933	Nazi government appoints him director of the Reichsmusikkammer
1890s	Series of tone poems establishes his reputation as a composer; *Also Sprach Zarathustra*, Op. 30	1935	Removed from post due to his collaboration with Jewish librettist Stefan Zweig
1894	Marries soprano Pauline de Ahna	1938	Operas *Friedenstag*, Op. 81, and *Daphne*, Op. 82, produced
1898	Conductor of Berlin Opera	1943	Writes *Metamorphosen*, a "poem for 23 strings"
1904	Visits US and performs *Symphonia Domestica*, Op. 53	1947	Visits London and conducts own works

⌃ **Soprano Pauline de Ahna,** Strauss's wife, as Elsa in Wagner's opera *Lohengrin*.

KEY WORKS

FOUR LAST SONGS

SONGS	⏱ 24:00	📖 4	🎵 👤

Strauss wrote his *Vier letzte Lieder* (*Four Last Songs*) in 1948, and although they were not his last songs, they were among his last major compositions. The first three poems are by Hermann Hesse, and the last is by Joseph von Eichendorff. All four poems have an atmosphere of elegy, as the composer bids farewell to the world. Hesse himself is said to have been surprised by the project, and when he first heard the songs he claimed that they were "virtuoso, refined, full of well-crafted beauty, but lacking in core, merely an end in themselves"— although he admitted to only having heard them on the radio.

Beim schlafengehen (4:00) In the first song, "On Retiring to Rest," the poet, wearied by the day, is asking to be taken in by the starry night like a tired child. His hands and mind cease from working, and his five senses drift off into slumber. The soul hovers around the body, living on "in night's magic circle."

Frühling (5:00) In "Spring," the poet dreams of springtime, with its trees, blue skies, and birdsong, then sees it unfold in all its beauty.

September (6:00) At the other end of the year, the garden is in mourning, and summer comes to its end.

Im abendrot (9:00) This, the most moving of the four songs, sets words by Eichendorff's "In the Evening Glow." Now it is clear that Strauss is once again addressing his wife, Pauline, as they go hand in hand into the twilight, the larks still singing overhead as they go.

⌃ **Strauss always had a close relationship** with the Vienna Philharmonic Orchestra, seen here playing in the hall of the Musikverein.

 **Leontyne Price,** the acclaimed African-American soprano, made her debut as Ariadne at the San Francisco Opera in October 1977.

EIN HELDENLEBEN, OP. 40

ORCHESTRAL   ⏱ 51:00   📖 6   ✻

The title of this tone poem translates as *A Hero's Life* and the hero is Strauss himself, portrayed as a man of high ideals, surrounded by enemies. **Part one: The hero** (5:00) The first subject, the Hero's theme, makes it clear from the start that he is a noble character, a lively, confident individual, but not without a gentle side.

Part two: The hero's adversaries (4:00) The Hero's enemies (Strauss's critics) are portrayed as dull and petty-minded. They are contrasted with the Hero and his lofty, high-minded ambitions.
Part three: The hero's companion (14:00) This is a portrait of Strauss's loving but capricious wife, Pauline.
Part four: The hero's deeds of war (8:00) The Hero does battle to overcome his rivals in art and love.
Part five: The hero's works of peace (7:00) In this section, Strauss quotes from a number of his own earlier musical works.
Part six: The hero's retirement from the world and fulfilment (13:00) The Hero retires from the world of action (something Strauss never did) and spends his time in contemplation. In the conclusion, his life-force asserts itself once more.

> " There is no such thing as **Abstract music;** there is **good music** and **bad music**. If it is good, it **means something.** "
>
> **Richard Strauss**

DER ROSENKAVALIER, OP. 59

OPERA	⌛ 195:00	▭ 3	🎭 ♟ ♀

Strauss and his librettist Hugo von Hofmannsthal invented *Der Rosenkavalier* (*The Knight of the Rose*) as a fantasy of 18th-century Vienna at the time of the Empress Maria Theresa.

Act one (75:00) The heroine, the Marschallin—also called Marie Therese—is having an affair with young Octavian while her husband is away hunting. Her cousin, Baron Ochs von Lerchenau, interrupts their dalliance with a demand that she should provide a Knight of the Rose to present a silver rose to his fiancée, Sophie.

Act two (60:00) Octavian is chosen for the task and delivers the rose to Sophie, who immediately falls in love with him, and vice versa. When Sophie refuses to marry Baron Ochs, Sophie's snobbish father, von Faninal, tries to placate him, while Octavian fights the Baron and plots to have him disgraced.

Act three (60:00) Octavian, dressed as Mariandl, seduces Baron Ochs in a tavern of ill repute. They are interrupted, and the Marschallin and Sophie come to break up the fracas. The Marschallin recognizes the depths of Sophie's feelings for Octavian, and gracefully gives up her lover to the younger woman.

ALSO SPRACH ZARATHUSTRA, OP. 30

TONE POEM	⌛ 35:00	▭ 1	🎭

Strauss based this piece, *Thus Spoke Zoroaster*, on Friedrich Nietzsche's philosophical prose poem of the same title. Zarathustra (Zoroaster) is Nietzsche's ideal thinker, a leader of humanity. Strauss wrote the piece between 1895 and 1896, and conducted its first performance in Frankfurt. The film *2001: A Space Odyssey* brought its majestic opening bars to many new listeners.

ARIADNE AUF NAXOS, OP. 60

OPERA	⌛ 120:00	▭ 2	🎭 ♀

Strauss collaborated with Hugo von Hofmannsthal on a reworking of Molière's comedy *Le bourgeois gentilhomme*, to be performed with an operatic and vaudeville entertainment after the play. This six-hour show was not a success, but some years later Strauss and Hofmannsthal rewrote the piece, adding a Prologue in which Molière's comedy is hinted at and the situation is set up. Ariadne, lamenting the loss of Theseus on Naxos, is interrupted by Zerbinetta and her troupe of clowns, who try to cheer her up, before Bacchus arrives to take Ariadne with him to everlasting bliss.

SALOME, OP. 54

OPERA	⌛ 105:00	▭ 1	🎭 ♀

Strauss's *Salome* is a setting of Hedwig Lachmann's German translation of Oscar Wilde's play. The opera was first performed in Dresden in 1905, and was a great success throughout Europe. It tells the biblical story of how Herodias's daughter Salome persuaded King Herod to give her the head of Jokanaan, John the Baptist.

INFLUENCES

Strauss outlived his age of late Romanticism, and though he had taken on much of what had been discovered by Stravinsky and other avant-garde composers, his later work still remains tonal and late-19th century in its harmonic language Only now is it becoming clear how much influence his work has had on post-war composers.

⌃ **Costume designs for *Elektra,*** the opera that brought Strauss together with his librettist, Hugo von Hofmannsthal.

Romantic Opera
1810–1920

The 19th century provided the most popular of all operas—Verdi's *La traviata*, *Rigoletto*, and *Aïda*, Wagner's *Ring* cycle, Bizet's *Carmen*, and Puccini's *La bohème*. The popularity of these works is based on their universal themes, the huge emotions they generate, and the mastery of their writing for voice and orchestra.

The years between the death of Mozart in 1791 and the arrival of Rossini on the scene two decades later were comparatively barren for opera. Europe was too preoccupied with the Napoleonic Wars to have money to spare for this extravagant art form. 1813, when Rossini had his first great successes, was also the year in which two of the greatest Romantic opera composers, Verdi and Wagner, were born. Each revolutionized opera and polarized its enthusiasts into what even today can be—though should not be—two opposing camps.

Romantic opera covers over a century of composition. Up until World War I, Europe enjoyed a long period of relative peace, during which the revolutions of 1848 were a significant political upheaval. These involved Wagner directly (he was exiled for his participation in the Saxony riots) and several other composers indirectly.

International appeal

The other revolution to affect the century was the industrial one. By mid-century, railroads crisscrossed Europe and steamships plied the Atlantic, allowing composers, singers, and conductors to embark on the international careers that all now accept as the norm. Verdi traveled to Russia, Dvořák to the USA, Tchaikovsky to England (to pick up a doctorate), and Puccini to his eventual death in a Brussels hospital. The soprano Adelina Patti, greatest of bel canto singers, retired to a castle in south Wales; the tenor Enrico Caruso made his name in New York; and the Russian bass Chaliapin sang to audiences in Paris and London. In a century of nationalism, opera was a truly international art form.

Opera often springs from literary origins. Plays, epics, novels, and histories have always inspired librettists and composers, and 19th-century Romantic opera took its inspiration from a particular set of writers. Shakespeare's plays, Sir Walter Scott's novels, Goethe's *Faust*, and Schiller's historical tragedies all became sources for opera librettos.

Another great source of Romantic inspiration were the legends and poems of medieval Europe. Rossini took the old Swiss tale of William Tell for his last and possibly greatest opera, whereas Wagner drew on the great medieval German epics *Tristan und Isolde*, the *Nibelungenlied*, and *Parsifal*.

◄◄ **This painting by Degas** depicts a scene from the third act of Giacomo Meyerbeer's *Robert le Diable*. Meyerbeer was the most successful exponent of French *grand opéra*.

» **Verdi drew on Shakespeare's plays** for three of his operas: *Macbeth* (1847), *Otello* (1887), and his one comic masterpiece, *Falstaff* (1893). This watercolor depicts a set design for *Otello*.

Powerful emotions

In Italy, Rossini's use of Romantic plots, often melodramatic and improbable, inspired his two immediate successors, Donizetti and Bellini, who took Romanticism still further. Donizetti drew on Sir Walter Scott for *Lucia di Lammermoor*, while Bellini told tales of Druid priestesses in *Norma* and of sleepwalking girls in *La sonnambula*. In each of these operas the central figure is that great Romantic icon, the damsel in distress. Lucia in her bloodstained nightgown and Norma in her priestess's robes are among the most hauntingly dramatic heroines in all theater, spoken or sung.

TIMELINE: ROMANTIC OPERA

1813 Rossini's *Tancredi* and *L'Italiana in Algeri*, his first great successes

1829 Rossini's *William Tell*

1835 Donizetti's *Lucia di Lammermoor*, based on Walter Scott's novel

1851 Verdi's *Rigoletto*, based on Victor Hugo's play *Le Roi s'amuse*

1864 Ludwig II of Bavaria becomes Wagner's patron

1810	1825	1840	1855

1813 Verdi and Wagner born

1815 Battle of Waterloo; Congress of Vienna

1821 Weber's *Der Freischütz*

1848 Revolutions in Paris, Vienna, and other European capitals

1858 Present Covent Garden Theater opens in London

Verdi made further revolutions in the writing of opera. His earliest works told stirring tales of nationalism and heroism (*Macbeth*, *Ernani*, *Nabucco*), while in his middle period, in works such as *Rigoletto*, he examined the relationship between parent and child, portraying vulnerable heroines with uncomprehending, overbearing fathers.

Verdi's successors, Mascagni, Leoncavallo, and Puccini, added the new element of "verismo" or realism to their operas, telling stories in music that were none the less Romantic for being drawn from everyday life.

Opera beyond Italy

The great Russian composers, from Glinka to Tchaikovsky, all produced operas, usually on Russian themes. In France, Parisian *grand opéra* employed huge stage sets, vast orchestras and choruses, and prodigious solo voices, with Meyerbeer the dominant composer. Offenbach wrote in the rival form of *opéra comique*, concluding his career with a masterpiece of Romantic opera, *The Tales of Hoffmann*. Other French works that have lasted well include Bizet's *Carmen*, Gounod's *Faust*, and Massenet's *Cendrillon*.

In Germany the first great Romantic opera was Weber's *Der Freischütz*, based on a folk tale set in the forests of Bohemia. Weber had learned much from his studies of Beethoven, and brought a new richness of orchestration to his score. *Der Freischütz* inspired Wagner, who decided that the German world needed its own form of music drama, and proceeded to invent it, writing both words and music. Richard Strauss followed the unfollowable Wagner, producing Romantic works until well into the 20th century. He was the last of the great Romantic composers.

■ **Puccini's account** of the death of Mimi in *La Bohème* remains one of the most popular of all Romantic operas.

BEL CANTO

The great vocal tradition of 19th-century Italian opera was bel canto, which simply means "beautiful singing." The three great bel canto composers were Rossini, Bellini, and Donizetti, and their works have been criticized by some for putting ornamented melodic line and florid coloratura embellishments before the job of telling a story. Two of the finest early exponents were Giulia Grisi (1811–69) and Giuditta Pasta (1797–1865). Later stars included Jenny Lind (1820–87) and Adelina Patti (1843–1919), who left a number of recordings, but these were made when she was past her vocal best.

■ **Jenny Lind,** the Swedish-born soprano, won acclaim for the naturalness of her performances.

Carl Maria von **Weber**

◐ **1786–1826**   🏳 **GERMAN**   ✍ **306**

Carl Maria von Weber was a composer, conductor, and pianist whose opera *Der Freischütz* marked the beginning of German Romantic opera. The huge success of *Der Freischütz* liberated German opera from the Italian influences that had bound it until then, and showed how a nationalist style of opera could be founded on folk tunes and folk tales. Weber was admired by Beethoven and influenced his disciple, Wagner.

Weber was the son of a town musician who set up his own opera company, with which the young Weber spent much of his childhood on tour. He studied with Abbé Vogler, an eminent teacher and music director at several German Electors' courts, and worked under Joseph Haydn's brother Michael. At 17 Weber took up the post of Kapellmeister at the theater in Breslau (Bratislava). Eventually appointed Kapellmeister in Dresden, Weber spent his life touring ceaselessly as a conductor to promote his own and other composers' music. He died in London at only 39, a few weeks after the premiere of his final opera, *Oberon*, succumbing to the tuberculosis that had undermined his health for years. Apart from his operas, he is noted for his brilliant clarinet works.

MILESTONES	
1807	Composes his two symphonies
1811	Composes two clarinet concertos
1813	Appointed director of Prague Opera
1823	Completes *Euryanthe*, opera
1826	Completes *Oberon*, opera

KEY WORKS

DER FREISCHÜTZ

OPERA   ⌛ **150:00**   📖 **3**   ♫ ♘ ♪

Weber set *Der Freischütz* (*The Freeshooter* or *The Marksman*) to a libretto by Johann Friedrich Kind based on a set of ghost stories. The overture opposes C major with C minor, setting up the world of goodness and light (major) against that of evil and darkness (minor). Hunting-horn calls are heard alongside Weber's favorite low clarinet, setting the atmosphere of Bohemian forest life and the black magic of the Wolf's Glen. The evocation of the glen is a superb example of tonal scene-painting.

⬈ **Weber's *Der Freischütz*** is the ultimate distillation of German Romanticism in opera. It portrays the struggle of good and evil and evokes the beauty of nature.

EURYANTHE

OPERA   ⌛ **165:00**   📖 **3**   ♫ ♘ ♪

Weber's "grand heroic-romantic opera in three acts" was commissioned by the Kärntnertortheater in Vienna as a result of the success of *Der Freischütz*. With one of the most ludicrously implausible plots in all opera (which is quite an achievement), it has not been performed as often as deserved by its superb music—a continuous flow without spoken word.

OBERON

OPERA   ⌛ **170:00**   📖 **3**   ♫ ♘ ♪

Oberon, Weber's last opera, is a setting of an English libretto by James Robinson Planché and it was first performed in London in 1826 at Covent Garden. Weber overcame the difficulties of Planché's unpromising, convoluted text about the elf-king Oberon, the Caliph of Baghdad, his daughter Rieza, and Charlemagne, and wrote an opera that contains some of Weber's best music, especially the inspired overture.

Ferdinand **Hérold**

● 1791–1833   ♙ **FRENCH**   ✍ c.160

After lessons from his father, a pianist and composer, Hérold attended the Paris Conservatoire, performed his piano works in public, and won the Prix de Rome in 1812. But it was as a composer of masterful comic operas in the French style that he gained renown. His *La jeunesse de Henry V* was a success in Naples, where he served as pianist to Queen Caroline.

MILESTONES	
1812	Wins the Prix de Rome
1813	Teaches royal princesses in Naples
1817	*Les rosières*, opera, premiered
1826	*Marie*, opera, staged
1827	Marries Adele Elise Rollet; becomes choirmaster at the Paris Opéra
1828	*La fille mal gardée*, ballet, premiered
1831	*Zampa*, opera, staged in Paris

A year after returning to Paris in 1816, he produced his opera *Les rosières*, the first of many resounding successes, punctuated by failures, mainly down to poor librettos. His ballets are also innovative in using new music, rather than old melodies. Shortly before the premiere of his last (and hugely successful) opera, *Le pré aux clercs*, he died prematurely from chronic tuberculosis.

« **The roguish pirate Zampa** is flung to his death by the avenging spirits of his former bride, Alicia, in the final scene of Hérold's enormously popular *Zampa*.

Jules **Massenet**

● 1842–1912   ♙ **FRENCH**   ✍ c.450

Massenet's early career followed the regulation path for a French composer in the 19th century. After studies with Ambroise Thomas at the Paris Conservatoire, he won the Prix de Rome, then spent three years in Italy before returning home to break into the Paris opera scene in 1866. Success came gradually as Massenet honed his technical skills. Although he staged his first opera in 1867, a decade passed before he achieved his first real success with *Le roi de Lahore*. Lasting fame came in 1884 with *Manon*, an international hit that established Massenet as France's leading opera composer. Now in control of his career, he continued producing successful, internationally staged operas, such as *Werther*, without needing to update his deft style. As a teacher at the Paris

Conservatoire, Massenet was admired for his meticulous, but kind, easy-going nature, apparently preferring family life to parties.

MILESTONES	
1863	Wins the Prix de Rome
1866	Returns to Rome and marries
1877	*Le Roi de Lahore*, opera, first success
1878	Becomes professor of composition at Paris Conservatoire
1884	*Manon*, opera, a huge success
1885	Writes *Le Cid*, opera, after Corneille
1892	*Werther*, opera, after Goethe, staged

» **In the bleak finale** to Massenet's blockbuster, *Werther*, Charlotte despairs at the suicide of her true love, Werther.

Giacomo **Meyerbeer**

● **1791–1864**   📖 **GERMAN**   ✍ **c.285**

Meyerbeer developed and dominated French Grand Opéra, the new epic and historic style that would influence the Romantics, from Verdi to Wagner. Although massively extravagant in scale, effects, casts, and costs, Meyerbeer's lavish melodramas are now being revived and recorded, graphically illustrating their spectacular and fashionable appeal in his day.

Born Jakob Liebmann Beer to a Jewish family in Berlin, Giacomo Meyerbeer Italianized his first name, and added "Meyer" to his second on receiving a legacy from a relative. A child prodigy on the piano, he performed in public from the age of seven. Nurturing a passion to compose, he turned out some disastrous oratorios until, inspired by Gioachino Rossini's operas in Italy, he produced *Il crociato in Egitto*, an instant hit in both Venice and Paris, where he settled. After a fallow patch during a spate of family tragedies in the 1820s, Meyerbeer experimented with the new style of Grand Opéra—epic in scale, drama, and effects—that he effectively invented with *Robert le Diable*. This and a run of similar box-office hits established him as a master of the genre.

MILESTONES

1810	Studies counterpoint with Abbé Vogler at Darmstadt in Germany
1815	Visits Italy to study vocal writing
1817	Produces his first Italian opera, *Romilda e Costanza*, in Padua
1826	*Il crociato in Egitto*, opera, staged
1831	*Robert le Diable*, opera, a huge hit
1836	*Les Huguenots*, opera, premiered
1837	Starts composing *L'Africaine*, opera
1842	Becomes Generalmusikdirektor (music director) in Berlin
1849	*Le prophète*, opera, premiered
1854	*L'étoile du nord*, opera, staged
1865	Posthumous premiere of *L'Africaine*

KEY WORKS

ROBERT LE DIABLE

OPERA   ⏱ **240:00**   📖 **5**   🎭🎵

Famous for its scandalous chorus of dancing nuns, its evocative orchestration, and brilliant writing for voice, *Robert le Diable* was the first product of a fruitful collaboration between Meyerbeer and the librettist Eugène Scribe. It tells the tale of the 13th-century Duke Robert of Normandy, whose love for Isabella saves his soul from the diabolic machinations of his demon father, Bertram.

◀ *Le prophète,* one of Meyerbeer's most dramatic and bombastic operas, is famous for its stunning light effects and explosive finale.

LES HUGUENOTS

OPERA   ⏱ **240:00**   📖 **5**   🎭🎵

Meyerbeer's moving opera explores the intense religious conflict that erupted in a massacre on St. Bartholomew's Day in 1572, when the Protestant minority of Huguenots were ruthlessly slaughtered by the Catholic majority. The historic drama is intensified by the fated love between a Protestant and Catholic, Raoul and Valentine, both doomed to die in the futile bloodbath. Tuneful, luscious, and inventive, it is probably Meyerbeer's finest opera for voices, displaying his melodic talents.

Gioachino **Rossini**

🌐 **1792–1868**   🇮🇹 **ITALIAN**   ✍ **c. 240**

Born a few months after Mozart's death, Rossini was the greatest opera composer of the 1810s through to the 1830s, when he took a premature retirement from opera composition. His comic operas bubble with invention and fun, while his serious operas have great melodic beauty and superb writing for both voice and orchestra.

Rossini was the son of Pesaro's town horn player and his wife, a singer. He entered Bologna Conservatory in 1806 and, by 1813, when he was 21, he had written ten operas. He was the first composer to write opera without recitative, so creating an uninterrupted flow of music. He went on to write for theatres in Milan, Venice, Rome, and Naples, and in 1824 moved to Paris where he wrote five further operas, culminating in *William Tell*. Then Rossini stopped writing operas and composed only very occasionally for his remaining 38 years.

MILESTONES

1813	Operas *Tancredi* and *L'Italiana in Algeri* produced in Venice
1814	Engaged as music director for the two opera houses in Naples
1822	Marries Isabella Colbran, soprano
1823	Composes *Semiramide*, opera
1824	Made director of Théâtre Italien in Paris
1829	Writes *Guillaume Tell*, his last opera

KEY WORKS

IL BARBIERE DI SIVIGLIA

OPERA   ⏱ **165:00**   📖 **2**   🎻 ♒ ♿

Rossini set Cesare Sterbini's libretto, based on the first of Beaumarchais's Figaro plays *Le barbier de Séville* (*The Barber of Seville*) in 1816 and wrote the music, it is said, in 13 days. The play had been set to music before, and the supporters of the most popular setting, by Paisiello, caused a riot at the first night of Rossini's rival version in Rome.

LA CENERENTOLA

OPERA   ⏱ **150:00**   📖 **2**   🎻 ♒ ♿

Rossini's take on the Cinderella story is full of satire and wit. Cenerentola, rejected by her stepfather and stepsisters, is protected by Alidoro, a philosopher, and falls in love with Prince Ramiro, who arrives disguised as his valet Dandini. Dandini, disguised as the Prince, wins over the family. The real Prince can then marry his beloved.

GUILLAUME TELL

OPERA   ⏱ **225:00**   📖 **4**   🎻 ♒ ♿

The overture to *William Tell* is perhaps Rossini's most famous work. Based on Schiller's play about the Swiss patriot, Wilhelm Tell, Rossini's opera was his first—and last—work in the style of French Grand Opéra with its grandiose sets, huge choruses, and ballets, bound together by Swiss alphorn melodies. The four-act opera depicts the story of Tell, who rescues Arnold, a fugitive from the Austrian army of occupation. In the final act, Arnold restores Switzerland to freedom.

INFLUENCES

Rossini directly influenced Donizetti, Bellini, Verdi, Meyerbeer, Offenbach, and Sullivan, and indirectly influenced film scores and musicals well into the 20th century. His ornate vocal lines defined bel canto throughout his lifetime and his comic genius was never eclipsed. His serious operas are now making a comeback.

🔼 **A brilliant comic opera,** Rossini's *La Cenerentola*, seen here in performance in London, also has some genuinely emotional scenes.

Gaetano **Donizetti**

🜂 1797–1848   📖 ITALIAN   ✍ c.550

In a life of extraordinary productivity, Gaetano Donizetti wrote 65 operas, a dozen of which are still an important part of the operatic repertory. Like his near-contemporary Bellini, Donizetti wrote bel canto operas that celebrated the beauty of the human voice in long, expressive melodies and vivid, elaborate coloratura ornamentation. He was equally successful with tragedy and comedy.

Donizetti was born into a poor family in Bergamo and studied with the great teachers Simon Mayr and Padre Mattei. He often produced four operas a year, writing in the widest variety of styles, though most of his works are based on historic or fictional figures. He made his name in Rome with *Zoraida di Granata*, and the success of *Anna Bolena* in Milan allowed him to concentrate on tragic opera, though he continued to write comedies. After working in Paris and Vienna, in 1844 he fell ill and returned to Bergamo, where he was nursed by his nephew and friends, dying there in 1848.

MILESTONES

1818	*Enrico di Borgogna* produced in Venice
1830	*Anna Bolena* commissioned by La Scala opera house; first international success
1834	Composes *Maria Stuarda*
1840	*La fille du régiment* and *La favourite* written for Paris
1844	Begins to suffer symptoms of syphilitic paralysis and insanity
1846	Enters a sanatorium in Ivry

KEY WORKS

⌃ **Celebrated buffo bass singer** Signor Lablache played quack Doctor Dulcamara in a 19th-century production of Donizetti's opera *L'elisir d'amore*.

LUCIA DI LAMMERMOOR

OPERA   ⏳ 135:00   📖 3   🎭 ♟ ♪

This opera is Donizetti's masterpiece. It is based on *The Bride of Lammermoor*, a novel by Sir Walter Scott. Donizetti used extraordinary orchestral effects (including a glass harmonica in the original scoring of Lucia's mad scene, later replaced by a flute), but the opera is most remarkable for his scoring for coloratura soprano in Lucia's scenes and arias.

DON PASQUALE

OPERA   ⏳ 120:00   📖 3   🎭 ♟ ♪

Written for the four great bel canto singers of the Théâtre Italien, this late opera buffa tells the tangled tale of Don Pasquale's intrigue to disinherit his rebellious nephew Ernesto while Dr. Malatesta schemes to marry Ernesto to the widow Norina.

L'ELISIR D'AMORE

OPERA   ⏳ 125:00   📖 2   🎭 ♟ ♪

Ranking alongside the comedies of Rossini, *The Elixir of Love* is one of the most enduring comic creations of the bel canto era. Felice Romani wrote the libretto, based on a text by Eugene Scribe, itself based on Silvio Malaperta's play *Il filtro* (*The Philtre*). *L'elisir d'amore* was first performed at the Teatro Canobbiana, Milan, in 1832. It is one of Donizetti's most popular operas.

INFLUENCES

Verdi learned much from Donizetti, and Puccini was also to benefit from the example of Donizetti's gift for melodic invention and the use of unusual instruments (such as the glass harmonica in *Lucia di Lammermoor*) to characterize scenes. Berlioz, too, admired Donizetti, in spite of the fact that his works monopolized opera in Paris for a decade.

Vincenzo **Bellini**

● **1801–1835**   🏴 **ITALIAN**   ✍ **c.60**

Vincenzo Bellini, with Rossini and Donizetti, was one of the three great composers of Italian bel canto opera. He wrote ten operas, many of which have remained in the repertoire. His reputation rests on the long-breathed, beautifully lyrical lines he gave to his singers, as well as on the great vocal agility his music demanded. His masterpiece, *Norma*, contains the supreme bel canto aria in the repertoire.

Bellini was born in Sicily, and educated in Naples at the San Sebastiano Conservatory, where he studied under Zingarelli. His first opera, *Adelson e Salvini*, was given in concert in 1825. He was immediately commissioned to write an opera for the prestigious San Carlo opera house in Naples, and soon after won another commission—*Il pirata*—for the even greater La Scala in Milan. Bellini followed this success with *I Capuleti e i Montecchi*, in which Romeo's part is written for female mezzo voice. *La sonnambula*, *Norma*, and *I puritani* followed. Bellini moved to Paris and died there, tragically young.

MILESTONES	
1826	Writes opera *Bianca e Gernando* (title changed to *Bianca e Fernando* in 1828)
1830	Opera *I Capuleti e i Montecchi* is staged in Venice
1831	Writes operas *La sonnambula* and *Norma* for Milan with huge success
1833	Writes opera *Beatrice da Tenda*; goes to Paris; meets Rossini who advises him to write for Théâtre Italien there

KEY WORKS

NORMA

OPERA   ⏳ **160:00**   📖 **2**   🎵🎭♂

The most famous aria in *Norma* is the priestess heroine's great invocation to the moon, "Casta Diva" ("Chaste Goddess"). Long believed impossible to perform as Bellini intended, it was revived by soprano Joan Sutherland, who did much to rediscover the great bel canto roles of Bellini and Donizetti. The opera, to a libretto by Romani, was based on a tragedy of 1831 by French playwright Alexandre Soumet.

Act one (90:00) The setting is Gaul under Roman occupation. Norma, daughter of Oroveso, high priest of the Druids, wants to avoid the war her father desires against the Romans because she is in love with the Roman proconsul, Pollione. She already has two children by him. However, he is having an affair with her best friend, Adalgisa (also her acolyte), who confesses this to Norma.

Act two (70:00) Adalgisa wants Pollione to go back to Norma. He refuses and is sentenced to death, but Norma offers herself, instead, as a sacrifice to her tribe and gives up her children. She mounts her own funeral pyre, where she is joined by a repentant Pollione. The role of Norma is one of the most demanding in the whole soprano repertoire.

I PURITANI

OPERA   ⏳ **140:00**   📖 **3**   🎵🎭♂

Bellini's last opera, *I puritani* (*The Puritans*) is based, at some distance, on Sir Walter Scott's novel *Old Mortality*. It is set during the English Civil War.

» **Maria Callas's performances** in the title role of *Norma* were a career highlight, showing her at her best, both as a singer and as an actress.

Giuseppe **Verdi**

⬤ **1813–1901**   📖 **ITALIAN**   ✍ **42**

Verdi composed opera throughout his long life, developing his art from the influences of Rossini, Bellini, and Donizetti, through his use of French Grand Opéra forms in operas written for Paris, and, eventually, to the creation of his Shakespearian masterpieces, *Otello* and *Falstaff*, in which he began to use some of Wagner's innovations in operatic form. Throughout, his originality and fecundity remained unparalleled.

» **The operas of Verdi** were generally based on historical or literary figures and settings; his love stories invariably ended in tragedy.

Life

Giuseppe Verdi was born in the village of Le Roncole, Busseto, near Parma, in 1813, the same year as Richard Wagner. His father was an innkeeper, his first music teacher was the church organist, and his first patron was a local grocer who was prepared to pay for him to study at the Milan Conservatory. Unable to enter the Conservatory because of his inadequate piano technique, he studied privately for two years, then returned to Busseto and married his patron's daughter. His first opera, *Rocester*, has been lost, but his next, *Oberto*, was performed at La Scala, Milan. Verdi lost his wife and his two children within two years of each other and, grief-stricken, was about to give up composing when he was commissioned to write *Nabucco*. The opera's theme of national independence inspired him, and its great chorus, "Hebrew Slaves," became an anthem for the Italian Risorgimento movement for unification. After years of composing, an opera a year, he achieved financial independence by the late 1840s, bought a farm, and settled down with the singer Giuseppina Strepponi, whom he eventually married. Verdi was elected to the first Italian parliament after independence was declared in 1860. He wrote operas for St. Petersburg, Paris, and Cairo, and then waited 16 years before another composer, Boito, provided him with librettos for his two final operas, *Otello* and *Falstaff*.

Music

Verdi's early operas, such as *Macbeth*, *Ernani*, and *Nabucco*, took themes of national independence and used choruses as the "voice of the people," making powerful political statements. His soloists were given highly taxing roles, such as Lady Macbeth, Elvira, and Abigaille, which heightened the dramatic effect of arias and ensembles.

In his middle years, his dramatic skills developed and his orchestration grew increasingly subtle. *Rigoletto* and *La traviata* took realistic plots and set them with great lyrical beauty and emotional depth.

In his old age, after *Aïda*, Verdi returned to his beloved Shakespeare for his last two operas, in which his vocal writing, especially in *Otello*, shows power and expression beyond anything he had written before.

❝ Verdi…has **bursts of** marvelous **passion.** His passion is **brutal,** it is true, but it is **better to be impassioned** in this way **than not at all.** ❞ **Georges Bizet** in a letter, 1859

MILESTONES

1839	*Oberto* produced at La Scala, Milan
1842	First great success, *Nabucco*
1847	*Macbeth*
1849	Buys a farm at Sant' Agata
1851	*Rigoletto* premiered in Venice
1852	*Il trovatore*
1853	*La traviata*
1858	*Un ballo in maschera*

1869	Soprano Giuseppina Strepponi becomes his second wife
1871	*Aïda* performed in Cairo
1874	Composes Requiem in memory of the writer Alessandro Manzoni
1884	Arrigo Boito persuades him to resume writing operas
1887	*Otello* performed at La Scala, Milan
1892	Composes *Falstaff*

KEY WORKS

RIGOLETTO

OPERA   ⏱ 120:00   📖 3   ♒ ⛨ ♿

Verdi based *Rigoletto* on Victor Hugo's play *Le roi s'amuse*. Rigoletto, the hunchbacked jester to the libertine Duke of Mantua, has a daughter, Gilda, whom the Duke has been courting in secret, disguised as a student. The Duke's men kidnap Gilda and take her to the palace. Rigoletto comes looking for Gilda, but when he finds her, she has already been disgraced. Rigoletto pays the assassin Sparafucile to murder the Duke. Gilda substitutes herself for the Duke, and is fatally wounded. Rigoletto takes a sack that he believes to contain the Duke's body and finds, instead, his dying daughter.

AÏDA

OPERA   ⏱ 150:00   📖 4   ♒ ⛨ ♿

When *Rigoletto* was performed in Cairo to celebrate the opening of the Suez Canal, the Khedive of Egypt was so impressed that he commissioned *Aïda* to be staged in his newly completed opera house.

Aïda is an Ethiopian slave to Amneris, daughter of Ramphis, the Pharaoh. Aïda is in love with the Egyptian general Radamès, who is sent to lead the Egyptian army against Ethiopia. When Radamès returns victorious, he is given Amneris as his bride. Amonasro, Aïda's father, is captured. He convinces Aïda to find out from Radamès the plan of his next campaign. Ramphis discovers this betrayal and Radamès is condemned to be walled up alive in a tomb, where Aïda joins him. They die together.

MACBETH

OPERA   ⏱ 150:00   📖 4   ♒ ⛨ ♿

Verdi's librettist Piave took some liberties with Shakespeare's tragedy (the three witches become an entire female chorus), but Verdi's opera tells the story in a skillful, moving way. Lady Macbeth's sleepwalking scene is one of Verdi's finest, with its spectral orchestration for high strings and its high-lying vocal line that disappears to a mere thread of voice. It was Maria Callas who helped rediscover the role and brought *Macbeth* back into the permanent repertoire.

LA TRAVIATA

OPERA   ⏱ 120:00   📖 3   ♒ ⛨ ♿

Based on Alexandre Dumas's play *La dame aux camélias*, the story is of the courtesan Violetta and her love for Alfredo, which is thwarted by Germont, Alfredo's father. Germont tells Violetta to leave his son for the sake of his sister. Dying of consumption, Violetta does as he asks, only to be reconciled with her lover and die in his arms.

REQUIEM

MASS SETTING   ⏱ 140:00   📖 15   ♒ ⛨ ♿

Verdi wrote his Requiem in 1874 in memory of the great Italian novelist Manzoni. The setting of the Latin Mass for the dead includes many highly operatic effects (like the trombone in "Tuba mirum"). The fiery "Dies irae" is one of his most dramatic choruses.

⌃ **Romanian soprano Angela Gheorghiu** and French/Italian tenor Roberto Alagna sing a duet in a performance of Verdi's *La traviata* at London's Covent Garden.

Richard **Wagner**

● 1813–1883　　📖 GERMAN　　✍ 43

Richard Wagner reinvented opera as music drama. His aim was to create a "Gesamtkunstwerk," a unified work of art combining poetry, drama, music, song, and painting. In writing the music dramas of his maturity, he wrote both text and music, and superintended staging and performance as his own director and conductor. He built the Festspielhaus in Bayreuth as a fitting home for his *Ring* cycle and his last great work, *Parsifal*.

》 One of the most influential composers of all time, Wagner changed the course of both opera and Classical music in general.

Life

Wagner was born in Leipzig, and was educated in Dresden and at the Thomasschule, Leipzig, studying literature as intensively as he studied music. He was appointed choral conductor at Würzburg in 1833, and then took conducting posts at Lauchstädt and Magdeburg. He married an actress, Minna Planer, but their marriage was strained by Wagner's extravagance and infidelities. After working in Riga, he went to Paris, living from hand to mouth, then returned to Dresden where he was appointed court opera conductor. In Dresden he studied German epic poetry, gaining the subjects for the rest of his life's work. His participation in

the Dresden uprising of 1849 led to his exile. In Switzerland he wrote several essays, including the important *Opera and Drama* and the anti-Semitic tract *Jewishness in Music*. Wagner visited London and Paris, and continued to travel until permitted to return to Saxony in 1862. The turning point in his fortunes came when King Ludwig II of Bavaria invited him to Munich and became his patron, allowing Wagner to stage *Tristan und Isolde*, conducted by Hans von Bülow. Wagner fell in love with von Bülow's wife, Cosima, and fathered two children with her before Minna's death allowed them to marry. In Bayreuth, Wagner built a house and a theater, the Festspielhaus, where he staged the *Ring* cycle. He completed his final opera, *Parsifal*, in 1882, and died in Venice in 1883.

Music

Wagner inherited an art of German opera that had been developed by Mozart, Beethoven, and Weber. He transformed it into his own definition of music drama, a unified work that combined poetry and music, the two being conceived together. Wagner's early operas, up to *Rienzi*, were influenced by the trends of the day, especially French Grand Opéra. From *The Flying Dutchman* onward, through *Lohengrin* and *Tannhäuser*, Wagner found his own unique musical language. Central to his new style of composition was the idea of the leitmotiv, or leading motive, a musical theme linked to a specific character, symbol, or concept that recurred throughout the work. By the time he completed the *Ring* cycle, this had become a system of melody, harmony, and counterpoint that derived all its materials from a simple chord or opening phrase.

> " If one has **not heard Wagner at Bayreuth,** one has heard nothing! "
>
> **Gabriel Fauré** in a letter, 1884

At the same time, Wagner experimented with modulation and the key system, discovering ways of moving seamlessly to the remotest of keys with enormous emotional effect. Wagner's mastery of the orchestra (he invented the art of the modern conductor, invented new instruments such as the Wagner tuba, and discovered new timbres and combinations of instrumental sound) reached the height of its development in *Tristan und Isolde*. His understanding of the voice allowed him to write roles of huge length and complexity that were still singable, and which were able to penetrate the heaviest of orchestral textures. With *Parsifal*, Wagner brought the art of his music drama to a point which, at the time, seemed likely to remain unsurpassable.

☑ **Wagner's left-wing ideals** led to his implication in the fighting of the Dresden Rebellion of 1849. A warrant was issued for his arrest, but he escaped to Zurich.

MILESTONES

1841	Completes *Der fliegende Holländer*
1842	Opera *Rienzi* produced in Dresden
1843	*Der fliegende Holländer* produced in Dresden
1845	*Tannhäuser* produced in Dresden
1854	Completes *Das Rheingold*
1856	Completes *Die Walküre*
1857	Completes first part of *Siegfried*
1859	Completes *Tristan und Isolde*
1865	*Tristan und Isolde* produced in Munich, conducted by Hans von Bülow
1866	Wife Minna dies
1867	Completes *Die Meistersinger von Nürnberg*
1871	Completes second part of *Siegfried*
1872	Building of Bayreuth Festspielhaus begins
1874	Builds villa, Wahnfried, in Bayreuth; completes *Götterdämmerung*
1876	Bayreuth theater opens; *Ring* cycle first performed
1882	*Parsifal* performed at Bayreuth

KEY WORKS

DIE MEISTERSINGER VON NÜRNBERG

OPERA   ⌛ **255:00**   📖 **3**   ♫ ♗ ♪

When Wagner decided to write a comedy in 1861, he turned away from the high drama of the *Ring* cycle to focus on the small tale of a competition organized by the Meistersingers, societies of singers who guarded the integrity of the German song tradition. **Act one** (85:00) In 16th-century Nuremberg, the knight Walther von Stolzing is in love with Eva, Pogner's daughter. Pogner will give her in marriage to whoever wins the singing contest of the Meistersingers' guild. **Act two** (85:00) Walther does not know the rules of the contest, but the (real-life) cobbler and poet Hans Sachs coaches him, and helps him fend off the town clerk Beckmesser, who also wants to marry Eva. **Act three** (85:00) Walther, singing a song composed by Hans Sachs, wins the contest and gains Eva's hand in marriage; he is then enrolled as a full member of the Meistersinger's guild.

☒ **Wagner's custom-built opera house,** the Festspielhaus in Bayreuth, Germany, has been used to host the Wagner Festival annually since its completion in 1876.

DER RING DES NIBELUNGEN

OPERA CYCLE ⏳ 885:00 📖 4

In its full form *Der Ring des Nibelungen*, Wagner's most ambitious masterpiece, is actually a complete opera festival in itself, taking place over three days and a preliminary evening.
Das Rheingold (1 Act, 150:00) The dwarf Alberich steals the Rhinemaidens' gold to make a magic ring. The giants, Fafner and Fasolt, agree to exchange Freia—the goddess whose golden apples keep the gods young—for the gold Alberich has gained through the power of the Ring. Fafner kills Fasolt, taking the Ring.
Die Walküre (3 Acts, 225:00) The two mortal children of the god Wotan, Siegmund and Sieglinde, fall in love. Sieglinde's husband kills Siegmund, although Brünnhilde the Valkyrie tries to protect him. Sieglinde is pregnant with Siegfried, the savior of the gods. To punish Brünnhilde for trying to save Siegmund, Wotan puts her to sleep on a rock ringed with flames.
Siegfried (3 Acts, 255:00) Siegfried, the son of Siegmund and Sieglinde, succeeds in forging his father's shattered sword. He goes to Fafner's lair (the giant is now a dragon), and, killing Fafner, gains the Ring. Finding Brünnhilde on her rock, he wakes her with a kiss.
Götterdämmerung (Prologue and 3 Acts, 255:00) Siegfried, in love with Brünnhilde, gives her the Ring, but his enemies Günther and Hagen give him a drugged potion. He brings Brünnhilde, with the Ring, from her rock. Hagen kills Siegfried and Günther as he fights for the Ring. Brünnhilde builds a pyre for Siegfried, and burns herself and Valhalla. The Rhine overflows and the Rhinemaidens drown Hagen and take back the Ring.

⏫ **Wagner's music** makes it clear from the start that the doomed love of Tristan and Isolde can lead to no other end but death.

TRISTAN UND ISOLDE

OPERA ⏳ 255:00 📖 3

Wagner's epic music drama of love and death, written in 1857–59, was first performed in Munich in 1865.
Act one King Marke's henchman Tristan is returning to Cornwall with the Irish princess Isolde, Marke's betrothed. Isolde's first husband died at Tristan's hand, and although she nursed the wounded Tristan, she now hates him for what he did. She orders her servant Brangäne to prepare a poison, but Brangäne substitutes a love potion. Each drink it, expecting death, but instead fall in love.
Act two While Marke is away on a night-time hunt, arranged by the treacherous Melot, who is also in love with Isolde, the lovers meet for an extended tryst. Tristan and Isolde express their passion in powerful, erotically charged music, but daylight comes, the hunting party returns, and Tristan is mortally wounded by Melot.
Act three The dying Tristan, who has been taken back to Kareol, his castle in Brittany, by the faithful Kurwenal, waits for Isolde to come to him. She comes, followed by King Marke, but Tristan dies in her arms. As she sings the "Liebestod," an astonishing Wagnerian *tour de force*, in which eternal love is consummated by death, Isolde is transfigured, then dies herself.

DER FLIEGENDE HOLLÄNDER

OPERA ⏳ 135:00 📖 3

The Flying Dutchman was Wagner's first attempt at reinventing opera. It has no distinct arias, and everything that happens, whether on the stage or in the pit, is there to enhance the drama. The Flying Dutchman himself is a man doomed to sail the seas alone until he finds the love of a true woman, which will save his soul.

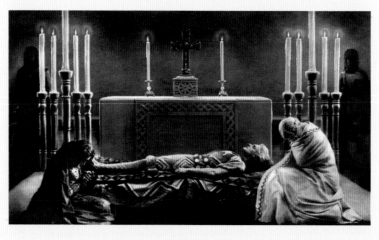

◀ **Fritz Lang's silent film** of 1922–24, *Die Nibelungen*, is split into two parts: *Siegfried* and *Kriemhild's Revenge*, dealing with the last two parts of the epic story.

TANNHÄUSER

OPERA   ☂ 180:00   📖 3   ♒ ⚒ ♨

Based on a poem by Ludwig Tieck, *Tannhäuser* received its first performance at Dresden in 1845. Its hero, Tannhäuser, returns to Germany from the realms of the goddess Venus and competes in a song contest for the hand of Elisabeth, his old love. Singing of the joys of the flesh rather than the spirit, he is banished. The pair are eventually reunited in death.

LOHENGRIN

OPERA   ☂ 210:00   📖 3   ♒ ⚒ ♨

Based on a German epic poem, and first performed in Weimar in 1850, *Lohengrin* tells of the rivalry between Telramund and Lohengrin over the succession to the dukedom of Brabant and the love of Elsa. Lohengrin's famous swan (on which he arrives to meet Elsa) turns out to be Gottfried, the missing heir to the dukedom.

PARSIFAL

OPERA   ☂ 250:00   📖 3   ♒ ⚒ ♨

As usual, Wagner wrote his own libretto for *Parsifal*, based on the epic poem by Wolfram von Eschenbach. Set in Arthurian times, it tells the story of the Grail knights. Their wounded king can only be cured by a "pure fool, wise through compassion." Parsifal arrives, and proves to be both a fool and pure. He fights the evil Klingsor, restores the holy spear to the Grail castle, and leads the rite of the Holy Grail.

INFLUENCES

Wagner's influence on subsequent composers was incalculable. His innovations transformed the harmonic language of the 19th century and helped bring about the abandonment of the system of tonality. Poets and novelists from Verlaine and T. S. Eliot to Thomas Mann and Marcel Proust referred directly to his inspiration.

⏶ **The operas of Wagner** work best on a massive scale, such as in this production of *Parsifal*, which, as is not unusual, makes use of massive sets and a large cast.

Léo **Delibes**

🌐 **1836–1891**   🏴 **FRENCH**   ✍ **c.70**

French composer and organist Léo Delibes achieved considerable fame as a composer of enormously successful operettas, operas, and ballets. His best-known work, the ballet *Coppélia*, was one of the first to use "national" dances, such as the Hungarian csárdás. *Lakmé* was written in the popular orientalizing style then fashionable in Paris.

Léo Delibes arrived in Paris from the provincial town of Saint-Germain-du-Val at the age of 12, after his father had died. While still a boy, he sang in the choir at La Madeleine and in the Opéra chorus. He studied organ and composition at the Paris Conservatoire and, at 17, became organist at Saint Pierre de Chaillot at the same time as working as an accompanist at the Théâtre Lyrique, where he began composing operettas. In 1865 he became chorus master at the Paris Opéra, and was eventually appointed professor of composition at the Paris Conservatoire. His last opera, *Kassya*, was unfinished at his death, and was completed by Massenet.

MILESTONES	
1848	Begins to study organ and composition at the Paris Conservatoire; taught by Adolphe Adam, theater composer
1853	Accompanist at Théâtre Lyrique
1855	Writes *Deux sous de charbon*, operetta
1866	Enjoys success with *Le source*, ballet, cowritten with Louis Minkus
1873	Composes *Le roi l'a dit*, opera
1876	First performance of *Sylvia*, ballet
1880	Writes *Jean de Nivelle*, opera
1883	*Lakmé*, opera, first performed in Paris

KEY WORKS

COPPÉLIA

BALLET   ⏲ 90:00   📖 2   ▟

Coppélia, with a libretto by Nuittier, is based on a story by the German fantasy writer E. T. A. Hoffman. Premiered at the Paris Opéra in 1870, it was one of the first ballets to include national dances. Delibes visited Hungary and returned with the famous csárdás, the Hungarian national dance, which he wrote into the score. The ballet tells the story of a mechanical doll, Coppélia, whom her creator passes off as his daughter.

LAKMÉ

OPERA   ⏲ 155:00   📖 3   ▟ ♙ ♟

Lakmé's libretto was based on a novel by Pierre Loti. Set in 19th-century India, it describes the hatred of the Brahmin priests for the British soldiers who suppressed their religion. The

elegance of Delibes's melodies, and the exoticism of the opera's setting, have made *Lakmé* a lasting favorite with singers and audiences alike. The role of Lakmé, with its coloratura display of the soprano voice, has drawn many great sopranos to interpret it. The "Flower Duet" in Act one, between Lakmé and her servant Mallika, is one of the most popular of all duets for soprano and mezzo.

LES FILLES DE CADIX

CHANSON   ⏲ 5:00   📖 1   🔊 ♟

Delibes's most popular song sets words by Alfred de Musset. It has been recorded by many of the world's greatest sopranos. Delibes uses the popular Spanish style in setting this song about girls and boys returning from seeing the bullfight and dancing the bolero.

🔼 *Coppelia* **was the last ballet** to be performed at the Paris Opéra before the Franco-Prussian War forced it to close.

Georges **Bizet**

● **1838–1875**   ᴾᵁ **FRENCH**   ✍ **c.120**

A precocious but short-lived talent, Bizet devoted the best part of his brief but creative life to opera, for which he wrote his greatest music. With *Carmen*, he changed the course of French opera, setting a style in lifelike drama and sensual music that reached its peak decades later.

The son of a singing teacher, Bizet read music at four, played the piano at six, entered the Paris Conservatoire at nine, and composed an accomplished symphony at 17. Although he produced some passable Italianate operas in the 1850s, real success did not come until 1863 with his sensual and melodic *Les pêcheurs de perles*. A fallow patch followed before Bizet turned out a string of instrumental successes, such as *Jeux d'enfants*, and started work on *Carmen*. The first critics reacted coolly, and Bizet died before it became a hit.

MILESTONES	
1857	Wins the Grand Prix de Rome; *Le docteur miracle*, operetta, staged
1858	Studies in Rome
1867	*La jolie fille de Perth*, opera, staged
1871	*Djamileh*, one-act opera, premiered
1872	Commissioned to write *l'Arlésienne*, incidental music, staged at Vaudeville
1875	*Carmen*, opera, premiered in Paris

KEY WORKS

LES PÊCHEURS DE PERLES

OPERA	⏱ **100:00**	📖 **3**	🎵 🎭 ♂

Bizet's first operatic hit, achieved in his 20s, never enjoyed *Carmen's* success, but still attracts audiences. Although written to an appalling libretto, its charm lies in its melodic music, sensual undertones, and exotic atmosphere, evoked by lively rhythms and spicy harmonies. The appealing vocal score, inspired by Bizet's mentor, Charles Gounod, also helps enthrall listeners, with such sweet, memorable songs as "Au fond du temple saint."

CARMEN

OPERA	⏱ **160:00**	📖 **4**	🎵 🎭 ♂

Bizet's *Carmen*, the first realistic opera, shocked the first audiences with its lifelike characters, sensual passions, and graphic on-stage murder. Set to a libretto by Henri Meilhac and Ludovic Halévy, the plot was inspired by Prosper Merimée's short novel about a passionate Spanish gypsy.

Act one (60:00) Soldiers arrest Carmen for assaulting a fellow worker at the cigarette factory in Seville. She escapes by seducing Don José, one of the guards, who is then imprisoned.
Act two (40:00) At Lillas Pastia's bar, Carmen attracts the bullfighter Escamillo. When Don José is released, she persuades him to desert the army and join a band of smugglers.
Act three (40:00) Don José, Carmen, and the smugglers march through the night. Carmen foretells her own death. Escamillo follows, fights Don José, and just escapes with his life.
Act four (20:00) In Seville, Carmen goes to the bullfight to watch her new lover, but Don José confronts and kills her.

JEUX D'ENFANTS SUITE, OP. 22

DUO	⏱ **30:00**	📖 **12**	🎹

A brilliant pianist, Bizet wrote this charming suite, based on children's games, for piano duet, from which he later orchestrated five movements as the *Petite suite d'orchestre* in 1872.

⌃ **The virgin priestess Leila** in *Les pêcheurs de perles* captures the hearts of two friends who vie for her hand.

Giacomo **Puccini**

● 1858–1924   𝔭𝔲 **ITALIAN**   ✍ 38

Giacomo Puccini was the last in the great line of Italian composers of Romantic opera. With *Turandot*, his unfinished masterpiece, the tradition can be said to have ended, although in it Puccini had already begun to explore much of the new musical language of the 20th century. His most popular operas, *La bohème, Madama Butterfly*, and *Tosca*, demonstrate his gift for capturing an audience's attention with pure dramatic intensity.

⟫ The operas of Puccini are based on passionate stories of love, revenge, and betrayal.

Life

Puccini was born in Lucca, Tuscany, into the fifth generation of a family of church musicians. His father died when Puccini was only five, but the position of organist at the church of San Martino was kept open for him until he was old enough to step into his father's shoes. However, a performance of Verdi's *Aïda*, which he saw in Pisa in 1876, convinced him that his true vocation was opera. He took up the position of church organist at the age of 19, but in 1880 went to study at the Milan Conservatory. When the publisher Sonzogno launched a competition for a one-act opera, Puccini entered *Le Villi*, which failed to win. Sonzogno's rival, Giulio Ricordi, commissioned another opera from Puccini, *Edgar*, and after its failure another, more successful: *Manon Lescaut*.

From that point on, Puccini devoted his life to composing opera, with country pursuits such as shooting and fishing as his recreations. In 1891, he bought a beautiful estate on a lake near Lucca. He was by then living with a married woman, Elvira Bonturi, whom he was unable to marry until the death of her husband. The relationship seems to have been a tempestuous one. In 1909, a servant killed herself after Elvira accused her of having an affair with Puccini.

During the writing of his last opera, *Turandot*, Puccini fell ill with throat cancer, and died while undergoing medical treatment in Brussels, leaving his masterpiece incomplete.

Music

Puccini's genius for melodic invention, his love for the pairing of soprano and tenor voices, and his gift for picking theatrically effective plots established him as the most popular of all opera composers. His Romantic lyricism is in the tradition of 19th-century Italian opera, but he took up 20th-century ideas of bitonalism and dissonance from Stravinsky and others.

❝❝ I shall feel [the story] **as an Italian,** with **desperate passion. ❞❞**

Giacomo Puccini

Throughout his career, his taste for the exotic led him to incorporate music from the widest of sources, from the Roman matins bells in *Tosca* to the Japanese melodies in *Madama Butterfly* (supplied by a friend) and the Wild West tunes of *La fanciulla del West*. In *Turandot* he went even further, using pentatonic and whole-tone scales to evoke a mythical China, and adding tuned percussion to an already rich orchestral palette.

MILESTONES

1880	Enters Milan Conservatory
1884	One-act opera *Le Villi* performed in Milan
1889	Second opera, *Edgar*, is a failure
1893	Third opera, *Manon Lescaut*, enjoys great success in Turin
1896	*La bohème* produced at Teatro Regio, Turin
1900	*Tosca* premiered at Teatro Costanzi, Rome
1904	Premiere of first version of *Madama Butterfly*
1906	Definitive version of *Madama Butterfly*
1910	*La fanciulla del West* premiered at Metropolitan Opera, New York
1917	*La rondine* performed in Monte Carlo
1918	*Il trittico* (three one-act operas)
1920	Starts work on *Turandot*, but work is left unfinished on his death in 1924

KEY WORKS

MADAMA BUTTERFLY

OPERA ⏱ 140:00 📖 3 ♫ 🎭 ♂

Puccini saw David Belasco's play about a Nagasaki geisha and her American naval officer lover, *Madame Butterfly*, and decided to turn it into an opera. Belasco's play was based on a short story by John Luther Long, which was itself based on an incident witnessed by his sister, Jennie Correll, a US missionary working in Nagasaki.

Act one (60:00) Pinkerton, an American naval officer, arranges to marry Madame Butterfly, a Nagasaki geisha. The marriage is attended by her family, the bride is deeply in love, but for Pinkerton his vows mean nothing.

Act two (50:00) Pinkerton has sailed back to the USA, and Butterfly, who has had a son by him, awaits his return. When her servant Suzuki suggests Pinkerton may never come back, Butterfly sings the aria "Un bel di" ("One fine day"). She sees his ship entering Nagasaki bay. Butterfly, her son, and Suzuki wait all night for Pinkerton's arrival.

Act three (30:00) The American consul tells Suzuki that Pinkerton has remarried. Pinkerton and his wife come to collect the child. On realizing the truth, Butterfly kills herself.

LA BOHÈME

OPERA ⏱ 120:00 📖 4 ♫ 🎭 ♂

Puccini and his librettists, Illica and Giacosa, based *La bohème* on Henry Murger's *Scènes de la vie de Bohème*.

Act one (40:00) Rodolfo the poet, Marcello the painter, and two other Bohemian friends share a Paris garret. It is Christmas Eve. They burn pages from Rodolfo's manuscript to keep warm. Mimì, a neighbor, knocks at the door. Rodolfo falls in love with her.

Act two (20:00) The four friends and Mimì are at the Café Momus. Marcello joins up with a former girlfriend, Musetta, a singer, who tricks her current lover, the elderly Alcindoro, into paying the bill.

Act three (30:00) Rodolfo is jealous of Mimì's infidelities, and at the same time feels they cannot continue living together in poverty, because she is dying of consumption.

Act four (30:00) The dying Mimì returns to the garret. The friends go off to buy her what comforts they can. They return to find Mimì dying in Rodolfo's arms.

>> **Luciano Pavarotti** enjoyed huge success in the 1990s with Calaf's aria "Nessun Dorma" from *Turandot*.

TURANDOT

OPERA ⏳ 120:00 📖 3

In ancient China, Princess Turandot has declared that she will marry the prince who can answer her three riddles. Anyone who fails will be beheaded. Prince Calaf declares that he wants to face the test. He answers correctly, but she refuses to marry him. He proposes that she should guess his name by morning; if she does, she can behead him. Turandot orders her servants to torture the name from Calaf's servant, Liù, who is in love with her master. Liù dies, and Turandot learns from her example what it means to love.

TOSCA

OPERA ⏳ 140:00 📖 3

Victorien Sardou wrote the melodrama *Tosca* as a vehicle for the great actress Sarah Bernhardt. Puccini turned it into a spectacular opera, its title role a magnificent vehicle for singers like Maria Callas. Its three acts are set in Rome, in the Church of Sant'Andrea della Valle, where the painter Cavaradossi helps the fugitive Angelotti; the Palazzo Farnese, where the villainous Scarpia has his torture chamber; and the Castel Sant' Angelo, where Tosca flings herself from the parapet.

MANON LESCAUT

OPERA 📖 4

This was Puccini's third opera, but the first to achieve the critical success he was looking for, and the work in which he found his own

verismo style. Based on the same Abbé Prevost novella as Massenet's *Manon*, which had been a huge hit only a few years before, Puccini's treatment of the story of eloping lovers was altogether more serious. He rejected the traditional arrangement of recitatives, arias, and choruses, and through-composed *Manon Lescaut* as a continuous unfolding of melodies following the dramatic structure, a technique he employed in all his subsequent operas.

LA FANCIULLA DEL WEST

OPERA 📖 3

The success of *Madama Butterfly* involved a lot of work for Puccini overseeing productions of the opera, and it was seven years before his next opera, *La fanciulla del West*. This was based on the play *The Girl of the Golden West* by David Belasco, which Puccini had seen in New York in 1907. The plot, which concerns the rivalry between a bandit and the sheriff for the love of Minnie during the 1850 California Gold Rush, gave plenty of opportunity for Puccini to develop his dramatic technique of continuous action. It was initially well received by audiences, but the lack of memorable arias or set pieces meant that its popularity soon waned, and interest in *La fanciulla* only revived after Puccini's lifetime.

GIANNI SCHICCHI

OPERA 📖 1

Just before World War I, Puccini had an idea for a group of three one-act operas of very different characters to be performed together. These were eventually performed in 1918 as *Il trittico* (*The triptych*): *Il tabarro* (*The cloak*) is a dark and violent piece of verismo, *Suor Angelica* (*Sister Angelica*) a tragic tale of suicide, and *Gianni Schicchi*, a comedy based on a story in Dante's *Inferno*, about the eponymous lovable rogue and his manipulation of a family after a contested will. Although Puccini was unhappy about these being performed separately, it soon became clear that *Gianni Schicchi* was by far the most popular part of the triptych, and has since usually been performed on its own, or coupled with another one-act comedy.

Jacques **Offenbach**

🌑 **1819–1880**   🏳 **FRENCH**   ✍ **c.100**

Jacques Offenbach created the French operetta. Many of his works have never left the repertory, with *La belle Hélène* and *Orphée aux enfers* (*Orpheus in the Underworld*) among the most popular ever written. But he also wrote one masterpiece of grand opera, *The Tales of Hoffmann*, left unfinished at his death. Set in Germany and Venice, it includes a gondola scene with the famous Barcarolle.

Offenbach was born near Cologne in Germany, the son of the cantor at the city's synagogue. He studied in Paris, becoming a brilliant cellist and playing in the Opéra-Comique orchestra. In 1853, he began writing operettas. He then became theater manager of the Théâtre Comte, which he renamed the Théâtre des Bouffes Parisiens. His light-hearted musical style, inventive in its melodies and enhanced by his choice of witty librettists as his collaborators, epitomized the style of the French Second Empire, while at the same time satirizing its excesses. He wrote more than 90 operettas, but also worked for many years on his grand opera, *Les contes d'Hoffmann* (*The Tales of Hoffmann*). He died before finishing it, but it was completed and orchestrated from Offenbach's sketches by Ernest Guiraud.

MILESTONES	
1849	Appointed conductor at Théâtre Français in Paris
1853	Begins composing operettas
1858	*Orphée aux enfers*, operetta, premiered
1864	Premieres of *Der Rheinnixen*, opera, in Vienna; *La belle Hélène*, operetta, Paris
1866	Writes *La vie parisienne*, operetta
1867	Writes *Robinson Crusoé*, operetta
1868	Writes *La Périchole*, operetta
1869	Writes *Princesse de Trébizonde*, operetta
1876	Moves to US; returns to Paris 1878
1880	Dies in Paris
1881	*Les contes d'Hoffmann*, opera, begun in 1877, given first performance

KEY WORKS

ORPHÉE AUX ENFERS

OPERETTA	⏱ 165:00	📖 2	🎭🎭🎭

This is a send-up of Greek mythology and a satire of French Second Empire society and its pretensions. Though openly caricatured in it, Napoleon III praised Offenbach for the piece. In the plot, Orpheus and Eurydice have each started affairs. Eurydice's new boyfriend, Pluto, takes her down to the Underworld, but Public Opinion forces Orpheus to get her back. The operetta ends with the *Galope infernal*, Offenbach's famous Cancan.

LES CONTES D'HOFFMANN

OPERETTA	⏱ 240:00	📖 5	🎭🎭🎭

Although Offenbach's last and greatest work is essentially quite dark and has much rich melody, it also offers moments of humor. Based on three tales by E.T.A. Hoffmann, its prologue, three acts, and epilogue follow Hoffmann's love affairs with Olympia, Antonia, and Giulietta. The Giulietta act, set in Venice, begins with the celebrated Barcarolle.

▷▷ **Offenbach's Cancan** is the most famous rendition of an Algerian dance popularized in the 1830s.

Johann **Strauss Jr**

◔ 1825–1899　　⚑ AUSTRIAN　　✍ c.250

Johann Strauss Jr, Vienna's "Waltz King," was the son of Johann Strauss Sr, who had taught the Viennese to waltz to the tunes of his famous band. His father forbade the younger Strauss to follow his profession, but Johann started his own orchestra and rivalled his father's success. When Offenbach's operettas were a hit in Vienna, Strauss followed his example and wrote for the opera house.

Johann Strauss Jr studied the violin against his father's wishes, and soon gained a reputation as a fine violinist, conductor, and composer. Throughout his career his output was prolific; he composed 15 operettas as well as popular polkas and waltzes, such as *The Blue Danube*. Strauss's superb operetta *Die Fledermaus* premiered in 1874, and within a year had been performed all over the world. Admired by Brahms and Liszt, he was considered to be the master of light music and became the most famous of the Strauss family.

MILESTONES	
1844	Forms his own orchestra
1855	Directs summer concerts in St Petersburg
1863	Conducts Austrian court balls
1871	First operetta produced in Vienna
1883	Composes *Eine Nacht in Venedig*, operetta
1885	*The Gypsy Baron*, operetta, performed
1888	Writes the *Emperor Waltz*

KEY WORKS

DIE FLEDERMAUS

OPERETTA　　⏱ 130:00　　▭ 3　　🎭🎻♂

The story begins with a practical joke that took place three years before the opening scene. After a costume ball, Dr. Falke is left by his friend Eisenstein to walk home through the city, drunk and alone, in his bat costume. In Act One, Falke invites Eisenstein, who is on his way to prison, to a ball at Prince Orlovsky's. There Eisenstein flirts with his disguised housemaid, Adele, and with his wife, Rosalinde (also in disguise, and herself having an affair with Alfred). When they all meet up in the prison the misunderstandings are resolved—it was all the fault of Orlovsky's champagne.

DER ZIGEUNERBARON

OPERETTA　　⏱ 120:00　　▭ 3　　🎭🎻♂

The Gypsy Baron is Strauss's other enduringly successful operetta, written to a libretto by Ignatz Schitzer. The story takes place in Banat, Hungary, in the 18th century, and begins when Baron Sándor Barinkay finds that his estates have been settled by gypsies. Zsupán, a wealthy pig-farmer, thinks Sándor would make an ideal son-in-law. However his daughter, Arsena, has her heart set on Ottokar, the son of her governess Mirabella. The gypsy Sáffi wins Sándor's love, and is revealed to be a wealthy princess descended from the last Pasha of Hungary. Sándor's fortunes are restored. Arsena marries Ottokar, and they are blessed by the Baron. They all live happily ever after.

TALES FROM THE VIENNA WOODS

WALTZ　　⏱ 13:00　　▭ 1　　🎭

Geschichten aus dem Wienerwald, written a year after *The Blue Danube*, was one of the most celebrated waltzes of the 19th century. Strauss's waltzes epitomized the essence of Viennese high society during the twilight years of the Austro-Hungarian Empire.

⬆ **Although Strauss wrote** such wonderful dance music, he always maintained he was unable to dance himself.

Franz von **Suppé**

● 1819–1895   🏳 AUSTRIAN   ✍ c.200

Suppé drily insisted that his successful style came about by accident, when his poor knowledge of German misled him into setting a yodelling song sentimentally in the style of Donizetti. Nevertheless, his first theater score in 1841 triumphed. During spells as Kapellmeister at the Theater an der Wien and the Carltheater, he conducted many historic performances of opera and wrote a succession of stage scores. He went on to become the first master of Viennese operetta—*Das Pensionat* was his first success, and *Boccaccio* was the work he considered his best. His light, fluent, and flexible music is most familiar now in overtures to operettas such as *Light Cavalry*.

MILESTONES

1819	Born in Spalato (now Split, Croatia)
1834	Writes first comic opera, *Der Apfel*
1835	Moves to Vienna
1841	Score to the play *Jung lustig* triumphs
1846	*Poet and Peasant*, incidental music
1860	Composes *Das Pensionat*, operetta
1866	Writes *Light Cavalry*, operetta

《 Suppé studied in Vienna with Ignaz Xaver von Seyfried, and conducted at various Viennese and provincial theaters, including the Leopoldstadt, from 1841 until his death.

Sir Edward **German**

● 1862–1936   🏳 ENGLISH   ✍ c.200

Edward German's promise as a gifted student of composition at the Royal Academy was amply fulfilled. Music for productions of Shakespeare at the Globe Theatre, where he was musical director, established his reputation, and he was soon besieged by commissions for concert works. He wrote operettas in the "Old English" style, such as *Merrie England*, though the appeal of Gilbert-and-Sullivan-esque music was diminishing. His elegant, warm, and romantic music—cosmopolitan yet always English—enjoyed both popularity and high regard (Elgar was an admirer). A meticulous conductor, German was also in demand to direct his own music.

MILESTONES

1885	*Te Deum* wins a prize at the Royal Academy of Music, London
1888	Becomes music director of the Globe Theatre, London
1902	*Merrie England*, operetta, performed
1904	Writes *Welsh Rhapsody*, symphonic suite
1907	Composes *Tom Jones*, operetta
1928	Knighted for his services to music

《 German's *Tom Jones*, based on Henry Fielding's novel, was a great success in 1907, although some were offended by the bawdiness of Tom's story.

Sir Arthur **Sullivan**

● 1842–1900   🏴 ENGLISH   ✍ c.300

Sir Arthur Sullivan, together with W. S. Gilbert, invented the Savoy Opera, and their names became inseparable. Gilbert and Sullivan's operettas parodied operatic convention and ridiculed the pomposities of British officialdom (even in the guise of Japanese in *The Mikado*). But Sullivan longed for recognition as a serious composer, and wrote many instrumental, choral, and operatic works.

Arthur Sullivan was the son of an Irish bandmaster and an Italian mother, and he published his first composition at 13. After studying in London at the Royal Academy of Music, and then at the Leipzig Conservatory, he wrote cantatas and symphonies before writing his first comic operetta, *Cox and Box*. In 1871, he met the playwright, W. S. Gilbert, and began a collaboration that lasted until the pair famously quarreled about a new carpet at the Savoy Theatre in 1889, only reuniting to write two final operettas. In the meantime, Sullivan had written his one opera, *Ivanhoe*, which he hoped would establish his reputation. This, however, rests firmly with the comic operettas he wrote with Gilbert.

MILESTONES	
1854	Chorister at the Chapel Royal
1862	Establishes reputation with incidental music for *The Tempest*
1876	*Trial by Jury*, first successful collaboration with Gilbert
1878	Composes *HMS Pinafore*, operetta
1879	*The Pirates of Penzance* produced
1883	Receives a knighthood
1889	Writes *The Gondoliers*
1890	Writes *Ivanhoe*, his only opera

KEY WORKS

HMS PINAFORE

OPERETTA   ⏳ 105:00   📖 2   ⚖ 🎭 👤

Filled with sea-shanties and nautical airs, *HMS Pinafore* is a satire on the British class system and its embodiment in the Royal Navy. Sullivan rose to the challenge of Gilbert's intricate meters and patter-songs with a lively, bustling score, setting the story of *The Lass that Loved a Sailor*.

THE MIKADO

OPERETTA   ⏳ 135:00   📖 2   ⚖ 🎭 👤

In the mythical Japanese town of Titipu, the strolling minstrel Nanki-Poo (the Mikado's son) is courting Yum-Yum, the ward of the Lord High Executioner. The wit of Sullivan's music is shown by his incorporation of a genuine Japanese tune, an English madrigal, and a Bach fugue in his score.

▲ *The Mikado*, first produced in 1885, ran at the Savoy Theatre for 672 performances.

Engelbert **Humperdinck**

● 1854–1921　　🏳 GERMAN　　✍ c.230

Engelbert Humperdinck was born in Siegburg in 1854 and studied architecture in Cologne before being encouraged to change his discipline to composition, piano, and cello. He continued his studies in Munich, winning prizes with his early compositions, including the Mendelssohn Prize, which took him to Naples. There he befriended Wagner, who brought him to Bayreuth as his assistant. Humperdinck assisted Wagner on *Parsifal*, and learned a great deal from him about orchestration and vocal writing, but he discovered his own original voice in his use of simple children's songs, especially in his masterpiece *Hänsel und Gretel*.

Humperdinck's sister suggested that he set the Grimm brothers' fairy tale *Hansel and Gretel* as a musical entertainment for her children. First he set songs, then a *Singspiel* with spoken dialogue, and finally in 1893 he produced the full operatic score of his first and most famous opera. It is also the one most clearly influenced by the music of Wagner, as heard in its complex orchestration and repeating musical themes. However, consistent with the composer's choice of traditional fairy tale as his subject matter, there is also fun and lightness, with passages inspired by folk dance and folk song, as well as musical originality. The story is well known: Hansel and Gretel are sent by their mother to pick strawberries in the forest. They get lost and fall asleep. They wake to find a gingerbread cottage. Its owner, a witch, tries to fatten Hansel for dinner, but Gretel bundles her into the oven and frees the gingerbread children.

MILESTONES

1876	Wins Mozart Scholarship, allowing him to study in Munich
1879	Writes *Humoreske* for orchestra
1881	Wins Meyerbeer Prize of 7,600 marks; goes to work for Wagner in Bayreuth
1910	Opera *Königskinder* (*Royal Children*) premiered in New York

⏏ **Humperdinck's** ***Hänsel und Gretel*** was premiered in Weimar by Richard Strauss, who called it "original, new, and authentically German." German audiences, such as this one in Berlin in 1895, took it to their hearts.

Franz **Lehár**

● 1870–1948　　🏳 HUNGARIAN　　✍ c.260

Franz Lehár was for 20th-century Viennese operetta what Johann Strauss Jr had been for the 19th century. He was the son of a military bandmaster and studied at the Prague Conservatory. He then led army bands, while starting his career as a composer with an unsuccessful grand opera, *Kukuška*. His waltz *Gold and Silver* was popular enough to allow him to leave band life and compose more for the stage. In 1902 he had two operetta premieres in Vienna, followed by his greatest success, *Die lustige Witwe* (*The Merry Widow*).

The libretto for *The Merry Widow* was adapted from *The Embassy Attaché*, a play by Henri Meilhac. Lehár used a larger orchestra than was until then usual for operettas. The music is a heady mix of Balkan folk dance, Parisian cabaret, and Viennese waltz. The operetta tells the story of a young "merry widow," Hanna, whose banker husband left her a fortune. To keep her from marrying a foreigner, the Pontevedrian Ambassador sends Count Danilo to woo her. He does so. Her money thus stays in Pontevedro, rescuing her from bankruptcy.

The Merry Widow was so successful that it spawned a craze for "Merry Widow" corsets, hats, and cocktails. The operetta made his fame in Europe and the US, as well as his fortune, and Lehár's income enabled him to buy an elegant villa in Bad Ischl in 1912.

Lehár's operetta career then flourished, but declined during World War I. Working with the tenor Richard Tauber, he found new success with *Frasquita* and *Paganini*, culminating in *The Land of Smiles*. Under the Nazis, he was forced to retire (his wife was Jewish), but his work was still performed.

MILESTONES

1902	Writes concert waltz *Gold and Silver*; *Wiener Frauen*, operetta, is a success
1920	Begins writing for Richard Tauber
1934	Writes a full-scale opera, *Giuditta*

⏏ **Lehár made his name** as a composer of Viennese waltzes before finding success with operettas.

National Schools
1830–1950

During the 19th and early 20th centuries, as modern nation-states emerged, music for many composers became a means of asserting their national identity. Other composers included in this section were not actively nationalists, but their music nevertheless reflects their countries or regions of origin.

Much of the music of the Baroque and Classical periods has a style that cannot easily be pinned down to a single country; styles and forms were international. In the 19th century, however, musicians began to define themselves in terms of their nationalities as well as the styles or genres in which they worked.

European politics in the 19th century was dominated by nationalist movements. These were of two main kinds. There were peoples united by a common language, such as the Italians and Germans, whose aim was to form a single nation-state, while other peoples—for example, the Hungarians, Czechs, and Irish—were subject to foreign rule and sought autonomy or independence. Music, along with language and literature, became a means of expressing their aspirations.

The most clear-cut example of musical nationalism, however, did not emerge in a country ruled by an oppressive empire. Russia was itself a great empire, but historically had been made to feel culturally inferior to Western Europe. European music had been imported into Russia by and for the aristocracy; the only truly Russian music was that of the folk tradition.

Russian nationalism

The catalyst for change in Russia was Mikhail Glinka. His opera *A Life for the Czar* was similar to Rossini in style, but recalled the Russian folk melodies he had heard in his childhood.

The so-called "group of five," who emerged in the middle of the 19th century, took Russian nationalism much further. Balakirev composed a symphonic poem *Russia* and Borodin wrote *In Central Asia*. A third member of the group, Mussorgsky, was not a formally trained musician; unfamiliar with Western harmonic progressions, he composed music that made full use of Russian folk harmonies. Later Russian composers, such as Rimsky-Korsakov, also made use of folk melodies and influenced future generations of composers, including Glazunov and Stravinsky.

The Habsburg Empire

Czech nationalist composers were less virulently anti-Western than their Russian counterparts. Their aim was to affirm their cultural difference from the Austrian

⟪ This painting of Spanish gypsy dancers by Ricardo Canals y Llambi expresses the fascination felt all over Europe in the late 19th century for vital folk traditions in music and dance.

✉ **The plot** of Glinka's groundbreaking opera *A Life for the Czar* revolved around the election of the first Romanov czar in 1613 and included a lively depiction of Russian peasant life.

Habsburg Empire, which had ruled Bohemia and Moravia for centuries, suppressing Czech language and culture. Smetana, Dvořák, and Janáček all contributed to the development of their country's national musical style. *Má Vlast*, Smetana's cycle of symphonic poems, is not only a portrait of the Czech landscape, but also an evocation of

Czech culture and history. The section *Tábor* includes a Czech Hussite chorale, "Those who are Warriors of God." Hungary's situation differed from that of Czechoslovakia because its folk music had been represented (or misrepresented) by Romantic composers, such as Liszt, Brahms, and Joachim. It was only in the 20th century that Bartók and Kodály began to collect Hungarian folk music more systematically and make use of it in a more authentic way.

TIMELINE: NATIONAL SCHOOLS

1848 Marx and Engels publish *The Communist Manifesto*

1861 Unification of most of Italy; emancipation of serfs in Russia

1861–65 American Civil War

1874 Mussorgsky's *Boris Godunov* performed in St Petersburg

1835

1850

1865

1836 Glinka's patriotic opera *A Life for the Czar*

1848 Revolutions in Italy, across the Habsburg Empire, and in Paris

1860s Balakirev and other members of the "Five" strive to create Russian style of music

1870 Franco-Prussian War; unification of Germany under Kaiser Wilhelm I

1876 Ibsen's *Peer Gynt* performed with Grieg's incidental music

Indian melodies. Charles Ives was a more distinctively American composer, and his quotations of music from his own environment provide a highly evocative if individual picture of his childhood in New England. Later on, Aaron Copland would create a highly recognizable American music, partly by appropriating rustic styles such as the "hoedown" in Appalachian Spring.

A revival of folk music in Spain coincided with that in Britain in the early 20th century. Composers such as Granados and Albéniz in Spain and Vaughan Williams in England used the folk music of their respective countries in similar nostalgic ways.

⌃ Mitrofan Belyaev was a rich lumber merchant who founded a Russian music publishing house in 1885. Among his guests pictured here are Rimsky-Korsakov and Lyadov.

⌃ Smetana was inspired both by Czech history and his country's landscapes, as in this piece, *From Bohemia's Woods and Fields*, part of *Má Vlast* (My Homeland).

Further afield

Political and cultural links between Germany and the Scandinavian countries took some time to loosen; Denmark's Niels Gade, for example, spent much time studying and subsequently conducting in Leipzig. It was left to Nordraak and Grieg (who also studied in Leipzig) to create a distinctive Norwegian art music. Grieg's *Peer Gynt Suite* was written as incidental music for Ibsen's play about the eponymous adventurer. In Finland, the music of Sibelius has nationalist tendencies only in that it quotes Finnish folk music.

In North America, most art music of the 19th century ignored folk material, although MacDowell's *Indian Suite* uses American

FOLK MELODIES

Just as languages and dialects differ from each other, so folk melodies have distinctive and often immediately recognizable characteristics. Different cultures tend to use different kinds of intervals in their melodies, which give them a particular flavor. In the case of the Jewish Klezmer music of Central and Eastern Europe, for example, this is a particularly exotic flavor. The use of rhythm in folk music also differs greatly from one culture to another, just as it does in spoken language.

◀ In the late 19th century, musicians, painters, and social historians across Europe were enthusiastic recorders of vanishing regional folk traditions.

1883 Opening of Czech National Theater with performance of Smetana's *Libuše*

1919 Treaty of Versailles; Hungary, Czechoslovakia, Poland, and Finland gain independence

1880   1895   1910

1888 Rimsky-Korsakov's *Sheherazade*

1890 First of Danish composer Nielsen's six symphonies

1900 Sibelius's tone poem *Finlandia*

1917 Russian Revolution

1919 Pianist Paderewski becomes first prime minister of modern Poland

Mikhail **Glinka**

◔ 1804–1857   ▥ **RUSSIAN**   ✍ c.195

Glinka is regarded as the father of Russian music and produced the first successful Russian national opera. Rejecting traditional German forms and harmony in favor of music developed from folklike melodies, his works display rhythmic exuberance, quasi-oriental chromaticism, and vivid clarity of orchestral textures, which epitomize a Russian sound that inspired successive generations of composers.

From a wealthy family, Glinka only dabbled in music until his late 20s, when he established himself as a pianist in Milan. Subsequent musical studies in Berlin were cut short by his father's death, and he returned home to start work on his opera *A Life for the Czar*. Its success established him as Russia's preeminent composer; however, his next opera, *Ruslan and Lyudmilla*, was less well received. Travels to Paris and Madrid inspired him to write the orchestral showpieces which now eclipse his many fine vocal and instrumental works.

MILESTONES	
1830	Arrives in Milan; meets Mendelssohn, Bellini, and Donizetti
1835	Marries Mariya Petrovna Ivanova; she remarries bigamously six years later
1837	Appointed Kapellmeister of Imperial Chapel
1844	First production of opera *Ruslan and Lyudmilla* arouses admiration of Liszt
1848	Composes *Kamarinskaya*, orchestral work

KEY WORKS

A LIFE FOR THE CZAR

OPERA   ⏱ 209:00   📖 5

A celebration of nationalist fervour, this opera was originally titled *Ivor Susanin* after its tragic hero, but was renamed in honor of Czar Nicholas I, to whom it was dedicated. When staged in Soviet times, the title reverted and the libretto was altered to expunge references to the Czar.

In a Russian village, Ivan Susanin's daughter is about to marry Sobinin, who has returned from fighting the Poles. Susanin approves the wedding only when he hears that a new Romanov Czar has been crowned. A messenger interrupts celebrations at the Polish court to tell the King that the Russians are fighting back under their newly crowned Czar. During the wedding Polish soldiers arrive and demand to know the Czar's hiding place. Susanin leads them in the wrong direction and his stepson, Vanya, rides to warn the Czar. Sobinin and a group of peasants follow Susanin to attempt his rescue. The Poles realize they have

been tricked and kill Susanin. The Russian people celebrate in Moscow whilst Susanin's family mourns. The opera ends with a hymn to the Czar.

KAMARINSKAYA

ORCHESTRAL   ⏱ 7:30   📖 1

Inspired by meeting Berlioz, Glinka started writing orchestral works with a nationalist character. The last of these, *Kamarinskaya*, proved highly influential—Tchaikovsky believed that the Russian symphonic school was "all in *Kamarinskaya*, just as the whole oak is in the acorn." Based entirely on two Russian melodies, the work begins, after a brief introduction, with a slow, traditional bridal-song repeated three times with different accompaniments. A lively dance tune (kamarinskaya) follows on the violin, and is repeated 13 times in increasingly complex orchestral combinations. Then the music slows to reintroduce the bridal song, but the kamarinskaya soon returns for 21 more variations.

⌃ **Glinka's** *Kamarinskaya* was the first important Russian work to have been based entirely on folk music.

Aleksandr **Borodin**

⬤ 1833–1887　　🏳 RUSSIAN　　✍ 21+

Born in St. Petersburg, Borodin was the illegitimate son of a Georgian prince who registered the child under the name of a servant. Although he excelled from childhood in both science and music, he chose a career in chemistry. While practicing as a professor and researcher at the Academy of Medico-Surgery in St. Petersburg, he composed in his spare time. Although he admired Schumann, it was his compatriot Mily Balakirev—with whom he studied in 1863—who had the most dramatic influence on his style. One of the "mighty handful" of Russian composers, Borodin was perhaps the most overtly Romantic, turning out highly charged music, full of choral and orchestral color. Of this circle of composers, he was also perhaps most able to assimilate Russian folk style with the European symphonic tradition. He left a small but polished oeuvre, including symphonies, songs, and chamber music. His Symphony No. 2 displays a peerless mastery of technique, while *Prince Igor* remains a landmark of Russian opera.

Eighteen years in composition, and completed posthumously by Rimsky-Korsakov and Glazunov, *Prince Igor* is Borodin's best-known work. Set in 12th-century Russia, it depicts the imprisonment of a Russian prince by an invading Tartar tribe, the Polovetsians. A notable feature is Borodin's unusual handling of the chorus, which functions almost as a separate character in the drama. The thrilling Polovetsian dances that conclude the second act are often performed on their own in concert.

MILESTONES

1869	Symphony No. 1 premiered unsuccessfully
1872	Lectures at the School of Medicine for Women, St. Petersburg
1876	Writes Symphony No. 2 in B minor
1880	*In the Steppes of Central Asia*, tone poem
1890	*Prince Igor*, opera, premiered posthumously at St. Petersburg

⬆ *Prince Igor,* imbued with Russian character, displays Borodin's flair for orchestral color and exotic motifs.

Mily Alekseyevich **Balakirev**

⬤ 1837–1910　　🏳 RUSSIAN　　✍ c.50

The driving force behind the Russian nationalist "school" of music, Balakirev formed, guided, and inspired the "mighty handful," a circle committed to the nationalist cause including Cui, Mussorgsky, Borodin, and Rimsky-Korsakov.

After receiving early musical training from his mother, Balakirev was spotted by the wealthy music patron Alexander Ulibishev, who sent him to St. Petersburg to meet Mikhail Glinka. A difficult and single-minded idealist, Balakirev brooked no opposition and antagonized many. Overwrought and overworked, he suffered a nervous breakdown in 1871, withdrew from public life, and turned to mysticism, before emerging again in 1883 when he was appointed to the Imperial Chapel. His career was thus punctuated by periods of inactivity, but he produced some striking works in an unmistakably Russian idiom.

Regarded as Balakirev's greatest work, *Tamara* is based on a poem by Mikhail Lermontov that relates the story of a siren who entices a traveler into her lair with her seductive song. After a night of passion, all is silent in the morning as the traveler's corpse swirls past in the tide of the river. Although Balakirev is not overtly descriptive, the plot can be discerned in the music. A quiet timpani roll evokes the fairy-tale atmosphere, while Tamara's voice is heard in the sinuous woodwind figure.

MILESTONES

1847	Studies music in Moscow
1855	Moves to St. Petersburg
1861	Writes incidental music for *King Lear*
1862	Founds the Free School of Music
1869	*Islamey*, fantasy, composed
1871	Suffers breakdown; turns to mysticism
1872	Works for the Warsaw railroad
1882	*Tamara*, symphonic poem, staged
1883	Director of the Imperial Chapel
1908	Writes Symphony No. 2 in D minor

⬆ **The concerted force** of the "mighty handful" changed the course of Russian music, creating a distinctive Russian style that successfully merged Classical forms with Russian folk idioms.

Modest **Mussorgsky**

🌑 **1839–1881** 📖 **RUSSIAN** ✍ **c.50**

A mercurial and brilliantly talented composer, Mussorgsky was also an incurable alcoholic who led a disordered and prematurely shortened life. As a member of Balakirev's circle, he strove to compose music that resonated with the Russian people. However, many of his works were left unfinished, or were completed by well-meaning friends in a manner that may not reflect the composer's true intentions.

Despite being a prodigy at the piano, Mussorgsky initially joined the army, but resigned his commission in 1858 for a life of "meaningful endeavor." Taking a job in the civil service, he began to work on a symphony and an opera, but these came to nothing. For the rest of his life a combination of unsettled personal circumstances, a nervous temperament, and serious alcoholism contrived to limit his creative endeavors. Of the Russian "Mighty Handful," Mussorgsky's music is perhaps the most rough-hewn, earthy, and immediate.

MILESTONES	
1852	Enters Imperial Guard Cadet School
1861	Forced to work family estate following emancipation of the serfs
1865	First serious alcoholic episode
1867	Writes *St. John's Night on the Bare Mountain*
1872	Composes *The Nursery* (song cycle)
1874	Revised version of *Boris Godunov*; *Sunless* (song cycle); *Pictures at an Exhibition*
1875	*Songs and Dances of Death* (song cycle)

KEY WORKS

BORIS GODUNOV

OPERA	⏳ 210:00	📖 5	🎭 ⚒ ♦

Mussorgsky produced two complete versions of this opera during his lifetime, and Rimsky-Korsakov famously took upon himself the task of smoothing Mussorgsky's characteristically abrasive orchestration. His version is colorful and attractive, and was popular for many years. Nevertheless, it is now broadly agreed that Rimsky-Korsakov's alterations do little to enhance the work. As a consequence, *Boris Godunov* is now usually performed in one or other of its original versions.

Musically, the most important innovation in the opera lies in Mussorgsky's use of the speech patterns of Russian language as the basis for his music. Rather than setting dialogue to precomposed melodies, Mussorgsky's vocal lines follow the pitch and rhythm of spoken Russian. This gives the opera a sense of "reality" because characters appear to converse with each other in a manner that the Russian audience would immediately have recognized.

PICTURES AT AN EXHIBITION

SOLO PIANO	⏳ 35:00	📖 4	🎹

Mussorgsky wrote this work as a musical tribute to his close friend, the artist Viktor Hartmann, who died in 1873. It was written in 1874, when an exhibition of Hartmann's works took place. This impressive work for piano opens with a *Promenade*, which recurs several times; with its steady pulse but alternating tempo, it seems to suggest a viewer wandering around the gallery, pausing to inspect pictures more closely. The remaining 11 pieces are vivid interpretations of the individual paintings. The breadth of Mussorgsky's musical inspiration is unparalleled, conjuring images that range from playful to eerie or majestic.

🔺 **St. John's Night on the Bare Mountain** is a dramatic musical portrait of the witches' Sabbath, held in the mountains near Kiev.

Nikolay **Rimsky-Korsakov**

● 1844–1908   RUSSIAN   ✍ c.130

Rimsky-Korsakov was a friend of Mily Balakirev and member of the "Mighty Handful," a group of five composers led by Balakirev who aimed to develop an authentically Russian art music. Rimsky-Korsakov's music, much of it based on themes from Russian folklore, is justly renowned for its brilliant, colorful orchestration. He was later important as a teacher and counted Prokofiev and Stravinsky among his pupils.

Following his elder brother into the navy, Rimsky-Korsakov began composing a symphony in his final year at naval college after making the acquaintance of Balakirev. This proved impossible to complete while at sea, and by the end of his three-year tour of duty he had almost resolved to give up music altogether. On returning to shore, however, he was persuaded to finish the symphony and, after its successful premiere, decided on a switch of career. A committed nationalist, Rimsky-Korsakov wrote 15 operas on Russian themes and used folk melodies in many of his instrumental compositions.

MILESTONES	
1861	Meets Balakirev; starts Symphony No. 1
1865	Symphony No. 1 premiered by Balakirev
1887	Composes *Capriccio Espagnol*
1888	Composes *Sheherazade* and *Russian Easter Festival Overture*
1889	Completes Borodin's opera *Prince Igor* with Glazunov
1896	Orchestrates Mussorgsky's opera *Boris Godunov*

KEY WORKS

SHEHERAZADE

SYMPHONIC SUITE   ⏱ 45:00   📖 4

Like many Russian composers and artists, Rimsky-Korsakov was fascinated by the Islamic cultures over Russia's borders. A large-scale suite in four movements, *Sheherazade* is based on the tale of *The Thousand and One Nights* in which a young woman changes a cruel sultan's character by recounting stories.

Whilst Rimsky-Korsakov was especially drawn to four of the stories, to which the four movements of his work correspond, *Sheherazade* is not strictly descriptive. (He was initially persuaded to include programmatic titles for each of the movements, but later withdrew them.) Neither is it symphonic, in the sense of containing extensive development of themes. Rather, Rimsky-Korsakov described it as a "kaleidoscope of fairy-tale images and designs of Oriental character," in which the music attempts to capture the mood of each story.

Certain melodies recur throughout the work, however: notably the austere theme that opens the first movement—associated with the Sultan—and the sinuous solo violin melody heard shortly afterward, representing Sheherazade herself.

CAPRICCIO ESPAGNOL

ORCHESTRAL   ⏱ 18:00   📖 5

Spanish music was popular with Russian composers as part of the general interest in the exotic, and Rimsky-Korsakov's enduringly popular *Capriccio Espagnol* is based on themes drawn from a volume of Spanish folk melodies. The main musical ideas are a morning, an evening, a Gypsy dance, and an Asturian song. In a sense, the work is Rimsky-Korsakov *par excellence*—limited musical argument, but brilliant orchestral color. He emphasized that it should be thought of as a piece for orchestra rather than an orchestration of a piece that could otherwise stand alone.

⬆ **After his first opera,** *Ivan the Terrible*, Rimsky-Korsakov wrote 14 others. They form his most important legacy.

Anton **Rubinstein**

◔ 1829–1894   📖 RUSSIAN   ✍ 200

One of the very few 19th-century pianists who could stand comparison with Liszt, Anton Rubinstein was also outstanding as a teacher and conductor. His brother Nikolay was also an important pianist and musician. Rubinstein toured Europe as a child virtuoso, and then as a mature artist was known for his huge repertoire and remarkable stamina (in the US he played 215 recitals in under nine months). He was also twice director of the St. Petersburg Conservatory. He composed prolifically—and lucratively, thanks to his fame—but many of the grandiloquent pieces he composed can feel glib and superficial. However, his opera *Demon* was a huge success, with the great Russian bass Fyodor Chaliapin often in the title role, and his *Melody in F*, Op. 3, No. 1, proved lastingly popular.

MILESTONES	
1848	Becomes chamber virtuoso to Grand Duchess Helena Pavlovna, Russia
1864	Composes Piano Concerto No. 4
1871	Conducts Philharmonic Concerts in Vienna
1872	Tours US with Henryk Wieniawski

⌃ **The founding of St. Petersburg Conservatory** put the city on a par with Vienna, London, Paris, and Berlin, and soon attracted world-famous musicians to Russia.

Anatoly **Lyadov**

◔ 1855–1914   📖 RUSSIAN   ✍ 100

Born into a highly musical family, Lyadov never completed any large-scale works. Talented but rather lazy, he was expelled from Rimsky-Korsakov's composition classes for nonattendance, idled his summers away at his wife's country house, and ignored Diaghilev's commission for *The Firebird*, which Stravinsky snapped up. Many of his pieces are arrangements of folk songs collected from various parts of Russia, and he brought orchestral color and characterization to these miniatures. He collaborated with Rimsky-Korsakov and Balakirev, and his student Prokofiev found him likeable, but pedantic.

MILESTONES	
1878	Starts teaching at St. Petersburg Conservatory
1890	Composes *Pro starinu*, piano ballade
1897	Commissioned to collect folk songs by Imperial Geographical Society
1909	*The Enchanted Lake*, Op. 62, and *Kikimora*, Op. 63, tone poems, published

⌃ **Lyadov described** *Baba Yaga* (1904) as a "tone picture after a Russian fairytale" and used a large orchestra, including a xylophone, to create sounds of the forest and other atmospheric effects.

Sergey **Liapunov**

◔ 1859–1924   〰 **RUSSIAN**   ✍ 80

Liapunov's modest composing success didn't come until he was in his 40s, and then mainly thanks to encouragement and promotion from his friend Balakirev. In addition to conducting, Liapunov toured as a pianist and wrote with a complete understanding of the instrument. His best pieces were the works for piano, such as the Liszt-influenced *12 Transcendental Studies*, and his piquant songs, such as "The Mountain Peaks."

MILESTONES	
1893	Commissioned to collect folk songs
1905	Finishes *12 Transcendental Studies*, Op. 11, for piano
1910	Professor at St. Petersburg Conservatory
1913	Composes Prelude and Fugue in B minor, Op. 58, for piano

Mikhail **Ippolitov-Ivanov**

◔ 1859–1935   〰 **RUSSIAN**   ✍ 80

A craftsman in the Russian academic vein rather than an original genius, Ippolitov-Ivanov's style and technique changed little throughout his career, taking the form of folk song-based nationalism with an Oriental twist and, after the Revolution, hints of Uzbek, Kazakh, Turkmen, or Arabic music. His popular *Caucasian Sketches* shows the influences of Georgia, where he lived for a few years, teaching and conducting.

MILESTONES	
1884	Conductor of Imperial Opera, Tiflis
1893	Professor at Moscow Conservatory
1894	*Caucasian Sketches*, orchestral suite
1895	Writes *Armenian Rhapsody*, symphony
1900	Composes *Assia*, opera
1934	Publishes memoirs: *Fifty Years of Russian Music*

Anton Stepanovich **Arensky**

◔ 1861–1906   〰 **RUSSIAN**   ✍ c.80

Arensky was made a professor at the Moscow Conservatory immediately on graduating with a gold medal from St. Petersburg, having studied composition under Rimsky-Korsakov. He went on to teach Rachmaninoff and Scriabin. An eclectic composer, influenced by Chopin, Tchaikovsky, and Mendelssohn, among others, he worked unusual rhythms into his lyrical and sentimental music. In addition to writing operas, he also composed church music, songs, symphonies, and elegant piano pieces. Arensky's last years were spent successfully as a composer, pianist, and conductor, but were blighted by his addictions to alcohol and gambling.

MILESTONES	
1888	Directs Russian Choral Society
1891	*A Dream on the Volga*, opera, published
1894	Composes Piano Trio No. 1
1895	Becomes Director of Imperial Chapel, St. Petersburg
1900	Composes *Egyptian Nights*, ballet

≪ Arensky, seen here in his workroom, is best known for his charming, elegant, and melodically inventive Piano Trio No.1 in D minor.

Alexander **Scriabin**

● 1872–1915   🏴 **RUSSIAN**   ✍ **c.200**

Original to the point of eccentricity, Scriabin ranks among the 20th century's most important composers for the piano, and was one of its greatest musical innovators. In the later years of his short life, an all-consuming interest in mystical philosophy pervaded every aspect of his world. As his beliefs became ever more bizarre, he pushed the boundaries of harmony and performance to their limits.

Life

After setting out as a concert pianist, Scriabin injured his right hand, which put a temporary halt to his performing career but gave him more time to compose. Scriabin's early pieces, almost exclusively for the piano, show a clear affinity with the Romantics, with many works in characteristically Chopin-esque forms. In later years, however, Scriabin became increasingly interested in Helene Blavatsky's "theosophy." These beliefs came eventually to dominate his thinking about music, which in turn pushed his musical language in radically new directions. Nevertheless, he retained a curious reliance on classical formal principles.

Music

Scriabin's instrument was the piano, and the majority of his music was written for piano solo. His early pieces were heavily influenced by the Romantic style of Chopin, and to a lesser extent Liszt, and included numerous études, preludes, nocturnes, and "poèmes." Even in these early works, however, he showed a distinctive style, and quickly developed a very individual approach to harmonic color which took him increasingly further away from the conventions of tonal harmony. The progression is most clearly seen in his ten published Piano Sonatas, which are successively more chromatic and dissonant, and move from the classical sonata form in several movements to a more loosely structured single-movement piece. Sonata No. 5 in particular stands out as a turning point, when the complexity of his harmony verges on the atonal, and the subsequent sonatas are written without any key signature.

His harmonic language evolved hand in hand with his increasing interest in mysticism, and an ambition to write a large-scale work combining poetry, music, and visual elements. He also became fascinated with the connection between the colors of the spectrum and musical timbre and harmony, and explored this in his symphonic music, assigning different colors to each note of the scale.

The three symphonies, and the symphonic works *The Poem of Ecstasy*, and *Prometheus* (*The Poem of Fire*) show Scriabin as a superb orchestrator with a penchant for the dramatic and magical, which he hoped would reach its apotheosis in his sensual, quasi-religious *The Mysterium*, a forerunner of modern multimedia "events"; its performance, which Scriabin envisaged as being in the foothills of the Himalayas, was to bring about a form of armageddon, allowing "nobler beings" to replace the human race but, perhaps fortunately, the piece remained unfinished when he died.

MILESTONES	
1888	Studied at Moscow Conservatory
1896	Composes 24 Preludes, Op. 11; Piano Concerto, Op. 20
1898	Professor of Piano at the Moscow Conservatory
1903	Writes Piano Sonata No. 4, Op. 30
1907	*Poem of Ecstasy*, Op. 54, symphonic poem
1909	Composes *Prometheus*, Op. 60, symphony
1909	Moves to Brussels for two years
1911	Writes Piano Sonata No. 7, Op. 64 ("White Mass")
1913	Composes Piano Sonata No. 8, Op. 66; writes Piano Sonata No.9, Op. 68 ("Black Mass")

KEY WORKS

PROMETHEUS (THE POEM OF FIRE)

ORCHESTRAL   ⏱ 25:00   📖 1

Prometheus (*The Poem of Fire*) is the last of Scriabin's five symphonies, and one of the last pieces he composed before his death. It takes as its basis the Greek myth in which Prometheus defies Zeus to give mankind command of fire. For Scriabin, symbolism operated at every level in the work, from the so-called "mystic chord," on which much of the harmony is derived, to the specification of a wordless, white-robed chorus. Moreover, the work was intended to be an early—perhaps the first—example of a multimedia performance. Scriabin wrote a complete part for "Tastiera per Luce" ("keyboard of lights"), which would flood the performance space with different colored light according to which combination of keys was pressed. Considered for its purely musical merits, *Prometheus* is a striking work, and contains many moments of sensuous orchestration and bold, otherworldly harmony.

PIANO SONATA NO. 4, OP. 30

SOLO PIANO   ⏱ 8:40   📖 2   🎧

Scriabin's oeuvre consists in large part of piano works—he wrote many hundreds of preludes, études, and impromptus. Central to these is the series of ten sonatas, which began in 1892 in the sound world of Rachmaninoff and Chopin and ended in 1913 with a work that is on the very verge of atonality. Sonata No. 4 was composed during a summer of extraordinary productivity.
First movement (*andante*, 3:50) The first movement demonstrates some of Scriabin's most sensuous writing. It is based on one theme, introduced delicately and developed through a series of unexpected harmonic shifts.
Second movement (*prestissimo volando*, 4:50) The second movement explodes into life with a buoyant theme. A more lyrical second subject follows, then develops into a reintroduction of a theme from the first movement. After a recapitulation and coda, the sonata closes with a virtuosic flourish.

PIANO CONCERTO

ORCHESTRAL   ⏱ 28:00   📖 3

The Piano Concerto of 1896, Scriabin's first orchestral score, was well received by audiences and attracted him a degree of early fame. With distinct echoes of Chopin and Rachmaninoff, it stands as a fascinating contrast with his more extraordinary later works.

THE POEM OF ECSTASY

ORCHESTRA   ⏱ 20:00   📖 1   🎵

Sometimes referred to as Scriabin's Fourth Symphony, it is in fact a symphonic poem in a single movement, and the first of his orchestral works to make explicit reference to his mystical beliefs, in particular those of the Theosophists. Accompanying the score, but not intended for performance, is a philosophical poem by Scriabin on the subject of ecstasy and its connection with music as (in his view) respectively the most highly evolved emotion and art form. Written in 1905–07, it uses the highly chromatic harmonic language of his mature work, combined with continually shifting tone colors.

SONATA NO. 9, "BLACK MASS"

SOLO PIANO   ⏱ 9:00   📖 1   🎧

After Scriabin described his Sonata No. 7 as the "White Mass," the ninth was soon dubbed the "Black Mass." Whereas the former work is radiant, even joyous, the latter is among his most dark, knotty works, emphasizing the dissonant minor-ninth interval and ending with a grotesque march.

THE MYSTERIUM

MULTIMEDIA   ⏱ 7 DAYS

The Mysterium was left incomplete—Scriabin had barely begun work on it before his sudden death. Sketches indicate a seven-day-long multimedia spectacle intended for performance in the Himalayas. Scriabin believed that this performance would act as a purification ritual, leading to the rebirth of the world.

Scriabin was profoundly influenced by Helene Blavatsky's Theosophical Movement and, while in London, he visited the room in which she died in 1891.

Sergey **Rachmaninoff**

● **1873–1943**   ⚑ **RUSSIAN**   ✍ **96**

A highly praised conductor and outstanding pianist whose many recordings show his crisp technique, unostentatious approach, and outstanding clarity, Rachmaninoff was also the last major composer of the great Russian late-Romantic tradition. Most of his music was written before 1917, when he left Russia never to return; appropriately, some of his works radiate passionate yearning or nostalgia.

Tchaikovsky's support. However, a calamitous performance of his Symphony No. 1 (under an allegedly drunk Glazunov) drew savage reviews; for three years he could not face composing, and turned to conducting, with increasing success. However, a hypnotist doctor and musician, Nikolai Dahl, persuaded him to compose again. The Piano Concerto No. 2 was among the excellent works he now steadily produced. His reputation as composer, conductor, and performer grew. By his 40s he had toured the US, Russia, England, and Europe, but he lost his country estate in the Revolution and fled to Scandinavia. He spent his last 25 years in the US and Europe, working, touring, recording, and publishing music. Growing ill health made him cancel a concert tour, and he died of cancer aged 69.

》 To strangers
Rachmaninoff could seem unsmiling and aloof, but with friends and family in their homemade Russian enclave he was warm, content, and generous.

Life

After his father squandered the family fortune, Rachmaninoff's parents moved from a country estate to a crowded St. Petersburg apartment. His education was disrupted by their separation, so he was sent to the Moscow Conservatory. He boarded with his piano teacher in a severe routine of all-day practice, starting at 6:00am, and graduated with the highest possible marks for his composition and playing. His career started well: the opera *Aleko* was successfully premiered, and he enjoyed

Music

The piano figures prominently in Rachmaninoff's output, both solo and with orchestra. His orchestral works include three symphonies, and he wrote over 80 lyrical songs. There is little chamber music, and his three operas suffer from unpromising librettos. His choral work *Vespers* shows his liking for religious chant. His music up to the critically mauled Symphony No. 1 is energetic and highly competent, if sometimes derivative (the Tchaikovsky-ish opera *Aleko*, for instance). But when he started composing again after his years of self-doubt, Rachmaninoff's style developed significantly into the now-familiar sweeping melodies, subtly and richly scored—for example, in the long, seamless lines of the Piano Concerto No. 2 or Symphony No. 2. Among the few works he wrote after leaving Russia are the *Rhapsody on a Theme of Paganini*, Symphony No. 3, and Piano Concerto No. 4.

❝❝ Only **one place** is **closed to me,** and that is **my own** country—**Russia. ❞❞**
Rachmaninoff in an interview for *The Musical Times*, 1930

MILESTONES

1891	Composes Piano Concerto No. 1
1892	Graduates as composer; Prelude in C sharp minor, Op. 3, No. 2, composed
1893	Successful premiere of *Aleko*
1897	Disastrous premiere of Symphony No. 1; takes conducting post
1899	First international appearance, London
1900	Consults psychologist Dr. Dahl; receives auto-suggestive therapy to deal with nervous breakdown
1901	Piano Concerto No. 2 composed, dedicated to Dr. Dahl
1902	Marries cousin Natalia Satina
1908	Symphony No. 2 premiered
1910	Now an established composer-conductor-pianist; tours US
1918	Decides to live in US
1919	Makes his first recording; continues to record with Ampico for ten years
1936	Symphony No. 3 completed

KEY WORKS

PIANO CONCERTO NO. 2, OP. 18

ORCHESTRAL 35:00 3

The endlessly flowing lyricism of Rachmaninoff's first and most enduring success—the happy result of his confidence-building sessions with Dr. Dahl—has inspired direct and indirect use in pop music and films.

First movement (*moderato*, 11:00) Eight ominous piano chords introduce a somber first theme, contrasted with the more optimistic second; a strident, martial short figure is repeated as a device to link the two.

Second movement (*adagio sostenuto*, 12:00) An aching theme, sparsely woven between piano, solo winds, and strings, flows with a gentle sadness that seems to have no relief in sight.

Third movement (*allegro scherzando*, 12:00) After a bustling start, two minutes or so in comes the nostalgic and sincere theme that brought Rachmaninoff worldwide fame, played on oboe and violas and then taken up by piano. The theme recurs in more impassioned forms before the determined but unsettled finish.

SYMPHONY NO. 2, OP. 27

ORCHESTRAL 55:00 4

After the success of his Concerto No. 2, Rachmaninoff produced this, possibly his greatest orchestral work, to complete his comeback after the disasters of his first attempt at a symphony. Most of his works were composed in his idyllic country estate, Ivanovka, but the spacious No. 2 came from his time in Dresden.

First movement (*largo*, 19:00) A low, somber motto theme opens this broad movement. It turns into flowing and resolute, but tragic, long melodies, with sunnier sections and some impassioned climaxes.

Second movement (*allegro molto*, 9:00) A vigorous and bright movement, sparklingly orchestrated, containing a trademark yearning theme, and with an unexpectedly subdued finish.

Third movement (*adagio*, 14:00) Sumptuous, classic Rachmaninoff, that goes straight into a long-breathed, poignant clarinet melody against quietly intimate strings, and builds to some magnificently surging, almost triumphant, emotion with a tranquil finish.

Fourth movement (*allegro vivace*, 13:00) A bustling and vivacious rounding-off of a remarkable work.

Rachmaninoff's Piano Concerto No. 2 became famous when it was used to great effect in David Lean's 1946 film *Brief Encounter*.

INFLUENCES

Rachmaninoff's music was considered outdated and emotionally clichéd after his death by some, and has had little influence on Western composers (although Shostakovich's Piano Concerto No.2, for example, has a Rachmaninoff-like slow movement). However, his reputation is now secure as the last of a great line.

Alexander **Glazunov**

● 1865–1936　　▣ RUSSIAN　　✍ c.150

Glazunov was an important figure in early-20th-century Russian music: he taught Shostakovich and helped Rimsky-Korsakov complete Borodin's opera *Prince Igor*, which had been unfinished on the latter's death. Glazunov's own compositions, while popular in their day, were conservative—a likeable but unchallenging blend of Germanic Classical with a somewhat outmoded Russian nationalism.

Glazunov studied with Rimsky-Korsakov, and his Symphony No. 1 was performed when he was just 16. Much of his adult life was spent as professor, and then director, of the St. Petersburg Conservatory, and it was here that he had his most lasting influence as mentor to the "new" Russian school of composers. He was remembered as a strict teacher with a genuine concern for his students, but whose unabashed conservatism could jar with their progressive ideas; he famously walked out of the premiere of his student Sergey Prokofiev's Symphony No. 1.

Glazunov's compositions were highly polished, if slightly backward-looking. He achieved the most successful balance of Russian and European elements of any composer of the nationalistic school, led by Balakirev. Many of Glazunov's works were premiered by Balakirev.

MILESTONES	
1881	Composes *Stenka Razin*, symphonic poem, and Symphony No. 5
1884	Visits Liszt in Weimar
1897	Conducts Rachmaninoff's Symphony No. 1 while drunk, causing it to fail
1903	Writes Symphony No. 7 ("Pastorale")
1928	Leaves Russia for Paris
1934	Writes Saxophone Concerto

KEY WORKS

THE SEASONS

BALLET	⏱ 60:00	📖 15	♫

Written for the Russian Imperial Ballet, *The Seasons* is perhaps the last work in the Russian Classical ballet tradition before Stravinsky changed the genre forever. It is rarely danced, but has become Glazunov's most popular concert work: charming, inventive, and well scored.

《 Written with Rimsky-Korsakov, Glazunov's *Cleopatra* was performed by the Ballets Russes in typically exotic costumes.

VIOLIN CONCERTO

ORCHESTRAL	⏱ 20:00	📖 3	♫ ◉

Glazunov's Violin Concerto was written for violinist Leopold Auer, then taken up by Jascha Heifetz (a former pupil of Auer's), whose advocacy is chiefly responsible for its continued popularity. The first section develops a beautiful melody with strongly Russian overtones, before an extended cadenza links to the virtuosic finale.

SYMPHONY NO. 5

ORCHESTRAL	⏱ 35:00	📖 4	♫

Although clearly derivative, particularly of Mendelssohn in the Scherzo and of Tchaikovsky in general, this is a good example of Glazunov's blending of Russian themes with Classical forms.

Bedřich **Smetana**

● 1824–1884   ᴨ CZECH   ✍ c.150

More than any other composer, Smetana established a distinctively Czech national style which greatly influenced later generations of composers including Dvořák, Janáček, and Martinů. A native of Bohemia, at that time controlled by Austria, Smetana wrote several operas with nationalistic themes, and a magnificent cycle of symphonic poems depicting his homeland, in a distinctive Romantic style.

Smetana worked first in Prague and then Gothenburg, with moderate success, as a pianist and composer. By 1861, his nationalist sentiments compelled him to return to Prague. Unlike many "nationalist" composers, he made comparatively little use of folk melodies. Rather, he wrote operas and programmatic pieces based explicitly on Czech stories and places—his own colorful and dramatic musical voice thus came to embody Czech music. His breakthrough came with *The Brandenburgers in Bohemia*, which was premiered at the new Provisional Theater in Prague. Smetana was appointed principal conductor there, and established it as a Czech national opera house. Despite his success, particularly with his next opera, *The Bartered Bride*, he was frequently criticized for being too Wagnerian and not nationalistic enough (a grave accusation in those times of emergent Czech nationalism). The pressure on him coincided with encroaching deafness as a result of infection

with syphilis, and he resigned in 1874. He continued to compose, however, producing some of his most nationalistic music in his final years, including *Má Vlast* and the autobiographical String Quartet *From My Life*. Smetana had led a difficult life—his first wife and three of four daughters died, and the syphilitic infection not only deprived him of his hearing completely, but brought on a suicidal depression that eventually drove him to his death in a mental asylum.

MILESTONES

1848	Writes *Six Characteristic Compositions*; founds music school in Prague
1861	Returns to Prague
1863	*The Brandenburgers of Bohemia* performed
1866	Conducts Bohemian Provisional Theater Orchestra

KEY WORKS

THE BARTERED BRIDE

OPERA	⏱ 120:00	▭ 3	🎻 🥁 🎺

Smetana wrote his best known opera in reply to accusations of "Wagnerism" following the performance of his previous opera *The Brandenburgers in Bohemia*. Originally conceived as a light opera in two acts, *The Bartered Bride* was considerably revised after its first performance in 1866, and emerged as a more weighty three-act opera four years later. Smetana retained the lightness of touch, however, resulting in a tuneful comic opera in the Bohemian idiom.

MÁ VLAST

ORCHESTRAL	⏱ 75:00	▭ 6	🎻

Má Vlast ("My homeland") depicts in music scenes from Bohemia. *Vyšehrad* describes the castle on the hill in Prague; *Vltava* evokes of the river which flows through the city. It is followed by *Šárka*, the story of the heroine of the legend of the Maidens' War; *Z českých luhů a hájů* (*From Bohemia's Woods and Fields*); *Tábor*, the city of the Hussite warriors; and *Blaník*, the mountain where Czech legend says the army of St. Wenceslas sleeps.

Antonín **Dvořák**

● 1841–1904   ▣ CZECH   ✍ 189

Of all the 19th-century nationalists, Dvořák was perhaps the most successful in absorbing elements of national folk music into a sophisticated Classical idiom. Hailed as a champion of Slavic music, Dvořák also spent several years in America, where his ideas about national music had a profound impact on a generation of composers. His substantial output includes ten operas, nine symphonies, and much chamber music.

>> **A quiet, deeply religious ruralist** at heart, Dvořák was never happier than in the countryside of his native Bohemia.

Life

Dvořák's father was an innkeeper and butcher in a village outside Prague, and the young Dvořák was destined for the same trade. However, he showed promise as a viola player, and after studying at the Prague Organ School he took a position with the Bohemian Provisional Theater Orchestra. During this period he was also composing in a style increasingly influenced by the nationalist music of Smetana, who conducted the theater orchestra for a time.

Dvořák was awarded a Ministry of Education stipend for composition in 1875, by a panel that included Brahms. A couple of years later, he won it again; Brahms was once more one of the judges, and was now sufficiently impressed with Dvořák's compositions to recommend them to his publisher. Through this connection, Dvořák's name became widely known across Europe over the next decade, and he gained a strong following in England, where he conducted a series of concerts.

His fame now firmly established, in 1891 he was invited to become Director of the National Conservatory of Music in New York. Dvořák attacked this new role with gusto, and composed a series of works betraying the more or less explicit influence of American folk music. He returned to Prague in 1895, and lived there until his death.

Music

Dvořák is often compared with Brahms, no doubt in part because the two became good friends and were great admirers of each other's music. Dvořák wrote some of his greatest works in the Classical forms of the symphony, piano trio, and string quartet, of which Brahms is regarded as a master. Both had an interest in folk music, although in Brahms's case this was not the music of his native country but of the Hungarian

❝ I should be **glad** if something occurred to me **as a main idea** that **occurs to Dvořák** only **by the way.** ❞

Johannes Brahms

gypsies he had heard as a boy. Dvořák's musical temperament was rather different from that of Brahms. He never felt a weight of expectation from composing in the shadow of Beethoven. Even so, some of Dvořák's symphonies, especially the mighty No. 7, rank among the finest in the genre. Much has been made of Dvořák's capacity for

incorporating Bohemian folk music into Classical models, in works such as the "Dumky" Piano Trio, Op. 90. By the standards of the time, he was not progressive in terms of harmony or form, but his lyrical melodies—Bohemian in style, but rarely, if ever, taken from actual folk music— are wholly distinctive.

⚑ **The Bohemian Polka** was one of Dvořák's popular Slavonic Dances.

MILESTONES

1857	Attends organ school in Prague		**1885**	Symphony No. 7, Op. 70
1866	Joins Bohemian Provisional Theater Orchestra		**1892**	Director of the National Conservatory of Music in New York
1873	Cantata Hymnus, Op. 30, performed		**1893**	Symphony No. 9, Op. 95, "From the New World"
1874	Brahms recommends Dvořák to the publisher Simrock		**1900**	*Rusalka*, Op. 114
1877	Stabat Mater, Op. 58, completed		**1901**	Returns to Prague and becomes director of Conservatory
1878	*Slavonic Dances, Book 1*, Op. 46			

KEY WORKS

CELLO CONCERTO, OP. 104

ORCHESTRAL   ⏳ 33:00   📖 3   ♫ ◴

This concerto has become a central work in the cello's repertoire. Dvořák wrote it for his friend the cellist Hanus Wihan, but they fell out after Wihan changed the solo part and added two elaborate cadenzas, which Dvořák refused to include in the final version. Wihan eventually declined the premiere, which was given instead to Leo Stern.
First movement (*allegro*, 12:00) A lengthy orchestral introduction presents the main themes of the work before the soloist enters. Various development follows, before a radiant, full-orchestra rendition of the lyrical second theme and a triumphant close in B major.
Second movement (*adagio ma non troppo*, 10:30) The woodwind presents the expressive main theme before being joined by the soloist. A central section follows, quoting from a song Dvořák wrote in 1887. The main theme finally returns, this time led by the French horns.
Third movement (*allegro moderato*, 10:30) The rondo-form finale begins as a cheerful march, with plenty of opportunities for display from the soloist, before slowing to recall themes from earlier in the work.

SYMPHONY NO. 9, OP. 95, "FROM THE NEW WORLD"

ORCHESTRAL   ⏳ 42:00   📖 4   ♫

Dvořák believed America's folk music could produce a distinctive national musical voice, yet, surprisingly, the "New World" does not contain any authentic American tunes.
First movement (*adagio*, 9:30) Written in curiously strict sonata form, the movement builds to a rousing climax.
Second movement (*largo*, 12:30) The largo, with its famous cor anglais solo, is one of the most famous pieces of Classical music. Under the name "Going Home," the melody is often now mistaken for a genuine Negro spiritual.
Third movement (*scherzo*, 8:30) The thrilling scherzo was based on material from Dvořák's abandoned opera *Hiawatha*.
Fourth movement (*allegro con fuoco*, 11:30) This combines themes from earlier in the work with marchlike music to produce a thrilling climax.

Leoš **Janáček**

● 1854–1928   ⬛ CZECH   ✎ c.150

Janáček is among the most significant opera composers of the 20th century. A late developer in composition, he was nearly 50 before he completed his first successful opera, *Jenufa*, and all of his best-known works date from after this time. Aspects of his native folk music were a fully integrated part of his compositional voice.

After studying in Prague, Janáček moved to Brno, where he founded an organ school and made his living as a teacher. While dabbling in composition in a broadly late-Romantic idiom, he studied Moravian folk song and began to develop the idea that melodic lines should reflect the rhythms and pitch of Czech speech. This concept gave rise to the modal harmonies and seemingly disjointed, repetitive phrases of his mature style. In 1917, Janáček became infatuated with Kamila Stösslová. She inspired many of his late works, notably the opera *Káta Kabanová*.

MILESTONES	
1887	Writes first opera, *Sárka*, but rights to libretto are refused
1894	Begins work on *Jenufa*, opera; *Jenufa* performed for the first time
1916	Revised version of *Jenufa* premiered in Prague to great acclaim
1921	Opera *Káta Kabanová* receives premiere
1923	Completes opera *The Cunning Little Vixen*
1926	Composes *Sinfonietta* and *Glagolotic Mass*

KEY WORKS

FROM THE HOUSE OF THE DEAD

OPERA	⏱ 90:00	📖 3	♫ ♂

With a long-standing interest in Russian literature and culture, Janáček based his last opera (to his own libretto) on Dostoevsky's novel *The House of the Dead*, although the result is more a series of vignettes than a single story. After Janáček's death, parts of the score of Act three were found. Two of his pupils, believing the opera unfinished, "completed" it, adding a more uplifting finale and substantially changing the orchestration. It is now thought that Janáček's sparse orchestration and bleak ending were deliberate, and the opera is usually performed as originally written.

SINFONIETTA

ORCHESTRAL	⏱ 22:00	📖 5	♫

Janáček's last orchestral work, and probably his best known, grew out of an initial idea to write a series of fanfares for a gymnastic competition in

☑ **Janáček's entertaining opera** *The Cunning Little Vixen* was inspired by animal stories in a cartoon strip.

Brno. However, it developed into an exuberant tribute to the town he had lived in since his student days, with each movement (after the initial fanfare) portraying a part of it.

Fanfare (*allegretto–allegro–maestoso*) The *Sinfonietta* is notable for its bold inclusion of 12 trumpets. Nine of the them are heard here in chorus.

The castle (*andante–allegretto*) In reality a prison, this building is depicted by a sprightly, slightly sinister dance against a lyrical theme led by strings.

The queen's monastery (*moderato*) Beginning as a nocturne, the music builds to a dramatic climax, and then disappears as quickly as it began.

The street (*allegretto*) The bustle of a Brno street is announced by a trumpet fanfare which is then taken up in complex counterpoint by the orchestra.

The town hall (*andante con moto*) The most developed movement builds toward a climax: the 12 trumpets are finally heard together in a thrilling recapitulation of the opening fanfare.

Karl **Goldmark**

● 1830–1915   ▦ HUNGARIAN   ✎ c.60

Largely self-taught, Goldmark established himself as a composer during his 30s, while conducting, teaching, and writing reviews in Vienna. His eclectic musical style incorporated elements of Hungarian folk and Jewish culture (his father was a cantor). His exotic opera *Die Königin von Saba* (*The Queen of Sheba*) was a triumph in Vienna and later staged worldwide. His later works were more modest successes, but he became a noted musical figure in Budapest and Vienna, and a good friend of Brahms.

MILESTONES

1858	Organizes concert of own works
1860	Composes String Quartet, Op. 8
1876	New orchestral work *Rustic Wedding*, Op. 26, receives great popular acclaim

Ernst von **Dohnányi**

● 1877–1960   ▦ HUNGARIAN   ✎ c.120

Dohnányi was the most important Hungarian musical figure of the 20th century. By his mid-20s he was the greatest composer-pianist after Liszt. After ten years teaching in Berlin he returned home and reformed Hungary's musical life through teaching, conducting, radio, and concerts. His lyrical, vibrant works often show humor (his *Variations on a Nursery Rhyme* are often played), and his chamber music is particularly successful.

MILESTONES

1920	Performs all of Beethoven's piano works
1928	Head of piano and composition at Hungarian Academy in Budapest
1930s	Struggles against Nazi influences
1944	Composes Symphony No. 2
1949	Settles in US as composer-pianist at Florida State University

Bohuslav **Martinů**

● 1890–1959   ▦ CZECH   ✎ 383

Martinů was such a good violinist that his home town funded his studies at Prague Conservatory. Expelled for laziness, he moved to Paris, where he became recognized as a composer. Blacklisted by the Nazis for pro-Czech activities, he fled to the US, but later returned to Europe. His large output shows influences from Renaissance to jazz, using springy rhythms and themes generated from small fragments.

MILESTONES

1934	Writes Piano Concerto No. 2
1938	Composes String Quartet No. 5
1941	Flees to US as refugee
1953	Composes Symphony No. 6
1957	Moves to Switzerland
1958	Writes *The Greek Passion*, opera

Viktor **Ullmann**

● 1898–1944   ▦ CZECH   ✎ 70

The career Ullmann was building in Prague as a freelance composer, teacher, journalist, and broadcaster was cut short by Nazi anti-Jewish policies when he was sent to Terezín concentration camp in 1942. In two years of extraordinary musical life there, he directed the Studio for New Music, wrote reviews, performed, and composed satisfying and accessible music for concerts for prisoners, many being excellent musicians. Ullmann died at Auschwitz; his manuscripts were saved.

MILESTONES

1898	Born Teschen (now Český Těšín in the Czech Republic)
1933	Writes *Schönberg Variations* for orchestra
1943	String Quartet No. 3 composed
1943	Writes *Hölderlin-Lieder*, voice and piano
1943	Writes opera *Der Kaiser von Atlantis* (*The Emperor of Atlantis*) satirizing Hitler

Max **Bruch**

1838–1920   GERMAN   c.200

Bruch was an important figure in 19th-century German musical life, both as a composer and a conductor. He is chiefly remembered for his melodic Violin Concerto No. 1, although he also composed much choral music and several operas. Conservative by nature, Bruch believed music should be tuneful and accessible, and vehemently opposed the innovations of contemporaries such as Richard Strauss and Max Reger.

Bruch was born in Cologne and received his first music lessons from his mother. A musical prodigy, his Symphony No. 1 was premiered when he was just 14. After study in Frankfurt, he returned to teach in Cologne and began to establish himself as a composer and, chiefly, conductor. Various posts followed, including three years at the Liverpool Philharmonic Society, before he became professor of composition at the Berlin Academy in 1891. Bruch's straightforwardly Romantic idiom was essentially backward-looking, especially when compared with that of his later contemporaries. However, he had an undoubted gift for melody, and his best works, including his Symphony No. 3 and his famous Violin Concerto No. 1, make up for in beauty what they might seem to lack in depth.

MILESTONES

1863	Produces *Die Loreley*, the second and most enduring of his three operas
1866	Writes Violin Concerto No. 1
1867	Appointed director of court orchestra at Schwartzburg-Sonderhausen
1880	Appointed conductor of the Liverpool Philharmonic Orchestra
1881	Composes *Kol Nidrei*, orchestral work; marries the singer Clara Tuczek
1883	Conductor of the Breslau Orchesterverein; extensive US tour
1893	Honorary doctorate from Cambridge University
1898	Begins two years as conductor of Scottish Orchestra

KEY WORKS

VIOLIN CONCERTO NO. 1

ORCHESTRAL   22:00   3

This concerto, in G minor, is Bruch's best-known work, and one of the most popular violin concertos in the repertoire. The first movement is an extended dialogue between soloist and orchestra which flows without pause into the second, an idea Bruch adapted from Mendelssohn. The famous adagio shows Bruch's lyrical gift at its finest and has passages of quite exceptional beauty. The implications of the concerto's massive popularity were not lost on Bruch, who was known to muse (correctly, it transpired) that he would probably be remembered for this work alone.

KOL NIDREI

ORCHESTRAL   11:00   1

Written for solo cello and orchestra, this piece was written in Liverpool and premiered there by the cellist Robert Hausmann. Based on a Jewish prayer, Bruch's setting is remarkable for the cello's evocation of an anguished human baritone voice.

Kol Nidrei, with its richly emotional cello part, was inspired by the Jewish prayer sung on the eve of Yom Kippur.

Joseph **Rheinberger**

⬤ **1839–1901**   📖 **GERMAN**   ✍ **200**

Rheinberger's lavish talents as an organist and a composer, but primarily as a teacher, saw him progress quickly from student to professor at the Munich Conservatory, and he received many honors through a long and successful career. His wife was a poet, and he set many of her works—among his large output of orchestral, chamber, and vocal music—which were masterfully crafted in traditional styles. His work is most familiar to organists and Catholic choirmasters, with the 20 organ sonatas among his finest achievements. He is also remembered for his fine church music, which includes numerous Masses and three Requiems.

MILESTONES

1851	Moves to Munich to study
1859	After 100 unreleased pieces, publishes his Op. 1
1867	Becomes a professor; marries Franziska von Hoffnaass
1869	Writes *Der Tümers Töchterlein*, opera
1894	Is ennobled
1898	Composes Mass in F, Op. 190

« As organist and choral conductor at St. Michael's Church in Munich from 1860–66, Rheinberger composed many richly textured sacred works.

Alexander **Zemlinsky**

⬤ **1871–1942**   📖 **AUSTRIAN**   ✍ **c.70**

Zemlinsky was known chiefly as an excellent conductor and as a champion of Czech music. He held various posts in Vienna, Prague, and Berlin, before fleeing from the Nazis to New York. As a composer, his relatively traditional music was more successful in his early career than later on, when it was eclipsed by his pupils' modernism—he taught Berg, Schoenberg (his brother-in-law), and Webern. The intense, emotional quality of much of his music (such as in *Die Seejungfrau*) reflects his rejection by Alma Schindler, another of his pupils, in favor of Mahler. In his last years, Zemlinsky had to turn to composing hackwork to make ends meet. He suffered a series of strokes and died almost forgotten.

MILESTONES

1896	Opera *Sarema* wins major prize
1903	*Die Seejungfrau*, symphonic fantasy
1921	*Der Zwerg*, opera, performed
1923	Composes his *Lyric Symphony*
1924	Conducts premiere of Schoenberg's *Erwartung*
1938	Flees to New York

« The rise of the Nazi Party in Germany, in 1933, forced Zemlinsky to move to Vienna. In 1938, after the Anschluss, he emigrated to the US along with many other Austrian Jews.

Hugo **Wolf**

⬤ 1860–1903   🏴 AUSTRIAN   ✍ c.350

One of the greatest masters of Lieder, Wolf composed some 300 songs, developing and extending the tradition of Schubert and Schumann. A committed disciple of Wagner, his use of *Leitmotiv*—and his complete integration of music and text— transformed the Lied into a truly dramatic form. Wolf's music was very much affected by the depressive episodes from which his suffered throughout his life.

After briefly attending the Vienna Conservatory, Wolf scraped together an impecunious existence until he secured a job as music critic for the *Wiener Salonblatt* in 1884. Here he made a name for himself with caustic writing, an ardently pro-Wagnerian stance, and an implacable antipathy toward Brahms. From 1887 he resolved to compose full-time, and in the following nine years produced all of his most significant works. Eventually overcome by the mental illness that had dogged his adult life, he died in an asylum aged just 42. His musical significance rests on his songs, which are characterized by an unusual affinity with the poetic text, and an intensity of emotional expression redolent of large-scale dramatic forms, such as opera or symphony.

MILESTONES

1870s	Contracts syphilis
1875	Attends the Vienna Conservatory— dismissed in 1877
1880	Composes *Italian Serenade* for string quartet
1883	Writes *Penthesilea*, symphonic poem
1884	Becomes critic for *Wiener Salonblatt*
1887	First songs published
1889	Writes settings of *Goethe* (51), *Mörike* (53), and *Eichendorff* (20)
1890	Writes *Spanisches Liederbuch*
1891	Composes *Italienisches Liederbuch* (vol. 1)
1895	*Der Corregidor*, opera, performed
1896	Writes *Italienisches Liederbuch* (vol. 2)

KEY WORKS

🔊 **Wolf's admiration** for literature is shown by his setting of texts by many great poets from Shakespeare to Mörike.

GOETHE LIEDER

LIEDER	📖 51	🔊 🎵

Schubert made extensive settings of Goethe, and by choosing to set the same poet, Wolf consciously aligned himself with the great Lieder tradition. The Goethe songs date from Wolf's most productive period and typify his mature style. The texts were given prominence, and were thus acknowledged as the inspiration for his music.

SPANISCHES LIEDERBUCH

LIEDER	📖 44	🔊 🎵

For the Spanish songs, Wolf chose German translations of Spanish texts from the 17th and 18th centuries. He allowed his musical imagination free reign to capture the Mediterranean character of the texts, and the resulting songs are filled with dance rhythms and pseudo-guitar figuration. Admired for this colourful, evocative, and inspiring Spanish collection, Wolf was perceived, in certain quarters, to be one of the finest songwriters of his time.

Max **Reger**

1873–1916   GERMAN   500+

Despite being a prolific and wide-ranging composer, Reger's music has failed to capture audiences' imaginations. At its best, it has the authority of Brahms, allied with more progressive harmony; at its worst, it can seem dense, dry, and harmonically wayward. Much admired by his professional colleagues, Reger was nonetheless a difficult character who made many enemies and aroused strong opinions.

Reger led an unremarkable life. After studying with the great musicologist Reimann, he gained a post at the Leipzig Conservatory, where he remained until his death. He was famously hard-living and hard-drinking, partaking of everything (some would say composition included) to excess.

Reger's music can arguably be seen as the missing link between Brahms and Schoenberg because, like them, he venerated Bachian counterpoint. Often, however, the density of his contrapuntal writing and incessant shifts of harmony make his music hard to follow. His orchestral music can often feel almost impenetrable, but his large volume of chamber works is perhaps his most significant contribution to the concert repertoire.

MILESTONES

1886	Becomes church organist in Weiden
1890	Begins music studies with Heinrich Reimann in Munich and Wiesbaden
1899	Has mental and physical breakdown
1905	Appointed professor of composition at Munich Academy
1907	Appointed professor of composition at Leipzig; composes *Variations and Fugue on a Theme by J. A. Hiller*
1909	Has successful concert tour of UK
1911	Becomes conductor of ducal orchestra at Meiningen
1913	Composes *Introduction, Passacaglia and Fugue* in E minor
1915	Composes Clarinet Quintet

KEY WORKS

INTRODUCTION, PASSACAGLIA AND FUGUE IN E MINOR

ORGAN   30:00   3

Of all Reger's output, the works he composed for organ, most of which were written before he was 25, have established the most secure position in the repertoire. Indeed, in some quarters he is regarded as the most significant organ composer since Bach. The organ was the perfect medium for Reger to indulge his passion for counterpoint, as is well-illustrated in this monumental work, commissioned by the city of Breslau.

VARIATIONS AND FUGUE ON A THEME BY J. A. HILLER

ORCHESTRAL   40:00   13

Among the more approachable of Reger's orchestral works, this set of 11 variations and a fugue is based on a theme from Johann Adam Hiller's stage work *Der Aerndtkranz*. Somewhat akin to a longer, more austere version of Brahms's *Academic Festival Overture*, the work nonetheless bursts with invention and elaborate scoring.

⬆ Arnold Böcklin's *The Isle of the Dead* inspired Reger to compose his orchestral *Four Böcklin Tone-Pictures* in 1913 .

Franz **Schmidt**

🌑 1874–1939   📖 AUSTRIAN   ✍ 50

A highly regarded and much-honored pianist, cellist, conductor, and teacher in Vienna, Schmidt also found time to compose some impressive, large-scale works. These often show a Hungarian influence (he was from a Hungarian-speaking German family), as well as Classical-Romantic accomplishment and, in the fine works for organ, the influence of J. S. Bach. Schmidt's life was not easy: he battled against poor health all his life, his mentally ill first wife was murdered by the Nazis, and his daughter, commemorated in his Symphony No. 4 (his last), died shortly after birth. It was his symphonies that earned him most fame, although his opera *Notre Dame*, from which he drew an orchestral gypsy-style intermezzo, was also an international success.

>> **Schmidt's oratorio,** *The Book with Seven Seals*, composed between 1935 and 1937, was the only vocal work he completed apart from his two operas. It is inspired by biblical visions of the Last Judgment.

MILESTONES

1901	Starts teaching at Vienna Conservatory
1904	Completes *Notre Dame*, opera
1930	Composes *Variationen über ein Husarenlied* (*Variations on a Hussar Song*), orchestral
1932	Composes Symphony No. 4
1937	Completes *Das Buch mit sieben Siegeln* (*The Book with Seven Seals*), oratorio; composes *Solemn Fugue* for organ

Sigfrid **Karg-Elert**

🌑 1877–1933   📖 GERMAN   ✍ c.150

Karg-Elert's life was unusual: he married the daughter of the woman who had borne him an illegitimate son. His musical life was also unusual: despite being a talented pianist, he specialized in composing for the then popular art-harmonium, developed in France in the late 19th century. From 1924, he gave weekly radio harmonium recitals from his house in Leipzig. He also composed many works for organ, which were influenced by Impressionism and historical polyphonic styles. Popularity in England (a festival of his organ music was held in London) then made him unpopular in Germany. Short of money, he toured the US, but disastrously.

MILESTONES

1906	Composes Konzertstücke, harmonium
1910	Completes 66 Chorale Improvisations for organ
1912	Composes Sonata No. 2, harmonium
c.1918	Destroys 20 works in an artistic crisis
1919	Becomes professor at Leipzig
1930	Karg-Elert Festival held in London

⌃ **An excellent organist,** Karg-Elert also composed extensively for the harmonium. Among his best-known works are 33 stylistic studies inspired by the styles of composers as diverse as Palestrina and Schoenberg.

Fritz **Kreisler**

⬤ 1875-1962   🏳 **AUSTRIAN**   ⚰ **UNKNOWN**

A violin virtuoso of legendary sweet tone, expressiveness, and natural ability, Kreisler was a child prodigy who won the Paris Conservatoire's Gold Medal at 12. His virtuoso career—which lasted nearly 50 years—was disrupted by spells of fighting in World War I, fleeing the Nazis, and a traffic accident in 1941. Best-known for his evocative, rich-toned performances of the Brahms and Beethoven violin concertos, he also gave the

first recital of Elgar's Violin Concerto. An accomplished composer, too, he produced an operetta, a string quartet, and a variety of solos. More surprisingly, Kreisler proved also to be an imaginative hoaxer, admitting in 1935 that many of the 18th-century violin solos that he had "discovered," apparently by names such as Gaetano Pugnani or François Francoeur, had in fact been written by him. Not all critics were amused. But his dazzling, attractive forgeries continue to appeal to violinists and audiences, and they are frequently performed, although now are firmly attributed to him.

≫ **A virtuoso violinist** of effortless flair, Fritz Kreisler was widely renowned for his rich, insightful performances.

MILESTONES

1882	Enters Musikverein Konservatorium
1889	Tours the US before medical studies
1899	Starts his virtuoso career in Berlin
1910	Performs Elgar's Violin Concerto
1914	Fights for Austria in World War I
1919	Writes *Apple Blossoms*, operetta
1935	Admits to compositional hoaxes
1943	Becomes US citizen

Hanns **Eisler**

⬤ 1898-1962   🏳 **GERMAN**   ⚰ **UNKNOWN**

After receiving free lessons from Schoenberg in the 1920s, Eisler discovered Marx, and became a committed communist. Disaffected with new music, he wrote strongly political songs, theater, and cabaret music, and film scores in an easily understood, yet clever style. In the 1930s, playwright Bertolt Brecht became a

lifelong friend and collaborator. When Hitler came to power, Eisler's work was banned and he was exiled. He fled to the US, where he wrote songs and film music, including the score for Fritz Lang's *Hangmen Also Die*. In the 1940s he fell foul of McCarthyism, and was deported to East Germany, where he wrote music for stage and film.

MILESTONES

1923	Composes Piano Sonata No. 1, Op. 1
1925	Teaches music in Berlin
1930	Writes *Die Massnahme*, music for stage
1937	Composes the "German Symphony"
1948	Deported from the US
1949	Writes *Auferstanden aus Ruinen*, East Germany's national anthem
1957	*Schweyk in zweiten Weltkrieg*, for stage

⬆ **During America's "Red Scare,"** Eisler fell victim to the infamous witch-hunts spearheaded by Joseph McCarthy (center). Tried by the House Un-American Activities Committee, Eisler was found guilty and deported.

Carl **Orff**

◔ **1895–1982**　　◫ **GERMAN**　　✍ **20**

Despite composing countless large-scale stage works, Orff's fame rests almost entirely on just one, the hugely successful *Carmina Burana*. But perhaps his most lasting legacy lies in his innovative attitude to music education. Realizing the intrinsic relationship between music and movement, Orff stressed the value of playful participation, particularly through the use of voice and percussion.

Orff was born, raised, and educated in Munich, where in 1924 he cofounded a school for gymnastics, music, and dance. His hands-on approach emphasized direct experience and active participation, particularly through the use of voices and simple percussion instruments. Orff's own music reflects Stravinsky's influence and a passion for Classical texts. Striving for a musical language that would engage the listener's primitive impulses, Orff's sound-world is filled with pulsing rhythms, percussion, and direct vocal expression, achieving a powerfully visceral and sensual appeal.

MILESTONES	
1912	Attends Munich Academy of Music
1914	Leaves Academy to join army
1930	Writes *Music for Children*, Vol. 1
1937	*Carmina Burana*, cantata, premiered
1943	*Antigone*, opera, performed
1950	Appointed professor of composition at Munich High School for Music
1961	Founds Orff Institute, in Salzburg, providing courses for music teachers

KEY WORKS

CARMINA BURANA

CHORAL	⏱ 60:00	◫ 25	♫ 🎭 👤

Conceived for the stage, but more often performed as a concert oratorio, *Carmina Burana* is a setting of old German texts found at Benediktbeuern Monastery. However, its subject matter is rather less than holy, as the work's subtitle, *Cantiones profanae*, implies. For instance, *Bibunt Omnes*, which closes the central section, is a drinking song.

MUSIC FOR CHILDREN

ENSEMBLE	◫ 5	♫

While not strictly part of his serious output, Orff's *Das Schulwerk, Musik für Kinder* (*Schoolwork, Music for Children*) ranks with *Carmina Burana* as his most significant and lasting contribution. Written for very young children to play with simple percussion instruments, Orff's musical "schoolwork" shows his flair for and theory of teaching music.

» **The panoramic stage pageant *Carmina Burana*,** famous for its infectious rhythms and arresting vocals, enjoyed instant and phenomenal success.

Edvard **Grieg**

● 1843–1907   🏳 **NORWEGIAN**   ✍ c.80

Grieg is undoubtedly Norway's greatest composer and is responsible, together with Sibelius and Nielsen, for putting Scandinavia on the musical map. His exploration of Norway's folk music, and collaborations with Norwegian writers, helped him develop a style that was unmistakably nationalist in spirit. He wrote many songs, piano pieces, and chamber works.

After studying in Leipzig, Grieg moved to Copenhagen in 1863 to develop his career as a pianist. It was there that he met the young Norwegian composer Rikard Nordraak, who emphasized to him the need for a distinctive Norwegian music. On his return to Norway, Grieg began studying traditional folk music, and elements of this gradually pervaded his own romantic musical language. Sometimes derided as a miniaturist, it is nonetheless true—with the notable exception of the majestic Piano Concerto—that his best work is found in his lyrical songs, or his exquisitely crafted instrumental pieces.

MILESTONES

1865	Composes Violin Sonata, No. 1, Op. 8
1867	Marries Nina Hangerup, his first cousin
1868	Writes Piano Concerto in A minor
1874	Awarded a national artists' grant; moves back to Bergen
1880	Becomes conductor of the Harmonien Orchestra in Bergen
1884	*Holberg Suite*, Op. 40 (piano version)
1895	Composes *Haugtussa*, Op. 67

KEY WORKS

PIANO CONCERTO, OP. 16

ORCHESTRAL   ⏱ 27:00   📖 3

As a student in Leipzig, Grieg heard Schumann's Piano Concerto, and his own concerto owes a clear debt to that work. Premiered to great success in Copenhagen, the concerto is now among the most popular in the repertoire.
First movement (*allegro molto moderato*, 12:00) The opening bars of the Piano Concerto must be one of the most instantly recognizable in all Classical music—above a roll of timpani, the piano enters with a dramatic sequence of descending octaves. The remainder of the movement is a compressed sonata form, with a passionate cadenza appearing before the close.
Second movement (*adagio*, 6:00) This lyrical movement is deceptive in its simplicity, disguising a sophisticated command of harmony.

Third movement (*allegro moderato molto e marcato*, 9:00) Full of virtuosic writing for the soloist, the finale is its most distinctively Norwegian movement, with references to folk dances and imitations of the hardanger (a Norwegian instrument).

PEER GYNT SUITES NO. 1, OP. 46, AND NO. 2, OP. 55

ORCHESTRAL   ⏱ 32:00   📖 8

Based loosely on Norwegian fairy tales, *Peer Gynt* was originally written as an extended prose-poem; however, its popularity led Ibsen to produce a stage version in 1876.

Grieg's two *Peer Gynt* suites were drawn from 23 short pieces he composed as incidental music for the play's first production. For Grieg, a master of the miniature, incidental theater music was an ideal form—the perfect medium for his memorable short character pieces.

⬆ **Peer Gynt** tells the story of a young rogue who travels the world in search of fortune and fantastical adventures.

Carl **Nielsen**

● 1865–1931   🏴 DANISH   ✍ c.120

Nielsen was one of the most important symphonic composers of the 20th century, and certainly the most famous Danish composer in history. He developed a highly individual compositional voice, at times romantic and passionate, at others aggressive and almost atonal, but always highly charged. In addition to six symphonies, he wrote three concertos, two operas, quartets, and a popular wind quintet.

Despite a rural upbringing as one of 14 children, Nielsen learned piano, violin, and trumpet. After studying at the Copenhagen Conservatory, he became a violinist in the Danish Royal Theater Orchestra in 1886. Somewhat shielded from the European mainstream, and receiving little formal compositional training, his music developed along a highly individual path. His harmony, whilst essentially tonal, remains unique; he often created tension by using keys in opposing blocks, the work finishing in the "winning" key. The idea of struggle was central to his music, often explicitly so, as in his Symphony No. 5, where the drummer is instructed to improvise, as if to drown out the orchestra.

MILESTONES	
1894	Writes Symphony No. 1
1901	*Saul and David*, opera, performed
1902	Composes Symphony No. 2, "The Four Temperaments"
1908	Conductor of Royal Theater Orchestra
1911	Symphony No. 3, "Sinfonia espansiva"
1916	Appointed professor at Royal Danish Conservatory; writes Symphony No. 4, "The Inextinguishable"
1922	Composes Symphony No. 5
1925	Writes Symphony No. 6, "Semplice"
1928	Clarinet Concerto premiered

KEY WORKS

SYMPHONY NO. 4, "THE INEXTINGUISHABLE"

ORCHESTRAL   ⏲ 37:00   📖 4   🎵

Nielsen recognized his Symphony No. 4 as the beginning of a new, "organic" phase in his composing. The first movement pits an insistent triplet theme, introduced in counterpoint between wind and strings, against a radiant second subject in thirds. The second movement is a pastoral, led by the woodwind in a manner that is at once almost naively folklike and yet oddly unsettled. The slow third movement begins with a brooding theme on unison violins, punctuated by timpani beats and joined in a sparse counterpoint by the violas and cellos. A solo violin introduces a warmer theme before the stormy climax. The finale is a dramatic duel between two timpanists.

⌃ **As a young violinist** in the Royal Theatre Orchestra, Nielsen performed his own Symphony No. 1.

SAGA-DRØM

ORCHESTRAL   ⏲ 9:00   📖 1   🎵

This delightful work—based on *Njál's Saga*—describes the passage in which Gunnar Hlidarende dreams of being pursued by wolves. Low strings open the work with a dreamy melody over a pedal bass. After a chorale on the brass, accompanied by ostinato figures on the strings, a slightly faster section is led by the woodwind. Technically the most remarkable, the central section is a sequence of overlapping cadenzas for six instruments that enter one at a time and are left to play at their own tempo before being brought to a halt by the entry of the strings. A final passage of muted trumpet fanfares brings the work to a gentle conclusion.

Johan **Svendsen**

● 1840–1911   NORWEGIAN   ✎ 40

After an early career as a virtuoso violinist, Svendsen turned to composing. His music—which shows a natural mastery of large, traditional forms—complements that of his good friend and compatriot Grieg. However, he was also in such demand as a conductor that he composed little of importance after moving to Copenhagen in 1883. Although his style is Romantic, it has elements of Norwegian folk music. Only two of his symphonies survive; in 1882 the manuscript of the third was burned in a jealous rage by his American wife, from whom he was later divorced.

MILESTONES

1876	Composes Symphony No. 2, Op. 15
1877	*Norwegian Rhapsodies* published
1881	Writes *Romance* for violin and orchestra

Fredrik **Pacius**

● 1809–1891   FINNISH   ✎ UNKNOWN

After moving to Helsinki to lecture at the university, Pacius became a central figure in Finnish musical life. While organizing concerts and conducting choirs, he wrote pieces in the style of Mendelssohn and Louis Spohr that include a string quartet, a violin concerto, songs, stage music, and the beginnings of a symphony. His singspiel *Kung Karls jakt* (*The Hunt of King Charles*) was his most important work, and his patriotic song "Vårt Land" ("Our Country") became Finland's national anthem.

MILESTONES

1828	Violinist, court orchestra, Stockholm
1834	Settles in Helsinki
1848	Writes "Our Country," patriotic song
1852	*The Hunt of King Charles*, opera
1887	Composes *Loreley*, opera

Armas **Järnefelt**

● 1869–1958   SWEDISH   ✎ UNKNOWN

Järnefelt's working life was spent in Finland and Sweden. After studies in Helsinki, Berlin, and Paris, he held various significant posts as opera and court conductor in Stockholm before returning to Finland. He was especially well-known for his interpretations of Sibelius, who was his brother-in-law, and gave the first Swedish performances of works by Mahler and Schoenberg. Järnefelt's main fame as a composer rests on two lyrical pieces for orchestra: *Praeludium*—from music for the drama *The Promised Land*, and *Berceuse*. He also wrote choral works, piano music, and film scores in a Romantic style, often with evocative Finnish titles.

MILESTONES

1892	Sister Aino marries Sibelius
1903	Becomes director of Helsinki opera
1904	Writes *Berceuse* for small orchestra
1907	Conductor of Royal Opera, Sweden; composes *Praeludium* for small orchestra
1910	Takes Swedish nationality
1932	Returns to Finland

◀ **Situated in the heart of Stockholm,** the Royal Opera House was where Järnefelt delighted Swedish audiences as composer and conductor from 1907 to 1932.

Christian August **Sinding**

🌐 **1856–1941**　　📖 **NORWEGIAN**　　✍ **c.150**

Although now a rather distant second to Grieg, Sinding was very much the "other" Norwegian Romantic composer in his lifetime. He went to Leipzig to study violin, but quickly proved to be an adept and prolific composer, writing rich, strong music clearly influenced by Wagner and Liszt.

He stayed in Germany for many years, financed by the Norwegian government, and was also professor of composition at the University of Rochester, New York, for two years. Perhaps because of the Romantic density and heaviness of his music, his work declined in popularity after his death; however, the well-known piano piece *The Rustle of Spring* is often heard in recitals and found on CD.

MILESTONES	
1874	Studies at Leipzig Conservatory
1884	Composes Piano Quintet, Op. 5
1889	Piano Concerto, Op. 6, published
1890	Writes Symphony No. 1, Op. 21
1896	*The Rustle of Spring*, Op. 36, No. 6
1898	Writes Violin Concerto No. 1, Op. 45
1912	Composes *The Holy Mountain*, opera

« **Sinding wrote** many lyrical songs, principally of Norwegian texts, and was honored by the government in 1921 for his contribution to national music.

Rikard **Nordraak**

🌐 **1842–1866**　　📖 **NORWEGIAN**　　✍ **25**

Sent to business school in Copenhagen at 15, the young Nordraak studied music instead and became an ardent member of the new national movement in art. He founded Euterpe—a society to promote Scandinavian composers—with his friend Grieg. His simple, economical music includes Norway's national anthem, "Ja, vi elsker dette landet" ("Yes, We Love This Land"). Nordraak was still developing as a composer when he met his premature death from tuberculosis, but his influence on Grieg makes him a seminal figure in Norwegian music.

MILESTONES	
1859	Joins New Norwegian Society
1860	Writes *Four Dances* for piano, Op. 1
1864	"Ja, vi elsker dette landet" first sung, May 17
1865	*Maria Stuart i Skotland*, incidental music, published

Selim **Palmgren**

🌐 **1878–1951**　　📖 **FINNISH**　　✍ **c.500**

Palmgren is best-known for his evocative, wide-ranging, and graphic piano music: he wrote five concertos (No. 2 being an international success at the time) and more than 250 solo pieces. The works show a strong sense of mood and imagery: a fine pianist, Palmgren knew first-hand how to exploit the instrument's possibilities. After an early career conducting the Finnish Students' Choral Society, he concentrated on performing and toured widely across Europe and the US. For the last 15 years of his life he taught at the Sibelius Academy in Helsinki.

MILESTONES	
1907	Composes 24 Preludes, piano
1913	Piano Concerto No. 2, "Virta" ("The River"), completed

Jean **Sibelius**

🌑 1865–1957　　📖 FINNISH　　✒ 134

Sibelius ranks alongside Mahler and Carl Nielsen as one of the most important symphonists of the 20th century. His earlier, often fervently nationalist works were in a late-Romantic idiom, but in later years he developed a highly original musical language characterized by slow-moving harmony and distinctive, sometimes stark orchestration.

🔼 **An austere,** unsmiling, yet good-natured and humorous man, Sibelius found inspiration in the nature and landscape of his native Finland.

Born into a Swedish-speaking family, Sibelius went to Helsinki to study law, but soon abandoned this in favor of full-time music study at the Helsinki Music Institute (now the Sibelius Academy). After two years in Berlin and Vienna, Sibelius returned to Finland in 1892, taking a position at the Institute. Success came almost instantaneously with the vast symphonic poem *Kullervo*. Based on a character from Finnish mythology, it was a bald statement of nationalism at a time when Finland was itself a Grand Duchy under Russia's control. The Finnish cultural establishment took to Sibelius immediately. However, it was not until his Symphony No. 1 (1899) that he began to achieve international recognition.

In 1904, unable to concentrate on composition in Helsinki, he built a house in the country and lived there for the rest of his life.

MILESTONES

1899	Composes Symphony No. 1, Op. 39
1902	Symphony No. 2, Op. 43, composed
1907	Composes Symphony No. 3, Op. 52
1909	Composes String Quartet Op. 56, "Voces intimae"
1923	Composes Symphony No. 6, Op. 104
1924	Symphony No. 7, Op. 105, composed

KEY WORKS

FINLANDIA, OP. 26

TONE POEM	⏳ 8:30	📖 1	🎶

Finlandia opens with dramatic swells of brass and rumbling timpani, immediately conjuring images of the wild Finnish landscape. This music is developed by the strings and woodwind, before trumpet fanfares usher in a livelier section derived from the opening theme. This leads to the famous "Finlandia Hymn," sung first by the woodwind and then the strings, before the faster music returns to bring the work to a rousing conclusion.

SYMPHONY NO. 4, OP. 63

ORCHESTRAL	⏳ 38:00	📖 4	🎶

This symphony contains some of Sibelius's most difficult, stark music, and was described even by the composer himself as a "psychological" work.

SYMPHONY NO. 5, OP. 82

ORCHESTRAL	⏳ 30:00	📖 3	🎶

This piece remains probably Sibelius's most popular and accessible symphony, a good-natured work that stands in total contrast to the stark, brooding Symphony No. 4.

First movement (*tempo molto moderato—largamente—allegro moderato*, 13:00) An opening section scored for wind, horns, and drum presents the main theme, which is subsequently developed before a toccata-like section brings the movement to a grandiose close.

Second movement (*andante mosso, quasi allegretto*, 8:00) The Andante is a set of variations on a simple theme presented after a short introduction.

Third movement (*allegro molto*, 9:00) The finale is one of the most exciting movements in Sibelius's ouevre. Its second main theme, played by the horn, was likened by a critic to Thor swinging his hammer.

🔼 **Much of Sibelius's music** refers to stories from Finnish mythology collected in the *Kalevala*, such as the story of Lemminkäinen's mother in his *Lemminkäinen Suite*.

Sir Edward **Elgar**

● 1857–1934   ▣ ENGLISH   ✍ 79

For many, Elgar will always be associated with the imperial optimism of the late Victorian and Edwardian ages, yet his works are more complex than their bluff exterior often suggests. His music encompasses not only the outwardly confident tone of his grand public works, but also the intimate, spiritual outpourings of a deeply sensitive musician. He wrote relatively little after the death of his wife in 1920.

» **Elgar would often take** music manuscripts from his father's music shop into the countryside to study them, which forged his strong association between music and nature.

Life

One of the constants of Elgar's life was his love for the countryside of his native Worcestershire and the Malvern Hills. He and his family returned many times to this part of England, where he had spent his early career as a freelance musician, regularly traveling the countryside to visit his piano pupils. It was one of these pupils, Caroline Alice Roberts, whom he later married and who gave him much of the encouragement he needed to concentrate more fully on composition. Despite initial difficulties in gaining national recognition as a composer, Elgar soon built up a solid reputation during the 1890s

based on a series of choral works for festival performance. It was his "Enigma" Variations, however, that truly cemented his national reputation as a composer. Following this success, his other works were hugely anticipated: the masterly oratorio *The Dream of Gerontius*, the two symphonies, and the concertos for violin and cello, all of which confirmed his place at the forefront of British music. He often cast himself as an outsider due to his lack of academic training, his social status as the son of a shopkeeper, and his deep Roman Catholic faith in a largely Protestant society. Elgar was an extremely private man, never happier than when spending time with family or friends.

Music

A largely self-taught composer, Elgar absorbed elements of style from many different sources. There is a pervasive element of chromaticism in his music that adds color and unexpected, yet innovative, turns of phrase. This fluid musical language allowed him, for example, to move easily between depictions of heaven and hell in *The Dream of Gerontius*, yet conversely also provided one of the biggest stumbling blocks for musicians attempting first performances of his works.

Elgar was also a consummate master of orchestration, having learned his skills as a young man in his role as a jobbing musician. Many of his scores, such as the *Pomp and Circumstance Marches* and other public and ceremonial works, are full of the opulent, Edwardian textures for which he is best known. Other works, however, like the poignant miniatures in the *Serenade for Strings*, demonstrate his subtle understanding of the intimate in music.

❝ There is **music in the air. ** All you have to do is **take** as much **as you require.** ❞   Edward Elgar

MILESTONES

1872	Leaves school; works as organist, piano teacher, conductor, and violinist	**1904**	Is knighted
		1908	Symphony No. 1, Op. 35
1889	Marries Caroline Alice Roberts	**1910**	Violin Concerto, Op. 61
1890	Overture *Froissart*, Op. 19, performed at the Three Choirs Festival, Worcester	**1911**	Writes Symphony No. 2, Op. 63
		1919	Cello Concerto, Op. 85, composed
1899	"Enigma" Variations, Op. 36	**1924**	Appointed Master of the King's Music
1900	*The Dream of Gerontius*, Op. 38		

KEY WORKS

VARIATIONS ON AN ORIGINAL THEME ("ENIGMA"), OP. 36

ORCHESTRAL   ⏱ 30:00   📖 15   🎵

Elgar brought an unusual personal touch to his variations, using his original theme as a prism through which can be glimpsed his "friends pictured within." Over the course of 14 variations, Elgar provides musical character sketches of authors and poets (Richard Baxter Townshend in variation III, Richard Penrose Arnold, V), local dignitaries (William Meath Baker, IV; architect-pianist Troyte Griffith, VII), close friends (the calmness of Winifred Norbury, VIII; the delicate laugh of Dora Penny, X), and of course musicians (amateur pianist Hew David Steuart-Powell, II; violinist Isabel Fitton, VI; Hereford Cathedral organist George Robertson Sinclair, XI; amateur cellist Basil Nevinson, XII). In the case of Sinclair, the music is not a portrait of the man himself, but of the organist's bulldog, Dan. The most heartfelt variations describe Elgar's wife, Caroline Alice Elgar (I); his publisher, August Jaeger (IX), whose majestic and brooding variation goes under the pseudonym of "Nimrod," the hunter; and himself (XIV, forming the finale).

CELLO CONCERTO, OP. 85

ORCHESTRAL   ⏱ 27:00   📖 4   🎵 ◑

First movement (*adagio—moderato*, 7:15) The last major composition that Elgar completed opens with an anguished statement on the cello, momentarily soothed by the clarinet. A subtle, lilting melody gains in intensity to become the

◀ **English cellist Jacqueline du Pré** (1945–87) won fame for her performances of Elgar's Cello Concerto. Her life was tragically cut short by multiple sclerosis.

main theme, taken up by the soloist and orchestra in turn. Even the lighter moments in the second subject are haunted by the inevitable return of the opening.
Second movement (*lento—allegro molto*, 4:15) Querulous sixteenth notes and light, staccato orchestration mark the brief, elusive scherzo.
Third movement (*adagio*, 4:45) The cello takes center stage in the almost continuous elegy.
Fourth movement (*allegro—moderato—allegro, ma non troppo*, 10:45) The marchlike main theme gives way to the cello's passionate ruminations. The anguished statement from the first movement reappears briefly.

THE DREAM OF GERONTIUS, OP. 38

ORATORIO   ⏱ 95:00   📖 2   🎭 ♫ 🎵

Based on Cardinal Newman's 1861 poem, *The Dream of Gerontius* portrays the death of an old man and his journey to rebirth in the next world.

Sir Charles **Stanford**

● 1852–1924   ℿ IRISH   ✍ c.300

At the Royal College of Music in London, Stanford taught many future English composers. His religious music is familiar to Anglican churchgoers, and he also enjoyed success in Europe and the US, particularly with his Irish Symphony, which Mahler conducted in New York. His style is light and lyrical and definitely "British," though his love of Ireland is revealed in his use of folk melodies. Stanford's beautiful setting of Mary Coleridge's "The Bluebird" is a well-known choral piece.

MILESTONES

1879	Writes Service in B
1887	Composes Symphony No. 3, "Irish"
1896	*Shamus O'Brien*, opera, performed
1910	Writes "The Bluebird," part-song

Sir Granville **Bantock**

● 1868–1946   ℿ ENGLISH   ✍ 250

Between teaching at Birmingham University, traveling widely, and promoting the work of other composers, Bantock composed prodigiously: often works for large orchestra, but also brass band, choral, chamber, and piano pieces, and children's songs. Although popular in his lifetime, his music has since fallen out of favor. It is characterized by uncomplicated harmonies and pseudo-Oriental or Celtic subjects. His tone poem *Fifine at the Fair* (1901) and overture *Pierrot of the Minute* are sometimes heard.

MILESTONES

1915	Composes *Hebridean Symphony*
1924	*The Seal Woman*, Celtic folk opera
1928	*Pagan Symphony* performed
1933	Writes *Prometheus* for brass band

Sir Hubert **Parry**

● 1848–1918   ℿ ENGLISH   ✍ c.200

Parry's stirring Blake setting "Jerusalem," written in 1916, is one of the most familiar pieces of music in England, and shows his imaginative, craftsmanlike style. Educated, in the upper-middle-class way, at Eton and Oxford, Parry was a musical amateur working in insurance until he was almost 30. However, he rose to become a major figure in the revitalizing of English music: as a scholar working on the new *Grove Dictionary of Music*; as a professor at the Royal College of Music (and later at Oxford University); and as a highly accomplished composer. His first major success was the cantata *Blest Pair of Sirens*, which established him as one of England's leading composers and resulted in a string of commissions—plus a knighthood and baronetcy. Although an avowed agnostic, he produced some of Britain's finest sacred choral music.

MILESTONES

1877	Leaves Lloyd's of London
1880	*Prometheus Unbound* performed
1883	Professor of music history at RCM
1887	Composes *Blest Pair of Sirens*, cantata
1888	*Judith*, oratorio, performed
1898	Receives knighthood
1908	Created a baronet
1916	Writes *Songs of Farewell*

» **Parry's rousing and noble unison song** "Jerusalem"– a setting of words from William Blake's Preface to *Milton*—became almost a second British national anthem during and after World War I.

Ethel Mary **Smyth**

⬤ 1858–1944   📖 ENGLISH   ✎ c.100

Born into a military family, Smyth was a battler: a persistent champion of women's causes, and of her own vigorous, idea-filled works. Against her parents' wishes, she studied music in Leipzig, where she gained private and public success with early pieces. Back in England, "E.M. Smyth's" orchestral works impressed critics, but she struggled to have her operas staged. Germany premiered many, but World War I closed that avenue. A prominent member of the suffrage movement, Smyth had intense love affairs with women of note. She gained official recognition in her 60s—as conductor, broadcaster, writer, and campaigner, as well as for her revived music—but sadly, deafness stopped her composing.

✉ **When jailed** at London's Holloway Prison in 1912, Smyth led her fellow suffragettes in "The March of the Women," conducting with her government-issue toothbrush.

MILESTONES	
1877	Studies in Leipzig, Germany
1890	Debut of orchestral works, Crystal Palace, south London
1906	*The Wreckers*, opera, premiered in Leipzig
1911	Writes "The March of the Women," suffragette anthem
1922	Made a dame

Samuel **Coleridge-Taylor**

⬤ 1875–1912   📖 ENGLISH   ✎ c.160

The son of a black father from Sierra Leone, and a white English mother, Coleridge-Taylor fought racial prejudice all his life, but musically enjoyed great respect and popularity: his *Hiawatha's Wedding Feast* was England's most-performed choral work for ten years. His accomplished, sweetly Romantic style became unfashionable after his premature death from pneumonia, but is now enjoying a small revival.

MILESTONES	
1890	Studies violin at the Royal College of Music
1903	Becomes professor of composition at Trinity College, London
1904	Compose *24 Negro Melodies*
1906	Tours US; meets President Roosevelt
1907	Writes *Thelma*, opera

Roger **Quilter**

⬤ 1877–1953   📖 ENGLISH   ✎ 125

Trained in Germany, but English in style, Quilter was a shy, cultured, and well-traveled man from a moneyed family, with a wide circle of artistic friends. He was known in England as a songwriter—many of his works were performed by the major singers of the early 1900s. However, frequent illness meant composing was more difficult than the seemingly effortless results suggest. His wealth may have diminished when he was blackmailed about his homosexuality, but he had used it generously to help Jewish friends flee Austria before World War II.

MILESTONES	
1905	Composes *To Julia*, song cycle
1922	*Children's Overture* included in first broadcasted BBC concert

Frederick **Delius**

● 1862–1934   ⚐ ENGLISH   ✐ c.120

Although Delius spent the majority of his life abroad, he is generally remembered as a quintessentially English composer who wrote evocative and timeless orchestral tone poems. The mountainous wilderness of Scandinavia, the tropical orange plantations of Florida, and the delicate beauty of rural France all find a place in the haunting and harmonious music of this truly cosmopolitan composer.

outstanding orchestral works—particularly in the first decade of the 20th century—which show the influence of Wagner and Grieg. In later years, Delius's music was championed by the conductor Sir Thomas Beecham, even as his debilitating illness made it necessary for him to dictate his final works through his amanuensis, Eric Fenby.

Life and music

Enamored of music from a very young age, it soon became clear that, despite the wishes of his family, Frederick Delius was not destined to become a businessman, but would make music his life's work. Studying in Leipzig, and eventually settling in France, Delius produced a succession of

MILESTONES	
1884	Takes on an orange plantation at Solano Grove, Florida
1886	Studies at Leipzig Conservatory
1887	Composes *Florida Suite*
1897	Moves to Grez-sur-Loing
1901	Writes *A Village Romeo and Juliet*, opera
1903	Marries German painter Jelka Rosen
1904	Composes *Sea Drift*, choral work
1908	Writes *In a Summer Garden* for orchestra
1912	*On Hearing the First Cuckoo in Spring*
1914	*Requiem* to text by Friedrich Nietzsche

KEY WORKS

THE WALK TO THE PARADISE GARDEN

ORCHESTRAL   ⏱ 10:00   ▥ 1   ♣

This piece began life as an intermezzo in Delius's opera *A Village Romeo and Juliet*, which was based on a short story by the Swiss writer Gottfried Keller. Like the Shakespearean tragedy, the story tells of two families at odds over the rights to a piece of land between their farms. Despite the farmers' enmity, their children, Sali and Vreli,

begin to meet in secret, and eventually fall in love. The purpose of the intermezzo was to smooth the transition between scenes for a Berlin production of the opera in 1907, and represented Sali and Vreli making their way to the Paradise Garden, a rundown inn that stood on the disputed piece of land. Delius's music captures the very essence of the opera as the two leading characters come to terms with their hopeless situation of forbidden love.

A MASS OF LIFE

CHORAL   ⏳ 100:00   📖 2   🎵🎶♂

One of Delius's most ambitious works, this choral masterpiece was completed in 1905 and is a wholly secular affirmation of humanity—although even here there are moments of unease and despair. The text was carefully compiled by Delius and the German conductor Fritz Cassirer from Friedrich Nietzsche's *Also Sprach Zarathustra*. Together they selected a balanced sequence of 11 soliloquies that were particularly well suited to Delius's musical temperament. It is a huge and vigorous work with powerful choral writing and some imaginative orchestration, particularly in the evocative "Night Song."

ON HEARING THE FIRST CUCKOO IN SPRING

CHAMBER   ⏳ 8:00   📖 1   🎵

Written for small orchestra, this is one of two pieces composed by Delius between 1911 and 1912, the other being *Summer Night on the River*. In each work, the composer's colorful orchestration is strikingly suggestive of a pastoral idyll in France that appealed strongly to the English imagination; the subtle rhythms and instrumentation create a benign sense of rural tranquility. As its title clearly implies, *On Hearing the First Cuckoo in Spring* is liberally interspersed with the call of the cuckoo, represented in the ensemble by the clarinet. The piece also introduces a Norwegian folk song, "In Ola valley, in Ola dale," which Delius found in a collection published by Grieg as *Norske Folkeviser*.

BRIGG FAIR—AN ENGLISH RHAPSODY

ORCHESTRAL   ⏳ 19:00   📖 1   🎵

Introduced to the Lincolnshire folk song "Brigg Fair" by his friend Percy Grainger, Delius used it as the basis of a series of orchestral variations.

IN A SUMMER GARDEN

ORCHESTRAL   ⏳ 15:00   📖 1   🎵

Inspired by Delius's own charming garden in Grez-sur-Loing, this evocative work even has a central episode to represent the gentle Loing River. The piece is dedicated to the composer's wife—painter and avid gardener Jelka Rosen.

VIOLIN SONATA NO. 3

DUO   📖 3   ♇

This was one of Delius's last works, and was completed with the assistance of Eric Fenby. It was first played to the composer by the celebrated British violinist May Harrison, accompanied by pianist and composer Arnold Bax.

« **Delius and his wife, Jelka,** made their home in Grez-sur-Loing, near Fontainebleau, and received a steady stream of friends and admirers.

Ralph **Vaughan Williams**

◐ 1872–1958　　🏳 ENGLISH　　✍ 82

A child of the late 19th century who received his training at the hands of the Victorian founders of the English musical renaissance, Ralph Vaughan Williams became one of the key British composers of the 20th century. Influenced by traditions as varied as English folk song and Tudor polyphony, he composed prolifically in many genres and continued to explore his own distinct musical style until well into his 80s.

》 Vaughan Williams was one of the great setters of English poetry, and vocal music comprises a large part of his output.

composers and it is true that some of his works, such as *The Lark Ascending*, the *English Folksong Suite*, and *Fantasia on "Greensleeves"* are infused with this style. He was, however, a Londoner and an urbanite, and scores for his symphonies and film music are as challenging and sophisticated as those of any 20th-century European composer.

Despite his prolific output, Vaughan Williams's creativity matured slowly. He was highly critical of his works, revising them until he was absolutely satisfied, and often shared sketches with his great friend Holst, whom he trusted to give honest opinions on his current music projects. An acknowledged agnostic, he nevertheless used Christian themes and morality as the basis for many works, including his opera *The Pilgrim's Progress*, based on Bunyan's novel.

Life

Although born into an affluent, professional family and educated both at Cambridge and London's Royal College of Music, Vaughan Williams firmly believed that music was for everyone. A socialist at heart, his dedication to music at all levels led him to devote his energies not only to the sophisticated high art of the symphony, but also to the simple beauty of everyday music like folk song and church hymns. He is often credited with leading the English "pastoral" school of

❝ What **we want** in **England** is **real music,** even if it be only a **music-hall song.** ❞

Ralph Vaughan Williams in *The Vocalist*, 1902

Music

Vaughan Williams's study at the Royal College of Music with Hubert Parry, Charles Stanford, and Charles Wood provided him with a thorough foundation in contemporary German music. His own compositional voice, however, was also inspired by the music of earlier traditions, such as the simplicity and directness of English folk songs and the modal music he encountered while editing *The English Hymnal* in 1904. He blended these elements with other styles and techniques—such as 16th-century polyphony and harmony, Baroque counterpoint, and the delicacy of French orchestration learned from Ravel—into his own musical language in his mid-30s. During his long life, Vaughan Williams composed in almost every genre and was still active in his 80s when the creativity of many similarly long-lived composers had long since dried up.

MILESTONES

1895	Meets Gustav Holst	**1923**	*Fantasia on a Theme by Thomas Tallis* revised
1897	Studies with Bruch in Berlin	**1924**	Writes *Hugh the Drover*
1903	Collects first folk song, "Bushes and Briars"	**1940**	Composes music for the film *49th Parallel*
1908	Studies with Ravel in Paris	**1943**	Symphony No. 5 composed
1910	*A Sea Symphony* and *Fantasia on a Theme by Thomas Tallis* composed	**1951**	Writes *The Pilgrim's Progress*
1914	*A London Symphony*; *The Lark Ascending*	**1953**	*Sinfonia Antartica* produced
1922	Writes Mass in G minor	**1954**	Tours US

KEY WORKS

FANTASIA ON A THEME BY THOMAS TALLIS

ORCHESTRAL   ⏱ 17:00   📖 1

Composed for double string orchestra and solo quartet, *Fantasia on a Theme by Thomas Tallis* is based on the third tune in the Phrygian mode, "Why fum'th in fight?", which Thomas Tallis contributed to Archbishop Parker's Psalter of 1567. Vaughan Williams first encountered the melody when editing *The English Hymnal*.

Written in one continuous movement, the *Fantasia* begins quietly as Tallis's melody is picked out in pizzicato notes by the lower strings against an ethereal, sustained note in the violins. The theme is soon taken up by the larger ensemble with a fuller accompaniment before more intimate sections in which members of the solo quartet take elements of the theme, weaving independently against each other between interpolations from the larger ensemble in the manner of a concerto grosso.

SYMPHONY NO. 5

ORCHESTRAL   ⏱ 35:00   📖 4

First movement (*preludio, moderato*) Scored for a smaller orchestra than Vaughan Williams had used previously, this symphony uses musical material the composer had earmarked for his opera based on Bunyan's *The Pilgrim's Progress*.
Second movement (*scherzo, presto*) The brief Scherzo passes quickly, yet demonstrates that Vaughan Williams's studies in orchestration with Ravel were hugely influential, with choralelike

moments for the brass and muted strings supporting a delicate and light texture peppered with ubiquitous cross-rhythms.
Third movement (*romanza, lento*) It is only in the Romanza that the composer allowed parallels to be drawn with the music for *The Pilgrim's Progress*, since it uses material destined for the scenes portraying "The House Beautiful" in the opera. As the true heart of the symphony, the music is heartfelt, expansive, and wistful.
Fourth movement (*passacaglia, moderato*) The final movement, a joyous ending to a meditative work, is cast in the mold of a passacaglia with its static, repeating ground bass while the other instruments provide rhythmic and melodic interest above.

THE LARK ASCENDING

ORCHESTRAL   ⏱ 15:00   📖 1

Taking George Meredith's poem as the inspiration for this one-movement work for violin and orchestra, Vaughan Williams created exquisitely beautiful music that draws upon the contours of English folk song. Weightless cadenzas for the violin that disappear into the distance act as both prologue and epilogue.

⌃ **Vaughan Williams used a vibraphone** in his Symphony No. 8. Invented in the US at the beginning of the 20th century, it was used mainly by jazz musicians.

INFLUENCES

One of the most important English composers of the 20th century, Ralph Vaughan Williams made a huge contribution to the development of Classical music. Benjamin Britten owes him a particular debt, as do Gustav Holst and numerous film composers, including Jerry Goldsmith.

Gustav **Holst**

◷ 1874–1934   🏳 ENGLISH   ✍ c.120

Mainly remembered as the composer of *The Planets*, Gustav Holst was a true musical eclectic. He approached every composition from a fresh angle and drew his inspiration from sources as diverse as astrology, English folk song, Sanskrit poetry, Algerian melodies, and the poetry of Thomas Hardy. He was also a natural teacher.

Like his lifelong friend Ralph Vaughan Williams, Holst studied composition at the Royal College of Music with Charles Stanford, a leading figure in the 19th-century renaissance of British music. After working as a trombonist and *répétiteur*, Holst became director of music at St. Paul's Girls' School and also taught adults at Morley College, both in London. At the root of his music, mainly composed during the school vacations, is rhythm, and many of his works are based on insistent ostinato patterns. His colorful harmonic style blends traditional tonality with inventive combinations of chords and spare, open intervals, giving his music a truly distinctive voice within his era.

MILESTONES	
1895	Meets Vaughan Williams
1906	Composes *Somerset Rhapsody*
1908	Visits Algeria
1910	Writes *Beni Mora* (*Oriental Suite*)
1913	Composes *St. Paul's Suite* for his pupils
1916	*The Planets* premiered
1917	Composes *The Hymn of Jesus*
1922	Completes *The Perfect Fool*, opera
1927	Composes *Egdon Heath*, tone poem
1932	Given a visiting lectureship at Harvard

KEY WORKS

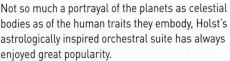

THE PLANETS

ORCHESTRAL SUITE   ⏱ 49:00   📖 7   🎻🎵

Not so much a portrayal of the planets as celestial bodies as of the human traits they embody, Holst's astrologically inspired orchestral suite has always enjoyed great popularity.

Mars, the bringer of war Mars opens with a menacing five-beats-in-a-bar ostinato over which music surges in waves through the orchestra with rising intensity before a sudden and abrupt ending.

Venus, the bringer of peace The mood is one of sensuous longing. Harps and woodwind solos emphasize the goddess's gentleness.

Mercury, the winged messenger Quicksilver reactions and sparkling agility characterize Mercury, a brief and light scherzo movement.

Jupiter, the bringer of jollity While depicting the majesty of this heavenly giant, the orchestra also emphasizes Jupiter's jovial spirit.

🔺 **Salisbury Plain was the inspiration** for the Egdon Heath Thomas Hardy described in his novel *The Return of the Native*. In turn, this inspired Holst to write his austere tone poem, *Edgon Heath*, considered one of his best works.

Saturn, the bringer of old age Tired, repeated patterns and heavy chords add weight to a solemn dirge on the brass.

Uranus, the magician This movement shows the quirky and changeable nature of the human spirit.

Neptune, the mystic As he reaches the outer edges of the solar system and the human psyche (Pluto had not yet been discovered), Holst allows mysterious harmonies and a wordless, offstage chorus of female voices to fade into nothingness.

ST. PAUL'S SUITE

STRING ORCHESTRA   ⏱ 13:00   📖 4   🎻

In the intermezzo, a broad, lingering melody is interrupted twice by a frantic melody Holst heard on a visit to Algeria, while the finale takes us back to London as two old English melodies, "The Dargason" (a dance tune) and "Greensleeves," are combined.

John **Ireland**

● 1879–1962 ⚑ **ENGLISH** ✍ c.100

A pianist and composer in equal measure, Ireland originally trained as a performer, but gravitated toward composition in his teens. His mature musical voice is reminiscent of the Impressionistic style developed in France by Debussy and Ravel. Although he wrote for orchestral and chamber forces, Ireland's main compositional legacy is for the piano.

Having spent eight years studying at the Royal College of Music in London from his early adolescence, it is not surprising that Ireland devoted most of his life to teaching, performance, and composition. His works often have a real sense of place that reflects the inspiration he found in the countryside and his enduring association with the county of Sussex and the Channel Islands. Ireland was particularly drawn to the verse of English poets, such as Alfred Edward Housman and Thomas Hardy. Ireland's thorough compositional training under Charles Stanford is reflected in his detailed and disciplined craftsmanship and his ear for tonal color.

MILESTONES

1904	Becomes organist at St. Luke's, London
1908	Composes *Phantasie Trio*
1909	Violin Sonata No. 1 wins Cobbett Prize
1917	Writes *The Forgotten Rite* for orchestra
1920	Composes Piano Sonata
1927	Sonatina for piano premiered
1930	Writes Piano Concerto in E flat major
1936	Writes *A London Overture* in B flat major
1937	*These Things Shall Be*, for orchestra
c.1947	Film score for *The Overlanders* released

KEY WORKS

SONATINA

SOLO PIANO   ⌛ 10:00   📖 3   🎵

It is possible to hear Ireland himself as pianist in this delicate work. A masterly moderato opening is followed by a deeply sombre Lento, culminating in a bubbling and rhythmic Rondo.

PIANO CONCERTO IN E FLAT MAJOR

ORCHESTRAL   ⌛ 26:00   📖 3   🎼 🎵

When Ireland heard the young pianist Helen Perkin play Prokofiev's Third Piano Concerto in 1930, he was so struck by her skill that he adapted his own Piano Concerto, making alterations to accommodate her small hands. Cast in the traditional three-movement concerto format, it still remains true to Ireland's characteristic, delicate style.

❰❰ **Ireland took great delight** in the English countryside, absorbing its mellow colors, soft tones, and lyrical sounds, which emerged in his music.

A LONDON OVERTURE IN B FLAT MAJOR

ORCHESTRAL   ⌛ 12:00   📖 1   🎼

Adapted from a comedy overture for brass, this orchestral version retains comic notes. A slow start leads to the main melody, based on a bus conductor's cry of "Piccadilly!"

Arnold **Bax**

🌐 1883–1953   📖 ENGLISH   ✍ c.300

Early in his studies, Bax's imagination was fired by the work of the Irish poet W. B. Yeats, whose Celtic verse and imagery provided the inspiration for some of the composer's most exquisite and atmospheric tone poems, such as *The Garden of Fand* and *Tintagel*. The breadth of his output, rivalling that of the recently acclaimed Vaughan Williams, has put Bax and his music back on the map.

Coming from an affluent family, Bax always had his own private income and never had to earn his living through teaching or performing. Once he had discovered his affinity for Yeats' work, Bax's music developed rapidly, and he also wrote novels under the pseudonym Dermot O'Byrne. His atmospheric tone poems, written during World War I, evoke the magic of nature, reflecting the Romantic mood of Richard Strauss and the impressionistic style of Debussy. By contrast, the lush, evocative music of his seven symphonies— each with three, rather than the more usual four, movements—incorporates the clarity and counterpoint he learned from Sibelius.

MILESTONES	
1893	Taken to concerts at the Crystal Palace, Sydenham, by his father
1900	Enrols at the Royal Academy of Music
1910	Visits Russia
1917	Writes *November Woods*, tone poem
1919	Composes *Tintagel*, tone poem
1922	Writes Symphony No. 1
1937	Receives knighthood
1939	Symphony No. 7 premiered

KEY WORKS

THIS WORLDES JOIE

CHORAL	⏱ 10:00	📖 1	🎵

This piece for unaccompanied choir, from 1923, takes its words from a 14th-century English prayer. The music builds from wistful homophonic textures in the first verse to passionate counterpoint underpinned by an insistent ostinato that is silenced only by the final note.

☑ **The otherworldly beauty** of the Celtic landscape, with its luminous skies and ancient stones, inspired the rhapsodic effects in Bax's tone poems.

TINTAGEL

ORCHESTRAL	⏱ 15:00	📖 1	🎻

This confident, evocative orchestral tone poem captures the powerful, elemental nature of the rough sea off the coast of Tintagel in Cornwall, set against the Arthurian story of Tristram and Iseult. It quotes briefly from Wagner's staged version of the legend, and mirrors Bax's passion for the pianist Harriet Cohen, whom he had met in 1912.

SYMPHONY NO. 6

CHORAL	⏱ 40:00	📖 3	🎻

It is hard to choose just one of the seven symphonies that Bax wrote between 1922 and 1939, but No. 6, from 1934, and dedicated to the conductor Adrian Boult, is a model of focused musical thought showing Bax at his peak.

George **Butterworth**

● 1885–1916   ⊠ **ENGLISH**   ✍ 15

In the English folk song revival of the early 1900s, no one set A E Housman's lyrical poetry to music better than Butterworth, who depicted the English countryside with haunting simplicity. A popular man, Butterworth was also a renowned folk dancer and collected folk songs. In World War I, he received a Military Cross for bravery in battle shortly before his death, and left a tiny output of high quality and unfulfilled promise.

MILESTONES	
1911	Writes *A Shropshire Lad*, six songs
1912	Composes *Bredon Hill* and *A Shropshire Lad*
1913	*The Banks of Green Willow*, idyll, orchestra
1914	Joins Durham Light Infantry
1916	Killed in action, Somme, 5 August

Arthur **Bliss**

● 1891–1975   ⊠ **ENGLISH**   ✍ 200

In some ways a natural successor to Elgar, whom he knew at Cambridge, Bliss wrote music that reflected his warm and outgoing personality. He served in World War I, and wrote his choral symphony *Morning Heroes* as a tribute to those who died. Mixing modern and Romantic ideas, he skilfully matched his music to the purpose or the players, from brilliantly orchestrated, dramatic work for the ballet *Checkmate* to simple pieces suitable for amateur choirs or brass bands.

MILESTONES	
1922	Composes *Colour Symphony*, orchestra
1935	Writes *Things to Come*, film score
1953	Master of the Queen's Musick
1969	Composes music for the investiture of Prince Charles

Gerald **Finzi**

● 1901–1956   ⊠ **ENGLISH**   ✍ 50

Finzi lived simply with his artist wife in rural Hampshire, and an individual, but English, accent runs through much of his music. When setting words, such as Hardy's verse, he captured the essential atmosphere perfectly. His songs for piano and voice work beautifully, though he was neither a singer nor an accomplished pianist. Hospitable, yet introspective, Finzi was also a notable scholar and researcher, and his amateur orchestra promoted new composers and performers.

MILESTONES	
c.1926	Writes *Dies Natalis*, cantata
1930	Teaches at Royal Academy of Music
1938	*Intimations of Immortality*, choral work
1949	Writes Clarinet Concerto, Op. 31
1956	Composes Cello Concerto, Op. 40

Peter **Warlock**

● 1894–1930   ⊠ **ENGLISH**   ✍ 125

Philip Heseltine was educated at Eton but received only an informal musical education. He enjoyed a lasting creative friendship with Delius, though his other relationships were often difficult, and he won public acclaim for the solo songs he wrote under the pseudonym Peter Warlock. A great admirer of early English music, he edited over 500 works, and set many songs in an idiosyncratic style, with influences from medieval music to Bartók.

MILESTONES	
1911	Meets Delius
1920	Edits *The Sackbut*, a music magazine
1922	Writes *The Curlew*, song cycle
c.1926	*Capriol Suite*, orchestra, published
1930	Dies in gas-filled flat, possibly suicide

Edouardo **Lalo**

● 1823–1892   ᴘᵁ FRENCH   ✍ c.70

Lalo's robust and inventive compositions impressed few people for most of his life. He worked as a teacher and violinist, playing in a string quartet and writing overlooked chamber music and an unperformed opera. But in his 50s, when his colleague Sarasate played Lalo's violin concerto and *Symphonie espagnole* (his most popular work today), his reputation grew, and other orchestral works were performed to great acclaim.

MILESTONES

1839	Abandons home to study in Paris
1873	Composes *Symphonie espagnole*, violin and orchestra
1882	*Namouna*, ballet, performed
1887	Symphony in G minor published

⌃ **In 1888 Lalo's opera,** *Le Roi d'Ys*, was performed seven years after its composition. It was popular and brought him the success he had hoped for.

Félix-Alexandre **Guilmant**

● 1837–1911   ᴘᵁ FRENCH   ✍ 100

It was inevitable that an outstanding organist such as Guilmant would settle in Paris, with its magnificent Cavaillé-Coll organs. As an energetic organ recitalist across Europe and America, known for his precision and clarity as well as his versatility in managing unfamiliar organs, he popularized and broadened the repertoire, exploring the work of both forgotten early composers and his gifted contemporaries. Guilmant succeeded Widor as organ professor at the Paris Conservatoire, and his compositional output includes eight attractive sonatas.

MILESTONES

1871	Becomes organist at Sainte-Trinité
1875	Composes Organ Sonata No. 1
1902	Organ Sonata No. 7 published

Cécile **Chaminade**

● 1857–1944   ᴘᵁ FRENCH   ✍ 400

Polished, colorful, witty, and typically French, Chaminade's music—much of it piano pieces or mélodies—was highly saleable. Popular in both England and the US, recognition in France was slower, and she often had to battle against negative perceptions of female composers. A large proportion of her 400 works were published in her lifetime, but her late-Romantic style faded in popularity after her death.

MILESTONES

1880	Writes Piano Trio No. 1
1888	Composes *Callirhöe*, ballet
1896	*Concertstück*, Op. 40, published
1913	First woman composer to be awarded the Légion d'Honneur

Camille **Saint-Saëns**

◐ 1835–1921　　🏳 FRENCH　　✎ 420

A composer, pianist, and organist, as well as being erudite in other fields, Saint-Saëns was one of the most significant French cultural figures of the 19th century. His long life and music career encompassed the Romantic era and its transition into the modern age. He acted as a vital bridge between the French light-opera tradition and the new Romantic dawn of Wagner, while advocating a Classical renaissance.

As a child prodigy, Saint-Saëns was hailed as the French Mozart. Classically inclined, but an admirer of Liszt and Wagner, he was influential in promoting new French music, although he rejected its later developments. His style was admired for its technical fluency, clarity of form, and sober elegance, but also charged with superficiality. However, there is much imagination, charm, and melodic inspiration in his vast and versatile output, which includes symphonies, concertos, chamber works for often unusual combinations, organ music, operas, secular and sacred vocal music, and songs.

MILESTONES	
1846	Official debut as solo pianist
1851	Enters Paris Conservatoire
1857	Appointed organist at La Madeleine; retains prestigious post for 20 years
1867	Writes *Les noces de Prométhée*, cantata, his first success
1868	Composes Piano Concerto No. 2
1871	Co-founds National School of Music
1880	Composes Violin Concerto No. 3
1915	Goes on triumphant American tour

KEY WORKS

SAMSON ET DALILA

OPERA　　⏳ 125:00　　📖 3　　🔊 🎭 🎵

This opera exemplifies the dual tendencies of the composer's style, the oratorio-like first act suggesting the influence of Bach and Handel, while the more dramatic and lyrical second and third acts are in line with the tradition of Meyerbeer and Gounod. Its novel combination of a grand symphonic style and memorable set pieces drew criticism from reactionary quarters, but made it much loved by a wider public.

LE CARNAVAL DES ANIMAUX

INSTRUMENTAL　　⏳ 22:30　　📖 14　　🎼

Worried that his "Grand Zoological Fantasy" might compromise his reputation as a serious composer, Saint-Saëns banned it from concerts altogether, excepting the 13th movement, "The

Swan." The ban was only lifted by a provision in his will. A royal lion, hens and cocks, tortoises, an elephant, kangaroos, an aquarium, birds, donkeys, pianists (told to play like beginners), fossils, and a swan are all described in *The Carnival of the Animals* before a rousing finale. "The Aquarium" and the finale are especially popular with the public, and the cello melody in "The Swan" is one of the most famous in all Classical music.

DANSE MACABRE

SYMPHONIC POEM　　⏳ 7:30　　📖 1　　🔊

Saint-Saëns's most famous symphonic poem is a quintessential blend of fantastical imagination and Classical rigour. At midnight, skeletons (depicted by xylophones, used for the first time in Classical music) emerge from their graves to dance in a churchyard.

▲ **Saint-Saëns's lifelong interest** in lepidoptery began in childhood. His musical talents were also evident early on: he started composing at five.

Gabriel **Fauré**

◉ 1845–1924   📖 FRENCH   ✍ c.255

Unlike his mentor Saint-Saëns, Fauré singularly succeeded in staying in tune with the artistic developments of his times, while retaining his own highly distinctive Romantic essence. Composer of a famous Requiem and widely regarded as master of the French song, he also created a very fine body of chamber and piano music. His gift for melody has tended to obscure the introspective, impassioned depth of his music.

The son of a country schoolmaster, Fauré was a protégé of Saint-Saëns's and took over from him as organist of the Church of La Madeleine in Paris. Prevented by financial struggles from composing regularly, his success was long in coming. While not obviously revolutionary, the stylistic independence that made him adaptable to the huge musical changes of his time also provoked the antagonism of reactionary peers. However, he was surprisingly made director of the Conservatoire and became venerated as the grand old man of French music. His musical spirit evolved from the sensuality of his youth to a darker, then a more forceful, and eventually a sparser style.

MILESTONES	
1871	Participates in foundation of the Société Nationale de Musique
1875	Composes Piano Sonata, Op. 13
1876	Composes Violin Sonata No. 1
1887	"Clair de lune," Op. 46, No. 2, song
1896	Becomes composition teacher at Paris Conservatoire
1898	Composes *Pelléas et Mélisande*, suite
1903	Experiences early signs of deafness
1913	*Pénélope*, opera, premiered
1921	Writes Nocturne No. 13, for piano

KEY WORKS

REQUIEM

MASS   ⏳ 39:00   📖 7   🎵 🎺 ♪

Fauré's most famous work was composed in stages and has existed in slightly different versions. Initial elements of its composition may be traced back to 1877. Work on the Requiem itself started in 1887. Its complete, seven-movement version was completed only in 1892, but just for a small, intimate orchestra. The full symphonic score was finally published in 1900.

Fauré's conception imbues the sober majesty of the Requiem form with a uniquely uplifting spirituality. Faced with criticism that, as a Mass for the dead, his work was not weighty enough, he responded, "It has been described as a lullaby of death. But that is how I perceive death: like a joyful deliverance, an aspiration to the bliss of the hereafter, rather than a painful experience."

⬆ **Fauré's lyric drama *Pénélope*** was a success in Monte Carlo in 1913, but is now little heard.

LA BONNE CHANSON, OP. 61

SONG CYCLE   📖 9   🎤 ♪

Fauré found his ideal poetic model for his melodies in the work of Paul Verlaine, setting nine of his poems in this song cycle. The free treatment of the poetic material, the expressive outpouring for the voice, and the prominence of the piano, seemed alien to the mélodie genre and disconcerted many listeners. However, the cycle was soon recognized as the most open and richest expression of Fauré's bold and fiery nature.

Inspired by his liaison with Emma Bardac, later Debussy's second wife, Fauré organized the poems to chart the journey of this love, described in the second song, as "toward paradise." He also created a musical unity by organizing the cycle around five recurrent themes, often stated by the piano, four of which are rejoined in the last song.

Henri **Duparc**

● 1848–1933   ◙ **FRENCH**   ✍ 25

Perhaps no composer's place in history is assured by such a small output as Duparc's with his 14 remaining songs. His reputation as the finest representative of the French mélodie genre, along with Fauré, rests on just a few songs in a life plagued by illness. An obsessive perfectionist, he destroyed most of what little else he produced, and an extreme neurasthenic condition gradually left him blind and paralyzed.

Originally set for a career in law, Duparc was swayed toward music by César Franck, who considered him his most gifted pupil. Duparc was a friend and admirer of Saint-Saëns, who introduced him to Liszt and Wagner. His poetic intensity, in part inspired by Wagner (whom he nonetheless did not seek to copy) and encapsulated in his phrase "I wish to be moved," was tempered by a taste for simplicity. It found its ideal context in the setting of songs, to which Duparc largely devoted himself. He wrote most of these for voice and piano, but some he later orchestrated. He nurtured plans for theatrical works, but a strange neurasthenic condition left him unable to compose after 1884. Blind and paralyzed for many years, he immersed himself in an increasingly mystical existence.

MILESTONES

1867	Produces his first composition
1868	Writes first songs, including "Chanson triste," "Soupir," and "Le galop"
1871	Writes "La vague et la cloche," song; participates in the founding of the Société Nationale de Musique
1873	Composes *Poème nocturne* for orchestra
1874	Composes *Lénore*, symphonic poem
1879	Song "Le Manoir de Rosemonde"
1882	Composes "Phidylé," song, and *Benedicat vobis Domine*, motet
1884	Composes "La vie antérieure," song
c.1886	Begins work on an opera, *Roussalka*

⯅ **Henry Duparc's song "Phidylé"** is a setting of a poem by Leconte de Lisle. Its long-spun melody rises to a radiant climax.

Vincent **d'Indy**

● 1851–1931   ◙ **FRENCH**   ✍ UNKNOWN

D'Indy was a conservative figure whose music school, the Schola Cantorum, rivaled the Paris Conservatoire with considerable success. A pupil of César Franck, whom he idolized, d'Indy was not admired by modernists who wanted to reestablish a tradition of pure French music free from any hint of the academic.

MILESTONES

1875	Graduates from Paris Conservatoire
1885	Wins Grand prix de la ville de Paris for cantata *Le chant de la cloche*; made secretary of Société Nationale de Musique promoting French music
1886	Writes *Symphonie cévenole*
1905	Writes *Jour d'été à la montagne*
1920	Marriage to much younger second wife inspires late-flowering creativity

He had some success as a composer in his day, but his compositions are nowadays seldom played.

Born into a military family, d'Indy never shed his reputation as a conservative musician. Parental pressure forced him to study law, but he tenaciously continued musical activities during his 20s. In his 30s he began to achieve acclaim, first with the cantata *Le chant de la cloche* (*The Song of the Bell*) and then with the *Symphonie sur un chant montagnard français* (*Symphony on a French Mountain Air*), both reflecting his interest in French folk song and its revival. The re-editing of past French music was another passion, for example the operas of Rameau. His teaching was based on the study of music history, while his compositions centred on Teutonic musical structure.

L'étranger, d'Indy's most successful opera, was first staged in 1903 in Brussels. He wrote his own libretto for it about a stranger arriving in a closed community. Though shot with modernism, the music still leans towards 19th-century techniques.

⯅ **D'Indy and his followers,** Déodat de Sévérac and Joseph Canteloube, inspired a revival of folk song in France in parallel with a similar trend in Britain led by Vaughan Williams.

Emmanuel **Chabrier**

● 1841–1894   ⚑ FRENCH   ✍ UNKNOWN

Chabrier could be considered an early Impressionist: he was admired by Debussy and Ravel, and was a friend of Manet. Gathering material for his most famous orchestral piece, *España*, he worked like an open-air painter, noting down dance melodies and castanet rhythms from the streets of Andalucia, and subsequently transforming them through kaleidoscopic scoring for a large orchestra.

Chabrier came from the Auvergne, and was pressed into studying law by his father. Although he spent 20 years as a civil servant, he managed to produce several comic operas during this time. He also became notorious for his alcohol-inspired improvisations in the bars and cafés of Paris. An ardent Wagnerian, he was moved to tears when he heard the love theme of *Tristan und Isolde* in 1880. Due to this experience and his growing success during the 1870s, he resigned from his job to devote himself to music. There followed his most productive period during which he wrote music in all genres.

MILESTONES	
1858	Begins studies in law
1862	Composes nine melodies
1873	Publishes an Impromptu dedicated to Manet's wife
1883	*España* premiered and subsequently arranged as a piano duet
1890	Begins work on *Briseïs*, an opera to a libretto after Goethe
1894	Dies as a result of syphilis

KEY WORKS

ESPAÑA

ORCHESTRAL   📖 1

España is a collage of Spanish dances collected in the streets of Andalucia. A precursor of Ravel's *Boléro*, it orchestrates the dances in a highly characteristic way. Chabrier described it as a "piece in F and nothing more." Stravinsky and Poulenc were particular fans.

PIÈCES PITTORESQUES

SOLO PIANO   📖 10

Chabrier's longest set of piano pieces incorporates elements of popular music, some Impressionistic pieces—for example "Sous bois" ("In the Woods")—and French regional folk dances that evoke his Auvergnat roots. They also contain some music in the "antique" style, reworking Baroque minuets, a technique that was later used by both Ravel and Debussy.

MARCHE JOYEUSE

ORCHESTRAL

Originally written as a two-part piano work in 1883, Chabrier orchestrated the two as a pastorale and march in 1888. Further revision resulted in the version that is frequently performed today.

» Chabrier had many friends among the writers and artists of Paris. An ebullient and colorful character, he wrote brilliant letters and many humorous songs.

Charles-Marie **Widor**

🌐 1844–1937   📖 **FRENCH**   ✎ **c.100**

Born in Lyon to a family of organ builders, Widor quickly gained a reputation as an organist in the French provinces. In his mid-20s, he replaced Lefebure-Wély at St. Sulpice in Paris, where he remained for 64 years, still performing in his 90s. He also taught organ and composition at the Paris Conservatoire, but his thorough Germanic schooling (his own teacher had come from a line extending back to Bach) led to clashes with the more Gallic, contemporary Fauré. Widor wrote many ballets, operas, songs, and orchestral works, but his greatest compositional achievement were the magnificent ten Symphonies for Solo Organ, which vary from the austere and demanding No. 7 and No. 8 to the popular Toccata—the finale from No. 5—a familiar component of wedding ceremonies.

MILESTONES

1870	Becomes organist at St. Sulpice, Paris
1872	Writes Organ Symphonies Nos. 1–4
1880	Composes *La korrigane*, ballet
1887	Writes Organ Symphonies Nos. 5–8
1891	Succeeds César Franck as organ professor at the Paris Conservatoire
1896	Succeeds Théodore Dubois as professor of composition

🔼 **In his hour-long monumental Symphony for Organ No. 8**, Widor pushed organ technique and artistic inventiveness to its absolute limit.

Ernest **Chausson**

🌐 1855–1899   📖 **FRANCE**   ✎ **c.75**

Growing up amid salon culture and in financial comfort, Chausson dabbled at writing and drawing, and qualified as a barrister, but then decided to become a musician, inspired by hearing Wagner in Germany. His talents impressed his teacher Massenet, and his reputation as a composer grew in Parisian musical circles through his 30s as he abandoned Wagner for a more intimate, exotically flavored personal style. After writing *Poème*, his most popular work today, he started to refine his style, but died in a cycling accident, aged 44. However, as secretary of the Société Nationale de Musique for ten years, he did much to encourage French contemporary music.

MILESTONES

1877	Sworn in as barrister; writes first song
1879	Studies under Massenet
1882	Writes *Viviane*, symphonic poem
1883	Marries (five children)
1895	Finishes *Le roi Arthus*, opera, after 10 years
1896	Writes *Poème* for violin and orchestra

◀◀ **Chausson led a quiet life** shared between his family and his salon, which drew figures such as Ysaÿe and Debussy. Here Debussy plays a piano duet with Mme. Chausson.

Claude **Debussy**

● 1862–1918   🏳 FRENCH   ✍ 227

Emerging as a radical innovator from within the conservative French music scene of the late 19th century, Debussy virtually single-handedly changed the course of European musical development. By dissolving traditional rules into a new language of unsuspected possibilities in harmony, rhythm, form, texture, and color, he created a rich body of work that would leave an indelible imprint on 20th-century music.

》 Debussy's works provoked sharply divided opinions and fierce controversies, but by the early 1900s he was established as the figurehead of a new music movement.

Life

Overcoming his simple background and his family's lack of affinity for music, Debussy entered the prestigious Paris Conservatoire at the age of 12. Early aspirations for a career as a concert pianist were unfulfilled, however, and his nonconformist tendencies were frowned upon. Although he was awarded the Grand Prix de Rome for composition in 1884, his earliest published works met with little success. Very much self-educated, Debussy traveled across Europe, absorbing the Oriental cultures that were being increasingly revealed to Westerners, and coming into contact with the leading artistic figures of the day. From 1892, his music started to attract wider attention, although it was not for another decade that the significance of his ground-breaking ideas became fully recognized. Debussy was also an outspoken music critic, writing under the pseudonym Monsieur Croche (Mr. Quaver). He had to endure trials in his private life, including financial struggles, the distancing of many friends after he left his first wife for the woman who would become his second, and a long battle with cancer. Debussy died just a few months prior to the end of World War I, by then an internationally celebrated composer.

Music

It was apparent early on that Debussy conceived music in a novel way, but it took him time to assimilate and crystallize his ideas. His *Prélude à l'après-midi d'un faune* marked the definitive spreading of his wings: thereafter, he took every genre—orchestral, vocal, piano, and chamber music—to new realms. His ability to perpetually build on his innovations and to renew himself creatively could leave even his most ardent followers confused. Although he has been called an Impressionist, Debussy's allusions to many idioms and movements, always masterfully integrated, are stamped with an individuality and inventiveness that defy all categorization. His interest in contemporary as well as ancient artistic currents, and in foreign, often exotic influences (including Spain and the Orient), reflected his insatiable curiosity and abhorrence of repetition.

> ❝ It is **unnecessary for music** to make **people think**... it would be **enough** if it **made them listen.** ❞
>
> **Claude Debussy,** 1900

MILESTONES

1880	Attends composition class of Ernest Guiraud	**1907**	Completes *Images*, for piano (2 sets)
1893	Composes String Quartet	**1908**	Success in England brings international fame
1894	Writes *Prélude à l'après-midi d'un faune*	**1912**	Completes *Images*, for orchestra
1899	Writes Nocturnes, for orchestra; marries Rosalie Texier	**1913**	Completes Preludes, for piano (2 sets); produces *Jeux*, ballet
1902	*Pelléas et Mélisande*, opera, completed and premiered	**1915**	Composes Cello Sonata
		1916	Sonata for Flute, Viola, and Harp
1903	Has affair with singer Emma Bardac; writes *Estampes*	**1917**	Violin Sonata completed

KEY WORKS

PELLÉAS ET MÉLISANDE

OPERA	⏱ 150:30	📖 5	🎵 🎭 ♂

Based on Maeterlinck's Symbolist play, Debussy's only opera has five acts, and its scenes are linked by orchestral interludes. Rejecting Italian conventions, it took opera beyond the sphere of Wagner's influence. The all but spoken style of the vocal parts and the delicacy of the orchestration lend the music an abstract quality that seemed almost scandalous at the time.

The opera tells the story of Golaud, grandson of King Arkel, his wife Mélisande, and his younger half-brother Pelléas. When Golaud feels that Pelléas and Mélisande are getting too close, he warns Pelléas to keep away from Mélisande and violently confronts her. When he surprises them again, he kills Pelléas. Wracked with guilt but still consumed by jealousy, Golaud pleads for Mélisande's forgiveness while seeking to find out the nature of her love for Pelléas. Having just given birth to a daughter, Mélisande dies without resolving the mystery.

LA MER

ORCHESTRAL	⏱ 24:30	📖 3	🎵

Debussy's largest purely orchestral work consists of three symphonic sketches of seascapes. It is the closest thing to a symphony that he would ever compose. Part one charts the morning progression of the sun, from the first glimpses of light, and its rise to its zenith. Part two explores the manifold perspectives

◀ **Debussy was influenced** by the gamelan, an Indonesian music ensemble that typically plays gongs, chimes, metallophones, and cymbals.

of the sea through the play of light on the water (the rise and fall of waves, shimmering surfaces, the rush of the surf). Part three reiterates fragments of the first part, and depicts the dramatic interaction of wind and water.

ESTAMPES

SOLO PIANO	⏱ 12:00	📖 3	🎹

Of these three works, "Pagodes" reflects the influence of Javanese gamelan music, "La soirée dans Grenade" evokes sultry Andalucia, and "Jardins sous la pluie" echoes the keyboard styles of Bach and Chopin. The three distinct pieces are united by their stylized clarity and economy, inspired by the prints—in particular from Japan—to which the title refers.

Louis **Vierne**

● 1870–1937   ⊞ **FRENCH**   ✍ c.70

Blind at birth, but given limited vision by an operation at six, Vierne became an outstanding organist and composer. A teaching assistant at the Paris Conservatoire, he was also organist at Notre-Dame for 37 years. Composed in enlarged symbols on huge sheets of paper, Vierne's six dazzling, wide-ranging symphonies for organ (inspired by the Cavaillé-Coll organs) are among the instrument's finest and most-played works. Vierne's later life was plagued by despair, illness, grief, and hardship; he died of a heart attack in mid-recital at Notre-Dame.

MILESTONES

1899	Writes Organ Symphony No. 1
1900	Becomes organist at Notre-Dame
1926–27	Pieces de Fantaisie, Vols. 1–4, organ

Reynaldo **Hahn**

● 1874–1947   ⊞ **FRENCH**   ✍ c.150

Hahn's songs powerfully evoke the cultured Paris salon around 1900, a milieu he knew well. Born in Venezuela to a German father, he came to Paris as a child, and by 16, having found fame with his charming songs (set to poems by Paul Verlaine), was moving in the city's artistic circles, eventually working as critic, composer, and singer. Although he wrote much incidental music, as well as ballets, operas, and operettas, he is best remembered for his songs. Hahn was a lover and lifelong friend of Marcel Proust, and his music is often about memories, such as the operetta *Ciboulette*, set in 19th-century Paris.

MILESTONES

1890	Writes *Chansons grises*, songs
1931	Writes Piano Concerto, No. 2
1934	Becomes music critic for *Le figaro*
1935	*Le marchand de Venise*, opera, staged
1945	Directs the Paris Opèra

Paul **Dukas**

● 1865–1935   ⊞ **FRENCH**   ✍ c.30

An intense perfectionist, Dukas composed scrupulously but slowly, turning out just a handful of choice, immaculately crafted pieces, much admired by Debussy. Among the most celebrated are the orchestral fantasy *The Sorcerer's Apprentice*, popularized by Disney's *Fantasia*; the widely acclaimed opera *Ariane et Barbe-bleue*; and the ballet *La Péri*, which established Dukas as a major modern composer.

A Parisian, Dukas was born into a musical family and made a career not only as a composer but also as a major music critic on the *Gazette des Beaux Arts* and other journals. Dukas's output was inhibited by his constant self-criticism: he destroyed much of his own work before dying. Piano pieces, such as the "Rameau Variations" and the Piano Sonata, still remain in the repertoire of specialists, as do many of the orchestral pieces. Dukas's broad-based teaching should not be forgotten, either, affecting such influential figures as Jean Alain, Maurice Duruflé, and Olivier Messiaen.

Dukas's dramatic and spirited opera, *Ariane et Barbe-bleue*, set to a text by the Belgian Symbolist Maurice Maeterlinck, ranks among the most important French pieces of the early 20th century. It recounts the story of the serial polygamist Bluebeard, who imprisoned his first five wives. It was an instant hit, due in part to the exotic orchestrations symbolizing the wives' bright jewels.

⌃ In *The Sorcerer's Apprentice,* when the apprentice sorcerer asks an enchanted broom to fetch water he is overwhelmed by the response.

MILESTONES

1871	Enrolls at the Paris Conservatoire
1888	Wins second prize in the Prix de Rome for his cantata, *Veléda*
1891	*Polyeucte*, overture, staged in Paris
1896	Composes Symphony in C major
c.1901	Writes Piano Sonata in E flat minor
1910	Teaches at the Paris Conservatoire
1926	Teaches at the École Normale

Erik **Satie**

◔ 1866–1925   ▣ FRENCH   ✎ c.50

An eccentric figure of enormous importance in French music and admired by Debussy and John Cage, among others, Satie described himself as a "medieval musician who had wandered by mistake into the 20th century." His early piano pieces are now popular classics and his later ballets for the Ballets Russes and Swedish Ballet are masterful collaborations between choreographers, designers, and costumiers.

Life and Music

Satie never embraced tradition. Like Chabrier, his youthful idol, he played the piano in cabarets, and popular music was important in his often irreverent compositions. Many had unusual titles: there is a *Bureaucratic Sonata* and some *Pieces in the Form of a Pear*, written in response to an accusation that his music was formless. In the 1890s he founded the Metropolitan Church of Jesus Christ the Conductor, associated with a mystical movement known as the Rose+Croix. In 1905 he enrolled as a returning learner in Vincent d'Indy's Schola Cantorum and was a model pupil. He secured fame after World War I with his ballet commissions.

MILESTONES	
1878	Enters Paris Conservatoire and hates it
1887	Takes up bohemian lifestyle in Montmartre; publishes *Sarabandes* for piano—first characteristic work
1911	Ravel performs some of Satie's pieces at Société Musicale Indépendante
1914	Publishes *Sports et divertissements*, piano pieces, in facsimile of own handwriting
1917	Collaborates with Cocteau, Massine, and Picasso on *Parade*, ballet
1920	Composes *Socrate*, symphonic drama

KEY WORKS

GYMNOPÉDIES

SOLO PIANO	⏲ 7:45	▥ 3	🕭

These piano pieces have become Satie's most celebrated work. Orchestrated by Debussy and arranged by many others, the dreamy, dismembered waltzes are easy to play, and have a magic rarely matched.

SOCRATE

TEXT SETTING	⏲ 30:15	▥ 1	🕭 ♟

Considered to be the apex of his work, here extracts from Plato are set in a bare, simple style which inspired the modernist group known as Les Six, to which Satie was something of a father figure.

PARADE

BALLET	⏲ 14:30	▥ 1	🎭

Satie's fullest ballet score, the music contains a typewriter, the siren of the *Titanic*, and a *bouteillophone*—a set of bottles played by a Chinese conjuror.

FURNITURE MUSIC

SOLO PIANO	▥ 1	🕭

Satie's great statement, which would now be called conceptual art, is music for a concert interval: a short phrase played over and over again. It is surpassed only by his 24-hour-long, repetitious *Vexations*.

⏶ **In** *Entr'acte* by film maker Réné Clair, Satie and French painter and designer Francis Picabia load a cannon in slow motion. The film was conceived by Picabia for showing during the interval of Satie's ballet *Relâche*.

Albert **Roussel**

🌑 **1869–1937**   🏳 **FRENCH**   ✍ **100**

After a stint in the navy, Roussel decided on a career in music at the unusually late age of 25. Despite not having enjoyed the widespread attention it deserves, his output is considered by many to be the finest French music to have been written between the wars. It shows Roussel's subtle and highly personal absorption of diverse styles, together with a great atmospheric sensitivity and rhythmic drive.

Having resigned his naval commission to devote himself to music, Roussel was still studying when his early works caught the music world's attention around 1906. His training with the conservatively inclined Vincent d'Indy, traces of Debussy's influence, and exotic musical ideas gained from travels to India and Southeast Asia in 1909 are reflected in the first period (1898–1913) of his creative output. After World War I, he gradually left these early influences behind. The works of his mature period (1926–37), which show an increasing interest in chamber music, are often described as neo-Classical. They have a new, austere mood with strong Stravinsky-like rhythms and innovative harmonies.

⏩ Roussel's opera-ballet *Padmâvatî* successfully combined his own style with Indian modes that he heard during his travels in India and Southeast Asia.

MILESTONES	
1894	Leaves navy; begins music studies
1902	Begins 12 years' teaching at Schola Cantorum in Paris
1909	Travels to India and Indochina
1913	Writes *Le festin de l'araignée*, ballet
1918	Completes opera-ballet *Padmâvatî*
1930	Composes Symphony No. 3
1931	Composes *Bacchus et Ariane*, ballet
1935	Completes Symphony No. 4, his last

⏫ These costumes were designed for one of the first performances of *Le festin de l'araignée*.

KEY WORKS

SYMPHONY NO. 3

ORCHESTRAL   ⏲ 22:15   📖 4   🎵

This bright and vigorous work, shaped in a conventional four-movement form, breathed new life into a genre that had seemed in decline.

BACCHUS ET ARIANE

BALLET   ⏲ 36:15   📖 2   🎵

Composed in 1930, this ballet has a rhythmic vitality and melodic inspiration that make it a worthy successor to Debussy's and Ravel's works in the genre. Roussel adapted each of the two acts into an orchestral suite, the second suite being one of his more popular works.

LE FESTIN DE L'ARAIGNÉE

BALLET   ⏲ 32:00   📖 2   🎵

The Spider's Banquet, Roussel's best-known work and his first masterpiece, shows traces of Debussy's influence. The plot of this ballet is set in a garden, where a spider, preparing to feast on insects caught in its web, is killed instead by a praying mantis.

Maurice **Ravel**

● 1875-1937   🏳 FRENCH   ✍ 88

Following in Debussy's path, Ravel established a distinctly French style that broke away from Romantic conservatism. A blend of sober refinement and luxuriant exoticism, his work is characterized by exquisite craftsmanship: Stravinsky described him as "the most perfect of Swiss clockmakers." This has sometimes obscured the moving quality of his melodies and the troubled undercurrents of his music.

Faced at first with a reactionary establishment, Ravel soon came to be recognized as the most significant French composer of the early 20th century after Debussy. His attachment to Classicism was fused with eclectic and adventurous tastes. While preserving the integrity of his own style, he drew inspiration from many idioms, and boldly—often wittily—blurred the boundaries between serious and light music. Much of his work plays on the contrast between chiseled technical perfection and fantastical imagination. A meticulous perfectionist, his output was only moderately sized, but of consistently high quality, covering chamber music, songs, piano works, and orchestral and stage scores, often originally written for piano.

MILESTONES	
1889	Enters Paris Conservatoire as a piano student
1898	Begins composition studies with Fauré; first published works
1905	Writes *Miroirs* for piano
1908	Composes *Rapsodie espagnole*, orchestra
1911	*L'heure espagnole*, opera, produced
1912	*Daphnis et Chloé*, ballet, performed
1920	Completed *La valse*, ballet
1925	*L'enfant et les sortilèges*, opera
1928	*Boléro* first produced

KEY WORKS

DAPHNIS ET CHLOÉ

BALLET	⏱ 49:00	📖 3	🎭 🎬

This ballet was commissioned in 1909 by Serge Diaghilev for his legendary Ballets Russes company. The reception of the first production, in 1912, was lukewarm. However, the work was soon hailed not only as one of Ravel's masterpieces, but also as one of the high points in a golden age for ballet.

The plot is set in a fanciful pastoral setting of Greek antiquity. The lovers Daphnis and Chloé are separated by a lively dance of nymphs, shepherd lads and lasses. Chloé is seized by pirates and Daphnis implores the god Pan to rescue her. Pan arrives just in time to scatter the pirates, and the reunited lovers dance in Pan's honor in a closing bacchanalia.

PIANO CONCERTO IN G MAJOR

ORCHESTRAL	⏱ 26:30	📖 3	🎭 🔊

Composed in 1929, this much-loved piece proved to be Ravel's last large-scale work. The two exuberant outer movements frame a lyrical slow movement of haunting beauty.

In the first movement, brilliant and bawdy exuberance, brimming with impish humor and surprising twists and turns, displays Ravel at his most carefree. Inspired by the slow movement of Mozart's clarinet quintet, the extended theme of the second movement is one of Ravel's most elaborate and moving melodic ideas, at once serene and elegiac. The third movement then shows Ravel at his most mercurial, with the chase between piano and orchestra providing dazzling virtuoso fireworks spiced up with jazzy inflections.

◹ **Bright, imaginative costumes** and colorful orchestration were integral parts of Diaghilev's Ballets Russes.

Joseph **Canteloube**

🔘 1879–1957   🏳 **FRENCH**   ✍ **c.150**

Born into a musical family of the Auvergne, the young Canteloube was fascinated by the folk music he heard on country walks. Not until his early 20s—now married, having lost both parents—did he study music seriously (with d'Indy). He moved to Paris to further his studies and built a career, moving in circles passionately dedicated to rediscovering, preserving, and popularizing folk music. He collected folk tunes and harmonized them, sometimes simply for amateur use, sometimes in a more elaborate, Impressionistic style. He also gave piano recitals—impressing Debussy—and lecture-recitals. Canteloube had limited success with his original compositions, but his very popular *Chants d'Auvergne*, while only "arrangements" of folk songs, are so exotically orchestrated that they are virtually original works.

>> **Canteloube's most well-known works** are arrangements of folk songs from the volcanic hills of the Auvergne.

MILESTONES

1902	Meets composer Vincent d'Indy
1907	Studies at Schola Cantorum, Paris
1923	Writes *Chants d'Auvergne*, series 1 and 2
1933	His second opera, *Vercingétorix*, produced
1941	Writes article defending complex orchestrations
1954	Writes *Chants d'Auvergne*, series 5

Lili **Boulanger**

🔘 1893–1918   🏳 **FRENCH**   ✍ **54**

Lili Boulanger's life was brief—in contrast with that of her sister, Nadia, the renowned teacher of composition, who lived into her 90s. But Lili made history, aged only 19, as the first woman to win the prestigious Grand Prix de Rome (her father had won it in 1835) with her cantata *Faust et Hélène*, which thereafter had great success in Paris. She wrote many of her finest works—mostly with mystical or biblical themes—in her gravely beautiful, clear, and dramatic style, during her stays in Rome, but these were cut short by World War I. After arriving home, she became terminally ill as a result of her immune system having been destroyed by childhood pneumonia. With remarkable serenity thanks to her strong faith, she dictated her intensely poignant *Pie Jesu* to Nadia on her deathbed in 1918.

>> **Lili Boulanger's mother** was a singer and her father taught at the Conservatoire. Her sister Nadia (right, with fellow competitors), won second prize in the Prix de Rome in 1908.

MILESTONES

1913	Composes *Faust et Hélène*, cantata; wins Grand Prix de Rome
1914	Writes *Clairières dans le ciel*, song cycle
1916	Visits Italy for second time
1917	Completes two symphonic poems
1918	Composes incidental music for Maeterlinck's play *La princesse Maleine*; dictates *Pie Jesu* on deathbed

Jacques **Ibert**

● 1890–1962　　　🏳 FRENCH　　　✍ UNKNOWN

Ibert was an important French composer of the first half of the 20th century. He was dedicated to the idea of continuing the French traditions of lightness, conciseness, and clarity, and adopted to this end a neo-Classical style. His most celebrated works are a flute concerto and an orchestral divertissement. Several operas, some remarkable chamber music, and songs complement these more celebrated works.

Ibert was a Parisian and played an important part in French musical life. He devoted himself to composition in his late teens, working as a piano teacher and accompanist to support himself. He also played for the silent cinema, an activity which was later to result in several film scores. His first major successes were in the 1920s, when several of his works were performed in Paris. Work at the Paris Opéra—for both ballet and opera—earned him further success. The latter part of his life was spent as director of the French Institute in Rome, where winners of the Prix de Rome (a prize awarded to musicians and which he himself had won) were awarded a subsidized year of working on their own projects. Works for the ballet, opera, radio, and film make up a considerable part of his output.

MILESTONES	
1910	Is admitted to Paris Conservatoire, and later studies with Paul Dukas
1919	Wins Grand Prix de Rome at first attempt with *Le poète et la fée*, cantata
1922	First public concert of his works given at Concerts Colonne in Paris
1924	Impressionistic orchestral pieces *Escales* premiered with great success
1927	One-act opera *Angélique* received well at the Paris Opéra
1926	Composes *Divertissement*, for orchestra
1933	Composes Flute Concerto
1937	Appointed director of Académie de France in Rome (until 1960)
1955	Begins two years as director of Paris Opéra-Comique

KEY WORKS

FLUTE CONCERTO

ORCHESTRAL　　📖 3　　🎵 🎶

One of the challenges of the concerto repertoire, this piece builds on the French tradition of flute-playing, arguably the best developed and most advanced in the European tradition.

ANGÉLIQUE

OPERA　　📖 1　　🎵 🎭 🎤

This farcical opera tells of a woman who has been put up for sale by her husband. To portray the irony, Ibert claimed to have used "the minimum of instruments for the maximum result."

DIVERTISSEMENT

ORCHESTRAL　　📖 6　　🎵

If neo-Classicism means using modern harmonies and phrase lengths within the frame of Classical forms, then Ibert's *Divertissement* is a masterpiece of the genre. It was written as incidental music for Eugène-Martin Lebiche's play *The Italian Straw Hat*, and has a joyous mood typical of the 1920s.

» **Among the film scores** that Ibert wrote is one for the 1948 film *Macbeth*, starring Orson Welles.

Frank **Martin**

● 1890–1974　　♙ SWISS　　✍ 73

Although Martin lacked any formal musical training, he became one of the foremost teachers and composers of his generation. Initially drawn to theory, his early works, now mostly forgotten, were excessively theoretical. With maturity, he developed a personal language, based on the 12-tone system, and a personal style, delicate and expressive, reflected in such masterpieces as *Petite symphonie concertante*.

Born into an extended Swiss Calvinist family, Martin's music was initially suffused with craft and workmanship, quite the reverse of the more hedonist style adopted by his French peers. Martin's work for the Institut Jaques-Dalcroze (where the teaching method was based on rhythm) affected his compositions profoundly. Rhythmic innovation became one of his hallmarks. Although his music evolved through a variety of styles—sometimes tonal, and for a time

⌵ **In Martin's *Le vin herbé***, Tristan and Isolde fall in love, provoking the jealousy of King Mark (far right), with tragic results, played out by a dark-toned chorus.

12-toned—all bear the composer's personal stamp, transcending his shifts in style. Martin's studies of Indian, Ancient, and Bulgarian music colored his work throughout his life, particularly with regard to rhythm. While he composed profusely, his work remains largely undervalued.

MILESTONES	
1918	Shuttles between Zurich, Rome, Paris
1922	Starts work on his Mass for two choirs, eventually staged in 1962
1923	Settles in Paris
1926	Returns to Geneva to study; writes *Rhythmes*, symphonic suite
1928	Teaches at Institut Jaques-Dalcroze in Geneva, Switzerland
1933	Piano Concerto No. 1 premiered; founds and directs the Technicum Moderne de Musique in Geneva
1941	Writes *Le vin herbé*, secular oratorio
1945	*In terra pax*, cantata for Armistice Day, broadcast on Swiss radio
1946	Settles in Amsterdam
1950	Teaches at the Cologne Conservatoire

Arthur **Honegger**

● 1892–1955　　♙ SWISS　　✍ 221

Although born in Le Havre, France, Honegger took his parents' Swiss nationality and studied for a while in Zurich, but moved to Paris while still a teenager and spent the rest of his life there. He studied at the Paris Conservatoire, and while there met up with a group of like-minded young composers who came to be known as "Les Six," and included Poulenc and Milhaud. Honegger was perhaps the most conservative of the group, and his music is generally in a neo-Romantic style.

Honegger wrote comparatively little chamber music, and preferred composing on a large scale; some of his finest works are the oratorios, including *Le Roi David* and *Jeanne d'Arc au bûcher*, for chorus and orchestra, and five symphonies. He is probably best known, however, for *Pacific 231*, a musical depiction of a steam locomotive, which

was the first of three "Symphonic Movements" written in the 1920s and '30s (the second was *Rugby*, the third untitled), which show his mastery of orchestral color. Despite steadily moving further away from the antiromantic ideals of Les Six, especially in his later compositions, he remained a close friend of both Poulenc and Milhaud until his death.

MILESTONES	
1921	Makes his name with the "dramatic psalm" *Le Roi David*
1923	*Pacific 231* is published
1927	Composes a score to accompany Abel Gance's film *Napoléon*
1938	The massive oratorio *Jeanne d'Arc au bûcher* is premiered in Basel
1940s	Remains in Paris during the Nazi occupation and joins the French Resistance
1950	Completes the last of his five symphonies
1951	Writes autobiography *I Am a Composer*

Ferruccio B. **Busoni**

◉ 1866–1924   ⚑ ITALIAN   ✍ 325

A multi-talented musician best known in his own lifetime as a brilliant piano virtuoso, Busoni was also a leading avant-garde critic, theorist, and teacher at the forefront of the new microtonal and electronic music. Renowned for his creative transcriptions of J.S. Bach for the piano, his music is now highly acclaimed as both visionary and progressive.

Born to musical parents in Tuscany, Busoni showed early promise and toured widely as both performer and conductor. Espousing the "Young Classicism," based on the styles of J.S. Bach, Mozart, and Liszt, he promoted the music of young composers, such as Schoenberg, while also taking an active interest in ethnic folk music, such as the Native American melodies that surge through *Indianisches Tagebuch*. It is hard to distinguish his original music from his transcriptions because he tended to quote existing music in his own works. Although he taught in many musical centers, his home for much of his adult life was Berlin.

MILESTONES	
1875	Concerto debut; enrolls at the Vienna Conservatory
1880	Studies in Graz with Wilhelm Mayer
1890	Wins the Rubinstein Prize for piano and composition; teaches in Moscow
1891	Teaches at Helsinki Conservatory
1907	Writes *Sketch of a New Aesthetic of Music*
c.1911	*Die Brautwahl*, opera, staged
1916	Composes opera *Turandot*

KEY WORKS

PIANO CONCERTO IN C MAJOR

ORCHESTRA   ⏱ 71:35   📖 5   🎵 🎼 🎹

A massive work, demanding stamina and skill from the pianist, Busoni's epic concerto, with its strong male chorus and huge orchestra, sounds more like a choral symphony than a concerto. A particularly unusual element is the inclusion of a choral setting of the "Hymn to Allah" from Adam Oehlenschläger's play *Aladdin*.

Prologo e introito (15:40) The strings open with a long melody interrupted by a horn-call. The Introito follows with the entry of the soloist. A cadenza is heard before the second subject enters on the woodwind, then another cadenza and a recapitulation follow before the movement ends with a serene coda recalling the Prologo.

Pezzo giocoso (9:45) The second movement opens with wild upward runs on the piano and a grotesque Turkish dance. After a short cadenza, the clarinet plays a traditional and lyrical Neapolitan song, "Fenesta che lucivi" ("The light through the window"), interspersed with piano figuration. The lively dance is revived before the movement dies away.

Pezzo serioso (23:00) After the Introito, the first section unfolds into a powerful, grand chorale with a variation. In the second section, the piano opens with a new theme, quickly followed by a resurgence of the opening music. The third section subsides into tranquillity.

All'Italiana (12:00) Italian songs, dances, and marches fuse with a dazzling piano cadenza, evoking "the crowded Roman street."

Cantico (10:50) The uplifting finale opens in E minor, recalling earlier themes. The male chorus sings "Hebt zu der ewigen Kraft Eure Herzen" ("Lift up your hearts to the Eternal Almighty") to the tune of the first movement's Introito, providing a glowing end to this grand concerto.

⚠ **Native American music** inspired Busoni's radical *Indianisches Tagebuch*, with its sonorous Hopi tunes and flowing rhythms.

Ottorino **Respighi**

◔ 1879–1936   ▥ ITALIAN   ✍ c.35

Respighi is the first Italian composer after Scarlatti whose fame does not rest on opera. He was a leading member of the so-called "generation of 1880," which tried to revive Italian music by going back to its roots in the Renaissance and Baroque eras. At one time hugely popular, his star has fallen since World War II.

The son of a piano teacher, Respighi grew into a man of wide culture in many languages, as well as a gifted violinist, pianist, and composer. A shy man, he shrank from the controversies between Classicists and Modernists in Italian music in the 1920s and 1930s, although by temperament he sided with the former. After an uncertain start as a composer, he established the essential elements of his style in *The Fountains of Rome*. This showed an orchestral mastery learned from studying under Rimsky-Korsakov, and later from Ravel and Strauss, as well as a passion for old music, mostly Italian, which worked its way into nearly everything he wrote.

MILESTONES	
1891	Starts studying violin, viola, composition
1906	Begins lifelong research into old music
1913	Settles in Rome to teach composition
1923	Appointed director of Conservatorio di Santa Cecilia, but resigns in 1926
1924	Completes *The Pines of Rome*
1927	Composes *Trittico Botticelliano*
1932	Fascist government honors him with membership of Reale Accademia; signs petition condemning Modernist trends in Italian music

KEY WORKS

ANCIENT AIRS AND DANCES

ORCHESTRAL SUITES   ⏲ 48:00   ▥ 4   ♫

Based on a collection of Renaissance-period lute music, this work consists of three suites for chamber orchestra, each in four movements. The first was so successful that Respighi wrote two more, in 1923 and 1928. The dances are based on dance forms popular at courtly entertainments and masques that Respighi found in ballets and dance manuals of the 16th and 17th centuries.

THE FOUNTAINS OF ROME

TONE POEM   ⏲ 16:00   ▥ 4   ♫

This was Respighi's first completely successful work, and perhaps his best. Here, the ponderous quality of his early work has been replaced by a new lightness of touch. The "silver rose" music from Richard Strauss's *Der Rosenkavalier* can be heard in the bright, celeste-colored orchestral sound, but it is absorbed into something entirely personal. The four pieces portray various fountains in Rome at "the hour in which their character is most in harmony with the landscape." The final "Villa Medici Fountain at Sunset," for example, simply evokes the scene, painting tolling bells and rustling leaves, whereas "The Triton Fountain in the Morning," in which naiads and tritons join in a frenzied dance, depicts the myths associated with that fountain.

» **This set was designed** for the premiere in 1934 of *La fiamma (The Flame)*, one of Respighi's eight, rarely staged operas.

Pietro **Mascagni**

⬤ 1863–1945   🏴 **ITALIAN**   ✍ **60**

The son of a baker, Mascagni studied law before moving to Milan to study at the Conservatorio, which he left after three years to pursue a career conducting opera. After some minor successes, his reputation was made overnight when his opera *Cavalleria rusticana* won the prestigious Sonzogno competition. Remembered today as the first verismo (realistic) opera, this work overshadowed the rest of his output, such as the lyrical comedy *L'amico Fritz*, and although he wrote some 15 operas, all well received, none attained the lasting popularity of *Cavalleria rusticana*.

One of the leading Italian composers and conductors of his time, Mascagni is renowned chiefly as an opera composer, although he also wrote songs, piano pieces, and orchestral music. He is often cited as the first composer of verismo opera, a term referring to the authentic depiction of everyday life in artworks; in fact, he wrote in a range of styles and forms, such as comedy, and some of his works were unashamedly populist in tone. Mascagni's reputation became somewhat tarnished through his close links with Mussolini's fascist regime.

MILESTONES

1881	*In Filanda*, cantata, wins first prize in a music competition in Milan
1882	Enters Conservatorio di Milano
1885	Leaves Conservatorio to conduct operetta season in Parma
1886	Becomes master of music at the Philharmony of Cerignola
1890	*Cavalleria rusticana*, opera, wins Sonzogno contest in Rome
1891	*L'amico Fritz*, comic opera, staged
1902	Incidental music for Hall Caine's *The Eternal City* premiered in London
1903	Becomes director of the Scuola Musicale Romana in Rome
1929	Directs La Scala in Milan

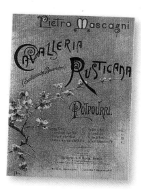

🔺 **A smash-hit** at its premiere in Rome, Mascagni's tense, racy opera thrilled the audience and received 60 curtain calls.

Ruggero **Leoncavallo**

⬤ 1857–1919   🏴 **ITALIAN**   ✍ **c.80**

After a musical training in Naples, Leoncavallo led a bohemian existence in Paris, playing the piano in cafés and composing sporadically. He moved to Milan's artistic circles, earning money from writing. On seeing the success of Pietro Mascagni's *Cavalleria rusticana*, he composed his own short realist opera, *I Pagliacci*, a polished piece calculated to appeal.

MILESTONES

1890	Collaborates on the libretto for Puccini's opera *Manon Lescaut*
1892	*I Pagliacci*, opera, successfully staged
1897	*La bohème*, opera, staged
1900	*Zazà*, opera, premiered successfully
1904	Enrico Caruso records arias "Vesti la giubba" and "Mattinata"

It was an instant hit in Milan, and the aria "Vesti la giubba" was the first recording to sell a million copies. But he found problems in Italy, partly due to his litigious nature and partly to bad luck. His *La bohème* was eclipsed by Puccini's, and Leoncavallo faded from public view.

◀ **The dramatic climax** to the intense, verismo opera *I Pagliacci* shocked its first audiences with the graphic, on-stage murder of Canio's faithless wife.

Ermanno **Wolf-Ferrari**

◒ 1876–1948   ᴾᵁ **ITALIAN**   ✍ **c.50**

Wolf was his German father's name, Ferrari his Italian mother's, and he always felt torn between the two cultures. He shuttled between Munich and Venice, and his operas combine German graveness with Italian lightness. Switching to music after first studying painting, Wolf-Ferrari won international fame fairly early with his cantata *La vita nuova* and opera *Le donne curiose*. For six years he headed the Liceo Benedetto Marcello in Venice, then left for Munich to compose in seclusion. During World War I he wrote little, but resumed with success in the 1920s, until war loomed again at the close of his life.

MILESTONES

1901	*La vita nuova*, cantata, succeeds widely
1906	*I quatro rusteghi*, comic opera, staged
1909	Writes *Il segreto di Susanna*, comic opera; moves to Munich to compose full-time
1927	Composes opera *Das Himmelskleid*
1939	Becomes professor of composition at the Salzburg Mozarteum in Austria

⏏ **In the witty and fast-paced opera** *I quatro rusteghi*, the rebellious beau Filipeto balks at his arranged marriage, with unexpectedly comic consequences.

Pablo de **Sarasate**

◒ 1844–1908   ᴾᵁ **SPANISH**   ✍ **55**

Born in Navarre to an artillery bandmaster, Sarasate was a child prodigy who gave his first public concert in Caruña at the age of eight and went on to play regularly at the court of Queen Isabel II in Madrid. Sarasate's compositions, mostly fantasies on Spanish melodies or themes from popular operas, were written primarily for his own performances and he was renowned for his sweet tone and pure style. Following the lead of many performer-composers before him, Sarasate wrote several concert fantasies on themes from popular operas including Mozart's *Don Giovanni* and *The Magic Flute*, and Verdi's *Forza del destino*. Sarasate's *Carmen Fantasy*, based on Bizet's hot-blooded opera *Carmen*, is essentially a set of variations on five of the best-known melodies, such as the emotionally charged Habanera. His *Zigeunerweisen* (literally "Gypsy Airs"), is a showpiece for violin and orchestra based on Spanish folk melodies. After a lively start full of technical trickery, a slow central section demands absolute control and tone, before closing with a breakneck finale.

MILESTONES

1856	Travels to the Paris Conservatoire to study with Jean Alard; mother dies of a heart attack en route; he catches cholera
1861	Wins the Conservatoire's prestigious Premier Prix; makes London debut
1874	Performs Lalo's *Symphonie espagnole*

» **A spectacular showcase** for violin, *Zigeunerweisen* demands the utmost sensitivity and virtuosity.

Isaac **Albéniz**

🔴 1860–1909   📑 SPANISH   ✍ c.150

Albéniz was a key figure in the Spanish musical renaissance of the late 19th and early 20th centuries. Through his indefatigable efforts as impresario, conductor, pianist, and composer, he became the first Spanish musician since Tomás Luis de Victoria to enjoy an international reputation. His piano music, above all the masterly series of tone poems *Iberia*, enlarged the domain of piano color and expressivity.

Albéniz was pushed into the role of traveling virtuoso at the age of eight by his needy family. His amazing facility as pianist and improviser won him worldwide fame, and by the 1880s he was pouring out a stream of piano character pieces, most hardly more than written-out improvisations. But his ambition grew; in the 1880s he wrote two piano concertos and a symphonic piece and, in the 1890s (by then living in London), tried his hand at operetta. In 1894, Francis Burdett Money-Coutts, the banking heir, became his patron. Albéniz then divided his time between operatic projects based on Money-Coutts's Arthurian libretti, works on Spanish themes, and concert tours.

MILESTONES	
1865	Gives first public concert
1882	Conducts a Spanish zarzuela company
1886	Writes *Suite española* No. 1 for piano
1887	Performs first concert of his own music
1896	*Pepita Jiménez* premiered in Barcelona
1900	Returns to Spain; discouraged by poor reception of his zarzuelas, moves to Paris
1902	Completes opera *Merlin*; moves to Nice to ease symptoms of Bright's disease
1998	First-ever full concert performance of *Merlin* with orchestra

KEY WORKS

IBERIA

SOLO PIANO	🕒 37:00	📖 12	🎧

These 12 character pieces—each a portrait of a Spanish locale—are Albéniz's masterpiece. Some, such as El Albaicín (an old quarter of Granada) or Málaga, are conventionally picturesque choices; others, such as Lavapiés (a poor district of Madrid), are surprising. All of them weave extraordinarily subtle webs of sound, in which a simple skeleton (such as an ostinato, or an accompaniment figure with typical guitar-inspired Spanish harmonies) is encrusted with layers of chromatic decoration. The influence of these works on later piano music was immense. No less a composer than Olivier Messiaen ranked *Iberia* alongside Bach's *The Art of Fugue* and the late sonatas of Beethoven.

MERLIN

OPERA	🕒 137:00	📖 3	🎭 🎻 👤

Wagner's influence can be heard in the grandeur of the first-act finale and the pervasive use of leitmotifs. There is even a direct quotation of the "peace motif" from *Siegfried*. All this will surprise anyone who knows Albéniz only through his "Spanish" piano music, but some of the *Merlin* music, notably the "Saracen Dances," recalls the more familiar Albéniz of *Iberia*.

INFLUENCES

Albéniz's subtle use of folklike idioms, and his amazingly refined use of the piano's resources of color and chromatic decoration, inspired later Spanish composers such as Granados and Falla, and were much admired by Debussy and Ravel.

🔼 **Composer Felipe Pedrell** taught Albéniz, inspiring him with his own enthusiasm for folk music.

Enrique **Granados**

● 1867–1916   ⩗ SPANISH   ✍ 25

Granados was one of a group of composers who were interested in developing a peculiarly Spanish form of art music by distilling the essence of Spanish indigenous folk music and blending it with the Romanticism of Schumann and Liszt. A virtuoso pianist as well as a composer, Granados died tragically at the peak of his career, before his potential had been completely fulfilled.

Granados studied in Barcelona under Felipe Pedrell, then in Paris, where he met the important French composers of the day, including d'Indy, Dukas, and Saint-Saëns. In 1890 he returned to Barcelona and began developing his career as a concert pianist. His music, much of it for piano and intended for his own performance, was strongly influenced by the nationalist ideas of Pedrell, as shown by his use of folk themes. But it was also Romantic in nature, with an advanced appreciation of chromatic harmony. Granados died when the liner taking him home from the premiere of his opera *Goyescas* was sunk in the English Channel.

MILESTONES	
1887	Goes to study with Charles Wilfrid de Bériot at Paris Conservatoire
1892	Gives Spanish premiere of Grieg's Piano Concerto
1892	Three orchestrated pieces from *Danzas españolas* given premiere
1901	Founds Granados Academy (later Marshall Academy) in Barcelona
1911	Composes *Goyescas*, suite for piano
1915	Completes *Goyescas*, opera
1916	Drowned with wife when English liner *Sussex* hit by German torpedo

KEY WORKS

GOYESCAS

SOLO PIANO   ⏱ 55:00   📖 6   🎧

Perhaps Granados's greatest work is his piano suite *Goyescas*, a set of pieces inspired by the dramatic paintings and tapestries of Goya. Granados makes full use of the rich late-Romantic harmonic palette, whilst incorporating distinctively Spanish rhythms and melodic shapes.

» **Describing his piano suite *Goyescas*,** Granados said that in his music he wanted to create "a palette of emotions such as appear in Goya's paintings."

GOYESCAS

OPERA   ⏱ 70:00   📖 1   🎭

Although Granados had already written several zarzuelas, he had long wanted to expand his piano work *Goyescas* into an opera. He finally began to arrange and extend the music with librettist Fernando Penquet, fitting the words around it. The resulting one-act opera was produced successfully in New York.

DANZAS ESPANOLAS

SOLO PIANO   ⏱ 65:00   📖 12   🎧

The *Spanish Dances* are a set of 12 short pieces evoking the folk music of Spain, without being literal arrangements of folk tunes. In 1892, three of the pieces were performed in an orchestral version, bringing Granados's name to wider notice.

Manuel de **Falla**

● 1876–1946　　📖 SPANISH　　✎ 25

The greatest Spanish composer since the Golden Age of Cristóbal de Morales and Tomás Luis de Victoria, Falla took the picturesque, Romantic Spanish style forged by Albéniz and Granados and imbued it with the Modernism of Debussy and Stravinsky. In his later works, he turned his back on the gorgeous, Impressionist sound world of his ballets to create a very Spanish form of neo-Classicism.

Precocious as a pianist but slow to start as a composer, Falla's real fame came with his ballets, particularly *The Three-Cornered Hat*. Composed for Diaghilev's Ballets Russes, it is strongly influenced by French Impressionism. An intensely religious man, Falla retreated to the calm of Granada in the 1920s, where he developed a new, spare style, in which the influence of old Spanish music replaced picturesque "Spanishisms" (a trend begun in *The Three-Cornered Hat*). Distressed by the Spanish Civil War and murder of his friend, the poet Lorca, Falla accepted an invitation to Argentina, where he then remained. His last 20 years were spent writing the huge, unfinished *L'Atlántida*.

MILESTONES

1905	*La vida breve* wins opera competition
1913	*La vida breve* finally premiered, in Nice
1922	Manages flamenco festival with the poet Federico García Lorca
1926	Finishes Harpsichord Concerto; begins *L'Atlántida*, opera-oratorio
1939	Moves to Buenos Aires

❰❰ **The first work** to result from Falla's blending of French Impressionist and Spanish national styles was his luxurious *Midnight in the Gardens of Spain* of 1915.

KEY WORKS

LA VIDA BREVE

OPERA	⏱ 60:00	📖 2	🎭

This passionate, fast-moving zarzuela tells of a gypsy girl who dies of a broken heart after her fiancé marries another. Despite the influences of Wagner and contemporaries such as Puccini, the mature Falla can already be heard.

EL SOMBRERO DE TRES PICOS

BALLET	⏱ 38:00	📖 2	🎭

The premiere of *The Three-Cornered Hat*—a story of mistaken identities—at the Alhambra Theater in London in 1919 was one of the greatest triumphs of Diaghilev's Ballets Russes. The sets were by Picasso and choreography by Massine. Deriving its style from flamenco *cante jondo* (deep song), Falla's music was praised for freeing itself from Debussy and Ravel.

HARPSICHORD CONCERTO

CHAMBER	⏱ 13:00	📖 3	🎹

Written for the great harpsichordist Wanda Landowska, and much admired by Stravinsky, this ranks among the masterpieces of 1920s neo-Classicism. The first movement quotes from a 15th-century Spanish song, and the second from Tomás de Victoria's Tantum Ergo.

Heitor **Villa-Lobos**

◉ **1887–1959**   ℙℕ **BRAZILIAN**   ✍ c.1,000

Astonishingly prolific, the composer Villa-Lobos was a larger-than-life character who has attained legendary status in Brazil. He made an extensive study of the folk music of his native country, which he incorporated into an eclectic musical style. This knowledge later formed the basis for sweeping reforms in the Brazilian music education system under the nationalist government of the 1930s.

Villa-Lobos's influences were as diverse as his own musical style. As a young man he played as a café musician, toured Brazil exploring indigenous music, and studied in Paris. Almost inevitably, for a composer who wrote with such ease and fluency, the quality of his output is variable. His best works are perhaps those in which his reverence for the Baroque is most obvious, such as the *Bachianas*

brasileiras series. Rarely seen without a cigar and a broad smile, Villa-Lobos was renowned for his rumbustious character and passionate advocacy of Brazilian music, an area in which he had an enormous impact as an educator.

MILESTONES	
1905	Visits northeast Brazil to collect folk music
1917	Writes *Amazonas*, tone poem
1918	Composes *A Prole do Bebê*, No. 1, suite
1923	Moves to study in Paris, funded by government grant
1929	Completes *Chôros series*
1930	Returns to Brazil and becomes director of music education for new nationalist government
1940	*Five Preludes for Guitar* performed
1944	Composes *The Green Mansions*, film score
1945	Completes *Bachianas brasileiras* series
1951	Writes Concerto for Guitar

KEY WORKS

CHÔROS NOS. 1–14

SUITE   📖 14   🎭

The *Chôros* date from the 1920s and were Villa-Lobos's own take on the "chorinho," a style of music that evolved in Rio de Janeiro in the late 19th century, blending European music with Afro-Brazilian rhythms. Scored for different instrumental ensembles, they present a kaleidoscope view of Brazilian music, as filtered through the young composer's active imagination.

CONCERTO FOR GUITAR

ORCHESTRAL   ⏱ 18:00   📖 3

The popular guitar concerto is one of comparatively few of Villa-Lobos's works to have taken a firm hold in the repertoire. An exciting piece, the finale in particular is full of syncopation and brilliant scoring. Villa-Lobos advocated the use of an amplifier to lift the volume of the guitar, but very few performers choose to use one.

FIVE PRELUDES FOR GUITAR

SOLO GUITAR   ⏱ **17:00**   📖 **5**   👁

Villa-Lobos's characterful guitar music has helped establish his international reputation, no doubt thanks to his idiomatic writing for the instrument (he was an excellent guitarist himself). Each of the *Five Preludes* is a portrait of a different aspect of Brazilian life, and—as ever with Villa-Lobos—they are quite stylistically diverse.

Number one (4:30) A typically Brazilian-sounding melody is played in the mid-range of the guitar, accompanied by plucked chords.

Number two (2:30) This Prelude depicts the *Capadocia*, a cocky native of the city of Rio. The first part is filled with light-hearted swagger, while the central section is a flurry of fast picking and parallel chords.

Number three (3:00) Prelude No. 3 is a homage to Bach, opening with a figure in almost bitonal counterpoint, and leading to a middle section of toccata-like figuration.

Number four (3:30) A haunting melody in the lower reaches of the instrument depicts the rain forest, returning—after a dramatic central section—in shadowy form using guitar harmonics.

Number five (3:30) The final Prelude, a homage to the lively and sophisticated social life of Rio, is a playful waltz that recalls themes from some of the earlier Preludes.

BACHIANAS BRASILEIRAS NO. 5

SUITE   ⏱ **8:30**   📖 **2**   ♟ ♻

The series of *Bachianas brasileiras* are, like the *Chôros*, scored for a variety of different ensembles. Written as a homage to Bach, Villa-Lobos makes a thorough attempt to fuse the composer's contrapuntal procedures with the spirit of Brazilian music. The fifth of the series is perhaps his best-known work. Villa-Lobos was a fine cellist, and it is surely his affinity for the instrument that enabled him to conjure a wide range of textures and sounds from this unusual ensemble of eight cellos and solo soprano.

Aria (*cantilena*) The Aria begins with a pizzicato bassline accompanying a gentle counterpoint. The soprano enters with a wordless *vocalise*,

shadowed by one of the cellos, intoning a vocal line with a distinctly Brazilian flavor. The central section is a setting of a poem in Portuguese, an impassioned paean to the moon. The opening material then returns, the soprano now humming the melody.

Dança (*martelo*) The second movement is a lively dance. The soprano sings a poem describing a native Brazilian bird, and has to negotiate all manner of fast, repeated words and sudden leaps.

☑ **In his tone poem *Amazonas*,** Villa-Lobos uses an array of ethnic percussion instruments.

Joaquín **Rodrigo**

● 1901–1999   ◗ᴺ SPANISH   ✍ c.200

Rodrigo is among the most significant Spanish composers of the 20th century. His approachable style, with its echoes of Spanish folk music, changed little throughout his long career. However, his influence has been significant and, while he wrote in many genres, he is remembered mainly for his guitar music. Blind from childhood, Rodrigo's prodigious output was composed using braille.

An attack of diphtheria rendered Rodrigo blind from the age of three. Nonetheless, as a child he showed great aptitude for music, studying firstly in Spain and then, following his fellow Spaniards, Granados and Albéniz, in Paris.

While hardly progressive, Rodrigo's music is an appealing blend of Spanish-inflected melody (although often without direct-reference folk sources) with a subtlety learned from his studies with Dukas, and, at times, a certain Stravinskian coolness—characteristics epitomized in the celebrated *Concierto de Aranjuez*. Not a guitarist himself, it is notable that his large output contains many works for the instrument, and as such he played a significant role in establishing the guitar in the Classical mainstream.

MILESTONES	
1918	Studies composition at Valencia
1927	Moves to Paris to study with composer Paul Dukas
1933	Marries the Turkish pianist Victoria Kamh
1935	Writes *Sonada de adiós* for piano, in memory of Dukas
1939	Returns to Spain; composes *Concierto de Aranjuez*
1942	Writes *Concierto heroica* for piano and orchestra
1947	Appointed Manuel de Falla professor of music at Madrid University
1954	*Fantasía para un Gentilhombre* produced
1963	Awarded Légion d'Honneur by the French government

KEY WORKS

CONCIERTO DE ARANJUEZ

ORCHESTRAL   ⏱ 20:00   ◫ 3   ♫ ◉

Inspired by the beautiful Rococo palace at Aranjuez, this is certainly the most famous work in the guitar repertoire, and one of the best-known pieces of Classical music of the 20th century. The two outer movements are full of dance rhythms, while the gorgeous second is a masterpiece of subtle scoring— the evocative melody shared between the guitar and cor anglais.

◀◀ **The guitar** is the instrument with which Rodrigo is most associated, but he never played it himself.

FANTASÍA PARA UN GENTILHOMBRE

ORCHESTRAL   ⏱ 22:00   ◫ 4   ♫ ◉

Rodrigo's second-best-known work for solo guitar and orchestra. Premiered in San Francisco by the renowned guitar virtuoso Andrés Segovia, the work is a fantasy on themes from the 17th-century Spanish composer Gaspar Sanz.

SONADA DE ADIÓS

SOLO PIANO   ⏱ 4:00   ◫ 1   ◉

Rodrigo studied with the renowned composer Paul Dukas. His death in 1935 affected him deeply, and the touching *Sonada de adiós* was written as a homage to his friend.

Carlos **Chávez**

● 1899–1978 　 MEXICAN 　 c.200

Composer, conductor, teacher, administrator, and writer, Chávez was a prolific and major figure in the development of Mexican music in the 20th century. Trained as a pianist, but self-taught as a composer, he directed the Conservatory and Institute of Fine Arts, created and headed major national orchestras, and promoted both radical new music and native Mexican music to all social classes. Chávez's works cover traditional genres (for example, his six symphonies) plus some of his own (such as the four "Solis"). They often show indigenous influences, sometimes using folk instruments—based on historical research, such as in the Aztec-influenced *Xochipilli*. His works are characterized by strong rhythms, a "Mexican accent," and spiky dissonance, but avoid repetition and cliché. He was also influenced by the music of Stravinsky and Schoenberg.

MILESTONES	
1921	Debut as composer: Piano Sextet
1922	Marries Otilia Ortiz, pianist
1925	Becomes head of OSM (Mexico Symphony Orchestra)
1928	Director of National Conservatory
1932	Composes *Caballos de vapor*, ballet
1947	Forms OSN (National Symphony Orchestra)

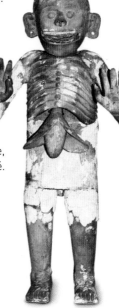

» *Xochipilli* **was written** to commemorate an exhibition of Mexican Art in New York.

Alberto **Ginastera**

● 1916–1983 　 ARGENTINE 　 c.100

Ginastera's *Panambi* made his name while still a student, and he went on to become the major Argentinian composer of the 20th century. He combined superb composing technique and eloquence with a strong sense of national identity: the virile rhythms and tough sounds of *Estancia* vividly suggest gauchos out on the ranch. However, his music also ranges from the charming (*Impresiones de la Puna*) to complex contemporary techniques (String Quartet No. 1). He directed the National Conservatory and taught—sometimes at loggerheads with the Perón government. In mid-career he wrote film music to support himself, but later commissions piled up: in his last 12 years, working in Switzerland, he composed prodigiously.

MILESTONES	
1941	Writes *Estancia*, ballet/orchestral suite
1948	Composes String Quartet No. 1
1954	*Pampeana No. 3*, orchestra, performed
1966	*Don Rodrigo*, opera, is a success in New York
1971	Remarries and moves to Switzerland

« **The atmospheric rhythms** and meditative effects in some of Ginestera's later works suggest the wild landscape of the Argentinian pampas.

Steven Collins **Foster**

● 1826–1864 📖 AMERICAN ✍ c.300

The American songwriter Stephen Collins Foster has become something of a cult figure. Perhaps because of his unrivaled ability to capture the essence of 19th-century American life and aspiration, he has come to be regarded as almost a folk hero, and his songs as authentic folk songs. In truth the bald facts of his life are rather mundane, rendering his achievements all the more remarkable.

Foster initially worked as a bookkeeper for his brother's steamboat business in Cincinnati, where he enjoyed his first major success with "Oh! Susanna." On returning to Pennsylvania in 1950, he decided to become a professional songwriter, a genuinely pioneering decision, as there was then no real "music business." Although almost wholly self-taught, Foster published his first song in his teens, and went on to write around 200 others. His songs were motivated by social purpose—both to capture the spirit of the American people, and to portray a world in which all were equal. At times, he deliberately adopted the musical and poetical style of immigrant groups, such as the cotton planters, which may be one reason why his works were mistaken for folk songs.

MILESTONES

1844	Publishes his first song, "Open Thy Lattice Love"
1846	Moves to Cincinnati to work as a bookkeeper for his brother
1848	Writes "Oh! Susanna," song
1850	Returns to Pennsylvania to become a professional songwriter; composes the song "Camptown Races"
1851	Writes "Old Folks at Home" ("Swanee River") and "Laura Lee," songs
1853	Visits friends in Bardstown, Kentucky, inspiring him to write "My Old Kentucky Home," song
1854	Composes "Jeanie With the Light Brown Hair," song
1862	Writes "Beautiful Dreamer," song

KEY WORKS

OH! SUSANNA

SONG   ⏲ 3:00   📖 1   🎵 🎶

The song "Oh! Susanna" achieved huge popularity when it was taken up as the unofficial anthem of the "forty-niners," the families traveling to California in the American gold rush. Most would not have known that it was written just a year earlier; as such, it stands as a fine example of Foster's ability to write songs with the timeless appeal of folk standards.

OH, SUSANNA.

« A rhythmic minstrel song capturing the ebullient spirit of the gold rush, "Oh! Susanna" was Foster's first and most enduring success.

BEAUTIFUL DREAMER

SONG   ⏲ 3:00   📖 1   🎵 🎶

Foster's later songs rarely rivaled his earlier ones for popularity, bar the serenade "Beautiful Dreamer," made famous by Bing Crosby in the 1940s.

MY OLD KENTUCKY HOME

SONG   ⏲ 3:00   📖 1   🎵 🎶

Foster wrote many evocative songs about the American South. "My Old Kentucky Home," inspired by a visit to friends in the region, has since been adopted as the official state song.

Louis Moreau **Gottschalk**

◗ 1829–1869   🏳 AMERICAN   ✍ 130

Arguably the first American nationalist composer, Gottschalk was a virtuoso pianist and performer whose flair won the praise of Chopin and Berlioz. Much of his life was spent touring outside his native country, yet the US remained his spiritual home and his music retained elements of the Afro-Creole qualities that shaped his early life. He composed much piano music, two symphonies, and two operas.

Gottschalk was born in New Orleans, of French-Creole descent. At the age of 13, apparently quite of his own accord, he determined to study in Paris. Although denied admittance to the Conservatoire, he studied privately, establishing himself as a pianist after a dazzling debut in 1844. Indeed, his playing was greatly admired by both Chopin and Berlioz, who described his "irresistible prestige and...sovereign power" at the keyboard. Gottschalk's composing, almost always secondary to his performing, has often been dismissed as mere light music, and his works have been largely forgotten today. However, his style can be seen as uniquely American in its exuberant integration of disparate influences.

MILESTONES	
1853	Returns to the US to tour widely
1856	New York concerts highly acclaimed
1854	Moves to West Indies for three years; composes *La Nuit des Tropiques*
1862	Returns to the US for the Civil War
1865	Forced to leave the US after scandal
c.1868	Composes *La Gallina: Cuban Dance*

◖ **A charismatic Creole virtuoso** from French New Orleans, Gottschalk dazzled audiences with his heady mix of Romantic idioms and Afro-Creole folk music and rhythms.

KEY WORKS

SYMPHONIE ROMANTIQUE: LA NUIT DES TROPIQUES

ORCHESTRAL   ⏱ 16:00   📖 2   🎷 🎵

La Nuit des Tropiques, written on the island of Guadaloupe during Gottschalk's three-year spell in the Caribbean, effectively fuses Romantic idioms with Afro-Creole folk music and Latin American dance rhythms, achieving striking coloristic effects. Although rarely performed nowadays, it has assumed a certain historical importance as the first genuine American symphony. That said, it bears little formal similarity to its European counterparts and is more akin to the freer form of symphonic poem. Its evocative mood and name probably derives from Félicien David's symphonic ode, *Christophe Colomb*, staged in 1847. A curious point of note is the fugue on a Cuban theme in the second movement.

THE LAST HOPE; THE DYING POET

SOLO PIANO   ⏱ 6:00   📖 1   🎵

The Last Hope and *The Dying Poet* are among the many overtly sentimental encore pieces that Gottschalk composed for use in his own performances. These two were particular favorites with his audiences, which were reported to have been largely made up of female admirers.

Amy Marcy Cheney **Beach**

● 1867–1944   ⚑ AMERICAN   ✐ 300

Amy Beach was one of the first US composers to gain a significant reputation outside her native country, and remains one of the foremost female composers of her time. Finding inspiration in Romanticism and the European folk-music tradition of her New England ancestors, she composed copiously throughout her life, and in later years developed a significant performing career.

Amy Beach would almost certainly have made a career as a concert pianist, but her husband encouraged her to limit her public appearances and concentrate instead on composition (she later returned to the platform following his death in 1910). In this she was immensely talented but largely self-taught, learning orchestration from a treatise by Berlioz and counterpoint by writing out fugues from

» **Beach composed music** for the opening of the Women's Building at the World's Columbian Exhibition, held in Chicago in 1893.

Bach's *Well-Tempered Clavier*. While not especially innovative, her music is well constructed and shows a sophisticated grasp of harmony. In works such as the Piano Concerto she demonstrated an ability (and willingness) to tackle large-scale forms. Her output is large and covers all the major genres.

MILESTONES	
1885	Debut with Boston Symphony Orchestra; marries Dr. Henry Beach
1896	Composes *Gaelic Symphony*, Op. 32
1898	Writes *Three Browning Songs*, Op. 44
1911	Concert tour to Europe; remains in Germany until 1914
1914	Settles in New York

KEY WORKS

GAELIC SYMPHONY, OP. 32

ORCHESTRAL   ⏱ 43:00   □ 4   ♫

Rather than follow Dvořák's example of using Native American and Negro music to forge a national style, Beach turned to Celtic folk music. Her *Gaelic Symphony* incorporates Irish melodies and was the first symphony by an American composer to garner significant attention in Europe.

PIANO CONCERTO, OP. 45

ORCHESTRAL   ⏱ 36:00   □ 4   ♫ ⌾

Beach's Piano Concerto is a large-scale, bravura masterpiece in the manner of contemporary late-Romantic concertos such as those of

Tchaikovsky and Grieg. Three of the four movements are based on material from Beach's own songs, including one to a poem by her husband. She premiered the work herself with the Boston Symphony Orchestra in 1900.

THREE BROWNING SONGS, OP. 44

SONG   ⏱ 7:00   □ 3   ⌾ ⚲

Beach composed over 100 songs, and it was for these that she was remembered until her revival in the mid-1970s in the wake of the US feminist movement. The *Three Browning Songs*, and in particular the delightful first song, "The Year's at the Spring," have proven enduringly popular.

John Philip **Sousa**

● 1854–1932 ⏶ AMERICAN ✍ 250

A composer, conductor, bandleader, and patriot, John Philip Sousa was known as the "March King." He composed many of the world's best-known military band pieces, including *The Stars and Stripes Forever*, the official march of the United States. In addition to his band music, which remains immensely popular, his output included some 15 operettas and many songs.

After Sousa attempted to run away with the circus at age 13, his father—a military trombonist—apprenticed him to the Marines. Following his discharge in 1875, and a spell conducting theater orchestras, he returned to the military to assume leadership of the US Marine Band. He went on to form his own hugely successful band in 1892, touring all over the world and setting new standards for the quality of marching band performance. From his first published composition in 1872 until the end of his life, Sousa wrote constantly, and his position as bandleader gave him ample opportunity to showcase his works. His 135 marches, many celebrating US places or events, are full of delightful melodies and possessed of a distinctive, good-natured swagger.

MILESTONES

1867	Father enlists Sousa in the Marines
1875	Discharged from the Marines
1880	Returns to the military to lead the US Marine Band
1888	Composes march *Semper Fidelis*
1889	*The Washington Post*, march, first performed
1892	Forms the Sousa Band
1895	Composes *El Capitan*, his first successful operetta
1896	Composes *The Stars and Stripes Forever*
1899	Composes march *Hands across the Sea*
1900	Sousa Band tours Europe
1901	Second European tour
1905	Third European tour
1910	Sousa Band's world tour

KEY WORKS

THE STARS AND STRIPES FOREVER

MARCH ⏱ 3:30 📖 1 ♇

Sousa and his wife were on vacation in Europe when they heard of the death of his manager, David Blakely. Thinking over the news while onboard the ship returning to the US, Sousa began to hear "a rhythmic beat of a band playing within my brain." That melody was in his mind for the remainder of the voyage, and was to become *The Stars and Stripes Forever*, perhaps his most enduringly popular march.

THE LIBERTY BELL

MARCH ⏱ 3:30 📖 1 ♇

The Liberty Bell is well known as the theme tune to the classic British comedy series "Monty Python's Flying Circus." It is a fine example of Sousa's musical craft—a rousing march, with a memorable theme and a hint of humor.

» **John Philip Sousa** was the inventor of the sousaphone, a now familiar instrument in the marching-band ensemble.

Edward **MacDowell**

● 1860–1908   ⚑ AMERICAN   ✍ c.70

One of the first US composers to establish a reputation outside his country, MacDowell was considered the most important US composer of his day. As a pianist and teacher he founded the music department of Columbia University and, with his wife Marion, the MacDowell artists' colony, which still exists. His musical style owes much to the influence of his teacher, Joachim Raff, but became more individual in later years.

Life and music

MacDowell studied first in New York, then Paris, but it was in Germany that he settled, teaching piano and establishing a career as a performer. Success as a composer followed his return to the US in 1888. After teaching at Columbia University, his final years were spent between New York and his house in Peterborough, New Hampshire. The artists' retreat he founded there with his wife in 1907 has flourished ever since. Inevitably, given his education, MacDowell's music was strongly influenced by the German Romantics, which may be the reason why it fell out of favor in the US between the two world wars.

MILESTONES	
1876	Moves to Paris to attend Conservatoire
1878	Dissatisfied with instruction in Paris, so moves to Wiesbaden
1879	Studies composition at Frankfurt Conservatory with Joachim Raff
1881	Made professor of piano at Darmstadt
1882	Composes Piano Concerto No. 1
1884	Becomes piano teacher at Wiesbaden
1888	Returns to US and settles in Boston
1896	Given first chair of music at Columbia University; writes *Woodland Sketches*
1907	Founds MacDowell Colony with wife

KEY WORKS

WOODLAND SKETCHES

SOLO PIANO   ⏳ 18:30   📖 10   🔊

Some of MacDowell's best-known music is contained in the late sets of short piano pieces *Woodland Sketches* and *New England Idylls*. Influenced by the American landscape, particularly that of his country retreat in New Hampshire, the musical language is sparse, direct, and even folksy compared with his earlier piano works. The individual pieces in *Woodland Sketches* are all evocatively titled.

The famous "To a Wild Rose," which opens *Woodland Sketches*, and the eighth piece, "A Deserted Farm," are perfect examples of pared-down piano writing—beautifully simple melodies arranged over poignant, mildly dissonant chords. "An Old Trysting Place" has richer harmony and the feel of an old choral setting, while "To a Water Lily" uses the full range of the piano to suggest a deep lake.

"Will o' the Wisp" is full of gleeful good humor. The most direct folk allusion is in "From an Old Indian Lodge," which imitates the rhythms of Native American chant.

Although some of the pieces are now performed separately, MacDowell intended them to be played together: in fact, the final piece, "Told at Sunset," quotes from some of the earlier movements as if in reminiscence.

PIANO CONCERTO NO. 2

ORCHESTRAL ⌛ 24:00 📖 3

Received with success at its premiere in 1889, this work was described by one critic as sounding "a model of its kind—the kind that Johannes Brahms gave the world over 30 years ago in his D minor Concerto." If this is a little over-stated, there is no doubt that the work cemented MacDowell's position as the foremost composer in the US. The Concerto No. 2 is a distinctive and interesting work, made unusual by its adoption of a slow first movement and a scherzo second, and by the many dance rhythms that feature throughout. It has also remained popular, largely thanks to US pianist Van Cliburn.

First movement (*larghetto calmato*, 10:00) After a short introduction led by the brass, the soloist enters with an intense, passionate cadenza. Cellos and clarinets introduce the lyrical second theme.

Second movement (*presto giocoso*, 7:00) This good-humored section is a rondo, filled with quicksilver passages for the piano and almost jazzlike in its constant syncopation.

Third movement (*largo—molto allegro*, 7:00) Beginning darkly with cellos leading a slow introduction, the mood lightens into a lively waltz, in which the soloist recalls themes from the first movement.

SONATA TRAGICA

SOLO PIANO ⌛ 26:00 📖 4

MacDowell's four substantial piano sonatas are all inspired by European mythology except this, his first one. It is his most personal—a tribute to the death of his teacher and friend, Raff.

SUITE NO. 2, "INDIAN"

ORCHESTRAL SUITE ⌛ 30:00 📖 5

MacDowell felt that native Indian music held far more potential than Negro music as a source of inspiration for an "American" style. In this large-scale work for orchestra he employed material that has been traced to the Iroquois and Chippewa tribes.

FIRST MODERN SUITE

SOLO PIANO ⌛ 30:00 📖 5

Despite its title, MacDowell's *First Modern Suite* for piano was resolutely in the European style he learned from his time studying with Raff. Nevertheless, it is full of charming music and extremely idiomatic for the piano.

◀ **The MacDowell Colony** at Peterborough, New Hampshire, is the oldest artists' colony in the US. Its oldest building was originally the composer's home.

Modern Music
1900–Present

Music since 1900 has developed in a wide variety of styles, many of them strongly influenced by ideological, social, and technological changes. Whereas composers of earlier times attempted to adopt and develop established styles, much music of the 20th and 21st centuries seems—at least on the surface—to break with the past.

The first half of the 20th century was dominated by two very different composers who both established themselves in Europe and ended their lives in California: the Austrian Arnold Schoenberg and the Russian Igor Stravinsky.

Schoenberg and his followers—raised on the high Romanticism of composers like Mahler and Wolf—saw themselves as building on the Austro-Germanic tradition. At the same time, Schoenberg's interest in painting indicates a close relationship between the Expressionism of artists such as Kokoschka and Kandinsky, and of his own music and that of his followers, such as Berg. Igor Stravinsky sprang to fame with his Russian ballets, such as *The Firebird* (1909) and *The Rite of Spring* (1913), and reinvigorated music with the primitive force of his rhythmic language, mirrored in the angular lines of the paintings of Picasso from the same period.

Neo-Classicism

Later, Stravinsky looked back to the past by drawing on styles and actual materials of the 17th and 18th centuries, and this style or spirit of "neo-Classicism" was embraced by many contemporary composers, especially in France. Stravinsky's *Pulcinella* (1918) was the seminal example of neo-Classicism, and even as late as his *The Rake's Progress* (1948–51), there is a sense of reverting to the traditions (and plots) of the past.

In France, Ravel's music was sufficiently objective in its poise and clarity to adapt to the neo-Classical ethos, as is shown in his *Le tombeau de Couperin* (1917–19), and even Debussy in his *Suite Bergamasque* succumbs to the charms of the past. In Britain, Walton and Constant Lambert took up the neo-Classical style, while in Germany, Hindemith explored the forms of earlier periods, most notably in his series of duo sonatas for orchestral instruments and piano.

Jazz

Just as many composers turned to the past to react against Romanticism, others found in jazz a perfect foil to the music of the previous century. Virtually no composer in Paris was immune to the influence of jazz: Stravinsky composed a Rag-time (1918); Milhaud composed the first jazz fugue in his ballet *La création du monde* (1923); and Ravel's Violin Sonata (1923–27) contains a

◄◄ **In the 20th century,** music continued to evolve, and new means of expression emerged. With advances in broadcasting and recording, popular music and jazz also had a significant influence on Classical music.

△ **For this production** of Stravinsky's *The Rite of Spring* by the Kirov Ballet in 2003, the original costumes and Nijinsky's choreography were reconstructed from contemporary records.

blues movement. At the same time, in the USA, Gershwin was creating concert works, such as *Rhapsody in Blue*, that bridged the divide between popular and "serious" music.

Folk influences

Elsewhere, composers explored their musical folk heritage. In eastern Europe, Béla Bartók and Zoltán Kodály both traveled extensively to make recordings of folk songs and dances. The Australian composer and pianist Percy Grainger was equally industrious, collecting

music from various parts of the world. In North America, Aaron Copland began to use cowboy songs, Quaker hymns, and Latin-American material in his own work, creating an immediately identifiable American style.

Later, European composers as diverse as Britten and Berio would make settings of folk songs of their own countries, and other composers such as Ligeti, Reich, and Volans would be influenced (in very different ways) by the music of Africa.

TIMELINE: MODERN MUSIC

1905 Einstein proposes Theory of Relativity

1907 Start of Cubist movement in the paintings of Picasso and Braque

1911 Stravinsky's ballet *Petrushka* with Nijinsky in title role

1914–18 World War I

| 1900 | 1905 | 1910 | 1915 |

1902 Debussy's opera *Pelléas et Mélisande*

1907–08 Schoenberg composes *Verklärte Nacht*

1913 Premiere of Stravinsky's ballet *The Rite of Spring*; noise of opposing factions in audience drowns the music

Music and politics

In Russia, several distinct and important voices emerged during the 20th century. Prokofiev spent some time in the West, and was influenced by the neo-Classicism he found in Paris, whereas Shostakovich remained in the Soviet Union and was forced to pay lip-service to the Socialist Realism of the Soviet authorities. Political interference also surfaced in Nazi Germany, where Jewish composers were banned during the 1930s and even the music of non-Jewish composers, such as Anton Webern and Alban Berg, was outlawed as "degenerate art." Among the potentially great composers who died or were killed in Nazi camps was the Moravian Gideon Klein and the Czech Viktor Ullmann.

Some composers remained resolutely independent from other movements. Olivier Messiaen took religion as an important unifying factor for his music and at the same time used exotic scales and birdsong.

SCHOENBERG AND SERIALISM

Schoenberg devised the 12-note process of composition, whereby a pattern of all 12 semitones (known as a "series" or "row") should be used in a particular order before any one is repeated. The relationship between the notes of the row would always be maintained, although it was permissible to transpose the row (start on a different pitch), to reproduce it in "retrograde" (in reverse) or "inversion" (upside-down), and the notes could be combined simultaneously in chords. The idea was to avoid any sense of key or tonality. This way of composing became known as "serialism" and dominated music in the mid-20th century.

» **Arnold Schoenberg's** *Harmonielehre* (*Treatise on Harmony*) was published in 1911, and proved to be an influential theory.

☒ **Writer Jean Cocteau** with "Les Six" in 1925. The group consists of (from left to right) Milhaud, a drawing of Auric, Cocteau at the piano, Honegger, Tailleferre, Poulenc, and Durey.

1920 "Les Six"—name given to group of six French composers including Poulenc and Milhaud

1924 Gershwin's *Rhapsody in Blue* performed in New York; death of Puccini

1931 Varèse's *Ionisation* scored for percussion and two sirens

1938 *Anschluss*: annexation of Austria by Germany; Prokofiev writes score for Eisenstein film *Alexander Nevsky*

1920

1925

1930

1935

1920 First commercial broadcasting, in Pittsburgh, Pennsylvania

1925 Berg's opera *Wozzeck* performed in Berlin

1929 *The Threepenny Opera* by Kurt Weill and Bertolt Brecht

1933 Hitler becomes Chancellor of Germany

1935 Gershwin composes *Porgy and Bess*

1939 Germany invades Poland; World War II starts in Europe

>> **Music plays** a key role in cinema. Ennio Morricone wrote the score for Sergio Leone's *Dollars* trilogy.

Pierre Boulez, meanwhile, was initially influenced by Messiaen, but later rejected his teacher and instead became a high priest of formalism, taking the principles of serialism to a new level.

Modern trends

In the USA, John Cage, who had studied with Schoenberg, turned his back on serialism and looked to the music and philosophy of the East for inspiration, while bizarre conceptual preoccupations inspired the work of Karlheinz Stockhausen, one of whose works involves a string quartet performing in midair in four helicopters. Technology impacted on all types of music, through recording and through the use of synthesized sound; Edgard Varèse, for example, created a tape-only piece, *Poème électronique*, for Le Corbusier's Philips Pavilion at the Brussels Expo of 1958.

A group of composers who emerged in the late 1960s were the minimalists. Terry Riley, Philip Glass, and Steve Reich composed music based on the repetition of simple motives that many found mesmerizing. Ultimately this style was taken up by composers who sought to reintroduce elements of development, such as John Adams, who has composed orchestral music and opera of romantic proportions both in scale and richness of expression. Just as the minimalists rebelled against the complexity of

MUSIC FOR STAGE AND SCREEN

The American stage musical has attracted composers from Gershwin (*Porgy and Bess*) to Bernstein (*West Side Story*) and Stephen Sondheim. Fugitives from Europe in the 1930s, including Erich Korngold and Miklós Rózsa, found work in Hollywood alongside American composers such as Bernard Herrmann (*Citizen Kane* and *Taxi Driver*). Well-known classical composers who have also written film scores include Vaughan Williams, Milhaud, Prokofiev, Copland, Walton, and Philip Glass. An especially successful modern film composer is John Williams (of *Star Wars* fame).

>> **Bernstein's** ***West Side Story*** demonstrated the composer's surefire popular touch.

TIMELINE: MODERN MUSIC

1944 Bartók's Concerto for Orchestra receives its first performance in Boston

1953 Death of Stalin allows Soviet artists slightly more freedom

1957 Bernstein's *West Side Story* opens on Broadway

1962 Britten's *War Requiem* performed in Coventry Cathedral

1976 Philip Glass's minimalist opera *Einstein on the Beach*

1940   **1950**   **1960**   **1970**

1941–44 Siege of Leningrad; Shostakovich dedicates his Symphony No. 7 to city's heroism

1953–55 Boulez composes *Le marteau sans maître*

1955–57 Stockhausen composes *Gruppen*

1968 Berio's *Sinfonia*

1976 Górecki's Symphony No. 3

serialism, so a group of European composers, including John Tavener, Henryk Górecki, and Arvo Pärt, developed music that was equally simple in its construction, but emerged out of a spiritual calm.

Crossover music

Popular music forms, such as jazz, rock, and folk music, inspired a great many modern classical composers, but musical cross-fertilization in the 20th century was by no means a one-way traffic. Jazz composers such as Duke Ellington used an adapted orchestral format, a trend that continued with arrangers such as Nelson Riddle, and even into rock and pop. A number of bands including Deep Purple and Pink Floyd dabbled with orchestral composition, and rock guitarist Frank Zappa earned the respect of the Classical establishment with his impressive catalog of avant-garde compositions. Some Classical composers, notably Mark-Anthony Turnage, have also felt at home in jazz and rock, and incorporated the styles into their music, and it is often difficult to separate "Classical" and "popular" in the work of minimalists such as Gavin Bryars, or the truly eclectic improvisatory style of composer-performers such as John Zorn.

≪ **Frank Zappa** rehearses with the London Symphony Orchestra for a concert at the Barbican in 1984.

1989 Fall of Berlin Wall; collapse of communism in Eastern Europe

1991 Breakup of the Soviet Union

2007 The Metropolitan Opera production of Tan Dun's opera *The Last Emperor* is broadcast live to cinemas around the world

1980

1990

2000

2010

1987 John Adams's opera *Nixon in China*

1990 Magnus Lindberg composes *Marea*

2000 Turnage's opera *The Silver Tassie*, based on the Sean O'Casey anti-war play, opens in London

2008 Elliott Carter's *Interventions* is premiered as part of his 100th birthday celebrations

Arnold **Schoenberg**

● 1874–1951   ⚑ AUSTRIAN   ✍ 213

Schoenberg has probably inspired more misunderstanding and controversy than any other 20th-century composer. His music broke with the past and yet he saw himself as part of a tradition of Germanic music and his abandonment of tonality as an inevitable step in music progress. He was also a great, self-taught teacher. His music can seem unapproachable, but he could also arrange Strauss waltzes.

» Schoenberg's death seemed to justify his superstitious belief in numerology: he died on Friday 13 July 1951, at 13 minutes before midnight.

Life

Schoenberg was born in Vienna, where his father owned a small shoe shop. He began composing as a child, but met Alexander Zemlinsky (his only teacher) when already a young adult, working in a bank. He converted to Protestantism from Judaism in 1898 and three years later married Zemlinsky's sister Mathilde. Their circle of friends included Berg, Webern, Mahler, and the painter Richard

Gerstl, who gave art lessons first to Schoenberg—himself a talented artist—and later to Mathilde. In 1908, Mathilde briefly left her husband for Gerstl, who committed suicide when she subsequently returned to Schoenberg. Mahler's death in 1911 was another blow to Schoenberg, and it was only when he moved to Berlin that he was able to regain some confidence. In 1933, horrified at the German anti-Semitism of the time, Schoenberg rejoined the Jewish faith in a ceremony witnessed by the painter Marc Chagall. Later that year he left Europe permanently, moving first to Boston and then to Los Angeles, where he took a teaching post at the University of California. Friends and near neighbors to his Hollywood home included George Gershwin and the writer Thomas Mann.

Music

After writing his early music in a late-Romantic style, Schoenberg developed a completely new musical language. Works such as the Chamber Symphony No. 1 and the String Quartet No. 2 took dissonance to levels which audiences had not previously encountered. The last movement of String Quartet No. 2 appropriately quotes the German poet Stefan George: "I feel the air of other planets." The Three Pieces, Op. 11, for piano confirm this new and strange planet: they are effectively atonal and expressionist. This "free atonality" liberated Schoenberg from writing in any particular key, and traditional melodies were replaced by expressive gestures and extremes of pitch or dynamics. He later pared his music down in a way that reflected the neo-Classicism of the day (for example the Six Little Pieces), and in his final years he strove toward some reparation with tonality.

> ❝ My **music** is **not modern,** it is merely **badly played.** ❞
>
> **Arnold Schoenberg**

MILESTONES

1898	Converts to Protestantism	**1911**	Meets Kandinsky
1899	Writes *Verklärte Nacht*, Op. 4	**1912**	*Pierrot lunaire*, Op. 21
1904	Berg and Webern become pupils	**1928**	Variations, Op. 31, for orchestra
1906	Chamber Symphony No. 1, Op. 9	**1933**	Emigrates to US
1909	Three Pieces, Op. 11, for piano	**1941**	Becomes US citizen
1911	*Gurrelieder* produced	**1942**	Writes *Ode to Napoleon Buonaparte*, Op. 41

KEY WORKS

PIERROT LUNAIRE, OP. 21

CHAMBER ⏳ 32:00 📖 3

Pierrot lunaire has gained a certain notoriety as one of Schoenberg's most radical works despite the composer's intention that it should be "light, ironic, and satirical." It is a setting of poems by Albert Giraud about the traditional commedia dell'arte character Pierrot. The work is scored for a female reciter and a chamber ensemble of eight instruments (flute, piccolo, clarinet, bass clarinet, violin, viola, cello, and piano) played by five performers, who play together for the first time in the very last song. The work's surreal quality is enhanced by the *sprechgesang* (speech-song) of the reciter, which appears to presage madness.

SUITE, OP. 25

SOLO PIANO ⏳ 24:30 📖 5

Schoenberg wrote little music for solo piano and tended to treat the instrument as a laboratory, experimenting with new compositional ideas on the instrument. As a result, the piano yielded many of Schoenberg's most interesting ideas, and the wonderfully fresh Suite for piano, composed in 1921, is no exception. It was the first work to be created in its entirety from a single note row—the first use of Schoenberg's influential 12-note technique that became known as "serialism." Nevertheless, the novelty of the compositional method is offset by the traditional dance forms used: there is a prelude, gavotte, musette, minuet, and trio, and an energetic gigue.

≪ The opera *Moses und Aron*—begun in 1932—was one of Schoenberg's unfinished works. Ever superstitious, he spelt "Aron" with one "r" to avoid a title with thirteen letters.

GURRELIEDER

CANTATA ⏳ 120:00 📖 3

This epic cantata was originally conceived as a song cycle based on a text by Jens Peter Jacobsen. It is the story of Waldemar, a medieval king of Denmark, and charts his doomed love for Tove, his blasphemy, penance, and the summer winds which sweep him and his ghostly retinue away in the dawn. The work is immersed in romantic symbolism and calls for a gigantic orchestra, choruses, soloists, and narrator. Significantly, it opens with an ethereal sunset, evoked by shimmering woodwind chords, and ends with a sunrise, symbolizing hope for the future.

INFLUENCES

Schoenberg was influenced by composers as diverse as Bach and Mahler. His own influence was immense, partly through his teaching (such composers as Berg, Webern, and John Cage were among his pupils), but also through the adoption of serialism on both sides of the Atlantic after 1950.

Anton **Webern**

● 1883–1945   ⚑ AUSTRIAN   ✍ c.31

Webern's legacy was relatively small in terms of works, but substantial in terms of subsequent influence. All of his music is immaculately crafted and he developed Schoenberg's 12-note procedures in distinctive ways. Most of Webern's compositions are extremely concise—he was able to compress a range of emotions into a few bars of music—yet they are among the most important works of the 20th century.

Webern was born into the middle class in Vienna (his father was a mining engineer). Although he studied musicology under Guido Adler at the University of Vienna, it was Schoenberg who was to be the decisive influence on his music. Webern enjoyed some success as a conductor in the 1920s but gradually withdrew from public life. His music was banned by the Nazis and his teaching activities were restricted after the Anschluss. During World War II he moved outside Vienna to escape the bombing of the city; ironically, he was shot one night (just after the war had ended) while smoking a cigar outside his daughter's house.

MILESTONES	
1906	Graduates with a doctorate from the University of Vienna
1911	Six Bagatelles for String Quartet, Op. 9; moves to Berlin with Schoenberg; marries Wilhelmine Mörtl
1913	Five Pieces, chamber orchestra, Op. 10; undergoes psychoanalysis with Alfred Adler
1925	Teaches at the Israelisches Blindeninstitute in Vienna
1938	Composes String Quartet, Op. 28

KEY WORKS

FOUR SONGS FOR VOICE AND INSTRUMENTS, OP. 13

SONG   ⏱ 7:00   📖 4   ♫ ♪

These four songs—which were composed during World War I—draw together poems of four different poets: *Lawn in the Park* by Karl Krause, *The Lonely Girl* by Wang-Seng-Yu, *In a Foreign Land* by Li Bai, and *A Winter Evening* by Georg Trakl. That Webern composed so many songs at this time shows not only that he was interested in literature, but also how important it was for composers of free atonal music to have a structure in which to work. Each song is accompanied by a chamber ensemble (including woodwind, brass, percussion, and string instruments), and the different combinations of instruments reveal Webern's fascination for variations in timbre.

PASSACAGLIA, OP. 1

ORCHESTRAL   ⏱ 10:20   📖 1   ♫

This is an early work, written while Webern was still a pupil of Schoenberg. It is Romantic in style and is one of the last works he wrote to have a key signature (D minor).

SYMPHONY, OP. 21

CHAMBER   ⏱ 8:00   📖 2   ♫

Although titled "Symphony," this work is for a small chamber orchestra (clarinets, horns, harps, and strings) and avoids the development principles to be found in traditional symphonies. The texture is transparent, mostly consisting of single notes with occasional chords, and the quality of tone changes continually.

Alban **Berg**

🌑 1885–1935　　🏴 AUSTRIAN　　✍ 83

Although he composed relatively few works, Berg is one of the most distinctive voices of the early 20th century. Much of his music employs the new 12-tone principles of his teacher Schoenberg, but still retains a Romantic generosity and the emotional intensity of Expressionism. His music is inherently dramatic.

Berg was born into a middle-class Viennese family, but his first formal training in music came from Schoenberg at the relatively advanced age of 19. The relationship with Schoenberg was always to be strained, as Berg attempted to please his teacher but rarely succeeded in doing so. Although his Piano Sonata, Op. 1, marked a new artistic confidence, it was not until the 1920s that his reputation became firmly established, particularly with the success of his opera *Wozzeck*. After completing his Violin Concerto, Berg spent time in the countryside, where an insect bite brought about the infection that was to result in his death.

MILESTONES	
1901	Takes job as a civil servant
1910	Marries Helene Nahowski
1912	Composes *Five Altenberglieder* for voice and orchestra
1915	Called up for service in the Austrian army
1923	Works performed in ISCM Festival in Salzburg
1926	The *Lyric Suite* for string quartet
1928	Begins opera *Lulu*, which remains unfinished

KEY WORKS

VIOLIN CONCERTO

ORCHESTRAL　　⏱ 25:00　　📖 2　　♒ 🎵

Soon after he began composing this 12-tone work, Berg was made known of the death of Manon, the daughter of the architect Walter Gropius and Alma Mahler. She had suffered from poliomyelitis, and was only 18 years old when she died. Berg decided to dedicate the Violin Concerto to her memory—the work is inscribed "To the memory of an angel."

First movement The first movement consists of two sections: a dreamy and quasi-improvisational andante and a dancelike allegretto. Berg used some preexisting melodies, such as a Carinthian folk song in the allegretto—this is played by the horn.

Second movement This also consists of two sections, allegro and adagio. The allegro is the most tortured and Expressionist part of the concerto and represents the suffering of Manon.

This culminates in a flourish for the violin, which gives way to another quotation, this time from Bach's harmonization of the Lutheran chorale "Es ist genug" ("It is Enough"). This chorale enters very quietly, played by clarinets, and this must surely be one of the most poignant moments in any concerto. The soloist soars above the orchestral parts (representing the soul of Manon rising to heaven). Symbolically, the folk tune from the first movement makes a return appearance as a flicker of life before the violin plays the entire note-row to end the work.

INFLUENCES

Berg was greatly influenced by his teacher, Schoenberg, but also by late-Romantic composers such as Wagner and Richard Strauss. Always the most popular of the Second Viennese School with audiences, his own influence on composers continued to grow since his death, particularly toward the end of the 20th century.

🔼 **Georg Büchner's 1914 play *Wozzeck*** gave Berg the plot for his opera of the same name, one of his most successful works.

Béla **Bartók**

◐ 1881–1945   ⚑ HUNGARIAN   ✍ 695

Hungary's most important composer of the 20th century and a major exponent of modern music, Bartók was also an outstanding specialist in music folklore and a teacher of wide repute. His music was invigorated by the themes, modes, and rhythmic patterns of the Hungarian and other folk-music traditions he studied, which he synthesized with influences from his contemporaries into his own distinctive style.

» **In 1907** Bartók was made Professor of Piano at the Royal Academy of Music in Budapest, and in 1911 he and Kodály founded the New Hungarian Music Society.

he entered the Academy of Music in Budapest, where he shone as a pianist: he was soon invited to perform in Vienna, Berlin, and Manchester, among other cities. In 1906 Bartók met his contemporary Kodály and discovered that they shared an interest in folk music. Eventually they collected music from all over eastern Europe. Bartók's first wife was Márta Ziegler, who assisted him in his field trips to collect folk music; the couple divorced in 1923 and Bartók subsequently married the pianist Ditta Pásztory, who bore him a son, Péter, in 1924. Bartók left Hungary after the German invasion of Austria and settled in New York in 1940. Life in the US proved precarious, although some financial security was provided by the intervention of friends such as Sergei Koussevitsky, who commissioned new works from him. After a long period of ill health, Bartók died in New York while completing his Third Piano Concerto.

Life

Bartók was born in southern Hungary to parents who were both teachers and amateur musicians. His idyllic childhood was disrupted in 1888 by the death of his father, and his mother was compelled to move between different towns in the region. The young Bartók composed enthusiastically, but suffered from various childhood illnesses. In 1899,

Music

Bartók's early music clearly shows the influence of German Romantics such as Richard Strauss. However, his interest in folk music exerted a strong pull and, even when he refrained from using actual folk tunes, his melodic and rhythmic language showed the folk character. Much of the music Bartók wrote around 1910 (such as the *Allegro barbaro* for piano) was percussive in style, mirroring the primitivism of Stravinsky's music of the same period. Bartók's music is meticulously crafted, with remarkably clear proportions: different parts often mirror each other, and the three sections of the ballet *The Wooden Prince*, for example, are arranged symmetrically. Bartók's most Expressionistic phase was after World War I in such compositions as the pantomime *The Miraculous Mandarin*.

❝ **Bartók's name**… stands for the **principle** and the **demand** for **regeneration** stemming from the people, both in **art** and in **politics.** ❞

Zoltán Kodály

MILESTONES

1899	Enters Academy of Music, Budapest	1928	First concert tour of the US
1906	Meets Kodály; plans folk-song collection	1936	*Music for Strings, Percussion, and Celesta*
1907	Professor at Academy of Music		
1909	Marries Márta Ziegler	1937	Begins Violin Concerto No. 2
1911	*Bluebeard's Castle*, Op. 11	1938	*Contrasts* written for Benny Goodman
1914	Begins *The Wooden Prince*, Op. 13	1940	Leaves Hungary for the US
1923	Divorces Ziegler; marries Ditta Pásztory	1943	Concerto for Orchestra

KEY WORKS

MIKROKOSMOS

SOLO PIANO   📖 153

Between 1932 and 1939, Bartók composed over 150 short piano pieces as part of a set called *Mikrokosmos*. Ranging from easy to concert-standard, they reflected his wish to introduce eastern European and Arabic folk tunes to a wider audience, as well as to create piano pieces for his young son Péter to learn. Many of these pieces show Bartók's interest in mirror images between left- and right-hand patterns.

MUSIC FOR STRINGS, PERCUSSION, AND CELESTA

ORCHESTRAL   ⏱ 34:00   📖 4   ♫

This piece was written for Paul Sacher and the Basle Chamber Orchestra in 1936. As with many of Bartók's works, percussion features strongly, not only as a means of rhythmic organization, but also as color. He integrates folk music and original material highly successfully in this work.

CONCERTO FOR ORCHESTRA

ORCHESTRAL   ⏱ 37:30   📖 5   ♫

Introduction (*allegro non troppo—allegro vivace*) The first movement begins mysteriously with a theme in the low strings accompanied by whispering violin tremolandos. Instrumental groups are gradually added until the bright and energetic allegro vivace begins with a theme from the violins. A second theme is introduced by solo trombone in regular meter.

Game of pairs (*allegretto scherzando*) The second movement features pairs of instruments, which move at all times in parallel: the bassoons (a sixth apart) are followed by oboes (a third apart), clarinets (a seventh apart), flutes (a fifth apart), and, finally, trumpets (a second apart). The choralelike middle section is given to the brass.

Elegy (*andante, non troppo*) Bartók called the third movement a "lugubrious death song." The opening theme on low strings recalls the first movement. The misty section for flutes and clarinets that follows is accompanied by string tremolandos and harp glissandos. The music becomes more and more agitated until the passionate material from the first movement reappears.

Intermezzo interrotto (*allegretto*) This movement was apparently influenced by a broadcast of Shostakovich's Symphony No. 7. Bartók thought that Shostakovich's patriotism was misguided and quoted a theme of that work in raucous parody. There is then an outrageous response from muted trumpets, clarinets, and trombones.

Finale (*presto*) Announced by a horn fanfare and athletic strings, the flurry never lets up, and the coda is a brilliant culmination to one of the great orchestral works of the 20th century.

INFLUENCES

Bartók was greatly influenced by the folk music of Eastern Europe. In his youth he admired the music of Richard Strauss and later in his career developed an interest in Baroque music as well as the compositions of contemporaries such as Stravinsky. He influenced Lutosławski and Britten.

✉ **In 1917,** Bartók (center) traveled through Romania with his fellow Hungarian composer Zoltán Kodály (right) and Joan Busitia to collect native folk songs.

George **Enescu**

● 1881–1955   ⚑ ROMANIAN   ✍ c.300

Despite his astounding memory for music—he knew every note of Wagner's *The Ring of the Nibelung*—and his prodigious ability as a violinist, Romania's greatest composer was a modest man. Perhaps too modest: he wrote prolifically, but published only 33 works with opus numbers. When he conducted his folk-inspired *Poème roumain* in Bucharest at 17, he instantly became a figure of national importance.

MILESTONES

1889	First public performance, aged eight
1893	Studies at Paris Conservatoire
1898	*Poème roumain* for orchestra triumphs
1926	Composes Violin Sonata No. 3
1936	*Oedipe*, opera, premiered in Paris
1946	Exiled from Romania; falls ill
1954	Writes Chamber Symphony

Enescu spent his long career moving between France and Romania, performing internationally, composing (his main love), and developing Romanian musical life. His music reflects the variety of stylistic changes he saw in his lifetime, and his chamber works are especially fine. A perfectionist, he spent ten years writing his opera, *Oedipe*.

⊗ **Although Enescu's work** transcends nationalism, he never abandoned his beloved native country.

Zoltán **Kodály**

● 1882–1967   ⚑ HUNGARIAN   ✍ c.250

An all-round, practical musician who needed little formal tuition, Kodály did his doctoral thesis on Hungarian folk song, which he collected in rural tours over many decades.

Like his friend Bartók, he used it to inspire his own melodic, inventive work, much of it choral. His flourishing career—as academy teacher, critic, scholar, and composer—was affected by the war, but was revived internationally by *Psalmus Hungaricus*. To the end of his life he toured worldwide, both lecturing and conducting his own works. Composing for 70 years, and constantly promoting Hungarian music, Kodály was lavishly honored at home and abroad. His logical step-by-step teaching methods are still highly influential today.

» **As a keen educator,** Kodály devoted much of his time to visiting Hungarian schools and was actively involved in the development of music for children.

MILESTONES

1915	Solo Cello Sonata Op. 8
1926	Composes *Háry János*, Singspiel
1927	*Psalmus Hungaricus* premiered in London
1933	Composes *Dances of Galánta*, orchestra
1939	Writes *The Peacock Variations*, orchestra
1945	Becomes president of the Hungarian Arts Council

Percy **Grainger**

● 1882–1971   ⚑ AUSTRALIAN   ✍ 186

Grainger was a virtuoso pianist, a collector, an arranger of folk songs, and a highly original composer. With an unusual breadth of creative vision, his interests spanned the ages—from medieval music to the latest developments by his contemporaries Delius and Grieg. He was a pioneer of what he called "free music" and was particularly determined that music should be available for all.

Grainger studied for a short time with Ferruccio Busoni in Germany, but despite a mutual admiration for each other's abilities, their temperaments were too different to remain on close terms. When he moved to London in 1901, Grainger began to establish a reputation as a concert pianist. During his 20s he became friendly with Edvard Grieg, who encouraged him to collect English folk songs; these form the basis for many of his inspired settings, such as *Country Gardens* and *Molly on the Shore*. Often experimental in his approach, Grainger's interest in "free music" led him to come up with the new idea of "elastic scoring"—meaning that a work could be played by whatever instruments happened to be available, rather than by a prescribed instrumentation.

MILESTONES

1894	Makes his debut in Melbourne
1895	Studies in Frankfurt
1901	Moves to London; composes *Hill Song No. 1*
1903	Tours Australia, New Zealand, and South Africa
1907	Writes *Molly on the Shore*, orchestra
1913	Composes *The Warriors*, orchestra
1914	*Tribute to Foster* published; moves to US
1917	Serves in US Army
1918	Composes *Country Gardens*
1922	Mother commits suicide
1928	Marries Ella Ström at premiere of *To a Nordic Princess*, Hollywood Bowl

KEY WORKS

HILL SONG NO. 1

CHAMBER   ⏱ 27:00   📖 1   ⚘

Grainger considered this to be his finest work, and it was originally scored for a highly unusual ensemble of wind instruments: with the exception of the piccolos, the group comprised double-reed instruments, which produce a nasal sound quality (he asked for oboes, cor anglais, bassoons, and contra-bassoon). He later felt that this was not realistic and rescored the work in 1923 for an even more diverse group. There are five main sections, and the "fast walking pace" is somewhat obscured by the frequently changing meter.

TRIBUTE TO FOSTER

CHORAL   ⏱ 21:00   📖 1   ♫♬♪

Late in life, Grainger recalled his mother having sung him to sleep with the tune of Stephen Collins Foster's "Camptown Races." His *Tribute to Foster* uses an up-tempo version of the tune in its outer sections and a slow lullaby version in the middle section, in which the choir play "musical glasses."

» **Grainger's close bond** with his mother was broken only when she committed suicide by jumping off a skyscraper in New York.

Igor **Stravinsky**

● 1882–1971   ﹏ RUSSIAN   ✍ 127

Generally considered to be the greatest composer of the previous century, Stravinsky's long life spanned continents, cultures, and eras. As an iconic figure in the modern arts, he was perhaps equalled only by Pablo Picasso, whose early innovations created the same shock and excitement. He also resembled Picasso in his gift for radical artistic transformations, yet, despite this quality, Stravinsky always remained ineffably himself.

》 Despite its "shocking" modernity, Stravinsky's music is also very structured, precise, and controlled, full of artifice and theatricality.

Life

Stravinsky was born near St. Petersburg, where his father was principal bass singer with the Imperial Opera at the Mariinsky Theater. Borodin, Dostoyevsky, and Stravinsky's future teacher, Rimsky-Korsakov, were family friends. Stravinsky's talent was not obvious at first, and he was forced to study law at St. Petersburg University, applying himself to music in his free time. Success came in 1910, with the commission of *The Firebird* from Serge Diaghilev, director of the Ballets Russes. The ballet's Paris premiere also launched the career of another Diaghilev protégé, the dancer Vaslav Nijinsky, and was hugely successful. Stravinsky joined Europe's artistic elite, with many of whom (Picasso, Gide, Cocteau) he went on to collaborate in further ballets. In mid-career, he fell increasingly under the influence of the European "Classical" heritage. Having fought off tuberculosis, he fled World War II, and moved to the United States.

Music

Stravinsky's musical output falls into three main periods: "Russian," "neo-Classical," and "serial" (or "12-tone"). From Rimsky-Korsakov, Stravinsky had learned to orchestrate in the exquisite, iridescent colors that characterize *The Firebird*. As Serge Diaghilev challenged him to find an ever-more Russian style, Stravinsky began to incorporate Russian folk tunes and to invent new sounds based on pounding, irregular rhythms and pungent harmonies. The result was an entirely original kind of music beyond simple tonality and which (especially in *The Rite of Spring*) could not be written in a constant time signature. Such music shocked and excited, flying in the face of the accepted rules of music composition. However, in time his music returned to the tonal idiom. Stravinsky created the "neo-Classical style," which its detractors called "classicism with wrong notes"; this made it all the more astonishing when, in the US, Stravinsky underwent his final metamorphosis, and himself took up the 12-tone method.

> **Music** is given to us with the sole purpose of **establishing an order** in things, including, and particularly, the **coordination** between man and time.
> **Igor Stravinsky**

MILESTONES

1902	Studies law at university, and composition with Rimsky-Korsakov
1909	Premiere of *Scherzo fantastique*; Diaghilev commissions *The Firebird*
1910	Debussy expresses his admiration; he and Stravinsky become friends
1913	Premiere of *The Rite of Spring*
1920	At Diaghilev's suggestion, arranges music by Pergolesi for *Pulcinella*
1921	Writes *Les noces* and embarks on love affair with Vera Sudeykina
1926	Returns to the Russian Orthodox Church after experiencing a "miracle" in Venice
1927	Premiere of *Oedipus Rex*; the work is poorly received
1928	US premiere of *Apollon Musagète*
1937	Adopts French citizenship; writes last piece in Europe, *Dumbarton Oaks*
1939	Sails for the US after the deaths of his eldest daughter and wife
1940	*The Rite of Spring* features in Walt Disney's animated film, *Fantasia*
1945	Writes "Ebony" Concerto for Woody Hermann's jazz band
1951	Premiere of *The Rake's Progress*, opera
1962	Revisits Russia
1964	Composes *Elegy* on the death of John F. Kennedy; completion of *Requiem Canticles*, his last major work

⊼ **In 1913,** with choreography by Vaslav Nijinsky, Stravinsky's *The Rite of Spring* received its premiere at the Théâtre de Champs-Elysées in Paris.

KEY WORKS

DUMBARTON OAKS

CONCERTO   ⧖ 11:00   📖 3

Written at a time of many crises in Stravinsky's life, *Dunbarton Oaks* is a reminder of his assertion that music "expresses nothing but itself." The work met with a mixed reaction on its premiere, being deplored by those who thought serious composers should be in the vanguard of a continuous musical revolution.

The opening movement is reminiscent of J. S. Bach's "Brandenburg" Concertos. The modest instrumental forces and the regularity of the meter all hark back to Baroque practice. The second movement has a sly, jazzy insouciance. It features flute and violin as solo instruments—plus the clarinet, an instrument that was unknown in Baroque times. The pronounced "finale" returns to the Baroque model, yet Stravinsky abandons counterpoint in favor of his characteristic games of deft chordal interplay, shifting accents, and sprightly syncopation.

PETRUSHKA

BALLET   ⧖ 32:00   📖 4

Stravinsky first intended *Petrushka* to be a concert work for piano and orchestra, but he became possessed by the idea of the piano representing "a puppet suddenly endowed with life, exasperating the patience of the orchestra with diabolical cascades of arpeggios." Diaghilev soon persuaded him that the work was destined to be a new ballet.

First part (10:00) *Petrushka* is set in St. Petersburg during the Shrovetide Fair. Superimposing a number of characterful instrumental lines and harmonies, the music evokes the ebb and flow of the crowd, interspersed with the antics of street entertainers.

Second part (4:00) Petrushka is in his cell. Hiccups of melody suggest the jerking puppet, while melancholy, discordant reveries of piano and clarinet evoke Petrushka's hopeless love for the heartless Ballerina.

Third part (5:00) Petrushka's rival in love, a handsome, scimitar-wielding Blackamoor, dances with the Ballerina. He is portrayed by a trumpet, she by a coy flute; mechanically tender, the music stutters and preens, evoking the reedy sonorities of a fairground organ.

Fourth part (13:00) Suddenly Petrushka is chased from a tent and cut down by the Blackamoor's scimitar. The crowd disperses, and in the eerie twilight Petrushka (or his ghost) returns to haunt the terrified showman—and to taunt anyone in the audience who might have been moved by the tale.

⊼ *Dumbarton Oaks* takes its name from the estate of Robert Woods Bliss, who commissioned the piece for his 30th wedding anniversary in 1938.

△ **The ecstatic rhythms** of *The Rite of Spring* have ensured its continuing popularity, both as a ballet and as a concert piece. This performance at Avignon in 1995 was choreographed by Pina Bausch.

△ *The Firebird* premiered in Paris in 1910. Its success transformed Stravinsky's career and strengthened his friendship with Diaghilev, with whom he produced two more balletic works: *Petrushka* (1911) and *The Rite of Spring* (1913).

THE RITE OF SPRING

BALLET	⏱ 32:00	📖 2	

The Rite of Spring, set in primeval Russia, portrays a ritual in which a young girl dances herself to death to win the favor of the god of Spring. The ballet is a work of savage ecstasy, driven forward by its powerful, primitive rhythms.

Part one (15:30) After the mysterious Introduction comes the "Dance of the Adolescents," in which young girls dance to the insistent stamping of a single chord repeated continuously with changing accents, while off-beat horn chords punch the air. After further ritual dancing, the first part of the ballet breaks off in midair like a terrifying cliff-hanger.

Part two (16:30) Both parts of the ballet begin quietly and end in pulsing violence. In the dawnlike introduction to the second part, some of the strings play delicate harmonics while others sound shudders of fearful anticipation.

As the girl chosen for the sacrifice dances herself to death in the final climax, the horns play "with bells up," projecting their exultant high notes straight over the heads of the orchestra and out into the auditorium.

APOLLON MUSAGÈTE

BALLET	⏱ 30:00	📖 2	

A ballet of Classical poise and restraint, scored for strings alone, *Apollon Musagète* began Stravinsky's connection with the inspired choreographer of so many of his later works, George Balanchine.

LES NOCES ("THE WEDDINGS")

BALLET	⏱ 25:00	📖 4	

The most startlingly scored of all Stravinsky's works, *Les noces* evokes both the earthiness of peasant life and the hieratic splendor of Russian Orthodox ritual.

AGON

BALLET	⏱ 24:00	📖 3	

An ingenious conflation of styles and periods, Agon takes inspiration from Renaissance dance and works by Boulez and Stockhausen.

THE RAKE'S PROGRESS

OPERA	⏱ 135:00	📖 3	

This work, with a libretto by W. H. Auden and Chester Kallman, was based on the series of engravings of the same name by English 18th-century painter and moralist William Hogarth. A "number opera" with arias and recitatives, it marked the end-point of Stravinsky's neo-Classical phase. It was Stravinsky's largest work, and premiered in Venice in 1951.

PULCINELLA

BALLET	⏱ 38:00	📖 1	

Inspired by the Italian commedia dell'arte, this work arranges music by Pergolesi and his 18th-century contemporaries. However, by slight changes of harmony and idiosyncratic orchestration, Stravinsky makes the music entirely his own.

THE FIREBIRD

BALLET	⏱ 45:00	📖 1	

The ballet tells of the battle between the magical Firebird and the demon Kashchey. Dancers who missed their cues at the premiere blamed their confusion on the unusualness of the orchestration.

OEDIPUS REX

OPERA-ORATORIO	⏱ 48:00	📖 2	

Stravinsky's collaborator Jean Cocteau based the text of this "opera-oratorio" on Greek tragedy, yet Stravinsky chose to set the text in Latin. Between movements, a spoken narration keeps the audience abreast of the story.

INFLUENCES

Stravinsky's impact on other composers was immediate. Edgard Varèse's *Amèriques* is full of reminiscences of *The Rite of Spring*. In fact, most music of recent times could not have been written without Stravinsky's innovations. Villa-Lobos, Hindemith, Messiaen, Britten, Poulenc, Bernstein, Pärt—all these composers owe him a profound debt.

Darius **Milhaud**

🌑 1892–1974　　📖 FRENCH　　✍ 426

Milhaud entered the Paris Conservatoire at 17 and then, in 1917, was taken to Rio de Janeiro by poet and diplomat, Paul Claudel, so that they might work on music theater projects together. The music of Brazil made a lasting impression on Milhaud. Despite deep-seated differences (he was unshakeably Jewish in his faith, Claudel a proselytizing Catholic), they collaborated for many years. In later life, Milhaud taught Xenakis, Stockhausen, and Dave Brubeck.

Some of Milhaud's first and finest music was for Claudel's translation of Aeschylus's *Oresteia*. Devising a way of setting texts of elemental force, Milhaud, in *Les Choëphores*, had passages spoken by the chorus or narrator to a purely percussion backing. The "Incantation" section is stern, bracing, rich, and atmospheric. *Le bœuf sur le toit*, Milhaud's most popular work, includes bi-tonal passages (music in two keys at once).

MILESTONES

1909	Studies violin at Paris Conservatoire, then composition there
1917	Composes *Les Choëphores* for stage; travels to Brazil with Claudel
1919	Writes ballet *Le bœuf sur le toit* in collaboration with Jean Cocteau
1920s	Is member of "Les Six," a radical young French composers' group
1921	Ballet *L'homme et son désir* premiered
1930	Opera *Christophe Colomb* is acclaimed
1940	Leaves Nazi-occupied France for US

◁ **Milhaud wrote** *Saudados do Brazil* in 1920–21 as a dance suite for piano, but later orchestrated it.

Francis **Poulenc**

🌑 1899–1963　　📖 FRENCH　　✍ 185

Poulenc was born into a cultured and wealthy Parisian family. Although he studied piano from childhood, he was 22 years old before he went to Charles Koechlin for composition lessons. He joined the group of young French composers known as "Les Six" and, in 1923, Diaghilev commissioned a ballet

MILESTONES

1913	Studies piano with Ricardo Viñes
1918	*La Rhapsodie Negre* performed in public; Stravinsky helps him find a publisher
1936	Makes pilgrimage to Notre-Dame de Rocamadour, and writes *Litanies à la vierge noire*
1957	Composes his great opera, *Les dialogues des Carmélites*
1958	*La Voix Humaine* to text by Cocteau

from him, *Les biches*, which achieved popular and critical success. From the 1930s, Poulenc gave concerts of his own songs with the baritone Pierre Bernac.

Poulenc's music faithfully reflects its composer—a manic depressive, a devout Catholic, and one of the few public figures of his time to be openly (and often turbulently) gay. His manner of blending neo-Classical harmonies with the bittersweet touches of French popular song gives his music a distinct and subtle charm, even when it touches on tragedy.

In 1938, when Poulenc wrote Concerto for Organ, Strings, and Timpani, he joked that it showed a "Poulenc who was on his way to joining a monastery." Yet the work's seven sections cover the gamut of his style, ranging from irreverent burlesque to gothic majesty. The key (G minor) is perhaps an indication of its debt to Bach's G minor Fantasia.

Poulenc wrote a number of sonatas for piano and wind, and Sonata for Oboe and Piano proved to be the last. Dedicated to Prokofiev, it is a plangent, elegiac piece—all the more haunting for being the composer's own swansong.

△ **Perhaps Poulenc's greatest success** was his surrealist comic opera, *Les Mamelles de Tirésias*, based on a farce by Apollinaire.

Paul **Hindemith**

● 1895–1963   ♊ GERMAN   ✍ 415

A prolific composer and amazingly gifted all-round musician, Hindemith wrote significant pieces for almost every known instrument in Classical music. He spent the first half of his life making his living as a full-time performer. He became first violinist at the Frankfurt Opera House while still a student and was soon playing viola in professional quartets. During the Nazi era, he lived in the US, teaching composition at Yale. His youthful exuberance sometimes surfaced even in later works such as his *Concerto for Orchestra* and *Symphonic Metamorphoses on a Theme of Weber*, but his style is generally characterized by his love of Baroque counterpoint and Classical forms.

Hindemith's *Kammermusik No. 1, Op. 24* is for a band of equals, playing—among other instruments—xylophone, accordion, trumpet, and siren. The music is inventive and uproarious.

⌃ *Kammermusik No. 6* is scored for the viola d'amore, a Baroque instrument favored by Hindemith.

His symphony *Mathis der Maler* consists of preludes and studies for an opera Hindemith later wrote on the life of the German painter Matthias Grünewald. It portrays panels from the Isenheim altarpiece. The last movement is an instrumental version of the opera's climactic scene, when the anguished painter identifies himself with the tormented saint.

MILESTONES

1921	Opera *Murderer, Hope of Women*, to a libretto by Expressionist painter Oskar Kokoschka, causes outrage
1923	Programs the Donaueschingen Music Festival, where his song cycle *The Life of Mary* is premiered
1929	Plays in string trio with cellist Emmuel Feuermann
1934	Fürtwangler premieres *Mathis der Maler* in Berlin, and defends Hindemith against Nazis in a newspaper article
1957	Conducts premiere of his opera *The Harmony of the World* in Munich

Sir William **Walton**

● 1902–1983   ♊ ENGLISH   ✍ 121

Sir William Walton owed much to his fortunate early connections. A boy chorister at Christ Church Cathedral, Oxford, he stayed at the university to study music, and was befriended by the Sitwells, an aristocratic family of writers who supported Walton while he established his career. His first famous work was *Façade*—an "entertainment" much influenced by the jazz of the "flapper" era—to which Edith Sitwell recited her melodious bohemian poetry. Walton's finest pieces were all written early in his career—the expressive Viola Concerto, the stupendous oratorio *Belshazzar's Feast*, and his renowned Symphony No. 1. His war-time film scores won him great popular acclaim. In later years, he lived with his Argentinian wife on the picturesque island of Ischia, near Naples.

Most of Symphony No.1 was composed between 1932 and 1933, and the white heat of its intensity owes much to a turbulent love affair with Imma von Dörnberg, a baroness with whom

⌃ **Sir William Walton's magnificent film score** for Laurence Olivier's *Henry V* was one of his most outstanding achievements.

Walton had been living in Switzerland. The four-movement work was premiered late in 1935 by the conductor Sir Hamilton Harty; its rapturous reception proved to be the zenith of Walton's life and achievements.

Belshazzar's Feast is a work of harsh splendor for orchestra, baritone soloist, and choir (for which, as a former boy chorister, Walton always wrote magnificently). Walton treats Belshazzar's story not as sacred scripture, but as a lurid tale of the supernatural, and the work crams all the drama of an opera or film score into just half an hour.

MILESTONES

1920	Moves in with the Sitwells
1935	Leaves the Sitwells, who disapprove of his liaison with Lady Alice Wimborne
1936	*Crown Imperial* for George VI's coronation
1939	Violin Concerto for Jascha Heifetz
1943	Writes film score for *Henry V*
1954	*Troilus and Cressida*, opera, performed
1956	Composes for the coronation of Elizabeth II

Henry Dixon **Cowell**

🌑 **1897–1965** 📕 **AMERICAN** ✍ **996**

An unorthodox upbringing by parents who were "philosophical anarchists" left its mark on the young Cowell, and he found himself on the margins of musical life. In 1914, this talented "wild child" met his greatest mentor, ethnomusicologist Charles Seeger, who taught him much about modern music and what we now call "world music." Cowell's early works explore the modernist devices described in his pioneering book *New Musical Resources* and include tone clusters, graphic notation, the use of several simultaneous tempi and proto-electronic instruments, such as the rhythmicon. In later works an interest in Irish mythology comes to the fore, as part of a general move toward a startlingly eclectic sound-world combining modernism, "world music," and naively simple diatonic melodies.

MILESTONES	
1914	Cowell's debut concert, includes *Adventures in Harmony*
1915	Composes *Quartet Romantic*
1923	European tour performing his ultra-modernist piano works
1927	Creates *New Music*—concert series, magazine, and record label
1933	Writes article *Toward Neo-Primitivism* about his interest, ethnomusicology
1936	Homosexual encounter leads to arrest and four-year imprisonment
1957	Composes *Persian Set*, chamber music

◄◄ **Cowell was a pioneer** of innovative piano effects, such as playing groups of keys together in "tone-clusters" and strumming the strings directly.

Carl **Ruggles**

🌑 **1876–1971** 📕 **AMERICAN** ✍ **40**

A slow and meticulous composer, Ruggles constantly revised his work and destroyed anything he wasn't entirely happy with. Consequently, he has left an oeuvre of only a handful of pieces, which can be performed in the space of a couple of hours, but his legacy rests on the pioneering individual style he developed. Uncompromising in his approach to harmony, melody, and rhythm, he composed mainly orchestral works in a dissonant atonal style, with evocative titles such as *Men and Mountains*, *Portals*, and *Sun-Treader* that give some clue as to their monumental proportions. His ear for original sonorities, a feature of his orchestral writing, led to probably the most approachable of his works, *Angels*, written for an unusual line-up of muted brass instruments.

At the beginning and end of his long composing career Ruggles also wrote two very personal songs: *Toys* (written for his son) and *Exaltation* (in memory of his wife). Despite being held in high regard by his experimentalist colleagues Charles Ives and Henry Dixon Cowell, his radical style was not appreciated by contemporary orchestras and conductors, and was seldom performed until he was well into old age—he heard his longest and best-known piece, *Sun-Treader*, only from a recording. An accomplished painter, Ruggles turned increasingly to the visual arts in later life.

MILESTONES	
1920s	Work published in Cowell's New Music Edition and is noticed by Ives
1924	Publishes *Men and Mountains*, orchestral
1931	Completes *Sun-Treader*, orchestral
1950	Finishes *Evocations*, piano, begun 1937
1965	First hears *Men and Mountains*

Charles **Ives**

1874–1954   AMERICAN   313

Charles Ives was a great pioneer Modernist who experimented with polytonality, multiple tempos, and many-layered textures decades before the famous European Modernists. However, in many ways he was a conservative, and a religious, hymn-singing vein runs through even his most radical pieces. The combination of experiment and sturdy affirmation gives his music a strenuous aspirational quality.

>> **The employees** at Ives's insurance firm pretended not to know about the "old man's" weekend composing, which continued at breakneck pace up to and beyond World War I.

Life

Ives was the son of a provincial bandmaster with adventurous musical tastes. George Ives's fondness for getting his children to sing a hymn in one key while accompanying them in another left an indelible mark on his son's music. Ives was a precocious child: by the age of 14 he'd become the youngest salaried organist in Connecticut and had composed dozens of works. He studied music for four years at Yale University under Horatio Parker, who succeeded in instilling some academic discipline into his unruly student. In 1898 Ives got a job as an actuary, and ten years later he married Harmony Twichell after a long courtship. Later he founded his own insurance firm with his old friend Julian Myrick, and his high-minded principles and hard work made it one of the most respected firms in New York. In 1912 the Iveses bought a farm, to which they invited poor families to stay. One of these agreed to have their daughter adopted; she became Edith Osborne Ives. In 1926 declining health forced Ives to give up composing and in 1930 he retired from the business. During the 1930s and '40s his music, which had been ignored, was rediscovered by younger admirers. During the '60s and '70s his music was championed by Stokowski, Bernstein, and others, and his key pieces are now firmly in the repertoire.

Music

Ives's style is made of many disparate things, but the elements aren't welded together; they keep their separateness. A typical Ives piece might have a sturdy hymn tune harmonized with sturdy chords (but in the wrong key), followed by a wildly rhapsodic line with tumbling piano chords, or it might feature a quick, all-American Stephen Collins Foster melody, next to slow, massive chordal clusters and Debussian shimmers. However, Ives doesn't just put these ideas side by side; he puts them on top of each other, so that they sound simultaneously.

" When you hear **strong, masculine music** like this, stand up and **use your ears** like a **man!** "

Charles Ives, to an audience member who was heckling a new piece by his friend Carl Ruggles

Ives was the first composer to write pieces that had radically different sorts of music going on at once, an effect apparently inspired by childhood memories of hearing brass bands approaching Danbury town square, each playing in a different key and at a different speed. The effect is joyously anarchic.

Ives has none of the anxiety of European modernists like Schoenberg. But, despite its democratic appearances, in the end his music affirms conservative values. Chaos is typically subsumed into a hymn tune and a sense of mystical affirmation.

KEY WORKS

THREE PLACES IN NEW ENGLAND

ORCHESTRAL   ⏱ 18:00   📖 3

Composed between 1903 and 1914, this much-played orchestral piece follows the typical Ives progression from bracing coexistence of different elements, through riotous complexity, to a radiant vision of eternity.
The "St. Gaudens" in Boston Common (8:00) This assemblage of marching tunes and songs sounds as if overheard from a great distance.
Putnam's camp, Redding, Connecticut (6:00) An amalgam of two preexisting pieces, *Overture 1776* and *Country Band March*, this part is a perfect example of Ives's layering of two tempos, one above the other.
The Housatonic at Stockbridge (4:00) This is a modern chorale prelude, the hymn tune heard through a beautifully woven orchestral mist.

SYMPHONY NO. 4

ORCHESTRAL   ⏱ 31:00   📖 4

This is the quintessential Ives work. The symphony is stuffed with quotations from hymns, marches, and songs. It also absorbs many of Ives's earlier and unfinished works.
First movement (*prelude, maestoso*, 3:00) According to Ives, this asks the question "Why?", to which the following movements offer three diverse answers. Stern fanfares are responded to by a beatific choir, with memories of "Bethany" and "Watchman, Tell us of the Night."

Second movement (*allegretto*, 12:00) This is the most extreme music Ives ever wrote. Crammed into this "comedy" is a riotous assemblage of melodies, quotations, polyrhythms, and quarter-tones which summon up the chaos of life itself.
Third movement (*fugue, andante moderato*, 8:00) A calm and correct fugue which, as Ives said, expresses "the reaction of life into formalism and ritualism."
Fourth movement (*very slowly, largo maestoso*, 8:00) Gathering everything heard so far into an affirmative apotheosis, a military-sounding dirge introduces memories of Ives's childhood, a chorus singing "Bethany" leads to a climax, and then the music fades into an evocation of eternity.

THE UNANSWERED QUESTION

ORCHESTRAL   ⏱ 6:00   📖 1

The first piece of *Two Contemplations* for chamber orchestra, this is a masterly example of Ives's ability to pile up different kinds of music moving at different speeds into a meaningful near-chaos.

⊠ **The *Fourth of July*** from *A Symphony: New England Holidays* (1913), which celebrates life in small-town America, was one of Ives's most popular works.

Edgard **Varèse**

🌑 1883–1965   🏳 **FRENCH**   ✍ c.50

One of the most original voices of 20th-century music, Varèse turned his back on both conventional tonal music and the mainstream of modernist composers, developing an individual style of "organized sound." His use of massive blocks of sound, exotic timbres, and jagged rhythms did not go down well with contemporary audiences; it was not until after World War II that his music got the recognition it deserved.

Varèse's driving ambition was to find radical new directions in music. After studying at the Paris Conservatoire, he spent much time in Berlin, befriending Busoni and Debussy (whom he introduced to Schoenberg's atonality). It was in New York, however, that he pioneered new sounds, treading the border between organization and noise. *Hyperprism* provoked audience outrage, but it, and pieces such as his percussion-plus-siren *Ionisation*, established his modernist credentials. His output was erratic, with many unfinished projects, and he suffered depression in the 1930s when refused research funds; but after World War II his advances in tape-based sound art proved revolutionary.

» **Varèse said,** "I refuse to limit myself to sounds that have already been heard." In the 1940s he adopted the ondes Martenot, (here played by Maurice Martenot).

MILESTONES

1915	Leaves Europe to settle in New York
1922	Composes *Hyperprism*, for wind and percussion
1931	Composes *Ionisation*, percussion
1936	Composes *Density 21.5* for solo flute
1953	Starts experimenting with electronics
1954	Completes *Déserts*, instruments and tape

KEY WORKS

AMÉRIQUES

ORCHESTRA   ⏱ 23:00   📖 1   🎵

The first work written after he moved to New York, *Amériques* marked a new beginning for Varèse and symbolizes "discoveries—new worlds on earth, in the sky, or in the minds of men." It is written for an enormous orchestra, with expanded woodwind and brass sections and a percussion section that, alongside almost every conventional instrument, includes sirens, lion's roars, and wind machines. Written in one continuous movement, the piece builds relentlessly to an ear-splitting climax.

POÈME ÉLECTRONIQUE

ELECTRONIC   ⏱ 8:05

Written to be played in the Philips Pavilion at the 1958 World's Fair in Brussels and commissioned by its designers Le Corbusier and Xenakis, the *Poème* was recorded on tape that was originally synchronized with a light show and projected images within the building. The very abstract sound world juxtaposes many different timbres, exploring the range of tone from conventionally "musical" notes to noise, which come to the listener from all directions.

Roger **Sessions**

● 1896–1985   ▥ AMERICAN   ✍ 42

Born in Brooklyn, New York, Sessions was an intellectual prodigy—he wrote an opera at 13, graduated from Harvard at 18, and spoke French, Italian, German, and Russian. An able symphonist, he wrote nine symphonies as well as four concertos, three piano sonatas, and many vocal pieces, and much of his work was written after he was 60. His technically difficult music has generally proved more popular with students and musicians than the public. However, this did not trouble the idealistic, good-humored composer, who inspired many important American composers during his long and distinguished teaching career.

MILESTONES	
1923	The Black Maskers, incidental music, first performed
1925	Moves to Europe for eight years
1957	Composes Symphony No. 3
1963	*Montezuma*, opera, produced
1965	Begins teaching at the Juilliard School of Music
1971	Writes Concerto for Orchestra

≪ **The cantata**
When Lilacs Last in the Dooryard Bloom'd (1970) is an imaginative setting of verse from *Leaves of Grass* by Walt Whitman, Sessions' favorite poet.

Virgil **Thomson**

● 1896–1989   ▥ AMERICAN   ✍ c.300

Educated at Harvard, Thomson continued his studies in Paris, where he met Satie, who became a major influence on his work. There he also collaborated with fellow expatriate Gertrude Stein on his most famous work, the opera *Four Saints in Three Acts*, setting Stein's wordplay and random remarks (tidied up by Thomson's close friend, the painter Maurice Grosser) to a mosaic of hymn tunes, chant, and straightforward harmony. Back in the US he wrote film scores (often using American ingredients, such as cowboy tunes and spirituals) and orchestral pieces in various styles, and collaborated again with Stein. A fearless but respected critic, he lectured throughout the US and Europe; he also continued to compose, and received many honors.

MILESTONES	
1928	Writes *Four Saints in Three Acts*, opera
1936	*The Plow that Broke the Plains*, film score
1940	Returns to New York; becomes music critic for the *Herald Tribune*
1947	Writes *The Mother of Us All*, opera
1948	*Louisiana Story*, film score, wins Pulitzer Prize
1968	Composes *Lord Byron*, opera

≪ **In his score for *Louisiana Story*—a documentary about life in the bayou seen through the eyes of a Cajun boy—Thomson included many folk melodies.

George **Gershwin**

🌐 **1898–1937**　　📖 **AMERICAN**　　✍ **369**

George Gershwin was one of the most exuberantly talented and successful composers of the 20th century, and its most tragically short-lived. He had his first Broadway success in 1919 and his first "Classical" success in 1924, and thereafter remained dominant in both fields, winning the respect of such severe "Classical" masters as Rachmaninoff and—amazingly—Arnold Schoenberg.

🔼 **A true crossover artist,** Gershwin's serious compositions remain highly popular in the Classical repertoire, and his stage and film songs continue to be jazz and vocal standards.

Life

Gershwin's parents were Russian Jews who emigrated to the US in the 1890s. From 1910 Gershwin studied piano seriously and soon progressed to Chopin, Liszt, and Debussy. In 1914 he abandoned Classical music in favor of Tin Pan Alley (although he returned to it later in life) by dropping out of high school to work for Jerome Remick and Co. In 1920 he had his first hit with "Swanee," recorded by Al Jolson. Over the next four years he wrote five Broadway reviews, two London shows, and three Broadway ones, one of which, *Lady Be Good*, was the first of many with lyrics by his brother, Ira. In 1924 he gave the premiere of his *Rhapsody in Blue*. His new wealth allowed him to move into an elegant townhouse on the Upper West Side, and to seduce innumerable women. During the late 1920s he followed up the success of *Rhapsody* with other "Classical" pieces including the Concerto in F and the Preludes. In 1928 he traveled to Europe and met Prokofiev, Milhaud, Ravel, and Berg. Throughout the '30s he divided his time between concert tours as a pianist and composing musicals, including *Strike up the Band* and *Girl Crazy*. In 1936 he and Ira signed a contract with RKO film studios, which led to *Shall We Dance?*, *A Damsel in Distress*, and *The Goldwyn Follies*. Gershwin died at the height of his fame in 1937.

Music

Gershwin's importance in the history of American "Classical" music should not obscure the fact that he was in essence a songwriter. His genius needed no more than the four-minute frame of the popular song, with its predictable verse-and-chorus structure. They fall into a number of types: the sturdy march song, such as "Swanee" and "Strike up the Band"; fast, syncopated songs, such as "Fascinating Rhythm" and "I got Rhythm"; the slow romantic ballad, of which the best known are "Someone to Watch Over Me" and "Embraceable You"; and the medium-tempo song with an irresistible swinging beat, like "Nice Work if You can Get It". Although formally simple, these songs are enriched by startlingly original modulations.

The regular two- and four-bar phrases of his songs recur in Gershwin's concert works and in his opera *Porgy and Bess*, as do the characteristic "blue-note" harmonies of African-American music. The concert works achieve their effect by their melodic appeal and accumulation of contrasts, although the Concerto in F major shows a remarkable subtlety of form.

MILESTONES	
1914	Starts work in Tin Pan Alley
1918	Has three songs accepted by Broadway shows
1919	First full Broadway show *La La Lucille* opens
1924	*Lady be Good* opens on Broadway
1930	*Girl Crazy* opens on Broadway
1932	*Cuban Overture*
1935	*Porgy and Bess* opens on Broadway

❝ I don't think there has been **such an inspired melodist** on this Earth **since Tchaikovsky...** ❞ Leonard Bernstein

KEY WORKS

PORGY AND BESS

| OPERA | 🕮 190:00 | 📖 3 | 🎵 ♻ ♂ |

Given Gershwin's love of African-American idioms, it is not surprising that his one "serious" music drama should be on an African-American theme. The piece is criticized today for its clichéd image of African-Americans, but Gershwin can hardly be blamed for accepting the mindset of his time. It remains a riveting and profoundly moving work.
Act one The action opens in Catfish Row, a poor fishing community. The drunken, brutal Crown kills a man during a craps game, then flees. The drug dealer Sportin' Life offers to take Bess, Crown's woman, to New York with him. Instead Bess goes to stay with the crippled Porgy.
Act two Porgy and Bess sing the love duet "Bess, You Is My Woman Now," then Bess leaves for a picnic on an island. Crown appears at the picnic to reclaim Bess and she stays on the island with him. Two days later she is found, delirious. She wants to stay with Porgy, but is afraid that Crown still has a fatal hold over her. The act ends with a hurricane starting to blow.
Act three Porgy kills Crown, but nobody gives him away. However, he is jailed for a week and, while he is away, Bess is drugged by Sportin' Life, who takes her to New York. When Porgy is freed, he vows to find her and prepares to leave on his quest.

RHAPSODY IN BLUE

| ORCHESTRAL | 🕮 13:45 | 📖 1 | 🎵 ◉ |

The premiere of this piece in 1924 propelled Gershwin into the history books as the man "who first brought jazz into the concert hall." In many people's eyes, the idea that the "low," socially disreputable popular music of African-Americans could fuse with Classical music was too shocking to contemplate. The combined frisson of being fashionably new and risqué drew a glittering audience to the premiere. The work has a sectional form, with a big slow central melody. The obvious jazzy elements in the score have obscured the distinctly Jewish tinge in the melodies, some of which recall synagogue chants.

CONCERTO IN F MAJOR

| ORCHESTRAL | 🕮 33:00 | 📖 3 | 🎵 ◉ |

Unlike the earlier *Rhapsody in Blue*, which was scored by an assistant, this piano concerto was scored by Gershwin himself. In the four years after composing *Rhapsody in Blue*, Gershwin made a close study of European Modernist composers, so it is not surprising that whereas the earlier rhapsody had relied on simple alternations of soloist and orchestra, the concerto makes use of thematic transformation (the recurrence of a main theme in different guises, lending unity to the piece). The result was the pinnacle of Gershwin's achievement as a concert composer.

AN AMERICAN IN PARIS

| ORCHESTRAL | 🕮 22:00 | 📖 1 | 🎵 ◉ |

Gershwin said of this piece, "My intention here is to portray the impressions of an American visitor in Paris as he strolls about the city, listens to various street noises, and absorbs the French atmosphere." An opening section of infectious gaiety leads to a slow, reflective blues, showing perhaps an attack of homesickness. However, cheerfulness returns, and at the end "the street noises and French atmosphere are triumphant."

 The film *An American in Paris* (1951), starring Gene Kelly and Leslie Caron, had a score by George Gershwin, lyrics by his brother Ira, and a screenplay by Alan Jay Lerner.

Aaron **Copland**

● **1900–1990**   ⊞ **AMERICAN**   ✐ **135**

Aaron Copland is probably the best known, and certainly one of the most profoundly gifted, Classical composers that America has ever produced. In the 1930s and '40s he synthesized jazz, neo-Classical, and folk elements into a style that for many people summons up the spirit of his native country. This, combined with his energetic entrepreneurial and organizational gifts, makes him the key figure in 20th-century American music.

» **Although best known** to the public for his "Americana," Copland was also a composer of jazz, avant-garde, and serialist works.

Life

Copland was born in New York into a prosperous family of Polish-Lithuanian Jews. During his teens he studied music privately, scoured libraries for scores of new music, took an interest in jazz and, from 1921, spent three years in Paris. While there he acquired a cast-iron technique and a neo-Classical esthetic from music teacher Nadia Boulanger, and was dazzled by Parisian artistic life. Back home, early works such as the Piano Concerto earned him the reputation of a hot-headed modernist. Lacking commissions, he

staved off destitution by teaching and writing, and threw himself into the cause of new music. He was codirector of the Copland–Sessions concerts and cofounder of the Yaddo Festival, the Arrow Music Press, and the American Composers' Alliance.

In 1934 he wrote workers' choruses and an article on proletarian music that got him into trouble with Senator McCarthy's House Committee on Un-American Activities in the 1940s. However, by then he had become the musical voice of America with populist works such as *El sálon México* and the ballet *Appalachian Spring*, which won a Pulitzer Prize. In the 1960s he became American music's wise, urbane father figure, dispensing advice and friendship to younger musicians like Bernstein.

Music

At first Copland behaved like a true avant-garde composer, shocking audiences with sharp dissonance and jazzy irreverence. But he was never an ivory-tower composer; he wanted his music to relate to contemporary issues, and to appeal to public taste.

In the 1930s, under the impact of the Depression and a wave of left-wing sentiment among artists, he found a new awareness of himself as an American and as a citizen. In a series of ballets, *Billy the Kid*, *Rodeo*, and *Appalachian Spring*, he crystallized the style that made him famous. It was a style rooted in the forms of Stravinskian neo-Classicism, but this was united with a specifically American lyricism and feeling for landscape, both rural and urban. In the later years of his career, in the 1960s, he even succeeded in marrying Schoenberg's 12-tone technique with his own personal sound world.

❝ I do not compose;
I assemble materials. 〞❞

Aaron Copland

MILESTONES

1925	Completes first major work, the ballet *Grohg*	**1958**	Debut with New York Philharmonic launches 20-year conducting career
1938	*Billy the Kid*, first of his three great ballets, premiered by Lincoln Kirstein's Ballet Caravan	**1961**	Moves to Peerskill NY, where he lives until his death
1954	Elected to American Academy of Arts and Letters	**1964**	Presidential Medal of Freedom
		1972	Ceases composing

KEY WORKS

APPALACHIAN SPRING

BALLET   ⏱ 35:30   📖 8   ♇

The third and most perfect of Copland's "American" ballets, the work was commissioned in 1943 for the choreographer Martha Graham. It was originally scored for only 13 players, though it's more often heard today in the arrangement Copland made for full orchestra. The ballet portrays a "pioneer celebration of Spring in a newly built farmhouse in Pennsylvania in the early 1800s." The young farmer and his bride-to-be act out their feelings of hope, excitement, and trepidation. Copland said he was inspired by Graham's choreography, which he described as "prim and restrained, simple yet strong... the music reflects, I hope, the unique quality of a human being, an American landscape and a way of feeling." Toward the end, the traditional Shaker tune "Simple Gifts" is first quoted and then subtly varied.

12 POEMS OF EMILY DICKINSON

SONG-CYCLE   ⏱ 28:00   📖 12   🎵

This setting of poems by the visionary, reclusive poet Emily Dickinson is one of the great song-cycles of the 20th century. They are set in Copland's lean mature style, the piano part often confined to single notes in each hand, a style perfectly suited to the poems, which deal with the grandest subjects in the simplest language. The wide-open sounds of the music match Dickinson's rural imagery, and the unfussy rhythms of the songs accords with the Biblical plainness of Dickinson's verse. Within these limits the range of moods is vast: homely simplicity in

"Nature, the gentlest mother," a funereal tread in "I felt a funeral in my brain," bugle-calls and rushing scales in "There came a wind like a bugle."

PIANO VARIATIONS

SOLO PIANO   ⏱ 11:00   🎵

Copland said "This was the first of my works where I felt very sure of myself." It is generally regarded as the most impressive product of Copland's "abstract" period in the early 1930s. The piece has an unusual combination of rhythmic propulsion derived from jazz and a very strict compositional logic, influenced by Schoenberg's 12-tone system.

SYMPHONY NO. 3

ORCHESTRAL   ⏱ 42:00   📖 4   🎶

Copland was aiming for a big statement in this work, appropriate to a time of national stress (he began writing the symphony during World War II). The "public" manner culminates in the grandeur of the finale, which begins by quoting Copland's earlier *Fanfare for the Common Man*.

CLARINET CONCERTO

ORCHESTRAL   ⏱ 17:00   📖 2   🎶 🎵

Like Copland's earlier piano concerto, this consists of two movements separated by a cadenza. The first movement is one of his most inspired pastoral melodies, which unfolds over a stately slow-motion waltz accompaniment. The second explodes in jazzy fireworks, inspired by jazz clarinettist Benny Goodman, for whom the piece was written.

⬆ **Copland wrote extensively** for films in the 1940s. His score for William Wyler's 1948 film *The Heiress*, starring Olivia de Havilland, won an Academy Award.

Samuel **Barber**

● **1910–1981**   ▥ **AMERICAN**   ✍ **c.50**

Barber's music defies easy classification. Effortlessly lyrical, Romantic, and yet unmistakably contemporary, he achieved huge popularity without aligning himself to any school of composition or appearing concerned with Modernist trends. His comparatively small output covered all genres, although he is best remembered for his vocal works and the *Adagio for Strings*, made famous by the conductor Toscanini.

Barber trained both as a composer and singer at the renowned Curtis Academy. At a time when music was dominated by European Modernists such as Schoenberg and Stravinsky, Barber's easy Romanticism struck a chord with audiences. His gift for flowing, memorable melody lines masked the more contemporary aspects of his composition, notably an acute handling of dissonance and highly inventive orchestration. His output, already less than prodigious, declined sharply after the failure of his opera *Antony and Cleopatra* at the New York Metropolitan in 1966.

MILESTONES

1931	Composes vocal work *Dover Beach*
1935	Fellow of American Academy in Rome
1936	Composes Symphony No. 1
1942	Serves in US Air Corp
1947	Composes *Knoxville, Summer of 1915*
1949	Piano Sonata premiered by Horowitz
1958	Opera *Vanessa* wins Pulitzer Prize
1962	Composes Piano Concerto

KEY WORKS

ADAGIO FOR STRINGS

ORCHESTRAL   ⏱ 8:30   📖 1   🎵

The poignant *Adagio for Strings* is Barber's most popular work. Composed in 1936, the *Adagio* originally formed the central movement of his String Quartet, Op. 11. Two years later Barber rescored it for a full string orchestra, taking advantage of the extra resources to add weight and sonority.

The form of the *Adagio* has been likened to a long arch, based on the gradual expansion of a single, simple theme. This is heard first in hushed tones on the violins, before a more strident presentation by the cellos. After a process of ascending development, an impassioned climax is reached, before the music breaks off abruptly, almost as if overcome by emotion. The work then concludes quietly, recalling fragments of the theme. Perhaps because of its profoundly melancholic, contemplative tone, the *Adagio* has

found wide resonance with the public and has been played at many funerals, including those of John F. Kennedy, F. D. Roosevelt, and Einstein.

VIOLIN CONCERTO

ORCHESTRAL   ⏱ 21:00   📖 3   🎵 🎶

First movement (*allegro*, 10:00) Unusually, Barber chose to dispense with an introduction, the soloist launching immediately into the lyrical main theme of this sonata-form movement.

Second movement (*andante*, 8:00) A haunting solo oboe introduces the first theme, which is developed by the strings before the soloist enters and leads into a darker and more impassioned section.

Third movement (*presto in moto perpetuoso*, 3:00) An astonishing *tour de force* for the soloist against a background of wild rhythms from the orchestra, the finale contrasts greatly with the first two movements.

⏏ **Barber's *Adagio for Strings*** owes its fame to Toscanini, who performed it with the NBC Orchestra in 1938.

John **Cage**

◕ 1912–1992   ⏴ᵁ AMERICAN   ✍ 229

John Cage may well be the most original composer in the history of Western music. His life's project was to repudiate the entire Western tradition, but not in a spirit of anger or negativity. Even at its most chaotic, his music comes across as exuberant and life-affirming. He used chance procedures to free sounds from the "bullying" effects of human intentions and rules, so that they could "be themselves."

Born in Los Angeles, John Cage became interested in Classical Indian music and Oriental philosophies. He formed a percussion orchestra before settling in New York in 1942 and beginning a lifelong collaboration with dancer Merce Cunningham's dance company. His life project began with a ruthless process of stripping away, starting with harmony and melody. (Cage's earliest pieces are built out of pure rhythm, played on percussion or the "prepared piano.") Then he stripped away intention and form by introducing chance operations into music, ending up with pure silence in his famous piece *4' 33"*. This led to a welcoming in, when any chance noises could become part of a "piece." This is why Cage's later music ranges from the simplicity of *Two* to the riotous complication of *Roaratorio*.

MILESTONES

1934	Meets Arnold Schoenberg and decides to dedicate his life to music
1938	Invents the "prepared piano"
1940s	Studies Zen Buddhism
1948	Completes *Sonatas and Interludes* for prepared piano
1950	Creates first "chance pieces" after reading the ancient Chinese text, *I Ching*
1961	*Variations II* premiered; *Silence* (collected writings) brings him world fame
1978	Starts to "write" music as graphic designs at Crown Point Press
1979	*Roaratorio*, with tape, premiered
1987	Employing randomness, writes *Two*, first of his late "time bracket" pieces

KEY WORKS

VARIATIONS II

CHAMBER   📖 1   ♟

This is perhaps Cage's most extreme experiment in notation. The "score" consists of 11 transparent sheets bearing lines or dots. These are tossed down and the resulting patterns used to determine the basic characteristics of the sounds.

SONATAS AND INTERLUDES

SOLO PIANO   ⏱ 64:00   📖 20   ☜

This sequence of 16 sonatas, intersperced with four interludes, attempts to represent the eight "permanent emotions" of ancient Indian thought, "and their common tendency towards tranquillity". It is scored for "prepared piano", Cage's invention whereby metal and rubber objects are placed inside a piano to alter the sound.

ROARATORIO

TAPE & VOCAL   ⏱ 75:00   📖 1   ♟♪

This exuberant work—a joyous cacophony—for electronic tape and live performers is an attempt to translate James Joyce's vast novel *Finnegans Wake* into sound.

▶ In *4' 33"* the pianist sits reading the score, shown here, for four minutes 33 seconds, but does not play.

Roy **Harris**

● 1898–1979   ⚑ **AMERICAN**   ✍ **c.200**

Harris's broad, sweeping melodies, robustly based on hymns and American folk tunes and with vigorous but unusual rhythms, suggest the Midwest landscapes he knew well (he grew up on a farm in Oklahoma and drove a truck during his college days). After winning a music competition, he went to New York, where he befriended Aaron Copland, and then to Paris to study under Nadia Boulanger. There, his Concerto for Piano, Clarinet, and String Quartet received acclaim. Back in the US, he established his "American" style with great success in his orchestral works. He taught at several institutes and was widely honored. His Symphony No. 3 is often called the greatest American symphony.

MILESTONES

1925	Andante for Strings wins competition
1926	Goes to study in Paris
1929	Injured in a fall; returns to US
1933	Conductor Sergei Koussevitsky commissions symphony from him
1934	Completes first of his 13 symphonies
1938	Composes Symphony No. 3

« **The rugged landscape** of the American West is reflected in a distinctly rugged quality in many of Harris's works.

Conlon **Nancarrow**

● 1912–1997   ⚑ **AMERICAN**   ✍ **c.75**

Turning his back on an engineering career, Nancarrow studied music privately, fought in the Spanish Civil War, and—escaping anticommunist feeling in America—moved to Mexico City permanently. There he composed in isolation an extraordinary series of studies for the player piano, which could be "programmed" to automatically play music punched into piano rolls. The 50 or so works use an astounding variety of techniques, such as inhumanly fast tempos, relentless accelerations, and unimaginably mathematical cross-rhythms. In the late 1970s Nancarrow's music was discovered and recorded, and he found fame: he was given commissions, he was invited to international music festivals, and he received a $300,000 award.

MILESTONES

1930	Starts composing conventionally
1939	Refused US passport after having fought in Spanish Civil War
1940	Moves to Mexico City
1947	Buys player piano
1948	Writes Study No. 1 for player piano
1992	Writes Study No. 52 for player piano

⌃ **In his early career,** Nancarrow notated all his mature compositions on player-piano rolls. Most of them are impossible for human hands to play.

Leonard **Bernstein**

◔ **1918–1990**   ⚑ **AMERICAN**   ✍ **90**

Bernstein was one of the most dazzlingly gifted musicians of the 20th century. He was also an immense personality, with huge intellectual curiosity. He achieved preeminence in two fields: conducting, and composing for Broadway musicals and dance shows.

Bernstein was the son of a family of rabbis, and Jewish themes feature prominently in his music. By the end of his student years, it was clear his talents would be divided between "serious" music and Broadway. His greatest successes as a composer came before he was 40, both in the musical theater (*West Side Story*, *Candide*) and in concert music (Symphonies Nos. 1 and 2 and *Serenade*). After becoming chief conductor of the New York Philharmonic, conducting took up more of his time. However, he strove to compose at the same pace, while leading a complicated love life and showing support for unpopular causes such as the Black Panthers. "I'm overcommitted on all fronts," he once said.

MILESTONES	
1939	Writes thesis "Race Elements in Music"; graduates from Harvard University
1943	Wins fame conducting New York Philharmonic when Bruno Walter is ill
1944	Symphony No. 1, ballet *Fancy Free*, and musical *On the Town* are big successes
1949	Composes Symphony No. 2
1953	Is first American to conduct at La Scala
1956	Completes operetta *Candide*
1973	Lectures at Harvard televised in US and abroad as *The Unanswered Question*
1983	Opera *A Quiet Place* premiered

⏶ **Bernstein** became a "giant of the podium," the only rival to Herbert von Karajan.

KEY WORKS

WEST SIDE STORY

MUSICAL   ⏱ 90:00   📖 2   ♫ ♬ ♪

Bernstein's masterpiece takes the idea of Shakespeare's *Romeo and Juliet* and transfers it to 1950s New York. Bernstein, choreographer Jerome Robbins, and writer Arthur Laurents together elaborated the story of a native-born Polish boy and a Puerto Rican girl newly arrived in America, describing how their love is thwarted by the constant warfare between rival gangs on the city's West Side. Bernstein offered the job of lyricist to the then-unknown Stephen Sondheim. The show's debt to Rodgers and Hammerstein's *South Pacific* can be seen in its mix of opera and Broadway idioms, the dramatic integration of dance, and the use of song to highlight social tensions. However, the hard-edged gang music, and the sheer range of Bernstein's invention, take this work far beyond its model. Bernstein later created a suite of orchestral Symphonic Dances from the musical.

SYMPHONY NO. 2, "THE AGE OF ANXIETY"

ORCHESTRAL   ⏱ 36:00   📖 2   ♫ ◐

This symphony takes its scenario from W.H. Auden's ingenious long poem *The Age of Anxiety*. For its relatively short length, the symphony has a very complicated form: it is a combination of piano concerto, and theme and variations. In addition, it is also divided into two parts. The combination of influences—Brahms, Hindemith, Berg, and jazz—makes for a fascinating mix.

INFLUENCES
Bernstein's blending of classical "Americana" with jazz elements and his concern for big metaphysical and social issues are echoed in contemporary American music. However, his sources—jazz, Jewish music, and "classic" American composers—remain more influential than Bernstein himself.

⏶ **Bernstein** was a noted conductor of Mahler, Brahms, and Copland.

Elliott **Carter**

● 1908–   ⚑ AMERICAN   ✑ 145

Elliott Carter is the oldest of that vanishing breed of modernists born before World War II. Since the late 1940s he has clung to the view that music has to be many-layered and full of complex cross-currents, because only then can it be true to the complexity of modern life. In his music of the 1980s and '90s the textures thinned out, but the thought behind it was as quick and subtle as ever.

Carter was born in New York into a prosperous lace-importing family that spent much of its time in Europe. Having got acquainted with new music through Charles Ives, he joined the long line of American composers who studied with the great Paris-based advocate of neo-Classicism, Nadia Boulanger. In the late 1940s Carter had a creative crisis that led him to abandon his populist American neo-Classical stance in favor of an uncompromising modernism. Until the 1980s and '90s this made him better known in Europe than America. Even after reaching the age of 100, Carter has continued to produce new work.

MILESTONES	
1926	Studies literature, Greek, and philosophy at Harvard, and music at the Longy School
1939	Marries sculptress Helen Frost; begins teaching in Annapolis, US
1960	String Quartet No. 2 wins Pulitzer Prize, New York Music Critics' Award, and UNESCO First Prize
1976	Premiere of *A Mirror on Which to Dwell*
1999	Premiere of opera *What Next?*
2008	*Interventions for Piano and Orchestra*
2010	*Flute Concerto*

KEY WORKS

A SYMPHONY OF THREE ORCHESTRAS

ORCHESTRAL   ⏳ 15:45   📖 1

This single-movement work was Carter's response to Hart Crane's magnificent poem "The Bridge," a mystical evocation of Brooklyn Bridge and the city of New York. In Hart's poem the bridge becomes a symbol which spans a river and a continent, and which unites an ancient past and a technological future. To capture this visionary quality, Carter created a dense, glistening soundscape for three orchestras, the first consisting of brass, timpani, and strings, the second of percussion, clarinets, and solo strings, and the third of winds, horns, and upper strings. Each orchestra has its own repertoire of chords and melodic shapes, and its own independent succession of tempos. These are unfolded simultaneously, creating Carter's most extreme experiment in collage. The piece begins

with a high trumpet solo, which has been described as the definitive portrait in sound of New York, and ends with a "factory-noise" coda that tumbles down to the depths of the orchestra.

CELLO SONATA

CHAMBER   ⏳ 21:45   📖 4   ⾕

In the 1940s, dissatisfied with the populist style of his early works, Carter began to grope his way toward a new style. The second movement of the Cello Sonata, originally intended as the first, is in a jazz-tinged style, but the next two movements introduce musical ideas moving at different speeds. He then composed a new first movement, which instead of starting with a "theme" presents chords and intervals that act as a "quarry" for everything that follows. The work is in the shape of an endless loop, with the "beginning" in the middle.

Milton **Babbitt**

◔ 1916–2011　　☷ **AMERICAN**　　✍ c.110

After playing jazz, Babbitt was a music graduate by 19 and continued to study privately. An early proponent of 12-tone music, he worked in music and mathematics university faculties, developing advanced theories of musical systems. He taught at Princeton and the Juilliard School, among others, and became a significant writer and lecturer—and, as well as being a major intellectual, he was also a sports fan and raconteur. Babbitt's highly structured and complex works makes them unlikely to gain popular success, but they and his teachings have proved very influential. Frequently honored, he continued composing and working into his 90s.

⌃ **Babbitt's exploratory compositions** involved at various times tape, synthesizer (including the 1960s model shown above), and conventional instruments.

MILESTONES

1940	*Composition for String Orchestra*, 12-tone work
1960	Professor of Music at Princeton
1963	*Philomel*, for soprano and synthesizer
1970	Composes String Quartet No. 3
1973	Starts teaching composition at Juilliard
1982	Pulitzer Prize citation for life's work

Lou **Harrison**

◔ 1917–2003　　☷ **AMERICAN**　　✍ c.220

Harrison was a US West Coast experimenter, synthesizing world native and Western styles, working in different tuning systems, and creating novel percussive sounds. With his partner William Colvig he developed "American gamelan," from items such as garbage cans, tins, and baseball bats. He also wrote for standard Western instruments, usually with a lyrical flavor, and collaborated with Ives and Cage. His opera *Young Caesar* shows his advocacy of gay rights.

MILESTONES

1946	Conducts premiere of Ives's Symphony No. 3
1974	Composes *Suite for Violin and American Gamelan*

Leon **Kirchner**

◔ 1919–2009　　☷ **AMERICAN**　　✍ 55

Alongside a distinguished teaching career Kirchner worked as a pianist and conductor. His music—sometimes agonized, sometimes driving and energetic—is firmly in the tradition of his mentor, Schoenberg, flowing and unfolding, but always governed by some underlying idea, and resistant to temporary musical fashions. He received a Pulitzer Prize for his Quartet No. 3.

MILESTONES

1958	Composes String Quartet No. 2
1962	Composes Piano Concerto No. 2
1973	Composes *Lily*, chamber ensemble and tape (arrangement of opera)
2008	*The Forbidden* for orchestra

Ned **Rorem**

◔ 1923–   🏴 AMERICAN   ✍ 550

Rorem studied with Virgil Thomson (for whom he was secretary and copyist) and Copland at the Juilliard School. After winning prizes with the Lordly Hudson (best published song of 1948) and his Overture in C (Gershwin Prize) he went to Paris, where he lived for several years and became part of the artistic circles of Cocteau and Poulenc, one of his inspirations. Back in New York, where the success of his songs drew him, he taught at various institutes and increasingly developed his reputation as an excellent song composer (he has written over 500, with natural word setting and harmonies that are advanced but never impossible) and as a writer (such as his elegant and frank diaries).

MILESTONES	
1958	Returns from Paris to New York
1965	Composes *Miss Julie*, opera
1966	Publishes *The Paris Diary of Ned Rorem*
1976	*Air Music*, orchestra, wins Pulitzer Prize
1997	Composes *Evidence of Things Not Seen*, song cycle
2005	*Our Town*, opera

⏶ **During his time in Paris,** Rorem wrote his entertaining journal *The Paris Diary of Ned Rorem* (1951–55).

Morton **Feldman**

◔ 1926–1987   🏴 AMERICAN   ✍ c.150

Spurning conventional academic training—he worked in the family business—Feldman was influenced by the new sounds of Varèse, the pioneering work of Cage, and especially New York's 1950s abstract Expressionist school of painters and their faith in directness and instinct. His Modernist pieces sometimes involve nonstandard notation (his series of pieces *Projections* and *Intersections* are written on graphical scores, with general directions rather than individual notes on a stave), and can be of immense length—his String Quartet II lasts almost six hours. One of his last works, *Palais de Mari*, is unusual for a late composition in that it is only 20 minutes long. It came about from a request for Feldman to sum up everything he was doing in his very long pieces and to condense that into a smaller piece. After some time in Berlin, where he gained several commissions, he returned to the US to teach composition in Buffalo.

MILESTONES	
1951	Composes *Projections* and *Intersections*
1971	Is granted a residency in Berlin
1971	*The Rothko Chapel*, singers and ensemble
1973	Appointed professor at SUNY, Buffalo
1984	Composes *For Philip Guston*, ensemble
1986	Composes *Palais de Maris*
1987	Marries composer Barbara Monk

⏵ **Blue Penumbra, 1957** (oil on canvas) by painter Mark Rothko, a friend of Feldman's and one who helped shape his sound world.

George **Crumb**

🌑 1929–　　　🏴 AMERICAN　　　✍ 65

Raised in a musical family accustomed to the classics, trained in the conventional way rounded off at Berlin's Hochschule, and having made a career in teaching, mostly at the University of Pennsylvania, Crumb was at home with the standard repertoire. After initially being influenced by Webern, he has become almost notorious for requiring unusual sounds and innovative techniques in his relatively small but refined output. *Black Angels*, for example, evokes the horrors of Vietnam by asking the string quartet players to shout and bow wine glasses, while *Vox Balaenae* (*The Voice of the Whale*) requires its musicians to wear masks and perform under a blue light (the latter also features an electric flute, an electric cello, and an amplified piano). Many of his works set texts by Lorca, and the theatrical nature of his music—sometimes trancelike, other times explosive—has made it popular with dance companies.

» Poem of the Deep Song, one of several poems by Federico García Lorca set to music by Crumb.

MILESTONES	
1965	Begins association with Pennsylvania University
1968	Wins Pulitzer Prize for *Echoes of Time and the River*
1970	Writes *Ancient Voices of Children*; *Black Angels*, string quartet, produced
1973	Writes *Makrokosmos II* for piano
2002	Joint residency at Arizona University

Frederic **Rzewski**

🌑 1938–　　　🏴 AMERICAN　　　✍ c.70

A prodigiously talented pianist and composer, Rzewski went from Harvard and Princeton to Europe, where he performed and taught through the 1960s. He worked on radical jazz-based improvisation and live electronic projects, some with a socialist theme. He has been based in Rome and Liège since 1976 and teaches widely. His popular *The People United* is a 50-minute set of virtuoso variations in an astonishing array of styles on a worker's revolutionary song; later works were more experimental, before a recent freer phase. Miles 49–56 of his mammoth seven-hour-long piano solo *The Road* involve playing the floor and stool, whistling, humming, screwed-up paper, and a radio, plus sections for each hand alone.

☑ **Rzewski's magnum opus,** *The Road*, is a musical "novel" composed of 64 parts, each marking a "mile" in the work's journey.

MILESTONES	
1960	Studies under Dallapiccola in Florence
1962	Premiere of Stockhausen's *Klavierstück X*
1975	Writes *The People United Will Never Be Defeated* for piano
1983	Professor of composition at Liège
1988	Writes *Triumph of Death*, oratorio
1998	*The Road* written for piano

John **Corigliano**

● 1938– 　ᴾᴵ AMERICAN 　✍ 100

John Corigliano belongs to the same generation as the minimalists Reich, Glass, and Riley. But whereas they took a long and winding route to Romantic expressivity, via the severities of minimalism, Corigliano knew from the beginning that expressivity was his true home. His eclectic language, which calls on the evocative power of musical memory, has won him a wide audience.

Corigliano was a somewhat slow starter as a composer, and after studying at Columbia University he worked in classical music radio and as a concert programmer. Corigliano describes his early works, such as the Violin Sonata and the earlier movements of the *Dylan Thomas Trilogy*, as "a tense, histrionic outgrowth of the 'clean' American sound of Barber, Copland, Harris, and Schuman." The later works, beginning with the Clarinet Concerto, present a very different musical palette, less driven and with many more layers. But Corigliano is not aiming for the intellectual complication of a composer such as Elliott Carter. Memory, nostalgia, and the evocation of different emotional worlds are what interest him, which is why he is a truly postmodern composer.

»» **A still from *The Red Violin***, which features a haunting, complex, and lyrical score by Corigliano.

MILESTONES	
1960	Works as music programmer at New York music station WXQR
1961	Starts work with Leonard Bernstein on the *Young People's Concert* series
1971	Starts teaching at Manhattan School of Music
1977	Clarinet Concerto premiered by Bernstein in New York
1991	*The Ghost of Versailles* premiered in New York
1992	Teaches composition at Juilliard School in New York
1999	*The Red Violin* wins Pulitzer Prize
2000	Premiere of Symphony No. 2
2004	Symphony No. 3 "Circus Maximus" for large wind ensemble

KEY WORKS

A DYLAN THOMAS TRILOGY

ORATORIO	⏱ 90:00	📖 3	🎵 ♗ 🎺

It took Corigliano around 40 years to complete this large-scale "memory play in the form of an oratorio," as he calls it. The trilogy consists of settings of three poems by Dylan Thomas that were particularly dear to Corigliano: "Fern Hill," "Poem in October," and the darker "Poem on his Birthday."

SYMPHONY NO. 1

ORCHESTRAL	⏱ 43:00	📖 4	🎵

"During the past decade I have lost many friends and colleagues to the AIDS epidemic... My first symphony was generated by feelings of loss, anger, and frustration." Each movement is a memorial to a different friend; the moment in the first when a memory of Albéniz's "Tango" floats through the orchestra is typical of Corigliano's directness.

Steve **Reich**

🌑 1936–   📄 AMERICAN   ✍ 51

One of the best-known American composers, Steve Reich is acknowledged as the most sophisticated of the four pioneer minimalists (the others being Terry Riley, Philip Glass, and La Monte Young). Like Glass, Reich has broadened the range of his work, embracing his Jewish heritage and musically tackling political and ethical issues.

Although Reich reacted against the serial orthodoxy taught in the US, his early music was no less rigorous in the way it took a few simple ideas and pursued them relentlessly. In the 1960s, he found that, when started together, identical tape loops in old-style tape recorders would soon move out of synchronization. He began to transfer these phasing effects to conventional instruments, elaborating on them in ingenious ways. By the mid-1970s, his technique of making music from repeating, slowly changing patterns was established. In the 1980s, he returned to speech recordings for inspiration.

MILESTONES

1962	Studies with Milhaud and Berio
1966	Creates *Come Out*, first loop-phase piece; starts concerts with own ensemble
1967	Composes *Violin Phase*
1970	Studies in Ghana with Ewe tribe
1971	Composes *Drumming*; first appearance in big concert venue with orchestra
2002	*Three Tales* premiered: dark multimedia exploration of new technologies
2009	*Double Sextet* wins Pulitzer Prize

KEY WORKS

MUSIC FOR 18 MUSICIANS

CHAMBER   ⏱ 55:00   📖 1   ♟

This big, single-movement piece, created in 1974 and 1975 for an enlarged form of Reich's own ensemble, has a good claim to be his masterpiece. What makes it so irresistible is the way the moment-to-moment unfolding of Reich's familiar "pattern games" is embedded in a convincing architectural frame. The division of the ensemble into "breathing" wind instruments and voice and "pulsing" instruments gives rise to a layered texture, with slow-moving phrases set against pattering activity.

THE CAVE

MULTIMEDIA   ⏱ 142:00   📖 1   ♟ ⛃

In this ambitious work created with his wife, video artist Beryl Korot, several of Reich's interests come together: the use of speech rhythms in recordings; a concern with Jewish themes; and a desire to create a new kind of multimedia experience involving music, voices, and images. What is striking about this piece is the way speech, music, and images are strictly coordinated in time. The work concerns the Cave of Hebron, the burial place of both Abraham and Sarah and thus sacred to both Muslims and Jews. Recorded in Israel and in the US, the work explores the troubled legacy of the cave through interviews seen on screens and heard over speakers.

INFLUENCES

Reich's effect on musical culture is perhaps not as great as Philip Glass's, although within classical circles his influence may be greater, owing to the modernist rigor of his music. Nonetheless, his characteristic pattering, marimba-and-winds sound has managed to spread further, appearing on pop remix albums.

⌂ **Profoundly influenced by African drumming,** Reich's music consists of "pattern games" that are concerned not with melody, but with changes in time.

Philip **Glass**

◗ 1937–   📛 AMERICAN   ✍ 195

Glass is one of the founding fathers of minimalism, along with Steve Reich, Terry Riley, and La Monte Young. He shares with Riley and Young a respect for Indian music, and with Reich an interest in repetitive patterns. He is the most famous of them all, because of his vast productivity, his eagerness to collaborate with artists in different media, and the increasing emotional range and lyricism of his music.

Glass said, "Taboos—the things we're not supposed to do—are often the most interesting. In my case, musical materials are found among the ordinary things, such as sequences and cadences." Those ordinary things were indeed taboo in Glass's formative years, when the techniques of Stockhausen held sway. Through meeting Ravi Shankar and, later, the great percussionist Alla Rakha, he liberated himself from modernism and forged a hypnotic, repetitive style that was exactly suited to the rhythmic sax-and-keyboard sound of his own ensemble. After a difficult start playing New York lofts and galleries, Glass gained a cult following.

MILESTONES	
1957	Enrols at Juilliard School of Music
1963	Studies in Paris with Nadia Boulanger
1980	*Satyagraha*, opera, performed
1984	Composes music to inaugurate Los Angeles Olympics
2002	Writes score for Stephen Daldry's film *The Hours*
2006	*The Passion of Ramakrishna* for chorus and orchestra
2011	*The Lost*, opera

KEY WORKS

⬆ **Philip Glass's soundtrack** of atmospheric simplicity for *The Hours* is based on common chords and arpeggios, and is played in strange, circulating patterns by piano and strings.

MUSIC IN 12 PARTS

CHAMBER   ⏱ 205:00   📖 12   ♟

The longest and most ambitious piece Glass ever wrote for the Philip Glass Ensemble, this work is the summit of his early minimalist style. It began in 1971 as a single piece in 12 horizontal parts (six on keyboards, three on woodwind, and three vocal parts). Glass played it to a friend, who remarked, "Very beautiful. What will the other 11 parts be like?" Glass took this misunderstanding as a cue to compose 11 more pieces.

AKHNATEN

OPERA   ⏱ 150:00   📖 3   🎭🪕♂

Glass's "character operas" deal respectively with a brilliant scientist (Einstein), a great politician (Gandhi), and an influential religious reformer (Akhnaten). The last of the three works is the closest to a conventional opera. The music has a majestic slowness, in keeping with the vast timescale of the Egyptian world.

SYMPHONY NO. 5

CHORAL   ⏱ 98:00   📖 12   🎭🪕♂

This ambitious work brings together texts from many different "wisdom traditions," as Glass calls them. The 12 movements describe a journey through Death to Enlightenment.

INFLUENCES
Glass's influence has been immense, entering the general consciousness in a way no other living composer can match. The most telling proof of this is the countless TV soundtracks and commercials that imitate his style. However, his reputation in the classical world is much less secure.

John **Adams**

● 1947–   🎹 AMERICAN   ✍ 68

John Adams has become the most frequently performed living classical composer in the US, and quite possibly the world, due to his brilliant transformation of the minimal language he inherited from Glass and Reich. He retains the relentless forward momentum of minimalism, but vastly expands its expressive resources, and imports an exuberant range of cultural references, both "high" and "low."

Adams's name evokes the USA of the Founding Fathers, and his birth in Massachusetts seems to confirm this East Coast orientation. But his music evokes a very different West Coast mindset, symbolized by his move to California, and it is shown by an openness both to high-flown culture and Americana. These elements are held together in an idiom that grew out of the continuities of minimalism, and which, in its quieter moods, has a laid-back "Californian" feel. However, this mood is increasingly inflected by other elements—from dark European Romanticism to bright US pop.

KEY WORKS

NIXON IN CHINA

OPERA   ⏱ 160:00   📖 3   ♒♒♒

In Adams's first opera, the music is scored for only 34 players, including saxophones and synthesizers. The narrative is based on the visit by US president Richard Nixon to China in 1972, and much of the action consists of big public set-pieces. There are also intimate scenes in which the characters reveal their hopes and fears.

HARMONIELEHRE

ORCHESTRAL   ⏱ 40:00   📖 3   ♒

This work marked the decisive shift in Adams's work from the minimalist purity of his early works to his mature, more expressive style. The title comes from Schoenberg's harmony textbook of 1911, but the first inspiration for the piece came from a dream in which Adams saw a huge tanker rise out of San Francisco bay and take off like a rocket. The music mirrors this "take off" in a series of hammered E minor chords which speed up and disintegrate.

GRAND PIANOLA MUSIC

ENSEMBLE   ⏱ 30:00   📖 3   ♒♒♒

Adams has often spoken of the folly of ignoring popular culture and the necessity of embracing his US heritage. Some of his works revel in that heritage to an exuberant, irreverent degree; this is one of them. As he put it, "Beethoven and Rachmaninoff soak in the same warm bath with Liberace, Wagner, the Supremes, Charles Ives, and John Philip Sousa." Much of the writing is delicate, with the two pianos playing slightly out-of-phase. The loud, bombastic finale, entitled "The Dominant Divide," applies minimalist techniques to the simplest possible chord progression.

Adams conducting his nativity oratorio *El Niño*—an impressive reworking of the Christmas story, based on texts from religious and multicultural sources.

Terry **Riley**

● 1935–   ᴾᵁ AMERICAN   ✍ 95

Terry Riley is one of the founding fathers of minimalism. His '60s piece *In C* is acknowledged as a key work in the emergence of a driving, repetitive style that was picked up by composers who are now better known than Riley, such as Steve Reich and Philip Glass. The success of this piece has obscured the great variety of Riley's music, which ranges from tape-delay montages to Indian-inspired lyricism.

Terry Riley's life has been as unorthodox as his music. After studies at the University of California, he led a rootless life, playing the piano in bars in Europe and America. An early influence on his music was the jazz of that period, especially improvisers such as John Coltrane, Miles Davis, and Charles Mingus, who were extending the boundaries of the form. In the early '60s he was a cofounder of the San Francisco Tape Music Center, where he created highly innovative pieces using montage and tape-echo techniques, some in collaboration with underground composer La Monte Young.

His 1964 piece *In C* defines the '60s like no other Classical piece, but Riley would say that the meeting with Kirana vocal master Pandit Pran Nath in 1970 was the real watershed in his life.

Since then his music has reflected the profound influence of Indian Classical music, in its incorporation of improvisation, in its use of unorthodox tuning systems, and in its yearning for mystical transcendence.

MILESTONES

1960	Collaborates with La Monte Young
1962	Begins two-year stay in Europe
1964	Premiere of *In C*
1970	Meets Pandit Pran Nath
1980	Starts writing for the Kronos Quartet
1989	Leads Khayal group until 1993
1993	Starts teaching at Christi Sabri School of Indian Classical Music in New Delhi

KEY WORKS

 Riley's main influence has been Indian Classical music.

IN C

EXPERIMENTAL

To be played "by any instruments," this is a joyous affirmation of the chord of C major. The entire score consists of a single page of melodic fragments, through which the players move at their own pace. The fixed element is a hammered octave C, which holds the key and the rhythm.

THE SAINT ADOLF RING

OPERA   ♇ ♙ ♂

Like several other contemporary composers, Riley has become fascinated by the strange visions of the Swiss schizophrenic artist Adolf Wölfli. In 1992 he founded the Traveling Avant-Garde Theater Company to perform his multimedia chamber opera *The Saint Adolf Ring*, in which he performed as player, singer, and actor.

CONCERT FOR TWO PIANOS AND FIVE TAPE RECORDERS

EXPERIMENTAL   ♇

Much inspired by the chance works of John Cage, this work was premiered by Riley himself and La Monte Young. It is a joyously anarchic collage of keyboard sounds (both live and on tape loops) and recorded sounds such as explosions, screams, and laughter.

Aram **Khachaturian**

1903–1978 | ARMENIAN | 76

Khachaturian was the first, and so far the only, Armenian composer to achieve world renown. This was due to his two Romantic ballets *Gayaneh* and *Spartacus*, and his attractively melodious concertos. Like many Soviet ballets, his recall the exotic Romanticism of Rimsky-Korsakov and early Stravinsky. The extra ingredient is an Armenian folk flavor, which can be heard in nearly all Khachaturian's works.

Khachaturian had a generous, optimistic nature. Throughout the horrors of Stalin's Terror in the 1930s and the denunciations of the cultural commissar Zhdanov, he conducted himself with dignity, refusing to point the finger at fellow composers. His music has a similar straightforward cheerfulness; even the tragic moments in the ballets are picturesque rather than moving. The influence of Armenian folk music can be seen in the frequent hectic ostinatos, in chords based on fourths and fifths (inspired by the open strings of the Armenian *saz*), and a rhapsodic improvisational form of melody.

MILESTONES

1929	Enters Moscow Conservatory
1932	Joins Composers' Union
1933	Marries fellow Conservatory student Nina Makarova
1936	Premiere of Piano Concerto
1939	Awarded Order of Lenin
1940	Premiere of Violin Concerto
1948	Denounced as a formalist by Zhdanov, alongside Shostakovich and others
1973	Appointed Hero of Socialist Labour

KEY WORKS

GAYANEH

BALLET | 150 | 4

The first of Khachaturian's two balletic masterpieces, *Gayaneh* contains the famous "Sabre Dance," which soon became a hit for, among others, the Andrews Sisters (a fact that, along with Khachaturian's risky habit of wearing double-breasted "American" suits, may have led to his problems with Zhdanov in 1948). Almost as famous is the "Adagio," used by Stanley Kubrick in *2001: A Space Odyssey.*

SPARTACUS

BALLET | 140:00 | 4

This ballet portrays the heroic efforts of the slave Spartacus to free himself and his comrades from captivity. Given the date of the piece (1956), the conservatism of the musical language is astonishing. But so is the music's sheer Hollywood-ish orchestral bravura.

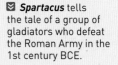

Spartacus tells the tale of a group of gladiators who defeat the Roman Army in the 1st century BCE.

Sergey **Prokofiev**

● **1891–1953**   ▥ **RUSSIAN**   ✍ **102**

Prokofiev had an immense natural gift as a composer and pianist. His pre-Revolutionary music is vivid, sarcastic, sometimes brutal; the later music is more measured and lyrical, and after his return to the Soviet Union, more conventional. Throughout his life Prokofiev kept his strong pictorial and dramatic sense, revealed as much in his "abstract" symphonies and sonatas as in his famous ballets.

>> **Though Prokofiev wrote** several "official pieces" for state occasions, his music was also criticized by the Soviet regime.

Life

An adored only child with a highly musical mother, Prokofiev had composed two operas by his 11th birthday. From 1905 he studied at the St. Petersburg Conservatory, where he quickly became known as an arrogant, rebellious composer of brashly modernist music. After the upheavals of the Bolshevik Revolution, in 1918 Prokofiev left for what he thought would be a short trip abroad. It turned out to be an 18-year sojourn, of which the first two were spent in the US. He scored an instant hit as a pianist, and received a commission for *The Love for Three Oranges*, the only one of his operas to win international fame in his lifetime. In 1921 his ballet *Chout* was a great success in Paris, and the following year he resettled, firstly in Bavaria, then Paris. The 1920s brought two further successes with the Ballets Russes: *Le Pas d'Acier* (*The Steel Step*) and *The Prodigal Son*. In between composing, Prokofiev made many successful tours as a pianist, to the US, Europe, and the Soviet Union. But he missed home. He started to accept Soviet commissions, and in 1935 returned to the Soviet Union, then in the grip of the Stalinist Terror. In the late 1940s he was criticized for "formalist tendencies" by the authorities. He died of a brain hemorrhage on the same day as Stalin.

Music

Up to the time of World War I there were two distinct strands in Prokofiev's music. There was a rich, post-Romantic mood, derived from Scriabin and Rachmaninoff, evident in works like the opera *The Fiery Angel*. Then there was a mood of biting sarcasm, revealed in such hectically rhythmic and dissonant pieces as the *Scythian Suite* and the piano work *Sarcasms*. Here the model was Stravinsky, with whom Prokofiev kept up a not always friendly rivalry. Prokofiev also had a quality all his own: this was a childlike playfulness, shown in a fondness for primary-color orchestration, and a tendency for the harmony to jump unexpectedly to distant chords, often within a single melodic phrase. But the chords themselves are not dissonant, and they always find their way back to their starting point. In the music of the Soviet period the dissonance and sarcasm withdraw, and the lyrical Prokofiev is revealed ever more clearly. The result in some people's eyes is disappointingly conventional, but the later works have their admirers too.

" I **abhor imitation** and I abhor the familiar. "

Sergey Prokofiev

MILESTONES

1913	Sensational premiere of Piano Concerto No. 2, Op. 16
1918	Travels to US via Siberia and Japan
1923	Settles in Paris after a year in Bavaria
1929	*The Prodigal Son*, Op. 46, premiered in Monte Carlo and Paris; *The Gambler*, Op. 24, premiered in Brussels

1935	Returns to Soviet Union in December
1936	*Peter and the Wolf*, based on a Russian folk tale written for chidren
1943	Completes draft of *War and Peace*, Op. 91, while evacuated to Alma-Ata
1945	Has serious concussion after a fall, which permanently weakens him

KEY WORKS

VIOLIN CONCERTO NO. 1, OP. 19

ORCHESTRAL   ⏱ 20:00   📖 3

Composed in 1917, in the same period as *Visions Fugitives*, the concerto was not premiered until 1923 in Paris. It has an unconventional form, with two slow movements framing a quicksilver, acid scherzo.

First movement (*andantino, andante assai*, 9:00) This begins with a radiantly lyrical theme, but soon the tempo quickens and the mood becomes brittle and strange, with a high-stepping balletic second theme. The reprise of the opening theme carries the music aloft to a shimmering, pianissimo ending.

Second movement (*scherzo, vivacissimo*, 4:00) The light-footed scherzo is brilliantly orchestrated. The contrasting second theme is a galumphing march, like a dance for trolls, whereas the ending is pure glittering color, the violin playing a stream of high harmonics.

Third movement (*moderato*, 7:00) A dry bassoon theme provides a neutral background for the lyrical violin. The bassoon theme's more emphatic return later on takes on a fugal texture. This leads to the climax, after which there is an exact reprise of the ending of the first movement.

ROMEO AND JULIET, OP. 64

BALLET   ⏱ 135:00   📖 3

Composed in 1934, this is a classic example of the Soviet taste for full-length, traditional ballets.

Act one The Prince of Verona's command that no one break the peace is portrayed in unusually sharp dissonance. Prokofiev lavishes three tender themes on Juliet, and portrays with great subtlety the moment when she sees herself in the mirror and realises she's no longer a girl. The ensuing "Masked Ball" where Juliet meets Romeo has some of Prokofiev's finest dance music.

Act two Juliet and Romeo are married in secret by Friar Lawrence in a marvelously tender and intimate scene. The fight scenes are full of restless, "cinematic" music.

Act three Prokofiev at first contrived a happy ending (this may have been a concession to the Soviet demand for optimism in art), but the original tragic ending was reinstated.

SYMPHONY NO. 5, OP. 100

ORCHESTRAL   ⏱ 42:00   📖 4

Composed in the darkest days of World War II, the premiere of this symphony in 1945 was heard against the thunderous background of an artillery salute. Prokofiev wrote that the piece portrayed "the grandeur of the human spirit." The affirmative final movement ends in jubilation, reflecting Soviet victories in the war.

VISIONS FUGITIVES, OP. 22

SOLO PIANO   📖 20

These 20 piano miniatures, by turns grotesque, tender, and sardonic, were written in 1915–17. The title comes from a line by the symbolist poet Balmont: "In every fugitive vision I see whole worlds: they change endlessly, flashing in playful rainbow colors."

⏏ **In this 1930s production** of Prokofiev's *Romeo and Juliet* by the Bolshoi Ballet, Galina Ulanova, creator of the role of Juliet, dances with Yuri Zhadonov.

Dmitri **Shostakovich**

🌐 1906–1975　　📕 RUSSIAN　　✍ 110

Alongside Benjamin Britten, Shostakovich is the most popular composer of the mid-20th century. His 15 symphonies are acknowledged as the greatest since Mahler's and his 15 string quartets the most significant since Bartók's. But he's also a controversial figure. Modernists dismissed him as a reactionary, or a lackey of the Soviet regime, and recent attempts to find anti-Stalinist messages in his music have aroused fierce debate.

⏏ **Though a controversial figure,** Shostakovich was the preeminent Russian composer of the Soviet era.

Life

Until the age of 11 Shostakovich lived a comfortable life in a well-off bourgeois Russian household. However, in October 1917 the Bolsheviks came to power, sweeping away the privileges of the middle class. After study at the St. Petersburg Conservatory, Shostakovich's first big success came with his Symphony No. 1, premiered in 1925, when he was only 19. He spent much of the 1920s and 30s writing film and theater scores to earn money, but, despite the frantic pace of work, he found time for a complicated love life. He married the physics student Nina Varzar in 1932, but had several affairs thereafter. Along with all creative artists in Russia at that time, Shostakovich's life was overshadowed by Stalin's repressive policies. In 1936 his opera *Lady Macbeth of the Mtsensk District* was attacked in the official newspaper *Pravda*. He eventually rehabilitated himself with his Symphony No. 5, but in 1948 he was attacked again for formalism. From the 1930s onward he was obliged to write optimistic "official" pieces alongside his "pure" symphonies and quartets. After Nina's death in 1954, Shostakovich remarried

twice, latterly to Irina Supinskaya, who outlived him. In the 1960s his health, which had never been strong, declined further, and much of his last years were spent in the hospital.

Music

Shostakovich's early works, such as the Symphony No. 1, have the exuberant balletic energy of Tchaikovsky and Stravinsky, and often a sarcastic spirit learned from Prokofiev. In the late 1920s and '30s two more ingredients entered the mix: the combination of grotesque parody and tragedy of Mahler, and the fierce Expressionism and social satire of Alban Berg's opera *Wozzeck*. At first the result was gleeful and exuberant, as in the opera *The Nose* and his 1936 hit *Lady Macbeth of the Mtsensk District*, an opera that proved to be the watershed in Shostakovich's life. After it was attacked, and he was disgraced, his music lost its high spirits. The parody was still there, but it had become anguished, and the general tone became angular, lean, and serious. In the Symphony No. 5, Shostakovich strikes a delicate balance between satisfying the communist regime's demand for simplicity and optimism (i.e., "representing contemporary reality in a musical language comprehensible to The People") and expressing his own views on the regime. What those views were is still a matter of debate, but there are many signs that in later life he hated it, as witnessed by the overblown fake triumphalism of Symphony No. 10's finale, the use of Jewish melodies (anti-Semitism was rife in Stalinist Russia) and his attraction to dissident poets, like Yevtushenko, whose verses appear in Shostakovich's late, bleak Symphony No. 13.

> ❝ To me he seemed like a trapped man, whose only **wish** was to be left **alone**, to the **peace of his own art** and to the **tragic destiny** to which he had been **forced** to **resign himself.** ❞
> **Nicholas Nabokov** on meeting Shostakovich in 1949 in New York

MILESTONES

1917	Bolshevik Revolution	**1949**	Visits US as part of Soviet-sponsored "Peace Conference"; forced to declare allegiance to Stalinist esthetics
1919	Enters St. Petersburg Conservatory		
1926	Symphony No. 1, Op. 10, wins acclaim		
1934	Composers' Union promulgates official esthetic of Socialist Realism	**1953**	Death of Stalin brings relaxation of controls on expression; premiere of Symphony No. 10
1936	*Lady Macbeth* condemned in *Pravda*		
1937	Premiere of Symphony No. 5, Op. 47	**1954**	Wife Nina Varzar dies; his mother dies the following year
1941	Hitler invades Soviet Union	**1960**	Joins Communist Party
1942	Premiere of Symphony No. 7 in Moscow; American premiere conducted by Toscanini; symphony becomes symbol of resistance to fascism	**1962**	Premiere of "Babi Yar"
		1966	Suffers heart attack; is made Hero of Socialist Labor and receives second Order of Lenin
1948	Accused of "antidemocratic tendencies" by cultural commissar	**1972**	Travels to East and West Germany, and England to meet his friend Benjamin Britten

⏏ **Shostakovich (right) worked as a fireman** during the Siege of Leningrad. In 1941, the first year of the siege, he composed his Symphony No. 7.

KEY WORKS

LADY MACBETH OF THE MTSENSK DISTRICT, OP. 29

OPERA   ⏳ 155:00   ▭ 4   🎭🎼🎵

Shostakovich's second opera was based on a brutal tale about a woman who murders her father-in-law and husband. He composed a brilliant score mingling tragedy, comedy, and satire. The seamless, symphonic texture incorporates tension-building orchestral interludes between scenes, inspired perhaps by Berg's *Wozzeck*. The erotic scenes shocked Prokofiev and the author of "Muddle Instead of Music" (in *Pravda*) who complained that "... 'love' is smeared all over the opera in the most 'vulgar' manner."
Act one Katerina is bored in her marriage to Zinovy. The new laborer, Sergei, arrives, tries to molest the cook, Aksinka, and is wrestled to the ground by the outraged Katerina. By the end of the act Sergei and Katerina become lovers.
Act two Katerina's father-in-law catches Sergei leaving Katerina's room and thrashes him. He orders Katerina to make a meal for him, which she poisons. Later Zinovy returns and is beaten to death by Katerina and Sergei.
Act three Katerina and Sergei are about to marry. An old peasant finds Zinovy's corpse and runs off to tell the police. At the wedding reception the police arrive and the couple give themselves up.

Act four Katerina and Sergei are now convicts in Siberia. Sergei rejects Katerina and makes advances to Sonyetka. At the end, the infuriated Katerina throws Sonyetka and herself into the river.

STRING QUARTET NO. 8, OP. 110

CHAMBER   ⏳ 19:00   ▭ 5   🎵

In 1960 Shostakovich witnessed the devastation wrought on Dresden by the Allies during World War II, and in a mere three days wrote this piece.
First movement (*largo*, 5:00) This begins with Shostakovich's personal musical "cipher," DSCH (the notes D, E flat, C, and B) in the cello, which slowly ascends through the parts in a canon. The bleak mood is sustained by a quotation of the first symphony.
Second movement (*allegro molto*, 2:00) This scherzo has a driving rhythm taken from the fifth symphony combined with DSCH in a canon. This builds to a climax in which the Jewish theme from Shostakovich's Piano Trio is played fortissimo.

⏩ *Lady Macbeth*, staged here by the English National Opera, was originally suppressed for being "too divorced from the proletariat."

>> **It was at the Composers' Union** at Nos. 10–11 Bryusov Pereulok that Shostakovich was forced to read an apology for works that deviated from Socialist Realism.

⬆ **Yevgeny Mravinsky** unveiled the Symphony No.10 with the Leningrad Philharmonic Orchestra.

Third movement (*allegretto*, 4:00) A varied reprise of the previous movement, refracted through the rhythm of a diabolical waltz.

Fourth movement (*largo*, 5:00) A high note on the first violin is accompanied by three terrifying chords followed by various themes from the Cello Concerto, Symphonies Nos. 10 and 11, DSCH, the revolutionary song "Tormented by grievous bondage," and *Lady Macbeth*.

Fifth movement (*largo*, 3:00) This reprise of the opening fugue combines with a new lullaby-like countersubject, which descends to C minor and the DSCH motive.

SYMPHONY NO. 10 IN E MINOR, OP. 95

ORCHESTRAL	⏳ 51:00	📖 4	🔀

This symphony was written in 1953, the year of Stalin's death. Some see its second movement as a menacing portrayal of one of Stalin's military parades. As is so often the case with Shostakovich, the work's apparently triumphal ending is deceptive.

First movement (*moderato*, 22:00) This immense sonata-form movement has a dark, uncertain first subject, and an anxious, wavering second subject like a distorted waltz.

Second movement (*allegro*, 4:00) The ruthlessly aggressive scherzo is played at breakneck speed.

Third movement (*allegretto*, 11:00) In the first part a forthright woodwind theme is framed by a quiet, enigmatic theme in the violins. Hidden in the woodwind theme is Shostakovich's personal music cipher DSCH (D, E flat, C, B), which is more prominent later in the movement, and in the quiet wistful coda.

Fourth movement (*andante—allegro*, 14:00) After an Andante introduction with a plaintive melody for woodwind, the Allegro bursts into life with a cheekily trivial theme. But the cheeriness is constantly undercut by memories of the Andante opening, and of Shostakovich's cipher, which entwines in majestic counterpoint with the main theme at the end.

CONCERTO FOR PIANO, TRUMPET, AND STRINGS, OP. 35

CONCERTO	⏱ 22:00	▭ 4	♫ ◉

This concerto is heavily influenced by the clean-cut neo-Classicism of composers such as Paul Hindemith. The first movement pits a nostalgic piano theme against a Baroque-sounding military fanfare on trumpet, while the second is an elegiac waltz. The third is full of busy neo-Classical counterpoint, and the last is one of Shostakovich's most effervescent finales.

SYMPHONY NO. 13, OP. 113

ORCHESTRAL	⏱ 45:00	▭ 5	♫ ♉ ♨

This piece, consisting of settings of poetry by dissident poet Yevgeny Yevtushenko, begins with "Babi Yar," which describes a massacre of Jews in Russia by the Nazis in 1943. The music has the bare, hollow style typical of Shostakovich's late

music. After the symphony's premiere, Yevtushenko was forced to add a stanza to his poem claiming that Russians and Ukrainians had died alongside the Jews at Babi Yar.

SYMPHONY NO. 5, OP. 47

ORCHESTRAL	⏱ 50:00	▭ 4	♫

The most played and discussed of all Shostakovich's works, this symphony encapsulates the agonies of his creative life. Subtitled "A Soviet Artist's Practical Creative Reply to Just Criticism," it begins with a great despairing outcry, followed by a long, numb lament. Of the apparently optimistic finale, Shostakovich said, "It's as if someone was beating you with a stick and saying, 'Your business is rejoicing, your business is rejoicing.'"

INFLUENCES

Because of his isolation from the West, Shostakovich's influence on the wider world of Classical music has been minimal. However, his influence on Russian composers, particularly Sofia Gubaidulina, Galina Ustvolskaya, and Alfred Schnittke, has been immense.

⬢ **Shostakovich** wrote several film scores, including this one for *The New Babylon*, directed by Grigori Kozintsev and Leonid Trauberg.

《 **The famous Russian violinist** Maxim Vengerov (left) performs Shostakovich's Piano Trio No. 2 at the Barbican in London.

Sofia **Gubaidulina**

● 1931–   ♙ RUSSIAN   ✍ 100

With a Tatar father and Russian mother, Gubaidulina mixes East and West in her deep, spiritual music. It found disfavor at times during the Soviet era, when she made a living from film scores. In 1990, however, she was invited onto the State prize-awarding committee and has received numerous prizes herself. Her affecting, mystic music mixes unusual textures and instruments in techniques ranging from microtones to mathematically generated rhythmic structures. Her violin concerto *Offertorium* helped establish her in the West.

MILESTONES

1978	Composes *De profundis* for accordion
1982	*Seven Last Words* for cello, bayan, strings
2000	Writes *The Passion According to St. John*
2007	*In Tempus Praesens*, concerto for violin and orchestra; *Ravvedimento*, for cello and guitar quartet
2011	*Labyrinth* for 12 celli

⬒ **The Kronos Quartet,** renowned for its love of the new, commissions work from Gubaidulina.

Rodion **Shchedrin**

● 1932–   ♙ RUSSIAN   ✍ 120

A virtuoso pianist, Shchedrin became professor of composition at the Moscow Conservatory in 1964 and stayed in official favor in the USSR, despite his refusal to endorse the invasion of Czechoslovakia in 1968. Since 1990 he has received many commissions and spends a lot of time in Germany. His compositions mix cultured music references with humor in styles from jazz to folk music and atonality. He has impeccable academic credentials, but his music (such as his ballet *Carmen Suite*) also enjoys popular appeal, both within Russia and increasingly outside. He has recorded his own vibrant, witty piano music, including five concertos and the 1972 *Polyphonic Notebook*. His output includes ballets and operas, orchestral, choral, and chamber works, and a Japanese musical.

» **Shchedrin is married** to ballerina Maya Plisetskaya, for whom he created the ballet *Carmen Suite*, an affectionately joking tribute to Bizet's opera.

MILESTONES

1970	Writes *24 Preludes and Fugues*, piano
1973	Succeeds Shostakovich as president of Composers' Union of USSR
1999	Composes Piano Concerto No. 5
2006	*Boyarinya Morozova*, opera
2011	*Double concerto* for piano and cello

Alfred **Schnittke**

● 1934–1998   🏴 RUSSIAN   ✍ 246

Alfred Schnittke is easily the best-known Russian composer since Shostakovich. He achieved that eminence through the shocking emotional rawness of his music, which to some people is the authentic voice of modern spiritual deracination. However, his critics say that this bleakness is only a reflection of the conditions peculiar to Soviet Russia, and that his hyperintensity veers close to musical chaos.

Schnittke grew up torn between different cultural roots: Russian, Jewish, and Austro-German. He also had to live with the Soviet hostility to anything that smacked of experimentation. The result is a music of spiritual torment that veers between Mahlerian irony and the bleakness of late Shostakovich. However, Schnittke goes much further than Mahler or Shostakovich, creating tension from the coexistence within single pieces of many stylistic references, a technique he dubbed "polystylism." In his music, as exemplified in his Concerto Grosso No. 1, a phrase of Mozartian sweetness can turn into a dissonant scream and a Vivaldi concerto Allegro can become a "danse macabre."

MILESTONES

1953	Enters Moscow Conservatory
1958	Union of Composers condemns his oratorio *Nagasaki*
1962	Begins career as freelance composer
1974	Composers' Union chief condemns his emblematic Symphony No. 1
1990	Moves permanently to Hamburg

◀ Schnittke's *Requiem* of 1975 expressed spiritual deracination at its most extreme. The fall of communism has allowed his music to be more widely heard in Russia.

KEY WORKS

CONCERTO GROSSO NO. 1

CHAMBER   ⏱ 32:00   📖 6   ♔

This piece reworks material from a film score. He achieves an alienating effect by sampling Baroque music, mixing microintervals and chromaticism, and quoting "banal popular music which enters as if from the outside with a disruptive effect."

SYMPHONY NO. 1

ORCHESTRAL   ⏱ 66:00   📖 4   ♫

One of Schnittke's most extreme works, his first symphony exemplifies, as he once said, all the ingredients of his life's music. It begins with the players arriving one by one and improvising chaotically until a signal from the conductor brings silence. Toward the end they leave, only to return and begin the work all over again.

VIOLA CONCERTO

ORCHESTRAL   ⏱ 35:00   📖 3   ♫ ✆

Written for the Russian violist Yuri Bashmet, this piece has a moment which starkly illustrates Schnittke's way of making familiar things seem strange. The violist launches a conventional-sounding phrase, which mounts higher and higher until it becomes a deranged scream.

Kurt **Weill**

◗ 1900–1950   🏳 GERMAN   ✍ c.100

Weill is one of few composers to make the transition successfully from modernist art music to the Broadway stage. With Bertold Brecht, he developed a sophisticated form of political theater that satirized contemporary life and incorporated popular music. After emigrating to the US, he adapted these ideas to the stage, writing several hit works and having a huge influence on the development of the musical.

During his early career in Weimar Germany, Weill embraced the *neue Sachlichkeit* (new objectivity) of Paul Hindemith and Ernst Krenek—music of cool modernism, consciously detached from the "excesses" of the Romantic era. Weill's interests became increasingly political, and he began a collaboration with left-wing playwright Bertold Brecht that revolutionized music theater by openly satirizing the establishment. After condemnation by the Nazis in 1935, he emigrated to the US and turned to composing for Broadway. His style, always deliberately referential and incorporating elements of popular music and jazz, proved ideally suited to this new medium.

MILESTONES	
1918	Attends Berlin's Hochschule für Musik; taught by Humperdinck and Busoni
1924	Composes Violin Concerto
1926	Writes *Der Protagonist*, opera; marries singer Lotte Lenya
1927	First collaboration with Brecht: result is *Mahagonny*, a Singspiel for radio
1928	Composes *The Threepenny Opera* and *The Tsar Has His Photograph Taken*, operas
1936	*Johnny Johnson* is his first Broadway work
1946	Elected as only composer-member of the US Playwrights' Producing Company

KEY WORKS

⤢ **The world of 1920s** Berlin lowlife and the theater were both inspirational to Weill.

THE RISE AND FALL OF THE CITY OF MAHAGONNY

OPERA   ⏱ 120:00   📖 3   🎭🎻🎵

This full-length opera, based on a radio Singspiel that was Weill's first collaboration with Brecht, is a biting satire on capitalist society. It tells the story of three escaped convicts, who, stranded in the US during the gold rush, decide to establish a city, Mahagonny, devoted to the hedonistic pleasures of drink, women, and gambling. Business booms and so do prices. Jim, a gold prospector, is unable to pay his debts and is executed by electric chair. The people demonstrate, while the city collapses in flames. Musically, *Mahagonny* is a curious blend of abrasive neo-Classicism in the mold of Hindemith, pastiche of grand opera, and popular jazz and cabaret. By juxtaposing these styles, Weill adds bite to the satirical libretto.

STREET SCENE

OPERA   ⏱ 130:00   📖 2   🎭🎻🎵

After success with stage musicals, Weill wanted to write an "American opera" in the mold of a verismo opera, with most of the dialogue sung, rather than acted, but still based on the musical virtues of Broadway. The story he chose was Elmer Rice's *Street Scene*, about a tragic murder in the immigrant community. A bullying husband catches his wife in flagrante with her lover, shoots them dead, and, after briefly escaping, is caught. The musical styles are diverse, from Anna's touching aria "Still I could never believe," reminiscent of Puccini, to pure 1940s jive and all manner of blues and jazz in between. Although this multiplicity of reference led critics to question whether Weill's vision of an American opera was truly fulfilled, *Street Scene* is well crafted and enjoyable.

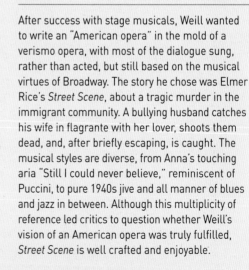

Olivier **Messiaen**

● 1908–1992   ◍ FRENCH   ◿ 74

Olivier Messiaen is one of the most paradoxical figures in music. A great radical of the 20th century, on a par with Debussy or John Cage, he was also a deeply traditional figure, serenely convinced of the truths of the Catholic faith. Messiaen saw no contradiction between these attitudes. He felt he had to develop his radically new language in order to give his fervently held beliefs the most vivid expression.

Messiaen's early influences were Wagner, Debussy, and Mussorgsky, and later, while at the Paris Conservatoire, Christian chant and folk music. His early piece "Le banquet céleste" already has the essential elements of Messiaen: it was scored for his own instrument, the organ; it has a Catholic subject; and it seems to bring time to a halt, through its incredibly slow tempo. Over the next 64 years Messiaen invented many other ways of loosening the grip of measured time on music, to give a foretaste of the eternity of heaven. Among these were rhythmic modes learned from ancient Indian sources, the use of patterned, repetitive forms, and imitation of birdsong.

MILESTONES	
1931	Becomes organist at La Trinité
1932	Marries violinist Claire Delbos
1936	Founds "La Jeune France" (with others) in opposition to neo-Classicism
1940	Interned in a POW camp in Poland
1942	Begins teaching at Conservatoire
1956	Composes *Réveil des Oiseaux*
1961	Marries Yvonne Loriod
1965	Begins work on *La transfiguration de notre seigneur Jésus-Christ*, choral
1984	Premiere of *St. François d'Assise*, opera

KEY WORKS

TURANGALÎLA SYMPHONY

ORCHESTRAL   ⧗ 70:00   ▥ 10   ♫ 🎵

One of a cycle of three pieces based on the Tristan legend and its theme of boundless love, this piece includes a prominent part for ondes martenot, whose tremulous, swooping melodiousness is an essential ingredient of its fascination. The ten movements alternate passionate love-music with austere rhythmic games.

QUARTET FOR THE END OF TIME

CHAMBER   ⧗ 50:00   ▥ 8   ✙

Messiaen composed this quartet for violin, cello, clarinet, and piano while being held in a German prisoner of war camp in Silesia in Poland during World War II. The premiere took place one freezing night, on a piano with faulty keys

and a cello with only three strings. The piece is full of Messiaen's apocalyptic imagery of angels, rainbows, and birds (for Messiaen, birds were God's true musicians). The opening "Liturgie de cristal" has repeating harmonic and rhythmic cycles of different lengths for cello and piano.

VISIONS DE L'AMEN

DUO   ⧗ 50:00   ▥ 7   ✙

A vast, tumultuous cycle of pieces for two pianos, first performed in 1943 by Messiaen and his wife-to-be, Yvonne Loriod, whose amazing virtuosity inspired the piece. It began a new era in Messiaen's creative life in which the piano became central. The titles "Amen of Creation" and "Amen of the Agony of Jesus" give a flavor of the apocalyptic imagery of the piece to glorify God in his creation.

⌂ **Organist at the church of La Trinité** in Paris for 60 years, Messiaen's work was both an expression of his Catholicism and a joyful celebration of earthly life.

Michael **Tippett**

🌑 **1905–1998**   📕 **BRITISH**   ✎ **73**

Tippett is the only rival to Benjamin Britten for the title of Britain's most significant composer since World War II, although he has only recently found a place in the hearts of music lovers. In his determination to articulate an all-embracing worldview in his music, he is almost unique; the only comparable figure is Olivier Messiaen. But unlike Messiaen, Tippett had to work out his own salvation.

» **Many of Tippett's works** explore a world illuminated by Jungian theories of psychology.

His socialist sympathies led him to found the South London Orchestra, composed of unemployed musicians. But in the mid-1930s he withdrew from politics, and after a personal crisis following the breakup of his first serious gay relationship, he began an intense engagement with Jungian analysis. By the late-1930s he'd formed his deeply spiritual and yet agnostic beliefs. For him life was a never-ending process of uncovering the dark and light aspects of the personality, and reconciling them into wholeness. From *A Child of our Time* onward, all his art was dedicated to articulating this worldview.

In the 1960s and '70s his delighted discovery of America and its music brought on an Indian summer of creativity. In his old age he gained the reputation of a sage, particularly among a new, young audience.

Life

The two important factors in Tippett's childhood were his rural surroundings (he spent almost his whole life in the English countryside) and his freethinking parents, who gave him a stubborn independence of mind. He was slow to develop, spending five years at London's Royal College of Music, returning for a further two years from 1928–30. During the 1930s he taught French to earn a living, and composed on the side.

Music

Tippett once declared that in an age of "shattered dreams" it was the duty of an artist to create images of "generous, abounding beauty." He achieved this many times, but not without an immense struggle, first to work out a worldview, and then to forge a personal musical language. At first this language took the form of a rich, very English Romanticism with a folklike flavor.

In the early 1960s, Tippett's music underwent a dramatic change. The new style consisted of accumulations of short, contrasted fragments and used a much more astringent harmonic language. But the urge to ecstasy and transcendence was still there. The works of the 1980s and '90s incorporated American pop influences into his earlier styles. The results were exuberant, if not always coherent.

❝ I like to think of **composing as a physical business.** I compose **at the piano** and like to feel **involved in my work with my hands.** ❞

Michael Tippett

MILESTONES

1923	Enters Royal College of Music in London
1928	Settles in Oxted, Surrey
1935	Joins British Communist Party, but leaves within a few months
1939	Undergoes Jungian analysis after personal crisis
1940	Becomes music director of Morley College, London

1943	Imprisoned for refusing to join armed forces during World War II
1965	Visits Aspen Summer School in Colorado, the beginning of his love affair with America
1970	Moves to rural Wiltshire; third opera, *The Knot Garden*, premiered
1983	Appointed to the Order of Merit

KEY WORKS

THE MIDSUMMER MARRIAGE

OPERA   ⏱ 150:00   📖 3   👐 ♿ ♫

Tippett's first opera was six years in the making. Written in his early lyrical style, it encapsulates his vision of life as a struggle to reconcile warring elements within the individual and between peoples. The protagonists of the opera, Mark and Jenifer, refuse to accept aspects of each other. Mark feels Jenifer is too emotional and intuitive; she feels he is too rational.

The action begins at dawn on Midsummer's Day. Jenifer, daughter of the manipulative and powerful King Fisher, has decided to elope with Mark. But at Jenifer's insistence their marriage is delayed by a spiritual quest, involving journeys to Heaven and Hell. In act two, the focus shifts to a second couple, Jack and Bella, and to the dance rituals of the supernatural beings who are the shadowy counterparts of the human characters. In act three, King Fisher's attempts to manipulate his daughter and Bella fail. Jack and Bella go off happily together. King Fisher tries to unveil the mysterious soothsayer Sosostris, but this causes his death. Mark and Jenifer reappear and are engulfed in the flames of an ecstatic ritual fire dance. Dawn then rises and they can celebrate their union.

A CHILD OF OUR TIME

ORATORIO   ⏱ 60:00   📖 3   👐 ♿ ♫

This piece established Tippett's reputation at the age of 39. It was prompted by the shooting of a German official by a Polish Jewish agitator in 1938, which became the pretext for a pogrom. In Tippett's piece this event becomes a symbol for the oppression of the individual by dark collective forces. But the libretto suggests that these forces are in fact our own faults, projected onto other groups, who are then perceived as hostile. Tippett followed the advice of T.S. Eliot to write his own libretto, a practice he always followed thereafter. The piece is a kind of modern Passion along the lines of J.S. Bach's *St. Matthew Passion*, with the Lutheran chorales replaced by Negro spirituals. The closing ensemble sums up Tippett's philosophy: "I would know my shadow and my light, So shall I at last be whole."

SYMPHONY NO. 3

ORCHESTRAL   ⏱ 55:00   📖 4   ♫ ♿

This is a bleak, questioning piece, cast in four sections. In the finale Tippett parodies the vision of universal brotherhood expressed in Beethoven's Symphony No. 9, setting it off against the blues. The soprano sings Tippett's own text, which embraces both humanism and the horrors of Auschwitz, and at the end offers a small ray of hope ("What though the dream crack, we shall remake it").

KING PRIAM

OPERA   ⏱ 125:00   📖 3   👐 ♿ ♫

King Priam marked a startling new departure in Tippett's style. The music is made of short, hard-edged, contrasting blocks—a "mosaic of musical gestures," as Tippett put it.

🔼 *King Priam,* first performed at the Coventry Cathedral Festival in 1962, has had several successful revivals. This is the English National Opera production of 1995.

Benjamin **Britten**

● 1913–1976   ⚑ BRITISH   ✍ 267

Benjamin Britten is the only British composer since Elgar to have achieved worldwide renown. He single-handedly created a school of British opera, and left a large body of instrumental and vocal music which gives fresh new life to the forms and harmonies of Western music. By the 1950s he had become a national institution, and today his popularity and musical influence seem more secure than ever.

» **Born in Lowestoft,** Britten was inspired by his native county of Suffolk, where he also began the institution of the Aldeburgh Festival at the Snape Maltings.

Life

A precociously gifted child, Britten began several years of study with Frank Bridge at the age of 11. They proved to be far more fruitful than his later years at the Royal College of Music. His plans to study in Vienna with Alban Berg were quashed on the grounds that Berg would be a bad influence, but in 1935 Britten found an equally bad influence at home, in the shape of the poet W.H. Auden. He collaborated with Auden on films for the GPO film unit, and on several mordant satires, including *Our*

Hunting Fathers. In 1939 he met the love of his life, the tenor Peter Pears. They set up home in 1945 in the Suffolk coastal village of Aldeburgh, where Britten would remain for the rest of his life. Many of Britten's greatest roles were created for Pears, including the lead in *Peter Grimes*, which reopened Sadler's Wells Opera in 1945. From 1947 the newly formed English Opera Group would be the center of Britten's operatic endeavors, although there were big commissions from Covent Garden (*Billy Budd*, *Gloriana*), BBC television (*Owen Wingrave*) and, most prestigious of all, the Anglican Church (the *War Requiem*, written for the reopening of Coventry Cathedral). His last decade was clouded by ill-health, although his very last works are among his greatest.

Music

The numerous works of Britten's childhood reveal one of the great prodigies of all time, with an amazing variety of styles ranging from Viennese Expressionism to modal lyricism. The stylistic uncertainty persisted into his 20s, although certain traits emerged that would be lifelong. There's a fondness for parody and stark funereal tragedy akin to Mahler, and a debt to the clear, clean textures of Stravinsky's neo-Classicism. In *Peter Grimes* all these things come together in a brilliant, miraculous synthesis. By this date nearly all of Britten's vocabulary was in place, the only major additions being the sound-world of Balinese music, as revealed in the ballet *The Prince of the Pagodas*, and in the 1960s a Japanese spareness and economy, expressed most directly in the *Three Church Parables*. These opened the final phase in Britten's music, in which he refined his style to its essence.

MILESTONES

1924	Meets adventurous composer Frank Bridge, who becomes his mentor
1930	Enters Royal College of Music, London
1935	Meets W.H. Auden
1939	Leaves wartime England for the US with tenor Peter Pears
1942	Reading Suffolk poet George Crabbe, especially "The Borough," brings on Britten's decision to return home
1945	June 7 premiere of *Peter Grimes*, Op. 33, makes Britten world famous

1948	Aldeburgh Festival founded: this soon becomes the center of Britten's musical life
1951	Premiere of *Billy Budd*, Op. 50, at Covent Garden
1962	Premiere of *War Requiem*, Op. 66
1964	Premiere of church parable *Curlew River*, Op. 71, the first of his late, lean works
1973	Premiere of Britten's last opera, *Death in Venice*, Op 88, with Pears in main role of Aschenbach

KEY WORKS

PETER GRIMES, OP. 33

OPERA 150:00 4

Britten's first opera has an anti-hero: Peter Grimes, an outcast from the Borough, a fishing village not unlike the Aldeburgh Britten had recently settled in. He's a sadistic bully, who wants to get rich and marry; but in Britten's opera he also has a poetic side. The wonderful orchestral interludes (known as the *Four Sea Interludes*) may have been suggested by Alban Berg's opera *Wozzeck*, while the saucy tavern music shows the influence of Gershwin's *Porgy and Bess*.

Act one The opening courtroom scene shows Britten's gift for comedy (later expressed more fully in *Albert Herring*). The following scene where Grimes recruits a new apprentice is a brilliant portrayal of village small-mindedness.

Act two Grimes's mistreatment of the boy becomes clear in Scene 1, and in Scene 2 the boy falls to his death (notice this appearance, early in Britten's career, of the theme of innocence abused). In the intervening interlude comes Britten's brilliant reinvention of an old form, the passacaglia.

Act three After a jolly dancing scene with a brilliant evocation of rustic bands, after which a posse is organized to hunt for Grimes. But his suicide (set to music which is brilliantly understated for some, and a disappointment to others) thwarts their revenge.

TURN OF THE SCREW, OP. 54

OPERA 103:00 2

With his small chamber orchestra, Britten invents a fascinating sound world that takes familiar symbols of innocence—the high tinkly sound of the celesta, children's voices, simple folk songs—and gives them a subtle twist that makes them appear sinister.

Act one (53:00) The Governess's arrival at the house to look after Miles and his sister Flora starts well, but soon the ghosts of the dead Quint and Miss Jessel appear, and the Governess is horrified to discover that the children are unafraid of them. The act climaxes in a sensuously uncanny duet between Jessel and Quint, one of the great moments in Britten's operas.

Act two (50:00) The Governess challenges the children to reveal their knowledge, but is rebuffed. She wrests Miles away from Quint's evil influence, but he dies, and the opera ends with her heartbroken rendition of Miles's song "Malo."

> It is **cruel,** you know, that **music** should be **so beautiful.** It has the beauty of **loneliness** and of pain… The beauty of disappointment and never-satisfied love.
> **Benjamin Britten**

SERENADE FOR TENOR, HORN, AND STRINGS, OP. 31

ORCHESTRAL	⏱ 25:00	📖 8	

Of Britten's five song cycles for voice and instruments, this is probably the greatest. It consists of six songs in a predominantly meditative or nocturnal mood, framed by a prologue and epilogue for solo horn.

YOUNG PERSON'S GUIDE TO THE ORCHESTRA, OP. 34

ORCHESTRAL	⏱ 16:00	📖 1	

One of Britten's most irresistibly ebullient works, this piece leads the listener through each section of the orchestra. It ends with a brilliant fugue, out of which the theme majestically emerges.

☑ **Britten's opera** for children *Let's Make an Opera!* in rehearsal at Aldeburgh in Suffolk, his home town.

BILLY BUDD, OP. 50

OPERA	⏱ 150:00	📖 4	

This profound exploration of Britten's favourite theme—the helplessness of innocence and goodness in the face of evil—contains some of his most gripping inventions, including the desperately sad chorus of seamen and Billy's lullaby sung the night before his execution—a perfect example of Britten's ability to plumb emotional depths with the most hackneyed materials.

INFLUENCES

Britten's influence has been most marked in Britain, where his interest in arranging Early Music and folk song has been as important as his own music. He is revered by composers who share his concern for reinvigorating simple tonal devices.

Yrjö **Kilpinen**

1892–1959 | FINNISH | c.750

Kilpinen was almost exclusively a composer of songs, writing over 700, but only half were published. After training in Helsinki, he traveled throughout Scandinavia and central Europe, and, in the 1930s, he was particularly popular in Nazi Germany, where he was seen as a Lieder composer in the tradition of Schubert or Wolf. However, his austere and bare style was neither modernist nor Romantic. Many of the poems he set were Finnish or Swedish, although he wrote 75 songs to German texts by Morgenstern.

MILESTONES

1920	Writes Leino songs; reputation grows
1922	Concentrates on Swedish poets
1923	First concerts of his works, Helsinki
1928	Composes Tunturilauluja; writes *Lieder der Liebe, Lieder um den Tod*
1954	*Hochgebirgswinter* published
1955	Starts Savonlinna Music Days

Elisabeth **Lutyens**

1906–1983 | ENGLISH | 190

Daughter of the architect Sir Edwin, Lutyens had a turbulent personal and professional life. She was a radical innovator and wrote uncompromisingly modern expressionist works, but also had to produce film and radio music to support her four children. Notorious for her dismissal of English pastoral music (such as that of Vaughan Williams) as "the cowpat school," she often felt isolated and met with incomprehension from the music establishment, whose recognition of her consistent achievement came late.

MILESTONES

1940	Composes Chamber Concerto No. 1
1952	Writes String Quartet No. 6
1957	*De amore*, cantata, produced
1972	*Time Off? Not a Ghost of a Chance!*, opera, performed

Elizabeth **Maconchy**

1907–1994 | ENGLISH | c.200

The only musician in her family, Maconchy studied at Prague Conservatory and was influenced by the urgent energy of Janáček and Bartók. Her suite *The Land* triumphed in a London Proms concert and launched a highly successful composing career, briefly interrupted by tuberculosis. Although a placid person, her music can be immensely passionate. Her ten string quartets—rhythmic and profoundly argued works—are a major achievement. She also wrote effective music for amateurs and children.

MILESTONES

1957	Writes *The Sofa*, first of three operas
1981	*My Dark Heart*, song cycle, performed

Gian Carlo **Menotti**

1911–2007 | AMERICAN | 70

Born and brought up in Italy, where he wrote two operas before entering the Milan Conservatory at 13, Menotti settled in the US, becoming a versatile director, librettist, and composer of stage works. He directed many film versions of his works, whose popular success is due to their light and open orchestral textures and memorable melodies. His TV opera *Amahl and the Night Visitors* has been broadcast annually since 1951.

MILESTONES

1946	Writes *The Telephone*, one-act opera
1950	*The Consul*, first full-length opera
1951	*Amahl and the Night Visitors*, first opera for TV, broadcast
1958	Founds Festival of Two Worlds, Italy
1976	Composes *The Halcyon*, symphony
1986	*Goya*, opera, performed

Roberto **Gerhard**

🌑 1896–1970　　🏴 SPANISH　　✍ 130

From a multicultural European background, Gerhard considered himself firmly Catalan, but settled in England to escape the Spanish Civil War. His music combines Spanish nationalism with modernism (he studied with both Pedrell and Schoenberg), and he wrote everything from innovative TV and radio incidental music to pioneering works for tape. All his work has imaginative genius and color—his Symphony No. 3 reflects the feeling of a transatlantic flight. After a precarious career, serious recognition eventually came in the 1960s, and his music was widely performed.

MILESTONES

1915	Teaches music in Barcelona
1939	Settles in Cambridge, England
1941	*Don Quixote*, ballet, performed
1947	Writes *The Duenna*, opera
1952	Composes Symphony No. 1
1959	*Lament on the Death of a Bullfighter*, speaker and tape

🔼 **In Barcelona,** Gerhard studied piano with Granados and composition with Carlos Pedrell, who aroused his interest in Catalan folk music.

Nikos **Skalkottas**

🌑 1904–1949　　🏴 GREEK　　✍ 100+

Now considered one of the most significant Greek composers of the 20th century, Skalkottas was largely unrecognized during his lifetime. After studying at the Athens conservatory, he moved to Berlin, where he studied composition with Weill and Schoenberg before moving back to Greece in 1933. In a tragically short career, he wrote an enormous number of works in all genres except opera, but struggled to get it performed and generally got a hostile reception. His idiosyncratic style, often using Schoenberg's 12-tone technique but also in a more traditional idiom influenced by Greek folk song, was too modern for conservative Greek audiences, and he was forced to earn his living as a rank-and-file violinist. Undeterred, he continued writing in his uncompromising style, bringing a Greek vitality to the dry academicism of serial technique, and applying the rigor of the German avant-garde to his beloved Greek folk music. In addition to complex large-scale works for orchestra, including six ballet scores, and the extensive concertos for piano and every member of the string family, he wrote a large number of smaller pieces for chamber groups and solo piano. In the 1950s and '60s a fresh appreciation of his work revealed colorful and energetic music composed with meticulous craftsmanship, and the tonal orchestral works in particular, such as the *36 Greek Dances*, gained the popularity they deserved.

MILESTONES

1940	Writes the last of his four String Quartets
1940s	Puts together a collection of essays on music and a treatise "The Technique of Orchestration"; published posthumously
1941	Works on the huge set of 32 Piano Pieces
1941-45	Germany occupies Greece and Skalkottas is held in an internment camp
1942-43	*The Return of Ulysses*
1948-49	*The Sea*, his last major work

Henri **Dutilleux**

🌐 1916–   📖 FRENCH   ✎ 50

Henri Dutilleux, one of France's most distinguished post-war composers, has led a quiet, reclusive life away from the public eye. Since he retired as head of music commissions at French Radio in 1963, he has focused all his energies on composition. His works have the typical French virtues of a subtle and sensuous palette of instrumental color and an

ornamented form of melody. They are like a series of subtle half-hints, where nothing is ever stated definitively—no sooner does a melodic or harmonic shape emerge than it is transformed into something new. Even though he has an international reputation, his ruthless self-criticism has kept his work list relatively small.

MILESTONES	
1938	Wins Prix de Rome with cantata, *L'anneau du roi*
1942	Conducts choir at the Paris Opéra
1946	Composes Piano Sonata, Op. 1
1951	Symphony No. 1 premiered
1985	Premiere of *L'arbre des songes*, concerto
2009	*Le temps l'horloge*, song cycle

◀ **After a year's service** as a stretcher-bearer in the French Army, Dutilleux returned to Paris in 1940 to work as a pianist, arranger, and teacher.

Hans Werner **Henze**

🌐 1926–   📖 GERMAN   ✎ 270

A prolific composer, in particular of music for the theater, Henze's career has taken him from an angry young man of the postwar period to an elder statesman of the 21st century. His style has evolved too, exploring various idioms and techniques, including neo-Classicism, serialism, jazz, rock, and pop, and often borrowing from music of other cultures, especially Arabic music. Despite this eclectic approach, his political stance has remained consistently Marxist, and is an important element in all of his music. Henze's father became a fanatical pro-Nazi during the

1930s, enrolling his sons in the Hitler Youth, and Hans Werner found his escape in music. After serving briefly in the German army during World War II, he became a professional musician and an avowed socialist. For some years he was associated with the German avant-garde composers at the Darmstadt New Music Summer School, but he found even postwar Germany politically intolerable and homophobic, and he moved to Italy in 1953, joining the Italian Communist Party. While in Italy, he slowly distanced himself from the serial style he had adopted in his early works, and began to collaborate with the poet Ingeborg Bachmann on the operas that established him as a major composer. In 1968, frustrated with European capitalist society, he moved to Cuba where he taught and composed for a couple of years before becoming disillusioned with Fidel Castro's regime and returning to Italy. From the 1970s his music, and especially his music for the theater, took on a much more aggressively left-wing tone, and made reference to various musical styles, but established his international reputation.

MILESTONES	
1958	Writes *Kammermusik*, tenor and guitar
1964	Composes *Der junge Lord*, opera
2007	*Phaedra*, opera

Einojuhani **Rautavaara**

● 1928–   ₪ FINNISH   ✍ c.220

After graduating from the Helsinki Academy, Rautavaara moved to the US in the 1950s where he studied at the Juilliard School in New York and with Sessions and Copland at Tanglewood. In his early work, he experimented with both neo-Classical and serial styles but found they did not suit his essentially Finnish character, and instead developed an idiosyncratic style, combining some avant-garde techniques with a melodic Romanticism. A superb orchestrator, he creates evocative sound worlds, often with mystical connotations that are hinted at by titles such as *True and False Unicorn* and *Angels and Visitations*. In addition to orchestral works and concertos for various instruments, he has written a number of operas, again exploring mystical themes, including *Vincent* on the life of Van Gogh, and *Rasputin*.

The basically melodic style makes his music more approachable than many other composers of his generation, and the unorthodox techniques he often uses are incorporated seamlessly into a Romantic framework; his *Serenades of the Unicorn* for guitar uses a teaspoon tapping the strings to suggest giggling nymphs, while his eerie Symphony No. 6 portrays van Gogh's troubled mind with a synthesizer. As a result, sombre, beautiful, and imaginative orchestral pieces such as *Cantus arcticus*, the mystical Symphony No. 7 "Angel of Light," and his Piano Concerto No. 3 have achieved international popularity and Rautavaara has gained respect as the foremost Finnish composer to follow Sibelius.

MILESTONES

1952	Writes *Pelimannit (Fiddlers)* for piano
1976	Begins 14 years as professor at the Sibelius Academy in Helsinki
1987	Completes *Vincent*, opera
2003–05	*Book of Visions*; *Manhattan Trilogy*
c.2005	*Before the Icons*
2007	*A Tapestry of Life*

Krzysztof **Penderecki**

● 1933–   ₪ POLISH   ✍ 150

At a time when avant-garde experimental music mainly avoided emotion, Penderecki made his name with the harrowing directness of *Threnody to the Victims of Hiroshima*—scored for 52 strings and using innovative notation and a shocking range of sounds. (The original title was *8' 37"*; the Hiroshima connection came after he first heard it played.) His *St. Luke Passion* resulted in invitations to work abroad and regular commissions. In the mid-1970s, his radical language softened and became more lyrical (his Symphony No. 3 of 1995 is mainly traditional-sounding) but the passion and anger at human injustice remains. His oratorios, in particular, reflect the struggle between Church and State in 1980s Poland.

⌃ **Often conducting his own music,** Penderecki was one of the pioneers of microtones and the use of whistles, hissing, shouting, and mechanical noise in music.

MILESTONES

1959	Wins the top three prizes in Warsaw composing competition
1960	Composes *Threnody to the Victims of Hiroshima* for 52 strings
1972	Becomes rector at Kraków Academy
1980	Writes *Lacrimosa*, choral, for Solidarity
2005	*Polish Requiem*

Witold **Lutosławski**

🌐 1913–1994   📛 POLISH   ✍ 86

Lutosławski lived in difficult times. His early works had to please the communist authorities and were largely inspired by Polish folk music. Later he was able to experiment publicly, expanding his harmony and incorporating passages in which performers were given some degree of rhythmic autonomy. In his last period, he strove to incorporate both worlds in his music, blending modernism with nostalgia.

Lutosławski's early years were darkened by the death of his father in Russia (where he had fought the Bolsheviks) and the loss of the family estate. Despite privations, he studied violin and piano, and entered the Warsaw Conservatory in 1927. By 1938 his music had been championed by Poland's leading conductor, Grzegorz Fitelberg, but World War II brought mobilization and capture by the Germans. Lutosławski escaped and returned to Warsaw, where he survived by playing dance music and piano duets with fellow composer Andrzej Panufnik. In later life, Lutosławski became Poland's preeminent composer, honored both for his music and his political integrity during the struggles against communism. His work was greatly influential both in his homeland and internationally.

MILESTONES

1918	Father and uncle executed as "counterrevolutionaries"
1927	Enters the Warsaw Conservatory, later studies with Maliszewski
1939	*Symphonic Variations* broadcast by Polish radio; mobilized
1940	Escapes enemy capture; returns to Warsaw; forms piano duo with Panufnik
1949	Symphony No. 1 denounced by the communist authorities
c.1958	*Musique funèbre* and *Jeux vénitiens* win international acclaim
1994	Awarded Poland's rare Order of the White Eagle weeks before his death

KEY WORKS

LES ESPACES DU SOMMEIL

ORCHESTRA & VOICE   ⏱ 15:30   📖 1

This sensitive vocal work, written for the acclaimed baritone Dietrich Fischer-Dieskau, evokes the mysterious world of sleep. The night is full of half-understood, hallucinatory images, but always "there is also you"—the beloved woman who haunts the poet's dreams.

MI-PARTI

ORCHESTRAL   ⏱ 15:00   📖 1   🎵

A compact work of great lucidity and visceral excitement, *Mi-Parti* moves from dreaming hesitancy toward a climactic tumult, peaking on a *sforzando* chord. The music then settles on a distant "icy" harmony, before melting away into a meditative coda. In archetypal Lutosławskian fashion, the piece alternates strictly conducted passages with *ad libitum* sections in which individual players repeat melodic motifs in free time.

◀◀ **The artistry** of violinist Anne-Sophie Mutter inspired many of Lutosławski's later pieces.

Karlheinz **Stockhausen**

◔ 1928–2007   ᛈ GERMAN   ✍ 313

Stockhausen won cult status thanks to a genius for music and publicity. Yet his stunts often had a serious point; even his *Helicopter Quartet*, in which a string quartet performs while airborne in four different helicopters, developed his long-standing fascination for music that moves in space, leading him to dream of concert halls in which the sound assails the listener from every direction.

Stockhausen was the first composer of the avant-garde to devote himself fully to electronic music. His teenage years were scarred by the deaths of his mother and father during World War II, leaving him to pay for his music studies in Cologne by playing in piano bars and accompanying a stage magician. He then studied with Messiaen in Paris and became involved in the birth of electronic music, producing seminal works such as *Gesang der Jünglinge*. Stockhausen became a leading figure at the Darmstadt summer schools, where John Cage introduced him to the use of chance processes in music. Toward the end of his life he concentrated on completing his vast opera cycle *Licht*. The seven operas are named after the days of the week. The first to be written, *Donnerstag* (Thursday), was staged in Milan as long ago as 1981; the last, *Sonntag* (Sunday), completed in 2003, premiered in Cologne in 2011. Although very different in character, all the operas are linked by three key melodies. The staging of the works has presented problems for conventional opera houses, especially when the composer requested such things as flying rockets, helicopters, or a pencil sharpener 13 feet high.

MILESTONES

1945	Serves in military hospital; father dies
1952	Studies with Messiaen; produces first electronic pieces
1956	Starts teaching at Darmstadt; writes *Gesang der Jüngling*, boy's voice and tape
1958	Hears John Cage lecture at Darmstadt
1960s	Forms his own ensemble; tours world
1968	Composes *Stimmung*, 70-minute work for six singers based on a single chord
1970	Complete works performed in Osaka
2003	Completes his 29-hour opera, *Licht*

KEY WORKS

GRUPPEN

ORCHESTRAL   ⏱ 22:00   📖 1   ♫

This early work remains truly epoch-making. It requires three separate orchestras and conductors, and is composed according to arcane rules linking pitch and rhythm, but the impact of the piece is spatial and, indeed, visceral. Few venues can place the musicians around the audience in the way Stockhausen intended, but to hear three massed orchestras in intricate three-way converse is still an unforgettable experience.

GESANG DER JÜNGLINGE

ELECTRONIC   ⏱ 13:00   📖 1   🎧

The power of this piece (which even influenced the Beatles, causing them to include a photo of Stockhausen on the cover of their *Sgt Pepper* album) lies not only in the use of early tape technology, but also in the emotional effect of a boy's voice singing the Benedictus among a welter of alien sounds. Stockhausen envisaged it as walking unharmed through a "fiery furnace," an image which surely has autobiographical wartime resonances.

Pierre **Boulez**

● 1925–   卪 FRENCH   ⚄ 55

For almost 50 years, Boulez has been the dominant force in contemporary music, not only as a composer, but also as a conductor, theorist, broadcaster, and as the founder of IRCAM, a Paris-based centre for research into music and technology. In his middle years, Boulez's composing seemed dangerously close to being stifled by other activities, but recent years have seen a steady succession of large-scale works.

Noting Boulez's youthful talent for math, his father sent him to study engineering. Boulez, however, defected to the Paris Conservatoire, where he was taught by Messiaen and gained a fearsome reputation for heckling at concerts of contemporary works that he judged insufficiently radical. He made his name as a composer in 1955 with *Le marteau sans maître*. With Stockhausen, he dominated the Darmstadt summer schools, the centre of new music in the 1950s. Having taken to the podium as an advocate of new music, Boulez began an international career as a conductor. His interest in technology resurfaced in the 1970s, when he founded IRCAM to find ways of extending music's frontiers.

MILESTONES	
1944	Studies with Messiaen
1955	Premiere of *Le marteau sans maître*
1962	*Pli selon pli* premiered
1969	Becomes chief conductor of BBC Symphony Orchestra
1971	Succeeds Bernstein as music director of New York Philharmonic Orchestra
1976	Founds Ensemble InterContemporain; conducts Wagner's *Ring* at Bayreuth
1977	Opens IRCAM at Pompidou Centre
1982	Premiere of *Répons* at London Proms
2000	Wins Grammy award for *Répons*

KEY WORKS

ÉCLATS/MULTIPLES

CHAMBER   ⧗ 37:00   ▢ 2   ⚘

This diptych actually consists of a "complete" piece (*Éclats*) and its open-ended sequel (*Multiples*). *Éclats* was intended to give its 15 players some freedom in choosing when and what they wished to play, in response to the contemporary music reducing musicians to the level of virtuosic machines. However, in performance Boulez did not always like the results of *Éclats*'s freedoms and soon began to eliminate them, giving all the decisions about the order in which sections would be performed to the conductor. *Multiples* is one of the first works which pointed to the use of what were to become more straightforward rhythms in his music—rhythms which audiences find easier to "hear," just as musicians find them easier to play.

RÉPONS

ELECTRONIC   ⧗ 43:00   ▢ 10   ⚘

Boulez's first major work to come out of IRCAM uses computers to produce real-time transformations of music played by two pianos, a harp, and bell-like instruments; background music provided by 24 string, brass, and wind players is unaffected.

The arrival of IRCAM's glittering new technology is announced majestically at the beginning of the second section; the group of soloists surrounding the pianos peals out a chord that is then seized on by the computer and is electronically treated and projected through six loudspeakers. The title *Répons* (*Responses*) refers to early Church music in which a soloist's music alternates with that of the choir.

⚈ **Boulez** was appointed director of the French government-sponsored IRCAM studio in 1977.

Iannis **Xenakis**

● 1922–2001   ▥ GREEK   ✍ c.160

Exiled in France for his involvement with the Greek resistance, Xenakis joined the group of avant-garde composers (including Boulez and Stockhausen) studying with Messiaen in the 1950s. His approach to composition was different from his contemporaries; he forged his own way, applying the principles of engineering and mathematics to produce some of the most strikingly original music of the late 20th century.

World War II disrupted Xenakis's education; he fought for the Greek resistance, fled a death sentence, and ended up penniless in Paris. He then worked in the great architect Le Corbusier's studio for 12 years, as an engineer and architect, while studying music privately. His ideas on electro-acoustic music established him as a pioneer, and he taught at many institutions.

His rigorous works are often intricately computer-generated by detailed mathematical processes, and generally written for combinations of conventional instruments, sometimes played unconventionally. Xenakis's explorations of the fundamentals of music continue to fascinate and influence advanced performers and listeners.

⯮ An architect with an understanding of advanced mathematics, Xenakis designed the Philips Pavilion for the Brussels World Fair in 1958.

MILESTONES

1947	Arrives in France as illegal immigrant
1953	Writes *Metastaseis* for orchestra
1957	Works with Schaeffer's electro-acoustic group
1962	Starts composing with a computer
1991	Writes computer program, GENDYN

KEY WORKS

METASTASEIS

ORCHESTRA	⏱ 7:00	♫

Metastaseis ("transformation," or "transition") was Xenakis's first major work, and the first he acknowledged as part of his oeuvre. Scored for a large orchestra, the piece evolves from a very quiet unison G through glissandoing strings to massive blocks of sound, in which the individual parts become subsumed by the whole. After a more fragmentary central section, the music returns to the glissandi of the beginning, and the piece dissolves once more into a unison.

PLÉIADES

SIX PERCUSSIONISTS	⏱ 46:00	🕮 4	

There is a strong emphasis on rhythm in much of Xenakis's work, and he wrote several pieces for percussion ensemble. The four movements of *Pléïades* can be played in any order. Each explores a different aspect of percussion music: *Métaux* (metals) is written for an instrument of Xenakis's own design made of metal plates, *Peaux* (skins) for drums, *Claviers* (keyboards) for xylophones, marimbas, and vibraphones, and *Mélanges* (mixtures) for a combination of instruments.

György **Ligeti**

● 1923–2006   ♙ HUNGARIAN   ♫ 117

One of the few great modernists to have reached a wider audience, Ligeti's own work bears the traces of a bewildering variety of styles and techniques, from late medieval Europe to the music of the pygmies of Central Africa. Other inspirations reflect the range of his intellectual curiosity, embracing the philosophy of Karl Popper, the paradoxes of Escher's art, and the intricacies of Mandelbrot's fractal geometry.

Ligeti was born in a small Hungarian-speaking enclave in Romanian Transylvania. At first intent on a career in science, his education was disrupted by anti-Jewish legislation, and he turned to composition. After World War II, Ligeti found his progress as a composer frustrated by communism, and in 1956 he fled to the West. Befriended by Stockhausen, Ligeti experimented with electronic music, but resisted pressures to adopt systematic methods of composition. The use of Ligeti's music in the film *2001: A Space Odyssey* won him a worldwide following.

MILESTONES	
1944	Deaths of his father and brother at the hands of the Nazis
1957	Works in Stockhausen's electronics studio in Cologne
1960	Premiere of *Apparitions*, orchestra
1961	Premiere of *Atmosphères*
1970	Granted a political "amnesty," Ligeti revisits Hungary
1978	Premiere of *La Grand Macabre*, opera

KEY WORKS

LONTANO

ORCHESTRAL   ⌛ 11:30   📖 1

Lontano is composed of countless barely audible canons. Great control is needed by orchestra and conductor to sustain the hushed flow of mysteriously shifting, infinitely delicate sound. A study in subdued restlessness, *Lontano* consists of quiet murmuring until a point two-thirds of the way through. A climax for a group of solo strings is followed by a second crescendo for the entire string section (except the double basses). The climax is suddenly cut off, movement almost ceases, and the music moves into catatonic retreat.

SAN FRANCISCO POLYPHONY

ORCHESTRAL   ⌛ 13:00   📖 1

Ligeti's career charted a gradual recovery of the musical language of the past. Each new piece reclaimed techniques which other modernists judged to have outlived their usefulness. He always liked polyphony (the overlaying of many voices in independent lines), but before *San Francisco Polyphony*, permitted himself to use it only on the microscopic level. Here the counterpoint comes to the surface in bold, characterful gestures, whose virtuosity once led orchestras to regard the piece as unplayable; moments such as the frantic conclusion, in which ostinato figures spin like tops as the horns yelp in excited syncopation, still test performers to the limit.

REQUIEM

CHORAL   ⌛ 25:00   📖 4

Ligeti's *Requiem* is a work of apocalyptic power, influenced by Renaissance polyphony and the choral works of Bach, but dividing orchestra and choir into so many individual parts that the intricate counterpoint dissolves into spectacular clouds of sound.

⬧ **Ligeti's atmospheric *Requiem*** (1965) was used on the soundtrack of *2001: A Space Odyssey* for scenes with strange visual effects and dreamlike sequences.

Luigi **Nono**

◐ 1924–1990   ᵱᵁ ITALIAN   ✍ c.60

An uncompromising modernist, Nono gained a popular following in his native Italy, not least because of the political convictions that inspired his music. Deeply affected by Mussolini's rule and the horrors of World War II, he joined the Italian communist party, and saw composing as a way of promoting his anti-fascist, Marxist views, and his progressive musical style as necessarily related to his politics.

Born into a family of artists, Nono was strongly influenced by painting, philosophy, and poetry. He established himself at the renowned Darmstadt summer school and became a key figure in the postwar avant-garde. His 1950s theatrical pieces, often with a strongly socialist theme, use innovative sounds and textures. Having rejected Darmstadt,

he turned to electronics and amplification in the 1960s, creating political works based on vocal material and centered around his performers. Through the 1980s, his experimentation in music theater—and with new technical resources— continued, moving occasionally from the political to the more private, and his concentration on the nature of music and communication made his work widely influential.

» The premiere of Nono's opera *Intolleranza 1960* with electronic sound, visual projections, and a political message, caused uproar in Venice.

MILESTONES	
1946	Meets Maderna
1955	Marries Schoenberg's daughter, Nuria
1959	Gives controversial lecture criticizing Darmstadt
1984	*Prometeo,* "aziona scenica," produced

KEY WORKS

IL CANTO SOSPESO

SOLOISTS, CHORUS, AND ORCHESTRA
⏱ 30:00   ◫ 9   ♫ ⛬ ♂

Using as its text a selection of the last letters from resistance fighters before their execution by the fascists, *Il Canto Sospeso* ("The Suspended Song") is written in a pointillistic style, with words and even syllables scattered around the various voices, using the 12-tone serial technique of Schoenberg and Webern to create an expressionistic atmosphere that enhances the poignancy of the testimony of the text. First performed in 1956, it established Nono's international reputation.

PROMETEO

OPERA   ⏱ 150:00   ◫ 9   ♀ ♂

Described by Nono as a *tragedia dell'ascolto* ("tragedy for listening"), *Prometeo* is not so much an opera as a collection of cantatas. The libretto draws various versions of the myth of Prometheus, and both the text and the music make frequent use of quotation. The singers and instrumentalists, scattered among the audience rather than on stage, are amplified, and their performance is electronically manipulated. *Prometeo* marked a turning point for Nono, the beginning of a period when he adopted a freer technique to combine personal expression into his political statement.

Luciano **Berio**

● 1925–2003   ▯ᴶ ITALIAN   ✍ 29

The leading Italian composer of the second half of the 20th century, Berio was a composer of formidable intellect and technique. He numbered among the pioneers of the avant-garde, yet even his most exuberant music had an undertone of Mediterranean melancholy. His ear for sonority, feeling for context, and knowledge of tradition helped to give whatever he wrote the rich hues of an old master.

Berio came from a family of musicians, and was taught piano and harmony by his father. In 1944, a hand injury sustained on his first day in the army put an end to his soldiering as well as his hopes of becoming a pianist. While studying composition in Milan, Berio met his first wife, American soprano Cathy Berberian. He spent the 1960s teaching across the US. After the breakup of his second marriage, he returned to Italy, developing an interest in Sicilian folk music and working with writers and personal friends such as Umberto Eco, Edoardo Sanguinetti, and Italo Calvino. His final marriage to Israeli musicologist Talia Packer is reflected in his works on Jewish themes.

MILESTONES

1955	Co-founds Italy's first studio for electro-acoustic music
1958	Begins solo-instrumental *Sequenza* series
1969	*Sinfonia* confirms his global reputation
1973	Begins *Points on a Curve to Find*
1974	Directs research at IRCAM electronics studio in Paris until 1980
1975	Joins Israel Chamber Orchestra
1980	Starts work on operas with Italo Calvino
1984	Composes *Voci: Folksongs II*

KEY WORKS

SINFONIA

ORCHESTRAL   ⧗ 32:00   ▭ 5   ♫♫ ♂

Berio's most celebrated work caught the mood of its time (the late 1960s) to perfection, and still crackles today with undiminished electricity. Eight voices supply a montage of fragmentary texts, acting like a section of the orchestra.

First movement (6:00) This evokes Brazilian myths on the origin of water. The music flickers with forest noises, summoning up a torrential river of orchestral sound.

Second movement: O King (5:00) The singers intone syllables from the name "Martin Luther King" while trumpets and a snare drum salute his memory.

Third movement (12:00) This dazzling montage of quotes from the Romantic and modern repertoires is carried along on the "river" of the third movement of Mahler's Symphony No. 2.

Fourth movement (2:00) A subdued interlude, in which the singers mull over fragments of their texts so far.

Fifth movement (7:00) The inspired finale samples music that has already been sampled from other music.

INFLUENCES

In postmodern style, Berio boldly advertised his influences: Mahler, Stravinsky, Berg, and Stockhausen are all detectable in the third movement of *Sinfonia*. However, Berio above all thought of music as a kind of speech. By analyzing speech and applying the post-structuralist ideas of thinkers like Eco and Calvino to music, Berio found his own musical voice.

⌃ **Berio often worked,** as here, with his first wife, Cathy Berberian. In 1958 he created *Thema* for electronics based on her reading from James Joyce's *Ulysses*.

Astor **Piazzolla**

🌐 1921–1992   🏳 ARGENTINE   ✍ c.750

The son of second-generation Italian immigrants, Piazzolla was born in Argentina but his family moved to New York when he was three. With such a cosmopolitan background, he picked up diverse musical influences, including jazz, classical music, and the tango. His father played the bandoneón, the Argentinian type of concertina, and Astor learned from him enough to get some work playing bandoneón with the tango composer Carlos Gardel. He returned to Argentina at the age of 16, and later played in tango bands in Buenos Aires. But he wanted to write classical music, and took lessons with Ginastera, who encouraged him to write orchestral music. His *Buenos Aires* Symphony was well received, and earned him a scholarship to study composition with Nadia Boulanger in Paris: this was a turning point in his career, because she advised him that his real talent lay in writing tangos. He went back and with his Octeto Buenos Aires developed a style of composition that incorporated the rhythms of jazz and dissonant harmonies of modern classical music into the traditional form of the tango.

Piazzolla found it hard to find a sympathetic audience at first, particularly during the 1970s when Argentina was under military rule, but European audiences proved enthusiastic. By the mid-1980s his *nuevo tango* style had become accepted in his home country and he had established a global reputation—not only among tango aficionados, but with classical listeners and performers too, earning him a prestigious commission from the Kronos Quartet to write the *Five Tango Sensations*.

MILESTONES	
1944	Forms the Orquestra del 46 to play his compositions
1967	Composes a "tango-opera" *María de Buenos Aires*
1976	Forms the Quinteto Tango Nuevo and develops the style known as *nuevo tango*

Mauricio **Kagel**

🌐 1931–2008   🏳 GERMAN–ARGENTINE   ✍ c.165

Kagel was born in Buenos Aires, where his German-Jewish family had settled after fleeing from Russia. He studied literature and philosophy at university, but took some private music lessons and through his membership of the *Agrupación Nueva Música* (New Music Group) developed an ambition to be a composer. As his interest was in the avant-garde, he moved to Cologne, a center of experimental music that had attracted composers including Stockhausen and Boulez, where he remained for the rest of his life.

His early works were very much in the style of the German avant-garde, but his anarchic and often irreverent approach to composition was not in tune with the rigidity and seriousness of postwar serialism, and he quickly found a more theatrical mature style. Running through all of his work is a sometimes bizarre sense of humor, comparable to the Theater of the Absurd, with which he pokes fun at musical conventions and institutions, and explores the meaninglessness of language. The result is some startlingly original music, often for "mixed media" including visual and theatrical effects. Some idea of the flavor of his music can be seen in titles such as *Unguis incarnatus est for piano and...* (meaning "ingrowing toenail is") or the ironic *Variations without Fugue on the "Variations and Fugue" on a theme by Händel for Piano Op. 24 by Johannes Brahms (1861–1862)*. Kagel also made several films for television, on mainly musical subjects.

MILESTONES	
1960	Founds the Cologne New Music Ensemble
1970	Makes the film *Ludwig Van* for German television
1985	The oratorio-like *Nach einer Sankt-Bach-Passion* has its premiere
2005	Composes *Fremde Töne & Widerhall* (Strange sounds and echo) for orchestra
2008	*In der Matratzengruft* ("In the Mattress Crypt") for tenor and ensemble remains unfinished when he dies

György **Kurtág**

● 1926–   ◪ **HUNGARIAN**   ✍ 85

After graduating from the Liszt Academy in Budapest and winning state prizes, Kurtág gained a name as a pianist, especially of Bartók, a major influence. In 1957–58 he encountered Western music in Paris, especially admiring Schoenberg, Webern, and their serial music. He then produced his String Quartet No. 1—a new starting point for his music. He returned to Hungary, becoming a renowned piano teacher, vocal coach, and repetiteur. In his mid-40s, he was commissioned to write children's piano music and the results inspired new creativity. Success with his *Troussova* songs in France made his name abroad, and since 1985 (having reached only Op. 23) he has composed more frequently.

MILESTONES	
1980	Completes song cycle *Messages of the Late Miss R V Troussova*
1987	Writes *Kafka Fragments*, voice and violin
1990	*Samuel Beckett Sends Word Through Ildikó Monyók...*, for soprano and piano
1994	*Stele*, for orchestra, premiered in Berlin
2003	*...concertante...* Op. 42 for violin, viola, and orchestra

⬙ **Many of Kurtág's works** are small scale, such as his 1980 *Messages of the Late Miss R.V. Troussova* for soprano and chamber ensemble with cimbalom.

Henryk **Górecki**

● 1933–2010   ◪ **POLISH**   ✍ 83

Górecki was born in Silesia, a part of Poland in which Polish, German, and Czech cultures exist side by side in a mix that has colored his musical interests. His studies at Katowice Academy of Music, where he embraced the radical "Polish School" (which also included Krzysztof Penderecki), resulted in his Symphony No. 1 and *Scontri*, both aggressively dissonant. He later taught at the Academy and became its rector, but resigned for political reasons in 1979. By the mid-1970s, influences such as a growing love of Polish folk music and medieval Polish chants caused him to adopt a far less astringent style, and his Symphony No. 3 shot him to huge international fame. Górecki's search in later decades for a pure, transparent style was inspired by a religious sensibility.

MILESTONES	
1973	Wins UNESCO first prize in Paris for *Ad Matrem*, choral work
1979	*Beatus Vir*, choral work, premiered at Kraków for visit of Pope John Paul II
1987	Completes *Miserere*, choral work
1988	*Already it is Dusk* for string quartet
1992	Soprano Dawn Upshaw's recording of Symphony No. 3 creates huge interest

◄ **In Górecki's spiritual and meditative Symphony No. 3,** a soprano sings poignant words written by a girl on a wall in a concentration camp.

Peter **Sculthorpe**

◕ 1929–　　　　🏳 AUSTRALIAN　　　　✍ 238

Despite his love and respect for the Classical, Sculthorpe has distanced himself from it, creating instead an Australian sound world by reflecting the continent's landscape and often basing his works on Aboriginal chants. He also incorporates elements from Japanese and Balinese music, reasoning that Australian art should link to a wider Pacific Rim culture, just as British music relates to Europe's.

Sculthorpe wrote music under the bedclothes by flashlight as a boy, after being rebuked by his piano teacher for composing rather than practicing. He was only 16 when he began studying music at the University of Melbourne. In 1955, his Piano Sonatina was selected to represent Australia at the International Society for Contemporary Music (ISCM) Festival in Germany and in 1958 he won a scholarship to study in England. On returning home, he wrote the desolate *Irkanda 1* for solo violin—a farewell to Europe as well as to his recently deceased father. It established the basis for a vivid new "Australian" soundscape, which he has explored ever more resourcefully in all his subsequent work.

MILESTONES

1955	Piano Sonatina played at ISCM
1961	Writes *Irkanda 1*
1963	Joins Sydney University staff (to 1999)
1965	Begins *Sun Music series* for orchestra
1986	Composes *Earthcry* for orchestra
1998	Elected one of Australia's 100 Living National Treasures by popular vote
2004	Premiers *Requiem*, large work for choir, soloists, orchestra, four didgeridoos
2006	Elegy for viola and strings
2008	*Tropic* for orchestra
2011	*Shining Island* for strings

» **Evoking the blazing heat** of the outback, Sculthorpe's typically rhythmic works sharing the title *Sun Music* include a ballet and chamber, orchestral, and vocal pieces.

KEY WORKS

PORT ESSINGTON

ORCHESTRAL　　⏱ 15:00　　📖 6　　♫

This is an unsettling, powerfully atmospheric piece that draws on music Sculthorpe wrote for a film about the history of a doomed, 19th-century British settlement in northern Australia. A string trio plays gracious, romantic, "civilized" music to represent the ill-fated settlers, while the string orchestra constantly encroaches with the wilder, eerier sounds of the bush. Both kinds of music comprise a series of variations on an aboriginal tune, *Djilili*, which occurs in many of Sculthorpe's works.

EARTHCRY

ORCHESTRAL　　⏱ 11:00　　📖 1　　♫

Earthcry brings together two of Sculthorpe's abiding concerns: the horror he feels at Modern civilization's abuse of the environment, and its dispossession of native peoples. The work recasts an earlier piece, *The Song of Tailitnama*, which was based on an Aboriginal chant for greeting the Earth at dawn. *Earthcry*, however, takes the material in new directions, working the music up into a fierce, mesmeric dance before reaching a final plateau of spectacular grandeur.

Sir Peter Maxwell **Davies**

● 1934– British ✍ 320

Intense energy is as apparent in Davies's charismatic personality as it is in his prolific output. Davies has dominated British music since the appearance of his explosive works of the 1960s, which gave exemplary expression to the anarchic spirit of the times. Responsible since then for works of the grandest integrity, his musical voice can be heard clearly, even in the many works he has written for children or film.

Davies's earliest memory of music is of being taken to see a local performance of Gilbert and Sullivan's *The Gondoliers*. He encountered very different musical experiences at the Royal Manchester College, however, where his friends included fellow composers Alexander Goehr and Harrison Birtwistle. Davies studied in Italy and America before returning to England to teach at a grammar school. He soon became known for eclectic music-theater works, like *Eight Songs for a Mad King*, but the direction of his work changed when he moved to Orkney and fell under the spell of its majestic seascapes.

MILESTONES	
1957	Studies with composer Goffredo Petrassi
1959	Teaches music at Cirencester Grammar School
1972	Premiere of *Taverner*, opera
1977	*Black Pentecost* performed; founds the St. Magnus Festival
1987	Receives knighthood
1997	Visits Antarctica prior to writing his *Antarctic Symphony*
2004	Becomes Master of the Queen's Music
2011	*Kommilitonen!*, opera

KEY WORKS

IMAGE, REFLECTION, SHADOW

CHAMBER	⏱ 36:00	📖 3	♟

This chamber masterpiece is written for six instruments, including piano and cimbalom (a Hungarian dulcimer whose strings are struck with mallets). It might seem an odd choice for a tribute to the Orkney landscape, but—as the title suggests—the music teems with echoes and doublings, and the cimbalom is the pungent, brackish double of the scintillating piano. The title comes from a poem by Charles Senior.

SYMPHONY NO. 3

ORCHESTRAL	⏱ 56:40	📖 4	🎺

Davies bases his pieces on numeric "magic squares." Here, the square contains the proportions of an Italian cathedral.

First movement (*lento*, 18:00) This majestic movement establishes D as the symphony's starting point, and quotes a medieval chant in praise of the Archangel Michael.
Second movement (*allegro*, 9:00) The first two scherzos centered on the vanishing point, which, in the Italian architect Brunelleschi's church nave, marked the position of the altar. The movement also expresses Davies's wonderment at a precipitous Orkney cliff-face thronged with a cloud of spiraling seabirds.
Third movement (*allegro vivace*, 7:40) Davies alters the angle at which the same nave is viewed: some elements are foreshortened, others magnified.
Fourth movement (*lento; adagio flessibile*, 22:00) Davies pays tribute to the last movement of Mahler's ninth symphony, and ends his impressive work with intimations of eternity.

🔼 **St. Magnus Cathedral on Orkney** offers perfect acoustics for players at Davies's summer festival.

Sir Harrison **Birtwistle**

🌎 1934–   📖 ENGLISH   ✍ 116

A few bars are all you need to hear to know that a piece is by Birtwistle. The quirky rhythms, the layered textures, and the immediate sense of theatre are unmistakable fingerprints. His music sounds idiosyncratically English, and often there is a dominant part for his favorite instrument—the clarinet. However, in recent years, Birtwistle has become known above all for his vocal music and his majestic, ritualistic operas.

Birtwistle studied clarinet at the Royal Northern College of Music, where he formed the New Music Manchester Group with fellow students, including Peter Maxwell Davies and trumpeter and conductor Elgar Howarth. After graduating, Birtwistle worked briefly as a professional clarinettist, but dedicated himself to composing on hearing that his first acknowledged piece had been selected for the Cheltenham Festival in 1959. Landmarks since that time have included his orchestral piece *The Triumph of Time* (inspired by Breughel), the parody opera *Punch and Judy*, and the mighty *Masque of Orpheus* with its elaborate stage spectacle and haunting electronics.

MILESTONES	
1955	Plays in the Royal Artillery band
1959	*Refrains and Choruses*, wind quintet, performed at Cheltenham Festival
1965	Composes *Tragoedia*; the music reappears in *Punch and Judy*, opera
1981	Composes music for Peter Halls' production of the *Oresteia*
1988	Receives knighthood
1991	*Gawain* performed at Covent Garden
2008	Composes *The Minotaur*, opera
2010	*Concerto for Violin and Orchestra*

KEY WORKS

GAWAIN'S JOURNEY

SUITE	⏱ 25:00	📖 12	🎵

This impressive piece is derived from Birtwistle's second epic opera, depicting Gawain's quest for the mysterious Green Knight. The earthy and evocative music draws on his rite-of-passage journey, the three attempts by the Green Knight's beautiful wife to seduce Gawain (each marked by a cockcrow), and the clopping horse hooves and whirling figures that characterize the encounters with her terrifying, if finally beneficent, husband.

THE MASK OF ORPHEUS

OPERA	⏱ 210:00	📖 3	🎵🎭♦

This complicated work retells three conflicting Greek legends about the death of Orpheus, enacted by singers and giant puppets. It is also a wonderfully baffling reconstruction of the rites once associated with the worship of Orpheus. Each act focuses on a specific ritual serving as a fixed point around which the opera revolves. Electronics are used to imitate the voice of Apollo and to create "auras" suggesting the sounds of tides and bees, both of which have rich symbolic connotations.

» **Each character in *Orpheus*** appears in three guises: as a singer, a dancer, and a mime.

Toru **Takemitsu**

◔ 1930–1996   ▥ JAPANESE   ✍ 104

Takemitsu first heard Western music when he was 14. After World War II, he listened to Classical music on US-forces radio, and it was mainly by listening to the works of composers like Debussy and Messiaen that he taught himself compositional technique. In 1959, Stravinsky heard Takemitsu's *Requiem for String Orchestra*, and declared it a masterpiece. It was only after talking to John Cage in 1964 that Takemitsu began to pay any attention to Japanese music, producing works like *November Steps* for orchestra and Japanese instruments. His most famous piece is probably *A Flock Descends into the Pentagonal Garden*. Takemitsu also wrote music for films, including Oshima's *The Empire of the Senses* and Akira Kurosawa's *Ran*.

MILESTONES

1944	Military service
1951	Founds an experimental workshop
1957	*Requiem for String Orchestra* wins acclaim
1967	Composes *November Steps*
1977	*A Flock Descends into the Pentagonal Garden*
1994	Wins prestigious Grawemeyer Award for Music Composition

≪ **A love of nature** and Japanese traditional culture are constant themes in Takemitsu's music.

Tan **Dun**

◔ 1957–   ▥ CHINESE-AMERICAN   ✍ 65

Tan Dun grew up during the Chinese Cultural Revolution, receiving no regular education and working as a rice planter. Later he was employed as a violinist and arranger at the Beijing Opera theater, only encountering Western music when he entered the newly reopened Central Conservatory of Music in 1976. His music began to show avant-garde influences and was even denounced as "spiritual pollution" by the Chinese government in 1983.

Three years later he moved to New York, and has since taken American nationality and has begun to write film scores. His music shows a wide range of influences, from jazz to Chinese opera, and often features unusual sounds, such as ancient Chinese bells or splashing water. As a conductor, Dun has created programs which reach a new and diverse audience.

MILESTONES

1976	Enters Beijing Music Conservatory
1998	Composes *Peony Pavilion*, opera
1999	Writes *Orchestral Theatre IV, The Gate*, for a Peking Opera actress, Japanese puppeteer, and string orchestra
2001	Wins awards for his score for Ang Lee's film *Crouching Tiger, Hidden Dragon*
2006	Composes *The First Emperor*, opera

≪ Dun's *Heaven Earth Mankind*, written to celebrate the reunification of Hong Kong with China, featured 65 ancient tuned bronze bells (excavated in 1978).

Arvo **Pärt**

◐ 1935–   ⚑ ESTONIAN   ✍ 93

Pärt has a following like few others in contemporary music. Starting out as a "progressive" composer, frequently in an atonal idiom, he stopped composing in the 1970s and emerged—after a period of creative silence—with an entirely new musical voice imbued with simplicity and devotional humility. Inspired by the sound of bells and the music of the distant past, his works seem to exist outside time.

As a child, Pärt attended evening music school. His early compositional experimentation was encouraged by necessity—only the lowest and highest notes on the piano at home worked properly. Having survived a serious illness, he entered the Central Tallinn Conservatory, and by the time he graduated he was already a successful film composer. His early serious music used a "collage" technique, mixing various styles. Although he achieved a national reputation, both his progressive and religious works were often banned by the authorities. In the early 1970s, Pärt joined the Russian Orthodox Church. He left Estonia in 1980 and settled in Germany.

MILESTONES

1957	Begins working for Estonian radio; writes film and television scores
1960	Composes *Nekrolog* for orchestra—the first piece of Estonian 12-tone music; it earns official disfavor
1962	Starts writing "collage" pieces, juxtaposing various styles, the final piece in this period being *Credo*
1977	Composes *Arbos*, *Cantus in memoriam Benjamin Britten*, *Fratres*, and *Tabula Rasa*
1980	Leaves Estonia for the West
2008	Symphony No. 4, "Los Angeles"

KEY WORKS

🔊 **Für Alina,** for piano, is based on a simple tonic triad; Pärt may have been influenced by St. Gregory of Palamas's book *Triads*.

FRATRES

CHAMBER   ⏱ 12:00   📖 1   ♟

The fact that *Fratres* can be heard in seven versions—for different instrumental combinations—reflects the fact that it is one of Pärt's most loved works. One of the early so-called "tintinnabuli" pieces, it sets the notes of an A minor tonic chord against overlapping scales in subtly shifting patterns—a technique which has some similarity to the compositional techniques of late medieval composers. That Pärt originally left the choice of instruments open to the performers also reflects the esthetics of an earlier time; the notes themselves were presumed to suggest a divine order, which could be communicated in any medium. Fratres means "brethren," perhaps suggesting a vision of society in which conflict and egotism has been supplanted by the "brotherly love" of communities living according to the Christian gospel.

CREDO

ORCHESTRAL   ⏱ 12:00   📖 3

The last work written in Pärt's earlier "collage" style, this piece was vilified by the communist authorities on account of its religious text. The music in Parts 1 and 3 is derived from the first C major prelude in J.S. Bach's *Well-tempered Clavier*—for, as in all the collage pieces, Pärt "borrows" the tonal material from older composers. The piece dramatizes the conflict between good and evil, with good being represented by pure C major and evil by dissonant note clusters.

Louis **Andriessen**

🌐 1939–   📖 DUTCH   ✍ 200+

As a reaction to the conservatism of his native Netherlands, Andriessen adopted a radical and overtly political approach to composition in the 1960s, and developed an idiosyncratic style more often than not for unconventional combinations of instruments.

Born into a well-known musical family in Utrecht, Andriessen studied with his father and others at the Royal Conservatory in The Hague, and then with Berio. Rejecting the serial style of his early work, he blended elements of jazz, electronic avant-garde, and American minimalism in an eclectic musical language. His style features driving rhythms and clashing dissonances, often amplified and exploiting extreme dynamics, first coming to public attention with *De Staat* for women's voices and large ensemble in 1976. His output ranges from pieces for solo instruments to works for various small groups of players, to concert pieces for voices and huge ensembles, and often includes parts for electric guitars and basses, synthesizers, and other electronic instruments. An interest in ritual and drama has inspired many stage works too, notably in collaboration with the British film-maker Peter Greenaway.

Respected as the foremost Dutch composer of the late 20th century, he has influenced a generation of younger composers who have played in the ensembles he founded in the 1970s, or studied under him as professor of composition at the Conservatory in The Hague.

MILESTONES

1972	Founds the street wind band Orkest de Volharding
1980s	Works on the music theater piece *De Materie* for amplified voices, amplified orchestra, and electric and electronic instruments
1996-97	*Trilogy of the Last Day*
2008	Completes the five part film-opera *La Commedia*

Jonathan **Harvey**

🌐 1939–   📖 ENGLISH   ✍ 100

After receiving doctorates from Cambridge and Glasgow universities and a fellowship at Princeton, Harvey's visionary experiments with electronic music impressed Boulez, who invited him to work at IRCAM in Paris. Harvey's innovative works, which include chamber, orchestral, and many choral pieces, have a meditative, spiritual, and ecstatic character (he has found the writings of Rudolf Steiner particularly inspirational) and have been widely recorded and performed across Europe. He is especially successful at combining conventional instruments with electronic or electronically modified sounds. Harvey has received honors in both the UK and US, and continues to fulfill constant new commissions, including some from the BBC Scottish Symphony Orchestra.

MILESTONES

1980	Writes *Mortuos plango, vivos voco*, tape
1981	Writes *Passion and Resurrection*, church opera; staged at Winchester Cathedral
1982	Composes *Bhakti*, 15 players and tape
1986	Composes *Madonna of Winter and Spring*, live electronics
1992	Composes *Scena*, violin concerto
2006	Composes *Body Mandala* for orchestra

《 **Jonathan Harvey's Hymn,** a piece for chorus and orchestra, was composed for the 900th-anniversary celebrations of Winchester Cathedral.

Gavin **Bryars**

🌐 1943–　　　🗣 ENGLISH　　　✎ 100+

A leading light in the British jazz and avant-garde improvisation scene of the 1960s, Bryars later emerged as a composer in a style that mixes elements of experimental and popular music. His early work, such as *The Sinking of the Titanic*, involved a large degree of indeterminacy, but also the idea of repetition of "found" sounds and music, comparable to Marcel Duchamps's use of found objects: *Jesus' Blood Never Failed Me Yet*, for example, is based on a tape loop of a tramp singing a hymn, and this very British interpretation of minimalist repetition became a surprise popular success. His preoccupation with fragments of music with particular associations continued through the 1980s, and was used to great dramatic effect in the opera *Medea*. In the 1990s, his approach has become in some ways more conventional, particularly in his operas, relying less on association and reference to external musical styles and composers, and exploring his own lyrical harmonic and tonal language. Bryars's style typifies the reaction against the complexity of much postwar classical music and the demands it puts on performers. A mark of his disdain for that sort of virtuosity was the formation of the intentionally untalented Portsmouth Sinfonia in 1970. Among his fellow cofounders was Brian Eno, whose recording company later released many of Bryars's works and helped establish his reputation.

MILESTONES	
1961	Studies philosophy at Sheffield University, then composition at the Northern School of Music
1970	Founds the music department at Leicester Polytechnic
1992	BBC Radio 3 commissions *A Man In A Room, Gambling*
1998	English National Opera perform *Doctor Ox's Experiment*
2010	Composes the ballet *The Third Light*

Sir John **Tavener**

🌐 1944–　　　🗣 ENGLISH　　　✎ 216

Tavener's first success came in 1968 with an avant-garde piece titled *The Whale*. In the following year a simpler work, the *Celtic Requiem*, appeared on the Apple label, thanks to contacts made by his brother, a builder, who was then working for Ringo Starr. Despite the religious nature of many early pieces, it took two events in the late 1970s to confirm Tavener in his pursuit of the harmonious simplicity for which he is now renowned: the failure of a musically and technically taxing opera at Covent Garden, and his reception into the Russian Orthodox Church. Since that time, Tavener has concentrated on writing devotional choral music—what he calls "icons in sound." By this, he means music that is "non-developmental"—that is, simple in texture and form, in the same way that religious icons are limited in their color palette and three-dimensionality, but yet inspire calm, spiritual illumination.

MILESTONES	
1968	*The Whale*, cantata, and *In Alium*, tape, soprano, and orchestra, are premiered
1969	Music is released on Apple label
1979	Opera, *Thérèse*, attracts hostile reviews
1980	Writes *Akhmatova: Rekviem*; has a stroke
2000	Knighted for "services to music"
2007	Composes *Requiem*; *The Beautiful Names* for tenor, choir, and orchestra

» **Tavener's work** includes a dance-opera, *Mary in Egypt*, with a libretto by Orthodox abbess Mother Thekla.

Michael **Nyman**

◗ 1944–   ⚑ ENGLISH   ✐ 100+

Best known for his scores for the films of Peter Greenaway and the award-winning soundtrack to Jane Campion's *The Piano*, Nyman has also had popular success with music he has written for his ensemble of amplified instruments, The Michael Nyman Band. Possibly his most enduring works, however, are his operas, which include *The Man who Mistook his Wife for a Hat*, based on a case study by Oliver Sacks.

MILESTONES	
1968	Credited with coining the term "minimalism" to describe a musical style
2007	*A Handshake in the Dark* for chorus and orchestra is premiered in London
2009	Releases the album *The Glare*, a collection of songs with words by David McAlmont superimposed on Nyman's music

Although Nyman studied composition at the Royal Academy of Music, he only settled into a career as a composer in his mid-thirties, after a decade of working as a music critic and editor. His interest in experimental music, and in particular John Cage, led him to explore the techniques of minimalism (a term that he claims to have coined), combined with frequent references to 16th- and 17th-century music and the insistent rhythms of rock music. This repetitive, mechanical style, played by his amplified "street band" (originally formed to provide music for a production of Goldoni's 1756 play *Il Campiello*) soon became something of a Nyman trademark, and was ideally suited for the soundtrack to Peter Greenaway's *The Draughtsman's Contract*, the first of several collaborations.

Through his work as a film composer, Nyman discovered a talent for, and love of, musical drama, which makes up a large part of his oeuvre alongside numerous chamber pieces for members of his band. Since the 1990s, his style has become less strident in tone, and more lyrical and reflective.

Michael **Torke**

◗ 1961–   ⚑ AMERICAN   ✐ 50+

Torke emerged in the 1980s as the leading American composer of the "postminimalist" generation, absorbing elements of pop and rock music into the minimalist style to produce music with great rhythmic vitality. Equally striking is his lush and inventive orchestration (he was described by the *New York Times* as "the Ravel of his generation")—a feeling for different tone colors which stems from his synesthesia, the connection between the senses that allows some people to "hear" color or "see" sounds. This was explicit in several of his early works, such as *Ecstatic Orange*, *Bright Blue Music*, and *Yellow Pages*, but has been a recurrent stylistic element in all his music. As a consequence, he has written mainly for orchestra or large ensemble, and the dramatic and rhythmic quality of his style has also made it particularly suitable for dance; many of his scores have been choreographed,

and recently he has written several ballets. A comparatively simple tonal harmonic language and an ability to write memorably expressive melodies makes his music very approachable, and has brought him considerable popular success, including commissions from the Atlanta Olympics (the orchestral "sonic olympiad" *Javelin*) and the Disney corporation (the massive oratorio *Four Seasons*) for millennium celebrations. He was also appointed as Associate Composer of the Royal Scottish National Orchestra in 1999, which brought him to the attention of audiences in the UK and the rest of Europe.

MILESTONES	
1996	Composes *Book of Proverbs* for voice and orchestra
2003	Founds his own record label, Ecstatic Records
2004	First performance of his ballet farce *An Italian Straw Hat*
2009	Composes *Mojave*, a concerto for marimba

Poul **Ruders**

● 1949–   ⚑ DANISH   ✍ 114

Ruders decided to be a composer at 16, when he heard Penderecki's *Threnody for the Victims of Hiroshima*. A Royal Danish Academy graduate in piano and organ, he became an acclaimed freelance composer, despite being mostly self-taught. He spent four years in London, after the Proms

MILESTONES

1967	Publishes first music
1980	*Four Compositions*, chamber concerto
1989	Composes Symphony No. 1
1994	Returns to Copenhagen
1998	*The Handmaid's Tale*, opera, produced
2005	Premiere of *The Trial*, opera
2007	*Dancer in the Dark*, opera
2008	*Kafkapriccio* for orchestra; *Concertino* for bass trombone and orchestra

success of his Symphony No. 1, and then returned to live and work in Copenhagen. The success of his opera based on Margaret Atwood's novel *The Handmaid's Tale* established his reputation worldwide. His music can be gloriously joyful and exuberant one moment and then change suddenly to introspection and despair. Using an expressive and flexible musical language— with passages of parody and quotation—Ruders has produced an impressive body of work.

⌃ **Ruder's opera,** *Kafka's Trial* (2005), was commissioned for the opening of the new opera house in Copenhagen.

Kevin **Volans**

● 1949–   ⚑ SOUTH AFRICAN   ✍ 100

Volans became popularly known in 1986 with the Kronos Quartet's bestselling CD of his work, *White Man Sleeps*. After university in Johannesburg, he studied in Cologne in Germany, became Karlheinz Stockhausen's teaching assistant, and was

commissioned to write for IRCAM. Associated with the New Simplicity school in the late 1970s, he became increasingly influenced by African music, incorporating its techniques into his original style, which established him in the 1980s. After further success with Kronos, Volans turned to dance in the 1990s, collaborating with British dancers such as Siobhan Davies, Jonathan Burrows, and Shobana Jeyasingh.

MILESTONES

1986	Moves to Ireland; writes *White Man Sleeps*, string quartet
1987	*Hunting: Gathering*, string quartet
1993	*The Man with Footsoles of Wind*, opera
2001	Writes *Zeno at 4am*, for puppets, actors, bass, string quartet, and chorus
2006	Piano Concerto No. 2 "Atlantic Crossing"

« **African drummers** perform at a dance on the Ivory Coast. African music inspired much of Volans's output, shaping his style and technique.

Wolfgang **Rihm**

● 1952–　　　　GERMAN　　　　✍ 300

Rihm's encyclopedic knowledge of Western music, and his affinity for the great Germans, has informed his enormous output of vocal and instrumental music. He studied under Stockhausen in 1972 and attended Darmstadt, where he is now a regular instructor. He is also professor of composition at Karlsruhe, where he was a student. Rihm started composing at 11, but his reputation was established in the 1970s with his cerebral but expressive music—particularly with the frequently staged *Jakob Lenz*, an opera on the descent of the eponymous poet into madness. He has frequently set texts by Nietzsche, and many of his works have historical allusions. Subjective in nature and emotionally powerful, yet retaining intellectual weight, Rihm's music enjoys high esteem with many serious listeners.

MILESTONES

1972	Studies with Stockhausen
1985	Professor of composition, Karlsruhe
1992	*Gesungene Zeit*, for violin and orchestra
1994	Premiere of *Séraphin*, music-theater
1999	Writes *Jagden und Formen*, orchestra
2010	*Dionysus*, opera; *Lichtes Spiel*, violin and orchestra

⌃ **Rihm's *Oedipus*,** seen here in performance with Andreas Schmidt in the title role, was written as a series of ten vignettes, two of which are pantomimes.

Kaija **Saariaho**

● 1952–　　　　FINNISH　　　　✍ 102

After studying at the Sibelius Academy, and in Freiburg, Germany, under the English composer Brian Ferneyhough, Saariaho moved to Paris where she has worked regularly at the IRCAM electronics studio. After writing melodious vocal works in the late 1970s, she started working with computers, exploiting techniques such as transforming synthesized sounds slowly into others. In recent years she has written for more conventional instrumentation, often in a dramatic and extrovert style, and occasionally using experimental effects like selective amplification. Saariaho has been involved in various multimedia projects, including a full-length ballet, *Maa*. In 2003, her lyric opera *L'amour de loin* won the Grawemeyer Prize, one of many awards that her works have received, and she continues to fulfill regular commissions across Europe.

MILESTONES

1986	Composes *Lichtbogen*, instruments and live electronics
1988	Records *Stilleben*, tape
1991	*Maa*, ballet, performed
1995	Violin concerto *Graal théâtre* premiered
2006	*La Passion de Simone*, oratorio/opera
2010	*Émilie*, opera

⌃ **Saariaho's opera,** *L'amour de loin* was first performed at the Salzburg Festival in 2000, and featured Vienna's highly acclaimed Arnold Schoenberg Choir.

Anne **Boyd**

◯ 1946–　　🏳 AUSTRALIAN　　✍ 70

On graduating from the University of Sydney, having studied under Peter Sculthorpe, Boyd spent several years in England (at York, under Mellers, then teaching at Sussex), and here she achieved success with her imaginative but disciplined, uncluttered music. Back at home she spent a period as a freelance composer, often setting Australian and Asian themes, as in her oratorio *The Death of Captain Cook*. Her interest in Asian music took her to Hong Kong for ten years, before returning to Sydney. As her academic career flourished, there was not always time for composing. However, she continues to produce works, such as the orchestral *Black Sun* and *Grathawai*, and lectures internationally.

MILESTONES	
1969	Moves to England
1974	Composes *Angklung*, for piano
1975	Writes *As I Crossed the Bridge of Dreams*, for 12 voices
1977	Returns to Australia
1981	Head of music at Hong Kong University
1990	Head of music, Sydney University
2005	*Yuya 2*, bassoon and string orchestra

⏶ **Anne Boyd explores** the music and tone worlds of a wide range of styles and cultures in her colorful works.

Carl **Vine**

◯ 1954–　　🏳 AUSTRALIAN　　✍ 62

Vine completed an electronic commission for West Australian Ballet while still at school, and won various music prizes while majoring in Physics at university. Now one of Australia's most performed and eminent composers, he has produced 20 vibrant, witty, and very danceable scores, as well as six symphonies, music for film and theater, and several other works. After winning many prizes in Australia, Vine worked as a freelance composer and pianist before embarking on a variety of composing residencies. He has appeared as a conductor and pianist in Europe, lectured widely on electronic music, and is Artistic Director of the Huntington Estate Music Festival in Australia.

⏵ **Vine's stirring score** for the closing ceremony of the 1996 Olympics invoked the heroic spirit of the Games.

MILESTONES	
1978	Composes *Poppy*, dance music
1979	Cofounds contemporary music ensemble Flederman
1984	Writes *Café Concertino*, chamber music
1985	Made resident composer at the New South Wales State Conservatorium
2000	Artistic director of Musica Viva Australia
2004	*Cello Concerto*
2011	*Violin Concerto*

Magnus **Lindberg**

◔ 1958–ㅤㅤㅤㅤ📖 FINNISHㅤㅤㅤㅤ✍ 65

In recent years, Finland has produced a throng of outstanding musical talents. Amongst its composers, Lindberg has one of the highest international profiles. The reasons are not hard to find: his music is dramatic, harmonically clear, colorful, ebullient (one of his major pieces is called *Joy*), and he uses the orchestra with prodigious skill to produce works of powerful immediacy.

Lindberg studied at the Sibelius Academy with composers Einojuhani Rautavaara and Paavo Heininen. Rautavaara would have encouraged Lindberg to see himself as a descendant of the founding father of Finnish music, Sibelius, but Heininen was interested above all in the works of the European avant-garde. Lindberg's early works, such as *Kraft* and *Action-Situation-Signification*, are bracingly modernist, in keeping with the exploratory aesthetics of Toimii, the performance group he helped found with the conductor Esa-Pekka Salonen in 1981. Lindberg's debt to Sibelius and other symphonic composers has become more audible, albeit with no dilution of his own musical voice.

MILESTONES

1970s	Works with Swedish electronics studio
1977	Cofounds the modernist "Korvat auki" (Ears Open Society)
1981	Goes to study in Paris
1985	*Kraft* is first successful orchestral work
1996	Directs Meltdown Festival in London
1997	Writes *Related Rocks* for IRCAM studio
2001	*Related Rocks* Lindberg Festival tours
2002	*Clarinet Concerto*
2006	*Violin Concerto*
2009	*Graffiti* for chorus and orchestra

KEY WORKS

AURA (IN MEMORIAM WITOLD LUTOSŁAWSKI)

ORCHESTRALㅤㅤ⏱ 40:00ㅤㅤ📖 4ㅤㅤ♫

Lindberg considered this massive work to be a cross between a symphony and a concerto for orchestra—both forms at which Lutosławski excelled. The four movements play continuously, the last building hypnotically to a climax based on repeating figurations, giving way to a strongly melodic epilogue for strings.

RELATED ROCKS

CHAMBERㅤㅤ⏱ 18:00ㅤㅤ📖 1ㅤㅤ♟

Related Rocks, for two percussionists, two pianos, and electronics, was inspired by a geological exhibition at which Lindberg was impressed both

by the variety and the ordered unity of the exhibits. The electronics provide a sonic "exhibition space" in which the instruments are presented. The work also develops an idea Lindberg had nurtured for some years: using electronically sampled recordings made during the demolition of a grand piano. The resultant sounds seem to have a symbolic power, perhaps the violence of events that formed the crystalline rocks.

◀◀ In the 1970s, Lindberg was impressed by energy of the English punk band The Clash and the destruction performances of Einstürzende Neubauten.

James **MacMillan**

🌑 1959–   📖 SCOTTISH   ✍ 180

MacMillan is one of the diplomats of contemporary music. His music can be challenging, but attracts a broad audience. He is Scottish and proud of it, but without being fanatical. A practising Roman Catholic, his theology is liberal and, though his music reflects his faith, it does not offer serenity by ignoring the "conflict and ambiguity" which is typical of most people's lives and on which, indeed, he believes music thrives.

MacMillan started composing while learning to play the trumpet as a child. He studied at Edinburgh and Durham universities, but began to find his personal voice as a composer only in his late 20s as he identified his national and religious sources of inspiration. His first success was *Búsqueda*

(*Search*), a music-theater piece that combined the Catholic liturgy with poems written by the mothers of the disappeared, women whose children went missing during the Dirty War in Argentina from 1976–83. *Búsqueda* and *The Confessions of Isobel Gowdie* set the course for his development, his works expressing religious conviction while still engaging with the "real world."

» **MacMillan has a strong interest** in Scottish and Irish folk music. In 1989 he was composer-in-residence at the St. Magnus Festival in Orkney.

MILESTONES	
1992	Completes *Veni, Veni Emmanuel*
1994	Writes Symphony No. 1 and *Vigil*
1996	Cello Concerto by Mstislav Rostropovich
1999	*Quickening* premiered at Proms
2004	*A Scotch Bestiary* for organ and orchestra
2007	*The Sacrifice*, opera
2008	*St John Passion*

KEY WORKS

VENI, VENI EMMANUEL

ORCHESTRAL   ⏱ 26:00   📖 1   ♫ ⦿

Veni, Veni Emmanuel (*Come, Come Emmanuel*) was written for leading percussionist Evelyn Glennie, who is also Scottish. As a percussion concerto, it allows a performer to demonstrate mastery of a vast array of instruments, but this presents a problem for the composer, because the number of sounds the soloist makes risks producing a fragmentary effect. MacMillan avoids this by turning the concerto into a set of clearly audible variations on one of the most glorious and familiar of all the liturgical chants for Advent.

VIGIL

ORCHESTRAL   ⏱ 40:00   📖 3   ♫

This work is part of an epic triptych titled *Triduum*. It was commissioned by Mstislav Rostropovich, who had come to know and admire *Veni, Veni Emmanuel*. Rostropovich premiered *Vigil* at the Barbican in London with the London Symphony Orchestra in 1997. *Vigil* was inspired by the Easter service, when Catholics anticipate Christ's Resurrection, and uses plainsong associated with the service. MacMillan describes *Vigil* simply, but graphically, as a journey from "despair to joy, from darkness to light, from death to life."

Mark-Anthony **Turnage**

● 1960– ♙ ENGLISH ✍ 102

Mark-Anthony Turnage has a gift for crossing boundaries. Many of his most striking works are infused with the spirit, harmonies, and rhythms of jazz. The energy this imparts to much of his music, together with his sense of drama and his commitment to contemporary social issues, commands attention from listeners of all persuasions, not only from those with "Classical" tastes.

Turnage began to win major composition prizes soon after completing his studies under John Lambert and Oliver Knussen. Hans Werner Henze commissioned an opera for the Munich Biennale in 1988, and the hard-hitting result, *Greek*, to a libretto by playwright Steven Berkoff, became an international success. In 1989, Sir Simon Rattle invited Turnage to become composer-in-association with the City of Birmingham Symphony Orchestra. The first result of the partnership was *Three Screaming Popes*, a work which proved that Turnage could be as aggressive and compelling in the concert hall as on the opera stage. Successes since then have come thick and fast, with operas such as *The Silver Tassie* and *Anna Nicole* playing to packed houses and arousing characteristic controversy.

MILESTONES

1978	Attends Royal College of Music
1981	Wins Guinness Prize for *Night Dances*
1988	*Greek* composed for Munich Biennale
1993	Composes *Your Rockaby*, concerto for saxophone, a favourite instrument
1996	Collaborates with John Scofield and other jazz musicians on *Blood on the Floor*, for large ensemble and jazz trio
1998	Turnage retrospective festival, *Fractured Lines*, held in London
2007	*Mambo, Blues and Tarantella*, concerto for violin and orchestra
2011	*Anna Nicole*, opera

KEY WORKS

THE SILVER TASSIE

OPERA	⏱120:00	📖 4	🎭 🎻 🎵

The opera takes its text from Sean O'Casey's pacifist play about a young Dubliner who wins a coveted football trophy before leaving to fight in World War I. The opera depicts the horrors of the trenches; but yet more disturbing are the consequences for the man who returns home to face betrayal and rejection because of his injuries.

BLOOD ON THE FLOOR

ORCHESTRAL	⏱70:00	📖 9	🎭 🎵

Commissioned as a ten-minute piece for an evening of jazz-inspired works by Gershwin, Bernstein, and others, *Blood on the Floor* outgrew the original brief. Like *Three Screaming Popes*, it takes its title from a haunted, visceral painting by Francis Bacon. With movements such as "Junior Addict" and "Needles," its subject is very personal, because Turnage's brother died from a drug overdose. Yet the work is an absorbing experience, a compelling blend of composed music and jazz improvisation.

❮❮ **Turnage is a great admirer** of the trumpeter Miles Davis and the jazz guitarist John Scofield.

George **Benjamin**

◔ 1960–   🏳 ENGLISH   ✍ 33

After studies with Olivier Messiaen in Paris and Alexander Goehr in Cambridge, Benjamin quickly emerged as a mature and confident composer. An early piece, *Ringed by the Flat Horizon*—written for an orchestra of 93—was played at the London Proms, making Benjamin, at 20, the youngest composer to have a piece performed at the Proms. His serious yet colorful, direct, even flamboyant style—compared by some to the mood of J. M. W. Turner's late paintings—led to frequent high-profile commissions through the 1980s. *Antara*, for Pierre Boulez, celebrated the 10th anniversary of IRCAM and won a major recording award. Benjamin has also been active as both pianist and festival organizer, and regularly conducts leading international orchestras. He has won numerous prizes and awards, including a CBE, membership of the Bavarian Academy of Fine Arts and the French Ordre des Arts et des Lettres, and since 1999 has built a close association with the Tanglewood Festival in the US.

MILESTONES	
1974	Studies with Olivier Messiaen
1980	Composes *Ringed by the Flat Horizon* for large orchestra
1984	Researches music at IRCAM
2001	Becomes Professor of Composition at King's College, London
2008	*Duet* for piano and orchestra

》 The evocative sound of Peruvian pan pipes (*antara*), manipulated electronically, gives the innovative composition *Antara* its futuristic and cosmic quality.

Thomas **Adès**

◔ 1971–   🏳 ENGLISH   ✍ 42

Winning "only" second prize as a pianist at the BBC Young Musician of the Year in 1989 proved a blessing in disguise for Thomas Adès. He concentrated instead on composing, becoming composer-in-residence for the Hallé Orchestra, shortly after leaving Cambridge University, and has since risen rapidly to prominence. His vivid, detailed, mightily assured style brought commissions from major orchestras, and his opera *Powder her Face* established his name worldwide. The orchestral piece *Asyla* was commissioned by Sir Simon Rattle, who conducted it at two seminal concerts, at Birmingham in 1998 and at Berlin in 2000, and the piece also won the coveted Grawemeyer Award, the largest international prize for composition. Adès is also active as a gifted conductor, teacher, and outstanding performer of his own and others' piano works.

》 The acclaimed production of *The Tempest*, conducted by Adès and premiered at London's Royal Opera House in 2004, starred Cyndia Sieden as Ariel.

MILESTONES	
1992	Double-starred first from Cambridge
1993	Performs first public recital in London
1995	*Powder her Face*, chamber opera, achieves international recognition
1997	*Asyla*, for orchestra, highly acclaimed
1999	Becomes artistic director of Aldeburgh Festival
2011	*Polaris* for orchestra and five video screens

Judith **Weir**

🌑 1954–   📜 SCOTTISH   ✍ 92

Judith Weir's music is accessible, unpretentious, and beautifully crafted. She is a tireless advocate of the "middle way" in contemporary music, rejecting both the extremes of simplicity (attributing much of the success of Górecki, Pärt, and Nyman to commercial forces) and intellectualism. She is best known for her operas, although theatrical wit and a strong gift for narrative inform all her work.

While still at school, Judith Weir studied with John Tavener, and later at Cambridge University with Robin Holloway. Since then, she has held teaching positions at universities in Britain and the US, but these have not deflected her from composing works of broad appeal, working with children and amateurs, and striving to build "wider musical communities." While director of London's Spitalfields Festival, she regularly programmed Indian music alongside contemporary pieces and community music-making events. Her own works draw inspiration from Chinese and Indian traditions (for instance, she has collaborated on projects with the Indian storyteller Vayu Naidu), as well as from her own Scottish roots. Her interest in medieval culture also shows in her music.

MILESTONES

1985	Composes *The Consolations of Scholarship* for ensemble and soprano, based on a Chinese drama of the Yuan period
1988	Completes choral work *Missa del Cid*; it is televised by the BBC
1999	*Natural History* (setting of Taoist texts) for soprano and orchestra premiered
2000	*woman.life.song* commissioned by Jessye Norman to words by Clarissa Estés, Maya Angelou, and Toni Morrison
2002	Collaborates with Vayu Naidu on *Future Perfect*, a blend of music and narrative
2007	*Concrete* for narrator, choir, and orchestra
2011	*Miss Fortune*, opera

KEY WORKS

MISSA DEL CID

CHORAL	⏱ 25:00	📖 6	🎵🎭🎶

This work blends the Latin Mass with extracts from a Spanish medieval epic recounting the exploits of El Cid—the fanatical slayer of the Moors. The brutality of his era is satirized by its absorption into the liturgy, but the work ends in desolation, portraying the aftermath of battle.

A NIGHT AT THE CHINESE OPERA

OPERA	⏱ 90:00	📖 3	🎵🎶

Judith Weir's first full-length opera is an expansion of her earlier *The Consolations of Scholarship*, which forms the central act

as a play within a play. The plot concerns the revenge of an orphan who has been unwittingly reared by a despot who killed his family. Act two echoes Chinese opera in providing music whose task is to support drama and stage gestures.

☑ **Sir Simon Rattle** commissioned Weir's *We Are Shadows* for the City of Birmingham Symphony Orchestra in 1999.

Glossary of music terms

A cappella Literally "in the style of the chapel" (Italian), the term describes a piece written for unaccompanied voice(s).

Atonal Describes any music without a recognizable tonality or key, such as serial music.

Aria Literally "air" (Italian), a vocal piece for one or more voices in an opera or oratorio, more formally organized than a song. Arias written in the 17th and 18th centuries usually take the form of "da capo arias," with a three-part structure, the third part being a reiteration of the first.

Ars nova Literally "the new art" (Latin), a term coined in c.1322 to refer to a style of music using new notation techniques, distinguishing it from the earlier "ars antiqua."

Basso continuo Harmonic, quasi-improvisatory accompaniment to a melodic piece used extensively in the Baroque period. The continuo usually comprised a harpsichord or organ and bass viol or cello, but was sometimes played on other instruments.

Cadenza Literally "cadence" (Italian). Originally an improvised solo passage by the solo performer within a concerto, from the 19th century onward cadenzas became more formalized and less spontaneous.

Canon Contrapuntal piece in which the separate voices or instruments enter one by one imitatively. If a canon is strict, the melody line is repeated exactly by all parts.

Cantata A cantata is in many respects similar to opera, being a programmatic piece generally for voice and orchestra that is designed to tell a story. The 17th and 18th centuries saw the rise of both the cantata da camera (a secular chamber piece) and the cantata da chiesa (its sacred equivalent).

Cantus firmus Literally a "fixed song" (Latin)—usually comprising very long notes and often based on a fragment of Gregorian chant—that served as the structural basis for polyphonic composition, particularly during the Renaissance.

Canzona Short, polyphonic part song popular in the 16th and 17th centuries. In many ways a canzona is similar to a madrigal, although the writing is lighter.

Capriccio Short piece in a generally free style. Capriccios written in the 17th century tend to be fugal in structure and rather more formalized than their Romantic equivalents—written by the likes of Brahms and Paganini, for example—which tend to be solo rhapsodic pieces.

Chamber music Music composed for small groups of two or more instruments such as duet, trios, and quartets. Chamber music was originally designed to be performed at home for the entertainment of small gatherings, but is now more often performed in concert environments. Similarly, chamber orchestras and operas are pieces written for small numbers of instruments, although all orchestral instruments are represented.

Chanson French part song of the Middle Ages and Renaissance similar to the canzona and often arranged for voice and lute. The term "chanson" later came to refer to any song to French words.

Chromatic Literally "of color" (Latin), based on the scale of all 12 semitones in an octave, as opposed to diatonic, based on a scale of seven notes.

Clavichord Early stringed keyboard instrument whose strings are sounded by being struck by metal "tangents," rather than felt-covered hammers (like a piano's), or plucked (like a harpsichord's).

Coda Literally "tail" (Italian), a final section of a piece of music that is distinct from the overall structure.

Concerto Derived from terms meaning both "performing together" and "struggling." Today, the term is given to describe a large piece for a solo instrument and orchestra, designed to be a vehicle for the solo performer's virtuosity on his instrument. In the earlier Baroque concerto grossos, however, there was a more equal interplay between the much smaller orchestra ("ripieno") and a group of soloists ("concertino").

Concerto grosso See *Concerto*.

Continuo See *Basso continuo*.

Contrapuntal Describes music using counterpoint, the simultaneous playing or singing of two or more melodic lines. Contrapuntal forms such as the ricercare, canzona, and

fugue evolved in the Renaissance, and reached their height in the work of composers such as Palestrina and J.S. Bach.

Counterpoint See *Contrapuntal*.

Crescendo Literally "growing" (Italian), a musical direction to play or sing gradually louder. The opposite is diminuendo.

Diatonic Based on a scale in which the octave is divided into seven steps, such as major and minor scales.

Diminuendo A musical direction to play or sing gradually more quietly. The opposite is crescendo.

Dissonance Sounding together of notes to produce discord (i.e. sounds unpleasing to the ear). The opposite of these terms are "consonance" and "concord." Dissonance is very subjective, and combinations of notes considered dissonant in one period are often heard as consonant by later audiences.

Divertimento Classical instrumental genre for chamber ensemble or soloist, often performed as light entertainment.

Dynamics Differences in volume of a piece or section of music.

Equal temperament System of tuning (or "temperament") whereby each note of the chromatic scale is separated from its neighbors by exactly the same degree. Equal temperament was introduced in the 18th century, and the new system made it possible to play in any key of the chromatic scale.

Fugato Passage written in the manner of a fugue.

Fugue A complex, highly structured contrapuntal piece in two or more parts, popular in the Baroque era. The separate voices or lines enter one by one imitatively: the first voice states a subject, then the second enters with an "answer" (the subject starting on a different note) while the first voice performs a countersubject. The process continues until all the voices have entered, and may be followed by freer "episodes," contrapuntal variations of the subject, or a repeated statement of the subject.

Galant A courtly musical style of the 18th century characterized by elegance, formality, and clarity, without ornamentation.

Grand opéra French development of opera, characterized by historic plots, large choruses, crowd scenes, ornate costumes, and spectacular sets.

Ground Composition developed on a ground bass (a constantly repeated bass figure, often melodic). Can also refer to the bass part itself.

Harmony The combination of two or more notes to form chords. In tonal music from the Renaissance onward, harmony has been based on the consonant interval of a third in three-note chords known as triads.

Homophonic Describes a style of writing popularized in the Classical period in which a lyrical melody line is supported by chordal harmony and a solid bass.

Intermezzo Light-hearted interlude performed between the acts of an opera seria. The intermezzo developed from the intermedio, a short musical drama performed between the acts of spoken plays in the 15th and 16th centuries.

Kapellmeister/Hofkapellmeister Choir master, or music director. The term Kapellmeister later became synonymous with the English "conductor," or US "leader."

Libretto Text of an opera or other vocal dramatic work.

Lied Traditional German song, popularized by the Lieder of Schubert.

Lute Early precursor of the modern guitar, of Eastern origin, popular in the Renaissance.

Madrigal Secular a cappella song popular in the Renaissance period, particularly in England and Italy, often set to a lyric love poem.

Masque Elaborate English stage entertainment chiefly cultivated in the 17th century and involving poetry, dancing, scenery, costumes, instrumental and vocal music. The masque was related to opera and ballet.

Mass Main service of the Roman Catholic Church, highly formalized in structure, comprising specific sections—known as the "Ordinary"—performed in the following order: *Kyrie, Gloria, Credo, Sanctus* with *Hosanna* and *Benedictus*, and *Agnus Dei* and *Dona nobis pacem*. Other movements can also be added, especially in the Requiem Mass.

Mélodie French equivalent of the German Lied and English song.

Minuet and Trio A graceful dance in 3/4 time, normally in three sections: the Minuet section (either binary or ternary form), then the Trio (originally intended for three musicians to play, and consisting of unrelated material), and finally a reprise of the Minuet. The piece appears as a movement of Baroque suites and Classical sonatas and symphonies, but was replaced with the faster Scherzo by Beethoven.

Modes Seven-note scales inherited from Ancient Greece via the Middle Ages, when they were most prevalent, although they still survive today in folk music and plainsong.

Modulation A shift from one key (tonality) to another—for example, C major to A minor.

Monody Vocal style developed in the Baroque period whereby the musical intent is conveyed by a single melodic line, either accompanied or not.

Monophonic Describes music written in a single line, or melody without an accompaniment.

Motet Originally, in medieval times, a vocal composition elaborating on the melody and text of plainsong. In the 15th century, the motet became a more independent religious choral composition, set to any Latin words not included in the Mass.

Motive Short but recognizable melodic or rhythmic figure that recurs throughout a piece, often used programmatically to refer to a character, object, or idea, as with Wagner's Leitmotiv and Berlioz's *idée fixe*.

Nocturne "Night piece." As a solo, one-movement piano piece, the nocturne originated with John Field, but was developed to a great degree by Chopin.

Opera Drama in which all or most characters sing and in which music is an important element. Traditionally, the writing is for full orchestra, soloists, and chorus, although examples exist that include fewer or more than these elements.

Opéra comique Exclusively French type of opera which, despite its name, is not always comic, nor particularly light. It is always based on original material, however, and always includes spoken dialogue.

Opera buffa Type of comic opera that was especially popular in the 18th century (e.g. Mozart's *The Marriage of Figaro*, Rossini's *The Barber of Seville*).

Opera seria Literally "serious opera," and the direct opposite of opera buffa. The style is characterized by heroic or mythological plots, and a formality of music and action.

Operetta Literally "little opera," and sometimes known as "light opera," this term refers to a lighter style of 19th-century opera that included spoken dialogue.

Oratorio Work for vocal soloists and choir with instrumental accompaniment originating in the congregation of Oratorians, founded by St. Philip Neri in the 16th century. Oratorios traditionally take biblical texts as their subject matter and are usually performed "straight," although they originally involved sets, costumes, and action.

Ornament An embellishment of a note or chord. This can be a simple added "grace" note, a trill, or a short melodic fragment such as a turn (the note above the main note, the main note, and the note below, played in quick succession before the main note).

Ostinato Repeated musical figure, usually in the bass part, providing a foundation for harmonic and melodic variation above.

Overture Literally "opening" (French), an instrumental introduction to an opera, which presents some of the main thematic material. In the Romantic period, stand-alone overtures were written, e.g. Brahms's *Tragic Overture* and Mendelssohn's *Hebrides Overture,* and performed in their own right. Overtures are usually in sonata form.

Pedal (point) A held note that usually occurs in the bass, above which harmonies change, sometimes even becoming discordant. A pedal point will often occur at the climax of a fugue.

Pizzicato Literally "pinched" (Italian), a style of playing stringed instruments that are normally bowed, such as the violin or cello, by plucking the string with a finger.

Plainsong Also known as plainchant, (from the Latin *cantus planus*), plainsong is medieval church music that still survives today in the

Roman Catholic Church. It consists of a unison, unaccompanied vocal line in free rhythm, like speech, with no regular bar lengths. Gregorian chant is a well-known type of plainsong.

Polyphony Literally "many sounds," in Classical music this refers to a style of writing in which all parts are independent and of equal importance, unlike homophonic music, and therefore implies contrapuntal music. Forms that typify this style include the canon, fugue, and motet.

Program music Any music written to describe a nonmusical theme, such as an event, landscape, or literary work.

Recitative Style of singing in opera and oratorio that is closely related to the delivery of dramatic speech in pitch and rhythm. The recitative sections are often used for dialogue and exposition of the plot between arias and choruses.

Rondo Piece (or movement) of music based on a recurring theme with interspersed material, following the form ABACADAE, etc.

Scherzo Lively dance piece (or movement) in triple time. During the Classical and Romantic periods, the third movement of a symphony or one of a sonata's middle movements was a Scherzo, usually paired with a Trio. The Scherzo and Trio replaced the Baroque Minuet and Trio.

Serial music System of atonal composition developed by Arnold Schoenberg and others of the Second Viennese School, in which fixed sequences of musical elements are used as a foundation for more complex structures. Most commonly these sequences comprise arrangements of each degree of the chromatic scale—known as a "tone row"—although shorter sequences may also be used. This tone row, or series, can then appear in four different ways: forward, backward (retrograde), upside-down (inversion), and upside-down and backward (retrograde inversion).

Singspiel Literally "song play" (German), Singspiel generally refers to a comic opera with spoken dialogue in lieu of recitative, as typified in Mozart's *The Magic Flute*.

Sonata Popular instrumental piece for one or more players. Appearing first in the Baroque period, when it was a short piece for a solo or small

group of instruments accompanied by a continuo, the Classical sonata adhered to a three- or four-movement structure for one or two instruments (although the three-instrument trio sonata was often popular), comprising usually three or four movements: an opening movement (in what later became known as "first movement" or "sonata" form), a slow second movement, a lively Scherzo, and finally a Rondo.

Sonata principle/form Structural form popularized in the Classical period, and from this period onward the first movements of sonatas, symphonies, and concertos were written mainly in this form.
1. A piece written in sonata form is traditionally comprises an exposition, comprising an object followed by a second subject (linked by a bridge section and modulated to a different key), after which the initial material is expounded on in the development section, and finally the recapitulation restates the exposition, although remaining in the tonic (main key).
2. A variation on sonata form is "rondo sonata form," in which the restated rondo theme is constructed around a similar developmental format, with a refrain (i.e. a section which returns regularly) alternating with contrasting sections called "episodes." If the refrain is labelled as A and the episodes as B and C, a typical rondo form will be as follows: ABACAD (with D being the coda).

Suite Multi-movement work (generally instrumental) made up of a series of contrasting dance movements, usually all in the same key.

Symphony Large-scale work for full orchestra. The Classical and Romantic symphony, popularized by Haydn and Mozart, contains four movements—traditionally an Allegro, a slower second movement, a Scherzo, and a lively Finale—but later symphonies can contain more or fewer. The first movement is often in sonata form, and the slow movement and Finale may follow a similar structure.

Symphonic poem Extended single-movement symphonic work, usually of a programmatic nature, often describing landscape or literary works. Also known as a tone poem.

Verismo Style of opera with thematic material and presentation rooted firmly in reality.

Index

Page numbers in **bold** refer to main entries.

Acknowledgments

The publisher would like to thank the following for their kind permission to reproduce their photographs.

Abbreviations: a = above; bg = background; b = below; c = center; l = left; r = right; rh = running header; t = top.

AKG = akg-images; AL = Alamy Images; ART = The Art Archive; BAL = www.bridgeman.co.uk; Co = Corbis; DK = DK Images; GI = Getty Images; KOB = Kobal Collection; LEB = Lebrecht Music and Arts Photo Library; MEPL = Mary Evans Picture Library; NPG = National Portrait Gallery, London; Red = Redferns; RGA = Ronald Grant Archive; SPL = Science Photo Library; TOP = Topfoto.co.uk.

2 Co/Mimmo Jodice; 4–5 GI/Taxi; 6 Co/Stephanie Maze; 8–9 AL/Vittorio Sciosia; 10–11 GI/Simon Watson;12t Co/John D. Norman; 12b LEB/Chris Stock; 13 bc DK; 13c DK/Dave King; 13bl DK/ Philip Dowell; 13br YAMAHA; 14t Red/David Redfern; 15 Co/David Stoecklein; 16b Co/ Sygma/Reuter Raymond; 17t GI/Stone; 18–19 Co/Sung-Il Kim; 20bl,cl,ccr,cr DK; 20ccl DK/ Dave King; 21bcb,bla,tr DK; 21blc DK/Dave King; 21cl,cr,tl DK; 22l DK/Andy Crawford; 22c DK/ Dave King; 22r DK; 23cr DK/Dave King; 23tl DK; 23br MEPL; 23l GI/Royalty Free; 24cl,r DK; 24al DK/ Dave King; 24cr YAMAHA; 25cr DK; 25far l DK/Dave King; 25cb2,cl1,cl2,r. DK/Philip Dowell; 25cb1 YAMAHA; 26c,tr DK; 26cra,crb DK/Dave King; 26–27b DK/Philip Dowell; 27r DK; 27al,bl DK/Dave King; 28bl,cl,cra,crb DK; 28bc DK/ Philip Dowell; 28cb GI/Photodisc/Royalty Free; 28ca YAMAHA; 28ar,cl LEB/Chris Stock; 29b GI/ Royalty Free; 29al1 YAMAHA; 30–31 GI: Yellow Dog Productions; 32tl LEB; 33c Co/Richard T. Nowitz; 33br AL/Ace Stock Ltd; 34b Bournemouth Symphony Orchestra/photo Chris Zuidyk; 35t Red/Andrew Lepley; 35b Clive Barda/ArenaPAL; 36–37 AKG; 38 Co/Gianni Dagli Orti; 40cl British Library, London, UK/BAL; 41crb,tl AKG; 42b Private Collection/BAL; 42tl LEB; 43crb AKG; 43cl The Dufay Collective/ photo Coneyl Jay; 44 AKG; 45t AL/John Arnold Images; 45b Co/Archivo Iconografico,S.A; 46b DK/Neil Lukas; 46t LEB; 47tr MEPL; 47tl LEB/ John Minnion; 47b Co/Bettmann; 48b AKG; 48c Co/Bettmann; 49tl Co/Kimball Art Museum; 49tr photo Scala, Florence/British Library, London; 49b AKG; 50 DK/Kim Sayer; 51b Bibliothèque Nationale,Paris,France/BAL/Lauros/Giraudon; 51t LEB; 52 LEB; 53 LEB; 54b AKG; 54t LEB; 55c AKG; 55tr AKG/Nimatallah; 55b LEB; 56b Co/ Archivo Iconografico, S.A; 56t LEB; 57b GI/ Stone; 58b Co/National Gallery Collection; By Kind Permission of the Trustees of The National Gallery, London; 58t LEB; 58c LEB/Colouriser AL; 59t LEB; 60–61 Lefevre Fine Art Ltd. London. / BAL; 62 LEB; 63bl AKG; 63c LEB; 64 LEB; 65 DK/John Heseltine; 66b Musée Ingres, Montauban, France/BAL/Giraudon; 66t LEB/ Colouris; 67br LEB; 67c LEB/ Colouris; 68tl AKG; 68cr Santa Maria del Soccorso (La Rotunda), Rovigo, Italy/BAL; 68b Co/David Lees; 69bl,cl AKG; 70br AKG/Erich Lessing; 70tl Co/ Stefano Blanchetti; 71b,t LEB; 72b ComedieFrancaise, Paris,France /BAL/Lauros/ Giraudon; 72tl LEB; 73c AKG; 73t Co/Bettmann; 74tr LEB; 74bl AKG/Nimatallah; 74br LEB; 75b Prado, Madrid, Spain/BAL; 75t Co/Archivo Iconografico,S.A.; 76t AKG; 76b AKG/British Library; 77t Co/Bettmann; 77b Co/Historical Picture Archive ; 78b AKG; 78tl Private Collection,Milan,Italy/BAL; 78c Co/Archivo Iconografico, S.A.; 79t Co; 79b Co/Robbie Jack; 80 LEB; 81 AL/Lebrecht Music and Arts Library; 82 LEB/Colouris; 83t Museum fur Geschichte de Stadt Leipzig/BAL; 83b Co/Ron Slenzak; 84 Co/ Archivo Iconografico; 86 AKG; 87tl Co/Archivo Iconografico,S.A; 87bl Co/Hulton-Deutsch Collection; 87br LEB; 88 Co/Bettmann; 89b AL/ Bildarchiv Monheim GmbH; 89tl LEB; 89tr AKG; 90 DK; 91 Red/Steve J.Sherman; 92 LEB/D. Hunstein/Sony; 93 LEB/Chris Christodoulou; 94 Co/Alfredo Dagli Orti/The Art Archive; 96bl,tr LEB; 97 AKG/Erich Lessing; 98b AKG; 98t LEB; 99b LEB; 99t LEB/ Colouris; 100cl,tl AKG; 100cr Co/Wolfgang Kaehler; 100b Dover Publications; 101cl AKG; 101t Co/Archivo Iconografico,S.A.; 101br Co/Stefano Blanchetti; 102 Co/Archivo Iconografico,S.A.; 103 LEB; 104 LEB/Laurie Lewis; 105bl,br AKG; 105tl Co/Archivo Iconografico,S.A; 105cr NPG; 106bl AKG; 106tl AKG/Nimatallah; 107tr AKG; 107bl AKG; 107br LEB; 108b,c,t Co/Archivo Iconografico,S.A; 109b,t LEB; 109r AL/Interfoto; 110t Co/Archivo Iconografico,S.A; 110c LEB; 111b,t AKG/Erich Lessing; 112 Co/Archivo Iconografico,S.A; 113b Co/Robbie Jack; 113t LEB; 114 Co/Archivo Iconografico,S.A; 115 Co/Archivo Iconografico,S.A; 116 AKG; 117 LEB/Suzie Maeder; 118tl,tr AKG; 118br Phillips, The International Fine Art Auctioneers, UK/BAL; 118cl LEB/Colouris; 119b,t AKG; 120 GI/Imagno/ Contributor/Hulton Archive; 122 LEB/Colouris; 123tr Co/Archivo Iconografico,S.A; 123tr, b LEB; 124t LEB; 124b LEB; 125 Co/Archivo Iconografico,S.A; 126 LEB/Decca/Hanak; 127 AKG/Ullstein Bild; 128tl Co/Hulton-Deutsch Collection; 128b LEB/Colouris; 130 Co/Archivo Iconografico,S.A; 131 AKG; 132 Co/Bettmann; 133 AKG/Erich Lessing; 134 Co/Austrian Archives; 135 LEB; 136bl AKG; 136cl Naxos rs International; 136t LEB/Colouris; 136tr AKG; 137tl,bl AKG; 138 Co/Hulton-Deutsch Collection; 139tr LEB; 139b LEB; 141 LEB/Suzie Maeder; 142 Co/Archivo Iconografico, 143 LEB; 144t Co/ Hulton-Deutsch Collection; 144b AKG; 145t AKG; 145b Co/Bettmann; 146 Co/ Hulton-Deutsch Collection; 147 LEB/G.Salter; 148 Co/Hulton-Deutsch Collection; 149t DK/ Demetrio Carrasco; 149br GI/Doug Gifford/ Contributor; 150 Co/Frank McMahon; 151t DK/ Demetrio Carrasco; 151b Co/Thierry Orban/ Sygma; 152 Co/Bettmann; 153 LEB; 154t Co/ Bettmann; 154b Co/Archivo Iconografico,S.A; 155t LEB; 155b AL/Photo Network; 156 Red/Ron Scherl; 158 GI/Edgar Degas/BAL; 160 ART/ Archivio Storico Ricordi Milan/Dagli Orti (A); 161 Co/Archivo Iconografico,S.A; 161 LEB; 162t Co/ Stefano Blanchetti; 162c LEB; 163br,ca AKG; 163bl Co/Bettmann; 163tl LEB; 164b,t AKG; 165t Co/Archivo Iconografico, S.A; 165b Co/Robbie Jack; 166b Victoria & Albert Museum, London/ BAL; 166t Co/Archivo Iconografico, S.A; 167t Co/ Archivo Iconografico,S.A; 167b GI/Gordon Parks/ TimeLife Pictures; 168 Co/Bettmann; 169 LEB/ Laurie Lewis; 170 Co/Hulton-Deutsch Collection; 171tr AKG; 171br DK/Pawel Wojcik; 172t LEB; 172b LEB; 173 AKG; 174b AKG/ Ullstein Bild; 174t Co/Bettmann; 175t Co/ Archivo Iconografico,S.A; 175b MEPL; 176 Co; 178 GI/Beatriz Schiller/Time Life Pictures; 179t AKG; 179b GI/Hulton Archive; 180b Historisches Museum der Stadt, Vienna, Austria/BAL; 180t Co/Archivo Iconografico,S.A; 181tl AKG; 181br Private Collection/BAL; 181cr ART/Museum der Stadt Wien/Dagli Orti (A); 181cl LEB; 182b,t AKG; 183tl, tr AKG; 183c AKG; 183br Co/Archivo Iconografico,S.A; 184 GI/Ricardo Canals y Llambi/BAL; 186 LEB; 187tl LEB; 187b ART/ Edward Grieg House, Nordas Lake, Bergen, Norway/ Dagli Orti (A); 187tr AKG; 188t Co/ Michael Nicholson; 188b ART/Bibliothèque des Arts Decoratifs, Paris / Dagli Orti; 189tl, br LEB; 189bl LEB; 189br TOP; 190c Hamburg Kunsthalle, Hamburg, Germany/BAL; 190t Co/ Michael Nicholson; 191b,t LEB; 192br Archives Charmet/BAL; 192cr DK/Demitrio Carrasco; 192cb,t LEB; 193b,tl AKG; 193tr LEB; 194 Co/ Bettmann; 195 MEPL; 196 LEB/Royal Academy of Music Collection; 197 RGA / Courtsey of Rank/ITV; 198t AKG; 198b ART/Private Collection/Marc Charmet; 199 LEB; 200 LEB; 201 LEB; 202t LEB; 202b LEB/Donald Cooper; 203b,t LEB; 204t AKG; 204b Private Collection/ BAL; 205br,cl AKG; 205cl Co/Michael Nicholson; 205tl LEB/Interfoto,Munich; 206b,t AKG; 207t AKG; 207b Peter Willi / Kunstmuseum, Basel, Switzerland/BAL; 208c Musée des Tapisseries, Angers, France/BAL/Lauros/Giraudon; 208br DK; 208cl,t LEB; 209c AKG; 209br Co/Bettmann; 209tr LEB; 210b AKG/Gert Schutz; 210t LEB; 211t Co/Michael Nicholson; 211b LEB; 212t AKG; 212b Co/Ludovic Malsant; 213tl AKG; 213b Co/Underwood & Underwood; 213cl,tr LEB; 214t AKG; 214c Co/Freelance Consulting Services Pty Ltd; 214br LEB; 215t Co/Hulton-Deutsch Collection; 215b Co/Archivo Iconografico, S.A; 216 Co/Hulton-Deutsch Collection; 217 GI; 218br AKG; 218cl Co/Hulton-Deutsch Collection; 218tl,tr LEB; 219bl Co/Bettmann; 219cr Co/ Hulton-Deutsch Collection; 219tl LEB/C. Lambton; 219br LEB/ Royal Academy of Music Collection; 220 Co/Michael Nicholson; 221 LEB; 222 Co/Bettmann; 223 DK/Dave King; 224t Co/ Bettmann; 224b Co/John Heseltine; 225b GI/ Design Pics/The Irish Image Collection; 225t LEB; 226b AL/Chromepix.com; 226t LEB/Royal Academy of Music Collection; 227tr Co/ Hulton-Deutsch Collection; 227br,cl,tl LEB; 228bl,tl,tr AKG; 228br Co/Hulton-Deutsch Collection; 229t Co/Bettmann; 229b Co/Michael Freeman; 30t Co/Michael Nicholson; 230b LEB; 231tl, tr LEB; 231bl AKG; 231br Co/Michael Busselle; 232t AKG; 232b Musée des Beaux-Arts, Reims, France/BAL/Lauros/ Giraudon; 233cr AKG; 233b,t LEB; 234 Co/ Bettmann; 235 Co/Michael Freeman; 236tl LEB; 236bl AKG; 236c LEB; 237t AKG; 237b "Les Ballets Suedois" Cinémathèque française, Paris; 238b,t AKG; 238c Co/Steve Raymer; 239t Co/Bettmann; 239b ART/Bibliothèque des Arts Decoratifs Paris/Dagli Orti; 240ca Co/Sylvian Saustier; 240b,cb,t LEB; 241t Roger-Viollet, Paris/BAL; 241 RGA/Courtesy Literary Classic Productions; 242t, cb Al/MEPL; 242c TOP; 243b,t Co/Bettmann; 244t Co/Bettmann; 244b LEB; 245tl, cl, br AKG; 245cr AKG; 46cl LEB; 246br LEB/Manchester Art Gallery; 246cr LEB/Sabine Toepffer/Deutsches Theater; 247t Co/Archivo Iconografico,S.A; 247b LEB; 248b Real Academia de Bellas Artes de San Fernando, Madrid, Spain/BAL/Giraudon; 248tl LEB; 369t Co/ Bettmann; 249c Co/O. Alamany & E.Vicens; 50 Co/John Springer Collection; 251 Co/Jeremy Horner; 252t Co/Bettmann; 252b DK; 53cl,tl Co; 253b Co/Craig Lovell; 253cr DK/conaculta-inah-mex—Authorised reproduction by the Instituto Nacional de Antropología e Historia; 254b LEB; 255b Co/Alan Schein Photography; 255t Co/ Bettmann; 256c Christie's Images/BAL; 256t LEB; 257t Co; 257b DK; 258 LEB; 259 Courtesy of The MacDowell Colony/Joanna Eldredge Morrissey; 260 Co/Jud Guitteau/Illustration Works; 262 LEB/Laurie Lewis; 263br LEB/Kurt Weill Foundation; 263cl Co/Bettmann; 64cr AKG/Mirisch-7 Arts/United Artists/ Album; 264t AKG/United Artists/Album; 265cb Co/Reuters; 266 LEB; 267 LEB/Private Collection; 268 Co/ Bettmann; 269t Co/Bettmann; 269b LEB; 270 Co/BBC; 271 AKG; 272clb AKG; 272cr Co/ Bogdan Cristel/Reuters; 272bl Co/ Hulton-Deutsch Collection; 272tl LEB; 273b,t LEB; 400 Co/David Cumming/Eye Ubiquitous; 274 Co/Hulton-Deutsch Collection; 275t Co/ Phillippa Lewis/Edifice; 275b Co/Kelly-Mooney Photography; 276b LEB/Laurie Lewis; 276t AKG/Niklaus Strauss; 277cr AKG; 277tl AKG/Paul Almasy; 277br AKG/©Sevenarts Ltd 2005. All Rights Reserved, DACS; 277cl AKG; 278tc AKG; 278tl DK/Dave King; 278bl Co/ Hulton-Deutsch Collection; 279ca Co/Bettmann; 279t, cb LEB; 280LEB; 281 LEB/© 1932 renewed by Associated Music Publishers BMI. International copyright secured. All rights reserved. Reprinted by permission; 415 GI/Taxi; 282tl Co/Bettmann; 282c GI/Hulton-Deutsch Collection; 283cr Private Collection/BAL; 283cl,t Co/Bettmann; 283b KOB/Flaherty Prods.; 284 Co/Underwood & Underwood; 285 RGA/ Courtesy MGM; 286 Co/Bettmann; 287 KOB/ Paramount; 288t Co/Bettmann; 288c Co/ David Lees; 289 AKG/Binder; 290cl Co/Joseph Sohm; Visions of America; 290tl LEB; 290cl LEB/Betty Freeman; 290br LEB/ R. Booth; 291cr Co/Ted Spiegel; 291br Co/Jon Hicks; 292 Co/Jacques M Chenet; 293br Co/Bettmann; 293bl Co/Christher Felver; 293t LEB/Betty Freeman; 293cr LEB/ Susurrea; 294cr AKG/Gert Schutz; 294tl AKG/ photo by Georgette Chadbourne/ © ADAGP, Paris and DACS, London 2005; 294br James Goodman Gallery, New York, USA / BAL/ © 1998 Kate Rothko Prizel & Christopher Rothko/DACS 2005; 294cl LEB; 295br AL/IMAGINA The Image Maker; 295t AKG; 295cr City Lights Bookstore; 295cl LEB/Betty Freeman; 296t Co/Reuters; 296b Kobal Collection/New Line/Ch 4/Telefilm; 297b Co/Tony Wilson-Bligh/Papillio; 297t LEB/ Betty Freeman; 298t Co/Piotr Redlinski; 298b KOB/Paramount/ Miramax/Clive Coote; 299t LEB/Betty Freeman; 299b LEB/ Laurie Lewis; 300t LEB/Betty Freeman; 300b TOP/HIP/The British Library; 301t Co/Dean Conger; 301b Co/ Robbie Jack; 302 LEB; 303 LEB; 304 GI; 305t LEB; 305b LEB/B.Rafferty; 306t DK/Demetrio Carrasco; 306bl LEB; 307t RGA /Courtesy Mosfilm; 307b LEB/Richard H Smith; 308tl AKG/ Marion Kalter; 308b Co/Galeb Garanich/ Reuters; 308cr LEB/Zdenek Chrapek; 309t AKG/ Marion Kalter; 309c Co/Peter Turnley; 310b The Stapelton Collection/ BAL/© DACS 2005; 310t LEB/Kurt Weill Foundation; 311t Co/ Hulton-Deutsch Collection; 312 Co/Hulton-Deutsch Collection; 313 LEB/B. Rafferty; 314 Co/Hulton-Deutsch Collection; 316 GI/Time Life Pictures; 317tr Co/Hulton-Deutsch Collection; 317bl LEB/Suzy Maeder; 318cr AL/Andrew Bargery; 318t Co/Hulton-Deutsch Collection; 318cl LEB/culture-images; 319tl AKG/Marion Kalter; 319cr Co/Bettmann; 319cl AKG; 320t LEB/Matti Kolho; 320b LEB/Forum; 321t AKG/ Horst Maack; 321b LEB/Laurie Lewis; 322 AKG/ Horst Maack; 323b Co/Catherine Panchoot; 323t Co/Philippe Caron/Sygma; 324c AKG/Paul Almasy; 324tl Co/Hulton-Deutsch Collection; 325b KOB/MGM; 325t LEB/Betty Freeman; 326c AKG/Bianconero; 326t LEB/Betty Freeman; 327b GI/Erich Auerbach; 327t LEB/Robin Del Mar; 328tl,bl Co/Niklaus Stauss/Keystone; William Coupon 329t LEB/Betty Freeman; 329cr DK; 329br AL/lookGaleria; 329t Co/Van Parys / Sygma; 330c Co/Charles & Josette Lenars; 330t LEB/Betty Freeman; 331b Co/Lawson Wood; 331t LEB/Richard H Smith; 332t AKG/Ullstein; 332b LEB/B.Rafferty; 333t AKG/Marion Kalter ; 333b Co/Liu Liqun; 333cl Co/Reuters; 333cr DK/ Demetrio Carrasco; 334b Richardson and Kailas Icons, London, UK/BAL; 334t LEB/Nigel Luckhurst; 335t TOP/Boosey and Hawkes/ ArenaPAL; 335b LEB/George Newson; 335cl LEB/ George Newson; 336t GI/ Eamonn McCabe / Redferns; 336cl LEB/Richard H Smith; 336br Kremlin Museums, Moscow, Russia/BAL; 337tl Co/Manuel Zambrana; 337bl TOP/Boosey and Hawkes/ArenaPAL; 338t LEB/Nigel Luckhurst; 338cr TOP/© 2004 Polfoto; 338bl Co/Cardinale Stephane/Sygma; 339t LEB/Betty Freeman; 339cr AKG/Horst Maack; 339cl LEB/Betty Freeman; 339b AKG/Marion Kalter; 340cr Co/ Penny Tweedle; 340b Co/Ales Fevzer; 341b Co/ Roger Ressmeyer; 341t LEB/Riichard Haughton; 342c DK/Paul Harris; 342t LEB/Jim Four; 343b Co/Bettmann; 343t LEB/Betty Freeman; 344tr DK/Andy Crawford; 344b LEB/Alastair Muir; 344cl,tl LEB/Betty Freeman; 345b Co/Catherine Panchout; 345t LEB/Kate Mount.

Dorling Kindersley would like to thank the following people.
Proofreading: Kingshuk Ghoshal.
Editorial: Sreshtha Bhattacharya and Neha Ruth Samuel.
Additional picture research: Sakshi Saluja and Sumedha Chopra.